Population, Consumption,
and the Environment

Population, Consumption, and the Environment

Religious and Secular Responses

edited by
HAROLD COWARD

STATE UNIVERSITY OF NEW YORK PRESS

Published by
State University of New York Press, Albany

Printed in the United States of America

For information, address the State University of New York Press,
State University Plaza, Albany, NY 12246

Production by Bernadine Dawes • Marketing by Bernadette LaManna

Library of Congress Cataloging-in-Publication Data

Population, consumption, and the environment : religious and secular
    responses / edited by Harold Coward
        p.   cm.
    Includes bibliographical references (p.   ).
    ISBN 0-7914-2671-8. — ISBN 0-7914-2672-6 (pbk.)
    1. Population policy — Religious aspects. 2. Population — Moral and
ethical aspects. 3. Population — Environmental aspects. 4. Man —
Influence on nature. 5. Consumption (Economics) I. Coward, Harold G.
HB849.42.P67   1995
291.1'78366 — dc20   95-81019
                                                                        CIP

Contents

Part III: Secular Responses

Part IV: Conclusions

Acknowledgments

This book is the result of the 1993 International Summer Institute, "Population and the Environment: Population Pressures, Resource Consumption, Religions and Ethics," held at Chateau Whistler, Whistler, B.C., 18–27 August 1993, which was organized by the Centre for Studies in Religion and Society, University of Victoria. This major event was made possible through financial support from the Social Sciences and Humanities Research Council of Canada (SSHRCC), the Canadian Global Change Program of the Royal Society of Canada, the International Development Research Centre (Ottawa), the World Council of Churches, the Canadian Conference of Catholic Bishops, the United Church of Canada, the University of British Columbia, and the University of Victoria.

Thanks are due to Christina Nordgren, Centre Secretary, for her efforts in organizing the Summer Institute and to the Centre's Research Associate, Ludgard De Decker, for preparation of the manuscript.

As always, it has been a pleasure to work with William Eastman and the staff of the State University of New York Press in the preparation of this volume.

1

Introduction

HAROLD COWARD

Any discussion of environmental ethics must begin with a statement of the scientific evidence as a baseline from which to begin the analysis. In chapter 2, Kenneth Hare suggests that the consensus of environmental scientists is that the chemical balance of the atmosphere is being upset by the introduction of alien chemical species — CFCs and the increased flow of greenhouse gases. Although the atmosphere is self-cleaning, its self-cleaning is too slow to cope with the excess gases pumped into the atmosphere, and so we will not be able to avoid their consequence — the greenhouse effect, which threatens human welfare.[1] This is a problem we have created for ourselves and that population increase will make worse. Indeed, some suggest that the rise of the world's population is rapidly outstripping the earth's carrying capacity and simultaneously fouling the atmosphere, so that the very survival of humans and other species, and the quality of our environment is in question.[2] To make things worse, demographic projections show a population increase of unprecedented magnitude continuing well into the next century.[3]

In chapter 3, Anne Whyte, in laying out the human context of the problem, warns that the earth's population rise is occurring at such a rate that it threatens to rapidly outstrip the earth's carrying capacity. In a recent *Atlantic Monthly* article, Charles Mann asks the question "How Many is too Many?" for the earth to sustain.[4] Mann shows that the answers to this question have varied since the 1700s between those who believe that continued population growth will eventually lead to an environmental catastrophe (e.g., the 1798 economist

1

Robert Malthus and the biologist Paul Ehrlich, in his 1968 book *The Population Bomb*) and those who argue that increasing technological efficiency and
changing social/economic patterns will solve the problem (e.g., the Marquis
de Condorcet in 1794 or A.L. Lovins in his recent article "Least-cost stabilization"[5]). At the Rio Earth Summit, the developing countries responded to
the developed countries on this issue by saying that the problem is not one of
overpopulation in the South but of excessive consumption of the Earth's resources by the well-off few in the North.

The debate has ranged across the disciplines of biology, economics, ecology, anthropology, philosophy, and demography. The brilliant summary of this
long, complex and crucial debate in *The Atlantic Monthly* is particularly significant in that *the role of religion is never mentioned.* Yet it is clear that religions can and do strongly shape people's attitudes and behavior toward the environment, toward the practice of fertility planning, and toward the sharing of
resources. Religion can obstruct or foster responsible behavior. The cooperation of the world's religions in helping civilization respond to our current global crisis is essential. Also, the religions may discover new vitality as they take
a fresh look at their sources of revelation for the wisdom their tradition may possess to guide our response to the problems that challenge us all. To respond to
this gap in knowledge, the Centre for Studies in Religion and Society at the
University of Victoria brought together some forty scholars from North America, Europe, Africa, India, Thailand, China, and Japan for an intensive ten-day
seminar to examine what the world's religions and secular philosophy, economics, law, and demography say about this debate.

In some ways, this seminar, held at Whistler B.C. in August 1993, was a
Canadian follow-up to Rio and the 1991 and 1992 meetings organized by Carl
Sagan, the Very Rev. James Parks Morton, and (as he was then) U.S. Senator
Al Gore. What made the Whistler seminar unique was the breadth of repre-
sentation present from Aboriginal and Eastern as well as Western religions —
and the fact that most religions were represented by women ethics scholars.
The papers presented on the religions, revised later to take advantage of the
working discussions at Whistler, form Part II of this book. Part III is composed
of the secular analyses from philosophy, demography, law, women and family planning, and post-Rio considerations — all referencing back to the religious issues raised in Part II, and the baseline analysis of Part I.

What follows in this Introduction is an analysis of points of convergence
and divergence in the responses of the various religions to the double-sided
question: "How can we respond to population pressure and excess consumption
and their degradation of the environment?"

POINTS OF DIVERGENCE

At the outset, it should be noted that most religions are just now beginning to systematically examine what their traditions have to say about threats to the environment from overpopulation and overconsumption. Various world events are prompting the religions to examine these issues. For example, the fact that the UN draft document for the Cairo 1994 summit on population has very little mention of religion is causing religious reflection on the problems being discussed, so that the voices of the religions will be heard. Often, it is women scholars who are taking the lead, and their work is proving to be a creative cutting edge of contemporary religious thought. At Whistler, for example, Judaism, Christianity, and Islam, the three patriarchical Western religions, were represented by female theologians. Buddhism, Chinese religion, and the Aboriginal traditions were also represented by women. Feminist scholars have paid particular attention to the issues. Let us now examine points of divergence under the three headings of Nature, Consumption, and Population Pressure.

Nature

While all the religions see nature as having varying degrees of intrinsic value, the Eastern and Aboriginal religions take a stronger stance on this issue. They emphasize that the cosmos is made up of interdependent parts, of which humans are simply one species among many. The Western religions are more anthropocentric, yet none of them give humans unchecked dominion over nature in satisfying their desires. Their various visions of a transcendent creator God place upon humans the responsibility of being co-stewards of the environment that God, the creator, has provided for their use. Yet today humans are destroying much of that which, in the view of the Western religions, has been created for their use. At the opening of our Whistler meeting, a group of Haida children and elders sang and danced a prayer-song of invocation in which we were reminded of the Aboriginal Golden Rule: each generation should meet its needs without jeopardizing the prospects for the next seven generations.

The Jewish tradition sees nature as having been created by God to give pleasure to humans, who have the responsibility to be careful stewards. As Sharon Levy points out in chapter 5, God's will was to build a world based on and functioning through *chesed,* or loving kindness. Our role in God's world is to be his partners in actualizing his will for the world as spelled out in the *Torah.* The observance of the sabbath is seen to play an important role in keeping humans balanced in their relationship with nature. By observing the sabbath, which God created as an integral part of creation, we step back from our potentially dominating role, and in peaceful ease, again become part of creation.

Then, with right relationships re-established, we resume our co-creator work in the new week. In a way the sabbath might be seen as an element that God built into creation to keep humans responsible and accountable. In the modern economy of seven-day shopping and consuming with no pause for rest or reflection, Judaism offers a compelling argument for the practice of *Shabbat* as a powerful means for changing our approach to nature and our overconsumption of its resources.

Jewish scripture and commentaries seem to agree with the practical position that humans should respect those aspects of the environment necessary to sustain life.[6] Less clear is the degree to which humans have duties to animals, plants, the environment, and its ecosystem, although feminist scholars are rereading the Talmud and Torah for texts that emphasize the earth and our connectedness with it. In this sense, they approach an extreme view held by some (e.g., Kabbalists and Hasidic thinkers like Martin Buber) whose mystical perspective endows all of creation with a divine spark that it is our duty as humans to liberate through engagement in I–Thou relationships.

Like Judaism, Islam sees nature as created by God for the benefit of humans, but not for their selfish use. The human role is to work to shape the world into the pattern God reveals in the *Qur'an*. Islam is more nature-affirming than Judaism or Christianity. It does not see nature as corrupted or discontinuous with God's purpose. As Al Faruqi puts it, the world "is innocent and good created precisely to the end of being used and enjoyed by man. The evil is not in it, but in its abuse by man."[7] Islam is unique among Western religions in two ways. First, there is no separation between humans and nature: they are both parts of God's creation, and join together in worshiping the one God, their creator. Indeed, there is the concept of a natural, cosmic *islām,* in which stars and molecules, plants, animals, and humans all "worship" God by conforming to the laws of their own being.[8] Nature not only joins humans in worshiping God, but, by its very existence, displays God's potentialities and attributes.[9] This leads to the second unique aspect, the idea that Nature is a revelation of God that in a sense parallels the revelation of the *Qur'an*. Islamic spirituality is based "not only upon the reading of the written *Qur'an [al Qur'ān al-tadwīnī]* but also upon deciphering the text of the cosmic *Qur'an [al-Qur'ān, al takwīnī]* which is its complement."[10] Some Sufis go so far as to describe the events of nature as "the book of nature" set before us to read.[11] Nature and the *Qur'an* are placed before humans as twin acts of God's self-revelation. But the relationship between the two books is not equal. It is only through the revelation of the *Qur'an* that humans can learn to "read" the book of nature; the cosmos is seen in its innocence to manifest God's compassionate breath through its regularity and beauty. Nature is thus a vehicle by which humans can be brought to see God's truth, beauty, and compassion. But the mystic and the scientist, through their respective disciplines, are understood by Islam as capable of seeing the divine truth inherent in nature.

Christianity views humans and nature as created by God, with nature's purpose being, at least partly, to provide for human needs (Ps.105). In this, Christianity is like Judaism and Islam. Again, as in Islam and Judaism, nature by its very existence praises God and manifests his awesome powers (e.g., Ps.148). However, unlike the Islamic view of nature as innocent in itself, Christian thought sees nature as having participated along with humans in the Fall.[12] A peculiarity of the Christian view is that the human fall from innocence recounted in Genesis 3 also drags down all of nature into a corrupt state. As Calvin puts it, "Through man's fault a curse has extended above and below, over all the regions of the world."[13] Paul speaks of humans and nature — the whole of creation — "groaning in travail together" toward the ultimate purpose for which God created it, namely the revealing of the sons of God, in which the whole creation will share (Rom.8:19–25). Thus, there is as well a strong teleological thrust in the Christian understanding of nature. For Christians, a special contribution of Jesus Christ was his exposure of nature as having value, not in itself, but only in relation to God's purpose. While the human misuse of our God-given freedom brought on the Fall (for both humans and nature), God's grace in Jesus Christ restores to us the opportunity to live a righteous life in relation to nature and God (Rom.8:1–14). Unlike Judaism, in which the revelation of the *Torah* provides all the help that is required, or Islam, in which the *Qur'an* gives the needed revelation, Christianity sees God's incarnation in Christ as essential to the re-establishment of right relationships after the Fall. It is the grace of Christ that enables one to see nature not from the selfish perspective of fallen humanity, but from the perspective of God. Only when this perspective is attained do humans function in the correct relationships among humanity–nature–God that bring forth the abundance of nature described in Genesis (1:26–31). It is in this context that the "human dominion over nature" mentioned in Genesis 1:28 is correctly understood from a Christian perspective.

When we shift to the Eastern religions and the Aboriginal traditions, we find a distinct difference in the degree of holistic interconnectedness assumed between humans and nature. Also, the divine is usually seen as present in, rather than separate from, nature. These traditions challenge the dominant Western view of a strong qualitative difference between humans on the one hand, and animals and plants (the Jainas push the position to its logical conclusion and include atoms of matter, e.g., air, water, and rocks) on the other. The basic Eastern position, to which all Hindus, Buddhists, and Jainas ascribe, is that just as humans are beings composed of a combination of spiritual and non-spiritual elements, so also are animals, and in the Jainas case, even plants, rocks, air, and water. To take the most extreme position (that of the Jainas) every animal, plant, or element of matter is a being in a different combination of the components that make up each of us. Thus, there is no radical break between humans and the non-human realms of nature. Consequently, as humans we should treat animals, plants, etc. with the same dignity and respect we accord other humans. Clearly, this approach has significant ethical implications. Exploitation of one part of nature (plants, animals, trees, etc.) by another part of nature (humans) is unacceptable — if it is unacceptable to exploit your child, wife, or neighbor because of their stature as "beings" then it is also unacceptable to exploit another being, who happens to be at that moment an animal (thus the Eastern practice of vegetarianism — to kill and eat an animal is to engage in cannibalism).

While this way of thinking seems strange and foreign to our Western minds, it is supported by a well worked out theory that follows with clear logic once its basic assumptions are granted. These assumptions involve the notions of rebirth and the law of karma. The law of karma maintains that every time you do an action or think a thought, a memory trace is laid down in the unconscious. A good action or thought leaves behind its trace as does an evil action or thought.[14] When you find yourself in a similar situation in the future, the previous memory trace rises up in consciousness as an impulse to do a similar action or think a similar thought once again. Note that this is merely an *impulse* (a disposition or desire), and in itself does not force us to repeat the good or evil action or thought. We still have free choice. We may decide to go with the impulse and repeat the action (in which case a new reinforced memory trace will be laid down in the unconscious), or to negate the impulse (in which case, using the analogy of the seed, the sprouting impulse will receive neither warmth nor nourishment and will wither away, leaving no further trace in the unconscious). Thus, by the exercise of free choice at each moment in life, we either reinforce or delete the memory traces in our unconscious. In theory, then, every impulse I experience in this life should be able to be traced back to actions or thoughts done since birth. But karma theory does not assume a *tabula rasa* or blank mind at birth. Not only does our unconscious contain memory traces of all actions and thoughts since birth, but also those from the life before this, and the life before that, and so on backward infinitely (since karma theory rejects any absolute beginning and assumes that life has always been going on). Consequently, each of us is thought to have a huge store of memory traces in our unconscious that is constantly bursting with ideas, impulses, desires to this or that good or bad action or thought. These impulses, however, can be controlled by the exercise of our own free choice. If a particular action or thought is repeated often enough, it becomes a habit. The result of this theory is a ladder of existence as follows:

Assume that you are a human being. If you use your free choice to act on the good karmic impulses that come up within consciousness, and negate the evil

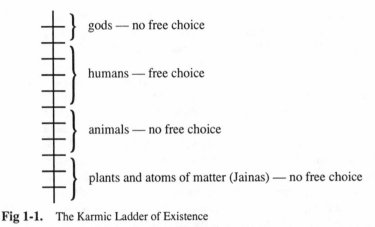

Fig 1-1. The Karmic Ladder of Existence

impulses, then, at the end of this life you will have increased the number of good karma (memory traces) in your unconscious and reduced the number of evil karmas. Using the image of a banker's balance, this will automatically cause you to be reborn higher up the scale. If, in your next and future lives, you continue to act on the good and negate the evil, you will spiral up the ladder of existence until you are eventually reborn as a god. Gods are beings just like us who, according to mythology, have the honor of superintending one of the cosmic functions, e.g., the sun god. But this is merely an honor and carries no free choice. Once the merit from all the good free choices made as a human is used up, you are reborn as a human being once again, with free choice.

But now let us follow through the other possibility, namely, that in this life you use your free choice to reinforce the evil impulses and negate the good. At death you will have increased the number of evil impulses and reduced the number of good impulses. This will automatically cause you to be born a step lower on the ladder of existence. If the same pattern is repeated again in the next life and the next, etc., you will spiral downward until eventually you are reborn as an animal. Animals are beings like you and me, but with a heavier composition of evil karmas (memory traces). Animals have no free choice, but simply endure the sufferings to which their animal instincts expose them. Through these sufferings, the evil karmas built up from years of evil choices (made freely as human beings) are expiated. Then one is reborn as a human again, with free choice and the ability to move up or down the ladder through karma and rebirth. In the Jaina view, plants and atoms of matter are treated as parallel to animals.

This is indeed a "long view" on life. After countless lifetimes it might well lead one to voice the sentiment, "Stop the world, I want to get off!" — or, in Eastern terms, "Is there not some way out of this beginningless and seemingly endless cycle of birth, death, and rebirth?" The Hindu religion gives one answer (one path out), the Buddhist religion another, and the Jainas a third — all quite different.[15] Before looking at the Hindu and Buddhist "answers" (paths of release) for their views of our human responsibility towards nature, let us first make some observations regarding environmental ethics from the karma-rebirth theory alone. First, there is no radical separation between humans and other forms of beings (animals, plants, atoms of matter). Instead, there is a radical equality presupposed. Second, according to karma theory, I have created the karmic impulses (good or evil) that I am now experiencing, as well as my current position on the ladder of existence, by my own freely chosen acts in previous lives. And the free choices I am making in this life will determine where I will end up in my next life. I alone, therefore, am responsible for the condition in which I now find myself, and for the condition I will create for the future. In this regard, karmic responsibility is seen to be both individual and cosmic. The way I make my choices conditions not only my future lives but also the future of all other beings — which, in the karma-rebirth perspective, includes all of nature. According to karma theory, our current environmental crisis is a direct result of the free choices made by humans to date — and it is up to humans to change the situation by the exercise of their free choice now, for the sake of both the present and the future.

In line with the theory of karma and rebirth, Hinduism sees all of nature as interconnected and capable of progressive transformation from matter to life to consciousness and finally to divine spirit. As Cromwell Crawford puts it, ". . . each stage is cyclically interlocked with the other stages. The dead stone is linked to life in the vegetable kingdom, plants are linked to consciousness in the animal kingdom, animals are linked to the intelligence of *homo sapiens,* and man is connected to the Life Force within the cosmos."[16] As to the character of this "Life Force," Hindu scripture is quite explicit:

> The essential self or the vital essence in man is the same as that in the elephant, the same as that in these three worlds, indeed the same as that in the whole universe (Brihadaranyaka Upanisad 1.3.22 as cited by Crawford[17]).

Crawford interprets the above Upanisadic verse as follows:

> The general idea behind this text is that the individual [self] *ātman* is one with the universal *Brahman. Brahman* literally means "the growing or increasing force" *(brih).* This *Brahman* force is manifest in the divinities of heaven, and in human, animal and plant life on

earth. All of these entities live an apparently independent existence, but they all emanate from *Brahman* and are finally reabsorbed into it.[18]

This emanation of the cosmos from the Divine is given detailed description in the *Bhagavad Gita,* where God's body is revealed as the whole Universe. Many Hindus (especially those of the Vaisnavite sect) see trees, cows, etc. as manifestations of God in nature, and therefore as fit symbols upon which to focus in worship. Nature, as God's body, is also seen by some to be a *guru* or guide to God, and therefore a fit subject for prayerful or scientific study.[19]

Like Hinduism, Buddhism adopts the karma-rebirth theory of nature and thus sees a continuity between human and animal life. Unlike the Jainas, Buddhists do not see plants and the inorganic elements of nature as composed of beings. There are some Buddhist schools, (e.g., Hua-yen) however, that see all of the cosmos as one interrelated web of existence within which there is no hierarchy. In the Hua-yen universe, says Francis Cook, "There is no center, or, perhaps, if there is one, it is everywhere. Man certainly is not the center, nor is some god."[20] This quotation identifies another distinctive feature of the Buddhist view of nature — it has no God. From the Buddhist perspective, the Universe has been going on beginninglessly according to its own inner laws, without the need for a creating, sustaining or supervising God. The Buddhist universe is one of identity and interconnectedness: what affects one part of the cosmos affects all parts. Therefore, the acts of humans, as part of the whole, are seen as intimately affecting the environment around them, of which they are a small but crucially interconnected part. Unlike the modern Western perspective, where people, and for some, God, stand separate from and above nature, from the Buddhist perspective there is only one level: nature, the cosmos, of which humanity, along with everything else, is simply a part.

Rather than thinking of the cosmos in terms of separate *entities,* Buddhism conceives of reality in terms of the relationships between entities. Rather than being conceived as distinct parcels of matter, reality is seen by the Buddhists to be the dynamic interrelationships that structure the whole. In this regard, Buddhist thought is often said to be close to that of modern physics and notions such as Einstein's theory, in which relationship is more fundamental.[21] The Buddha "taught that to exist in any sense at all means to exist in dependence on the other, which is infinite in number. Nothing exists truly in and of itself, but requires everything to be what it is."[22] The ethical implication of this viewpoint is that every single thing in the universe is important and thus deserving of respect. In the Buddhist view, interdependence is fundamental and all human interaction with nature occurs within that context. For the Buddhist, things do not exist in their own right, but only in interdependence. Things in nature, including humans, are said to be empty *(śūnya)* of any essence or self-existence

(svabhāva). Their existence arises from their relations of interdependence with
the rest of the cosmos, and it is within this context that all ethical reflection
takes place.

Indian thought provided the cradle for Hinduism and Buddhism. As evidenced above, Indian thought (although quite different in its basic presuppositions, such as karma and rebirth) shares with the West an approach to nature that
often emphasizes laws or principles by which nature is to be ordered and understood. When we shift from the West and India to China, we encounter a
radically different approach to nature. The Chinese give primacy to the concrete
particular in its aesthetic context, rather than to an a priori metaphysical theory. For example, whereas in Plato one proceeds by moving from the concrete
particular to the abstract universal (e.g., the "real" forms or ideas), in Chinese
Daoism there is no preassigned pattern. Rather, as Roger Ames puts it, "The organization and order of existence emerges out of the spontaneous rearrangement
of the participants."[23] The Chinese adopted a "this-worldly" focus on the details
of daily life as a basis for understanding nature and the cosmos. They emphasized the uniqueness of a particular person or event, and at the same time
stressed the interrelatedness of that particular to its cosmic context. The Chinese
sensibility, suggests Ames, leads to an approach to nature characterized by
"polarity" rather than the "dualism" of the West, in which humanity and nature,
or nature and God are seen as radically separate concepts. Polarity, by contrast, views such concepts as being interrelated in a way that each requires the
other for understanding. For example in the Daoist concepts *yin* and *yang,* "*yin*
does not transcend *yang,* nor vice versa, rather *yin* entails *yang* and *yang* entails
yin."[24] Darkness does not transcend light, nor vice versa; rather, darkness entails light and light entails darkness. In conceptual polarity each pole can only
be understood in relation to the other — as in the above example dark requires
light and vice versa. In dualist thinking, by contrast, the two concepts involved
are often seen in opposition (e.g., male versus female), thus leading to discrete
essentialistic interpretations of the world. From the dualist perspective it is relatively easy for humans to approach nature as a separate category of existence
— composed of things to be used as required. The polar character of Chinese
thinking and experience resists such a reification of nature by humans and conditions one into an intimate relational perception. All of this is well represented in Daoism. Nothing can be understood in independence of its context. In
fact, nothing exists by itself. All things such as humans and nature exist only
in interdependence and interpenetration.

De denotes the particular in its environment. It is both an individuating
and an integrating concept. Ames offers the illustration of the stew pot, "Just
as any one ingredient *[de]* in the stew pot must be blended with all of the others in order to express most fully its own flavor, so harmonization with other

environing particulars is a necessary precondition for the fullest self-discourse of any given particular."[25] For one to fully express or individuate oneself, it is necessary to harmonize and integrate oneself with other humans, nature and the whole cosmos. With such integration, one's particular humanness *(de)* will be realized. Contrary to what we might expect, Daoism does not see the necessity of integrating with the whole as militating against individual freedom and creativity. *De* as one's particular nature is understood by Daoism to have an inherent potency to self-expression and self-individuation. But such dynamic manifestation of the *de,* when integrated into the complexity of the larger whole, is called the *dao.* The distinction between *de* and *dao* therefore, is one of degree rather than kind. The *de,* when fully individuated and integrated, is but a particular aspect of the *dao.* For example, the *de* of a particular person, when fully expressed and integrated with his or her surrounding natural environment, is but an aspect of the *dao.* Ames says it better: "When *de* is cultivated and accumulated such that the particular is fully expressive of the whole, the distinction between *dao* and *de* collapses. . . ."[26] The result is harmony, regularity, and rhythm, and the action involved is described by Daoists as *wu-wei* (translated as "nonaction" meaning no self-willed action independent of the *dao).* It is also called *tzu-jan* (spontaneity or uncontrived action).

The Aboriginal perspective is in many ways very close to the Daoist viewpoint. However, rather than the theoretical *yin-yang* formulation, the Aboriginal tradition views the cosmos as a community of "peoples." Humans, animals, plants, rocks, trees, wind, and water are all seen as different species of "peoples," all of whom are suffused, unified, and transcended by the unseen presence of the Great Spirit. As Joseph Epes Brown puts it,

> Our animate inanimate dichotomy, or our categories of animal, vegetable and mineral, for example, have no meaning for the Indian who sees that all that exists is animate, each form in its own special way, so that even rocks have a life of their own and are believed even to be able to talk under certain conditions.[27]

As Daisy Sewid-Smith puts it in chapter 4, the hemlock tree, the bear, or the salmon all were seen as sacrificing themselves for the life of the people, and thus to be acknowledged and thanked. Such ritual practices helped to maintain human sensitivity to the social and natural limits within which life has to be lived.

Put another way, for the Aboriginal, all of the entities that make up nature share in the same consciousness that humans enjoy and thus are seen as different species of peoples. The consciousness that is possessed by all aspects of nature is described by Aboriginals in terms of manifesting divine spirit; all things are suffused, unified, and transcended by the unseen presence of the

Great Spirit. The Sioux Indian John Fire Lame Deer gives this notion meta-physical expression:

> You can't explain it except by going back to the "circles within circles" idea, the spirit splitting itself up into stones, trees, tiny insects even, making them all *waken* by his ever-presence. And in turn all these myriad of things which make up the universe flowing back to their source, united in one Grandfather spirit.[28]

There is of course *no one* Aboriginal religion or culture, but the many North American Aboriginal traditions share a common belief in the environment as composed of different peoples manifesting the one divine spirit (as expressed by Lame Deer). This idea leads to a genuine respect for the welfare of all forms of nature within the environment. Central to the notion of "person," for both Aboriginal and non-Aboriginal alike, is the idea that persons must be treated with respect and not be intentionally harmed. By seeing all aspects of the environment as different species of persons, the Aboriginal traditions manifest a strong and inclusive environmental ethic. Humans, together with all the component parts of nature (including the atmosphere), are seen as members of an intimately related family. As Callicot puts it, "Not only does everything have spirit, in the last analysis all things are related together as members of one universal family, born of one father, the sky, the Great Spirit, and one mother, the Earth herself."[29] Although the words are those of the Lakota sage Black Elk, the concept of the Great Spirit, as symbolized by the atmosphere (the sky), and the Earth Mother producing the family of creatures composing nature is so common as to be very nearly universal in North American Indian thinking. The ethic it generates is the necessity of treating all of nature as one would treat the members of one's own family, and the recognition that there is a spiritual aspect to all natural things. Human beings are part of a larger social and physical environment, belonging to both the human community and the community of all nature.[30] The ethical responsibilities and mutual obligations due to the members of one's own family or tribe are extended to include one's "natural relatives" that make up the environment. The cosmic kinship group enables the aboriginal, even when alone in nature, to feel as comfortable and secure as one would feel in the midst of a large family. Luther Standing Bear reports that the Lakota child never felt alone in nature. "Even without human companionship one was never alone. The world teemed with life and wisdom; there was no complete solitude for the Lakota."[31]

In their approaches to nature, all of the religions reviewed above would agree that the aggressive, self-centered attitude that has typified human interaction with the environment is unacceptable. Our misbehavior has brought upon us the environmental problems of fouled air and water, and the greenhouse effect, which threatens continued human welfare. The teachings of all of the religions require us to confess to the violation of nature and require from us nothing less than a changed attitude in which we value nature for its own sake — as a part of the cosmos of which we humans are but another part. The first place such a change must show itself is in our patterns of consumption — especially those of us who are well off. Such a change is important not only for the environment but also so that a fairer distribution of the earth's resources may occur.

Consumption

All the religions agree in warning against overconsumption and the dangers it would bring by damaging the environment and causing injustice between peoples. However, one religion, Christianity in its modern Western forms, is singled out as having the overwhelming responsibility for the imposition throughout the planet of unsustainable patterns of development. As Catherine Keller notes in chapter 6, it is not that Christianity has the worst ideas for the environment and the consumption of its resources, but that the modern Western Christian cultures have developed the ideological framework for unprecedented domination in the political, economic, and cultural spheres. It is this aggressive domination of peoples and nature by the ideological framework of the modern West that seems to be a root cause of much overconsumption.

In a widely quoted article, the historian Lynn White has pointed to the Christian understanding of the Biblical notion of humans as having "dominion over the earth" as a major factor in making possible the Industrial Revolution, its attendant overconsumption of natural resources, and the devastation of the environment that has followed.[32] Christian theologians (e.g., R. L. Shinn[33]) have responded by pointing out that White's thesis oversimplifies an extremely complex historical development. Nonetheless, no one denies that there is some truth to White's analysis. Quoting Genesis 1:28, in which humans are told to "fill the earth and subdue it, and have dominion over the fish of the sea and over the birds of the air and over every living thing," White suggests that such Christian ideas led directly to a human-centered and domineering attitude towards nature. Christianity established a dualism between humankind and nature and also insisted, says White, that God wills humans to exploit nature for their proper ends. Consequently, concludes White, Christianity, besides making possible the Industrial Revolution, also bears a burden of guilt for human alienation from nature and the overconsumption and environmental degradation that has resulted.

The Jewish conception of Yom Kippur, "The Great Shabbat," as described by Sharon Levy in chapter 5, seems helpful here. One day a year we are called to give an accounting. Our deeds are scrutinized. If there is error in our ways — if we have overconsumed — then we can only be forgiven by God if first forgiven by those we have slighted. Social justice and the Shabbat are tied together — we are required to put ourselves back into a right relationship with all of nature and with our neighbors.

Islam, Buddhism, Daoism, and the Aboriginal religions all have important wisdom on overconsumption. Indeed, for the Buddha, ego-selfish desiring (always wanting more) is the root cause of the constant frustration and lack of peace that typifies ordinary life. Overconsumption is its chief symptom.

Population Pressure

It is with regard to population pressure and its impact upon the environment that we find the greatest divergences among religions. Most of the religions in their traditional formulations have been solidly pro-natal. However, two religions, Buddhism and the Aboriginal traditions, appear to have taken different approaches. Rita Gross points out in chapter 9 that early Buddhist and Mahayana texts lay out three rules for response to the problems of population pressure (and overconsumption):

1. Buddhism assumes that humans must live within the limits of nature because they are a part of that web of life.

2. Morally there must be an equitable distribution of resources among the earth's peoples.

3. Population control is necessary to ensure (1) and (2) which are non-negotiable.

Buddhism requires moderation in reproduction to ensure that the carrying capacity of the earth is not strained. Therefore, the practice of birth control, but not abortion, is encouraged. Reproduction is not an accident or a duty, but is seen by Buddhism as a mature deliberate choice, which is to maintain the balance and harmony of the interdependent cosmic web of life. In this approach the emphasis on interdependence seriously challenges any notion of individual rights as overriding the greater value of the whole. Individuals, in other words, must not, as an individual right, choose to reproduce without concern for the overall impact on the biosphere.

Although Aboriginal traditions place a high value on the sacredness of life, contraception and abortion have historically been practiced but have become increasingly unacceptable as a result of the impact of European Christianity. As Aboriginal people adopted Christianity, the size of their families grew from an average of two children (widely spaced) to six (closely spaced). Methods employed included birth control by sexual abstinence during periods of war, hunting, or spiritual quest, and the knowledge of medicine people who specialized in contraceptive medicines and techniques. "The decision to abort or use contraceptives is initially an individual one; however, it was not carried out without the specialist [the medicine person] who acted as both counselor and doctor."[34] Overall guidance in such matters is provided by the aboriginal sense of needing to live in interdependence with nature — to maintain a state of equilibrium between humans and their natural environment. However, as Daisy Sewid-Smith points out in chapter 4, the impact of European society and its contagious diseases such as measles, along with infertility resulting from imported sexually transmitted diseases, radically reduced Aboriginal populations, so that today, like the Jews, the Aboriginals are concerned with maintaining their own decreasing population.

Chinese Religions should perhaps also be seen as divergent from the traditional pro-natal approaches of most religions. As chapter 10 by Jordan and Li Chuang Paper shows, throughout China's early history the concern was with underpopulation, therefore these sources offer little guidance with respect to overpopulation. However, during the past three centuries, overpopulation and its negative impact upon the environment have become a matter of serious concern. With the possibility of a doubling of the population every generation, China in 1980 adopted a one child per family policy. This policy is widely practiced and appears to have the support of the people, who see overpopulation as a threat to the future of the globe and to family well-being. The success of this policy is especially remarkable as it clashes directly with the fundamental imperative of Chinese Religion, namely the continuation of the patrilineal family. If the one child is not a son to conduct the family rituals then, according to traditional religion, the parents, grandparents, etc. will cease to exist upon the last son's death, and the family will come to an end. And in Chinese culture, familicide is the greatest moral crime.[35] However, changes are occurring which suggest that a gender neutral family is developing, in which a daughter *or* a son could perform the rituals required for the continuation of the family and the support of those in the afterlife.

Sharon Levy, in chapter 5, observes that from the Jewish perspective contraceptive methods are permissible if the carrying capacity of the earth has been reached. Following the directive of Isaiah that the world not become a "wasteland," population restriction practices may be necessary — although for a world Jewish population of thirteen million which is not currently replacing itself, and which was reduced from close to seventeen million by the Holocaust of World War II, the concern is in the opposite direction.

CONVERGENCES

While the points of difference noted above are significant, the Whistler Summer Institute also identified important points of convergence.

Nature

All the religions reviewed see nature as having varying degrees of intrinsic value, and all religions offer correctives to the exploitation and destruction of the environment that threaten the globe today. Each of the Western religions emphasizes that humans are to use their intelligence and the technology they create in being stewards of nature, according to God's plan rather than their own selfish interests. While Eastern and Aboriginal religions may not always conceive of God as separate from nature, their stress on the interdependence of all of nature, of which humans are simply one part, has a similar result — humans are morally responsible to live in harmony with nature, and this rules out selfish exploitation. The spiritual disciplines of meditation upon nature in the Eastern religions (e.g., Zen) are designed to keep this awareness front and center in human consciousness, so that it will guide all thought and behavior. These Eastern practices are resensitizing modern Westerners to a recovery of similar aspects of their own traditions. Thus, a common basis of respect for nature and humans, as being in a relationship of interdependence, is occurring. This is especially true when the Western religions are re-visioned through feminist eyes — e.g., Rosemary Radford Ruether, Sallie McFague, and Katherine Keller in Christianity.

Consumption and Population Pressure

The ethic of interdependence, now endorsed by all religions, requires a radical change in consumption patterns — especially from the well-off people in the developed and developing countries. This change, which would give up excessive consumption, is required for two reasons: (1) due to our respect for nature, of which we are an interdependent part; and (2) due to our commitment to social justice, which the ethic of interdependence entails. It is of interest to note that the 1993 Parliament of the World's Religions, held in Chicago just one week after the Whistler Seminar, also grounded its statement of "A Global Ethic" on the premise of "interdependence." Like the Whistler Seminar, the Parliament of World Religions found that a global ethic of interdependence requires respect for the Earth and its community of living beings (including people, plants, animals, air, water, and soil), and respect for others in the world-wide human family.[36] Effectively this ethic demands a "transformation of consciousness" that would give up excessive consumption with its attitudes of domination and exploitation. Instead, preservation of nature and concern for others (present and future generations) must be the new consciousness that directs our thinking and behavior. Such a transformed consciousness, both gatherings agreed, would produce a just economic order, for women and children particularly. For this to happen requires that in the developed countries especially, "a distinction be made between necessary and limitless consumption, between socially beneficial and non-beneficial uses of property, between justified and unjustified uses of natural resources, and between a profit-only and a socially beneficial and ecologically oriented market economy."[37] Such a transformation begins with the individual, for it is through changes in individual thinking and behavior that changes in government policy and business practice arise. And it is the stated goal of religions to bring about just such transformation of consciousness within individuals. Although techniques differ, the various religions all show a commitment to this common goal of limiting human consumption by transforming thought and behavior.

In Judaism, as chapter 5 makes clear, we are enjoined not to waste — the principle of *ba'al taschit*. This principle applies to resources of nature, such as energy, as well as to human-made things. The rich are those content with what they have. But every person has a right to shelter, food, water, and education (for both men and women). The world should not rely on reducing birth rates, but rather focus on reducing the overconsumption of the few and enabling all to live in dignity.

Judaism also employs the approach of requiring obedience to God's commands to offer the first fruits of harvest in thanksgiving, to let the land lie fallow every seventh year (Exodus 23:10–12), and to return everything to God for a fresh start every fiftieth year (Leviticus 25). These practices serve to remind humans that the land and its produce are not for their selfish use but are owned by God and given to humans as a trust to benefit all. Leviticus suggests a fifty-year cycle where all hierarchy is abolished and everything renews itself on the basis of harmony between God, humans, and all of nature. With regard to population pressure, many Jewish thinkers call upon the mystical thought of the Kabbalists, which suggests that humans must learn to limit themselves — their rate of reproduction, their use of natural resources, and their production of fouling wastes. The example to emulate is the Kabbalist vision of how God created the world. If God is omnipresent then, reasoned the Kabbalists, the only way God could create would be by an act of *tsimtsum* — of voluntary withdrawal or limitation to make room for creation. Similarly, we as humans must withdraw or limit both our reproduction and our wants, so as to make room for coexistence with our environment in this and future generations. As Schorsch put it:

The miracle of co-habitation with other living species, the beauty of collective I–Thou relationship with beings wholly different from ourselves, requires our self-limitation. If we were everywhere, our presence would herald the end of the teeming diversity of nature. Our fragile and unique habitat needs a reprieve from human assault.[38]

Nature's fragility and susceptibility to human greed is also emphasized by Islam. Nature's balance can easily be upset by human wickedness. Natural disasters such as floods, hurricanes, fires, and earthquakes are interpreted by some Muslims as warnings from God that people are embarked upon a fundamentally wrong course of action, and the disasters that the greenhouse effect threatens might be similarly understood. When seen as a kind of "wake-up call" from God, the greenhouse effect resulting from excessive consumption by humans poses a serious dilemma to Muslims around the world, but particularly to those Muslim countries such as Saudi Arabia, whose economy has come to depend upon the heavy use of oil. For such countries, and for the world at large, Islam's view of humanity as the "custodian of nature" *(Khalifa)* poses critical questions. Nawal Ammar, in chapter 7, describes how humans, as custodians of nature, are free to satisfy their needs only with an eye to the welfare of all creation. The harmony and beauty God gave nature must be respected by humans in their stewardship of nature, resulting in the following rules:

1. The use of nature resources must be balanced and not excessive.

2. Humans must treat nature and its resources with kindness.

3. Humans must not damage or abuse nature in any way.

4. Humans must share natural resources, for no one owns nature. All persons are benefactors and stewards. Therefore, population pressure will dictate limits to consumption so that there can be equal access to resources by all.

5. Conservation is enjoined by the *Qur'an.* Therefore, in Islamic law there are rules for the conservation of forests, water, and animals.

While the above rules served previous ages well, they are just now being enlarged by Muslims to address the modern issues of pollution, chemical warfare, and technological hazards, which are for the *Qur'an* clearly abuses of God's creation. While fertility control is generally forbidden by the *Qur'an,* and the production of children is encouraged, some Muslims now suggest that fertility control may be acceptable if seen as part of self-discipline on the part of humans to avoid upsetting the balance of nature.

Although there is great diversity within Christianity today (from conservatives to the radically progressive), many Christian thinkers are holding Christianity responsible for fostering much of the world's excessive consumption and overpopulation. Within Christianity, there are strong forces at work transforming Christianity's mainstream into a self-critical force for justice, peace, and the maintenance of the integrity of nature. As Catherine Keller puts it in chapter 6, planetary ecology cannot be separated from social justice, especially as seen through feminist theology. However, even in this perspective the traditional Christian opposition to fertility control has not yet been critically examined in relation to the looming crisis of overpopulation. Christian thinkers are recognizing, however, that it is overconsumption by the developed Christian countries of the North that is both polluting the environment and depriving the developing countries of the South of the resources they need. Keller suggests it is not the babies of the underdeveloped Asians, Africans, or Latin Americans who threaten the ecology, but rather the babies of well-off first-world parents. The first-world child will, due to excessive consumption, have thirty times the environmental impact of a third-world child. Therefore, it is the child who has most, the first-world child, that the world can least afford. This leads Keller to the radical conclusion that well-off Christians should choose to reduce their own populations and resource consumption, so as to make room for the migrating poor. Such an ascetic choice is not seen by Keller as a denial of pleasure, but as a responsible practice of fertility control in relation to others and to nature. It also challenges the traditional patriarchal family patterns basic to many Christian cultures, just as it has for the contemporary Chinese.

All of this is grounded in the teachings of the Hebrew prophets, who politicized the relationship of humans with nature, maintaining that "nature and man are bound together in a fateful history where the responsibility of man for his life and his world meets the demands of a new order in which basic justice is required."[39] In line with the prophets, the New Testament teaches that one must love one's neighbor in need (e.g., act as did the Good Samaritan). Christians today are realizing that their neighbor's welfare is strongly affected by the way they treat the environment and by the number of children they produce. The prophets addressed the issue of resource consumption from the vantage point of the poor. The lesson for Christians today, says Keller, is do not multiply the *quantity* of life, but enhance the *quality* of life through the sharing of nature's abundance. The result is an ethic of interdependence with the rest of creation, which may also mean an ethic of "non-creation" for Christians in developed nations — for the good of the whole. Although the prophets were quick to criticize human greed and sinfulness in its many forms, they also held out a hope for the future, a harmony that would include all of humankind and all nature. In the New Testament the idea of "the Kingdom of God" is seen as referring both to another world and to this world in its hoped-for state of harmony among persons and between humans and nature. For the early New Testament Christians, the notion of an immanent end-time (the second coming of Christ) led them to counsel "few possessions and no children." Christians today are hearing a similar counsel, not because the end (Apocalypse) is coming but in order to avoid another kind of end — an environmental catastrophe.

Like Christianity, Hinduism has traditionally opposed fertility control. The purpose of marriage is the production of children, and a childless marriage is grounds for divorce. A large number of children, especially sons, has been seen as both a social and an economic asset. Abortion or other means of fertility control have been condemned except when the mother's health is in danger.[40] In chapter 8, Klaus Klostermaier suggests that there have been times in India's history when the population pressure exceeded the earth's carrying capacity. At such times, many young people have chosen, or been urged by society, to enter *sanyassi* or celibate monastic life, perhaps to help ease the population pressure on the environment. Although Hindu leaders today would not advocate fertility control, most educated Hindus likely practice it. Indeed, with the social and economic emphasis on sons, there is evidence that the technologies which offer possibilities of sex selection and abortion to ensure the birth of sons are being used by some parents.

Traditional Hindu lifestyles, says Klostermaier, have used resources carefully and tried to conserve for the future. Possessions were kept to a minimum and fasting was popular. All of this was based on respect for nature as the body of God. For a Hindu, to overexploit nature through excessive consumption was to do damage to oneself, because oneself and nature were simply different aspects of the same whole — God. With the British came the modern Western idea of the exploitation of nature for profit, and the technological means to do so in abusive ways. With them also came modern medicine, which cut deaths dramatically, allowing the population to escalate, resulting in a vicious circle. According to Klostermaier, Hinduism has largely shut its eyes to these problems, with the exception of some women's movements and the aboriginal communities. Hindu-owned industry in India has not proven to be more environmentally responsible than were the British. And well-off Hindus have shown themselves just as open to engaging in unnecessary and conspicuous consumption as those in the modern West. One contemporary Hindu reformer, Mahatma Gandhi, attempted to bridge between India's traditional ideals of restraint and conservation. Gandhi attempted to guide India between the extremes of no growth at all and growth for material values only. In his view, Hindu ethics do not reject technology or material possessions, but see them as having a restrained but proper place in the cosmic order of God's body. His Hindu Vaisnava background — with strong Jaina influence — led him to advocate social models that balanced economic and environmental needs under spiritual values. Nehru, however, disagreed, and moved India quickly into the modern world. That action, together with India's population explosion, has resulted in the creation of huge cities (e.g., Calcutta and Bombay) whose rate of growth has far outstripped the expansion of infrastructure such as roads, water, and sewers. To such cities, which threaten to double in size in the next fifty years, the Hindu ethic of conservation and respecting nature as God's body poses a serious challenge. In spite of its fine ecological teachings, India, like the West, has ignored these teachings in its rush to modernization; it has not followed Gandhi's ideal of restraint.

Having reviewed the teachings of the religions on the double-sided problem of population pressure and overconsumption in the degradation of the environment, the volume turns to cognate analyses of the question from philosophy, economics, demography, law, and feminist theory — but without losing touch with the religious assessments.

In chapter 11, Michael McDonald examines the issue of global equity in the use of the earth's resources in the context of the moral diversity of the various secular and religious belief systems. Various prescriptions are examined for breaking the impoverishment / environmental degradation cycle. Mahendra Premi examines population projections and their impact upon the environment in chapter 12. As the population concentrates more and more in urban centers, he identifies water shortage as a serious problem. Global issues are contrasted with those of village India. Environmental degradation and "the religion of the market" is examined by Rodney Dobell in chapter 13. He contends that the market can be made to capture more of the social and environmental costs that must be taken into account in arriving at equitable resource use, but in the end our obligations to others and to Nature can only be sufficiently communicated through broadly accepted religious principles or social ground rules. These would require moving away from utilitarian calculation toward concerns for fairness and procedural justice.

The special contribution women can offer on the issues of population and resource distribution in the environment debate are explored by Jael Silliman in chapter 14. A "woman-centered" approach to population concerns is presented as a constructive way to address population and environmental goals simultaneously. In chapter 15, Elizabeth Adjin-Tettey examines the role that international law can play in dealing with intergenerational equity and issues of justice between the developed and the developing countries. She contends that the obligation to assist developing nations to deal with factors that compel them to degrade the natural environment is an emergent customary norm in North-South relations. As this obligation becomes binding in international law, enforcement will be possible and international law will be able to assist developing countries in breaking the cycle of poverty, population increase, and environmental degradation. In chapter 16, Yuichi Inoue exposes the myths of population and technology that keep Japan from taking the environmental crisis seriously. The first says that population problems belong to the developing nations of the South. The second assumes that constant economic growth and environmental protection can be made compatible by means of technological innovation and scientific resource management.Such myths were challenged by the Rio experience of the Japanese NGOs. Religions, including Japan's Shinto tradition, are seen to offer an important contribution to the environmental movement. Finally, in chapter 17, the conclusions and recommendations of the Whistler symposium are presented. Policy suggestions are offered for individuals, educators, religious leaders, business leaders, governments, and non-government organizations.

NOTES

1. F. Kenneth Hare, "The Challenge," in *Ethics and Climate Change: The Greenhouse Effect,* eds. Harold Coward and Thomas Hurka (Waterloo: Wilfrid Laurier University Press, 1993), pp. 11–22.

2. "Ethics and Global Population," *Philosophy and Public Policy,* Vol. 13, 1993, pp. 1–3.

3. Ibid., p. 2.

4. *The Atlantic Monthly* (February 1993).

5. A. B. Lovins, "Least-cost stabilization," *Annual Review of Energy and the Environment* 16: 433–531.

6. See Deuteronomy 20:10, which commands Israelite armies when attacking a Canaanite town not to destroy its fruit trees "by wielding an axe against them Although you may take food from them you may not cut them down." Segal notes the rabbis elaborated this practical rule to "the prohibition of *bal tash-it* which extends the ban on wastefulness to include other foodstuffs, clothing, fuel and water, or any other useful resource." E. Segal, "Judaism and Ecology," *The Jewish Star* (26 May 1989): p. 4.

7. I. Al-Faruqi, "Islamic Ethics," in *World Religions and Global Ethics,* ed. S. Cromwell Crawford (New York: Paragon House, 1989), p. 227.

8. K. Cragg, *The House of Islam* (Belmont, Calif.: Dickenson, 1977), p. 11.

9. W. C. Chittick, *The Sufi Path of Love: The Spiritual Teachings of Rumi* (Albany: State University of New York Press, 1983), p. 58.

10. S. H. Nasr, "The cosmos and the natural order," in *Islamic Spirituality: Foundations* (New York: Crossroad, 1987), Vol. 19: p. 345.

11. Ibid., p. 355.

12. D. Bonhoeffer, *Ethics* (London: Collins, 1955), p. 144.

13. J. Calvin, *Institutes of the Christian Religion,* transl. H. Beveridge (London: James Clarke, 1962), Vol. 2: p. 214.

14. The criteria for good or evil are determined as follows: For a Hindu, good and evil actions or thoughts are defined in the revealed scripture, the Veda. In Buddhism, where

there is no God or revealed scripture, good or evil is defined in terms of the intention motivating your action or thought (e.g. the intention to harm one's neighbour/dog/field produces an evil karma or memory trace). For a philosophical study of karma see B. R. Reichenbach, *The Law of Karma: A Philosophical Study* (Honolulu: University of Hawaii Press, 1990).

15. For a review of Hindu and Buddhist thought see my *Sacred Word Sacred Text: Scripture in World Religions* (Maryknoll: Orbis, 1988); and *Pluralism: Challenge to World Religions* (Maryknoll: Orbis, 1985).

16. S. Cromwell Crawford, "Hindu ethics for modern life" in *World Religions and Global Ethics,* ed. S. Cromwell Crawford (New York: Paragon House, 1989), p. 30.

17. Ibid. p. 33.

18. Ibid.

19. K. Klostermaier, "Spirituality and Nature," in *Hindu Spirituality,* ed. K. Srivaraman (New York: Crossroad, 1989), pp. 319–21.

20. F. H. Cook, "The Jewel Net of India," in *Nature in the Asian Traditions of Thought,* eds. J. B. Callicot and R. T. Ames (Albany: SUNY, 1989), p. 216.

21. Ibid., p. 219.

22. Ibid., p. 220.

23. Roger Ames, "Putting the *Te* back into Taoism," in *Nature in Asian Traditions of Thought,* p. 117.

24. Ibid., p. 119.

25. Ibid., p. 126.

26. Ibid., p. 128.

27. J. E. Brown, "Modes of Contemplation Through Action: North American Indians," *Main Currents in Modern Thought,* Vol. 30, 1973, p. 193.

28. J. B. Callicot, *In Defense of the Land Ethic: Essays in Environmental Philosophy* (Albany: SUNY, 1989), p. 186.

29. Ibid.

30. Ibid., p. 189.

31. Luther Standing Bear, as quoted by Brown, *op. cit.,* p. 194.

32. L. White, Jr., "The Historical Roots of our Ecological Crisis," *Science* 155 (1967): pp. 1203–7.

33. R. L. Shinn, "Science and Ethical Decisions: Some New Issues," in *Earth Might Be Fair,* ed. I. G. Barbour (Englewood Cliffs, N.J.: Prentice-Hall, 1972).

34. See information provided by Winona Stevenson on the Woodland Cree in Harold Coward, "World Religions and New Reproductive Technologies," in *Social Values and Attitudes Surrounding New Reproductive Technologies,* Vol. 2 of the Research Studies, Royal Commission on New Reproductive Technologies, 1993, pp.445–67. See also Daisy Sewid-Smith, "Aboriginal Spirituality."

35. Stevenson, *op. cit.,* p. 519.

36. *A Global Ethic,* Chicago: Council for a Parliament of the World's Religions, 1993.

37. Ibid. p. 6.

38. I. Schorsch, "Trees for Life," *Melton Journal* 25 (1992), p. 6.

39. D. D. Williams, "Changing Concepts of Nature," in *Earth Might Be Fair, op. cit.*

40. See Julius J. Lipner, "The Classical Hindu View on Abortion and the Moral Status of the Unborn," in Harold Coward, *Hindu Ethics: Purity, Abortion and Euthanasia* (Albany: SUNY, 1989), pp. 41–70.

I

Baseline Analysis

2

The Natural Background

F. KENNETH HARE

THE WORLD IS NOT MERELY PHYSICAL

In 1988, the International Council of Scientific Unions launched a long-term research enterprise entitled the International Geosphere/Biosphere Programme (abbreviated as IGBP). Its purpose is to bridge the gap between the earth and biological sciences — between those who study the physical earth and those who focus upon life. Since 1988, IGBP has blossomed in many countries. The Canadian Global Change Program is Canada's national equivalent.

The earth system is not merely air, water, soil, and rock. It comprises also the extraordinary phenomenon of life, of which human self-consciousness seems (to self-centered humanity) to be the supreme achievement. We share the planet with tens of millions of other living species. As far as we know, we alone are conscious of abstractions and obligations. Consciousness exists in many animal species; but consciousness in and of the abstract seems to be exclusively human. In that sense, we are unique. Moreover, we know of no life elsewhere in the universe (though most scientists believe that life must exist elsewhere, because the chemical elements on which it depends are scattered throughout the immensity of space and time).

It would be tragic if self-conscious life should bring about its own destruction — and in so doing, severely damage the stage on which the drama has been enacted — the planet Earth. Yet that is what is beginning to happen.

27

I write mainly as a scientist in the Western, empirical tradition. But the issues before us are not scientific; they are profoundly moral. For that reason, this volume brings together a diverse assemblage of individuals — from the major religions, traditions, or faiths; from several ethnic groups; from a variety of occupations; from differing age groups; and from North and South in economic terms. The Canadian Global Change Program also assumes that breadth is needed to solve our problems. From the first, it has included social scientists and humanists. The IGBP, its international equivalent, has stuck more closely to the natural sciences.

To scholars in the religious traditions, my scientific stance may seem alien. Like most biologists, earth scientists, and geographers, I value the planet for its own sake, quite independently of its role as the human habitat. The growth of the environmental sciences in the past two decades was not merely an intellectual movement; those involved were also quite passionate, in that the despoliation of nature angers us all. Scientists may aim at objective enquiry. They certainly assume that there is a truth about nature that does not depend on human emotions and values. Nevertheless, they share the anxieties of the rest of humanity; they are not bloodless Strangeloves. Most of us care about the earth, and about our species. We try to observe and understand things as they really are, and not however our prejudices might prefer them to be. We examine the role of human activities in global change in this objective light — not necessarily to condemn, but always to understand.

GLOBAL CHANGE

Global change has many components, with some of which this volume has little to do. Natural changes — such as biological evolution, landform changes, and astronomic variations (like the lengths of the day and year, and the strength of the sun) — are slow in human terms. Catastrophic events do occur, for example earthquakes, eruptions, landslips, atmospheric and solar storms, and high tides. But most such happenings are little more than spasms that soon relax. The physical and biotic worlds have until recently entered each century much as they began the last. We have shadowy evidence of more dramatic change, such as the possible asteroid impact at the end of the Cretaceous period, about sixty-five million years ago, with the extinction of a significant part of all life. Overall, however, we can usually assume that nature is conservative, and changes at a pace that is sedate in human terms. With such slow-moving phenomena we have few dealings in this account. Our concern is with anthropogenic change — with processes whose rapidity is often close to catastrophic, in that there are large effects within a single human lifetime, or even a single year.

We have concrete evidence of rapid changes in human numbers; in climate; in atmospheric and oceanic composition, such as carbon dioxide and ozone concentrations; in the extent and condition of forests, grasslands, wetlands, and deserts; in fish distribution; in soil; in hydrology; in the extent of snow and ice; and in the planetary gene-bank. In all these cases, the work of human beings is implicated. As a rule, the outcome is unintentional; it arises from the failure to see or care about the possible consequences of our actions. Human folly and ignorance easily outweigh malice.

Deliberate human intervention, though ubiquitous, operates on small geographical scales. But now, without delay, we have to devise globally effective remedies, as UNCED planned. If we succeed, it will be the first time our species has worked on the global scale to protect its inheritance. It is a huge challenge.

In the case of atmospheric and climatic change,[1] we have quantitative measurements to report, and, in addition, a large body of theoretical work, most of it concerned with simulation modeling of the atmosphere-ocean system. The measurements have established that real, though small, changes or fluctuations of climate have occurred during the past century. Modeling has given us predictions of what may happen in the future. I shall turn first to these findings, and then consider their implications for life.

MEASURED CLIMATIC CHANGE

Billions of measured values of temperature, precipitation, and other properties have accumulated in world archives.[2] After much effort to eliminate errors and confounding factors, several estimates of global and regional annual mean air temperatures are now available. Though there are other sources, the material analyzed by the Climate Research Group at the University of East Anglia, in Norwich, England, and by the UK Meteorological Office (whose files of marine data are indispensable), has been widely accepted as the best estimate of global temperature change since 1860. It is not, however, anything more than an estimate; the record is imperfect and uneven — and hence open to challenge.

Figure 2-1 shows the course of global annual mean surface air temperature from this source (World Meteorological Organization 1993). It suggests that temperatures have risen by about 0.5°C since 1910, with large year-to-year variations. Both hemispheres have been affected. The Intergovernmental Panel on Climate Change (IPCC), established in 1988 to assess the prospects for future climate, suggested (IPCC 1990, 1992) after examination of other evidence that the true value probably lay within the range 0.3° to 0.6°C.

This was not a large warming. Moreover, it was split into two periods of rising temperatures, 1910 to 1940, and 1975 to the present day, with three and a half decades of virtual standstill in between. Nevertheless, global warming has

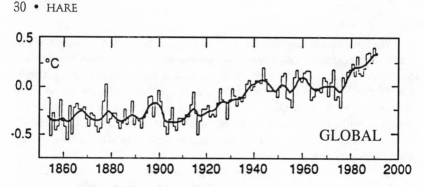

Fig. 2-1a. Mean global annual surface air temperatures, expressed as departures from the 1950–1979 normal.

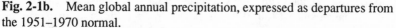

Source: Climate Research Unit, University of East Anglia, and Meteorological Office, United Kingdom (as printed in *World Climate News,* no. 2, World Meteorological Organization, Geneva).

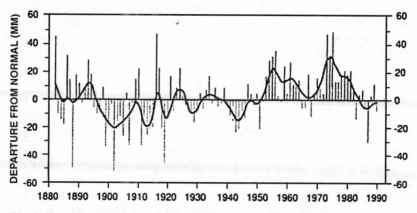

Fig. 2-1b. Mean global annual precipitation, expressed as departures from the 1951–1970 normal.

Source: Climate Research Division, NOAA Environmental Research Laboratories, United States (as printed in *World Climate News,* as above).

been widely recognized by members of the public and the media; the high political awareness of the effects rests on even wider acceptance by individuals, chiefly in the industrialized nations.

Several key features lie hidden within the simplicity of figure 2-1. One is the spatial unevenness of the warming. Some parts of the earth have actually cooled during the past century. Others have warmed more markedly. In parts of coastal Atlantic Canada and Greenland, for example, temperatures were highest in the 1920s, since when they have fallen progressively in many localities, culminating in recent cold summers in Newfoundland and the Labrador Sea (which may have been a factor in the decline of fish stocks). By contrast, in a wide belt from Alaska across the Yukon, the Mackenzie Valley, and the northern Prairie Provinces, temperatures during the past century have risen by 1.5°C or more (Gullett and Skinner 1992). In tropical countries the changes, if any, have been small. The spatial unevenness causes wide differences in public and political perception of the changes.

Another complexity, hinted at by the curves in figure 2-1, is the large year-to-year variation, which confuses an observer unaccustomed to the vagaries of climate. A single cool summer or cold winter invariably leads to the ironic question: "what's happened to global warming?" Major explosive eruptions such as Krakatoa in 1883, or Pinatubo in 1991, may inject enough particle-forming sulfur dioxide into the stratosphere to induce abnormal coolness for a few years — after which the warming resumes. Climatic change, if that is what we are seeing, is a faint signal behind clamorous short-term noise. Identifying the long-term signal is like tuning out lightning static on an old-fashioned AM radio.

Yet another complexity is that the warming has been essentially confined to the uppermost layer of the oceans (whose deeper waters are extremely cold worldwide) and the lower parts of the atmosphere (in general the bottom six kilometers). The lower and middle stratosphere (the atmospheric layers between fifteen and thirty kilometers) have actually cooled since 1960 (Angell 1988, 1991).

We cannot match this temperature record with as good a curve for global mean annual precipitation (rain and snow), because this is an exceedingly variable element, which we cannot measure accurately at sea. Nevertheless, the Climate Research Division of the US NOAA Environmental Research Laboratories has attempted an estimate, which is also shown in figure 2-1. Records of precipitation over land suggest small changes over the past century, but with much uncertainty. There have also been prolonged regional anomalies, like the disastrous desiccation of much of Africa in the past twenty-five years. Satellite observations are now being used to replace ground measurements, with increasing success; but it will be decades before we can claim to have proven what we all expect — that changing temperatures should lead to changing precipitation.

To assess the scale of the observed changes, we can compare them with events in the record of ancient climatic change, derived from a variety of sources — ecological, geological, geochemical, glaciological, and oceanographic. The bottom sediments of the oceans, inland lakes, and bogs, the layers of ice in the continental icesheets of Greenland and Antarctica, the growth rings of trees, and even the stalactites and stalagmites of caves, can be investigated to yield evidence of past temperature and precipitation regimes. From such sources, we have a picture of conditions back over 200,000 years (Jouzel et al. 1993), and from other geological evidence we can hazard informed guesses as to global climate back to the Pre-Cambrian era. From the fact that life existed in the oceans more than 3.5 billion years ago, and that liquid water appears to have been abundant throughout that period, we can assume in gross terms that the earth has always had a climate conducive to life, in spite of known changes in the intensity of the sunlight that provides nearly all the needed energy. On the other hand, we also have evidence — from the Greenland icesheet — of rapid short-term changes of temperature within the past 200,000 years (Dansgaard et al. 1993). Conservative as it may be, the natural climatic system appears capable of sudden, drastic shifts. We cannot rule out such dramatic change today — or tomorrow.

PREDICTED FUTURE CLIMATES AND SEA-LEVELS

The most widely discussed aspect of global change, at UNCED and elsewhere, has been the prospect of rapid future warming, because of the accumulation of greenhouse gases in the atmosphere. These are gases that allow warming sunlight to penetrate the atmosphere freely, but which retard the return flow of radiant heat to space. They warm the earth's surface and lower troposphere (below about six km above sea-level), and cool the stratosphere, at levels above about fifteen km. It is widely believed (but also questioned by some) that the recent observed warming is a forewarning of bigger things to come.

The greenhouse gases include water vapor and carbon dioxide, which are abundant, and much scarcer substances such as methane, nitrous oxide,[3] ozone, and various human-made compounds, such as the chlorofluorocarbons (CFCs) used chiefly in refrigeration. Because water vapor is naturally abundant (up to four per cent by volume of the atmosphere), and fluctuates even hourly, we treat it as part of the normal atmosphere, and include only carbon dioxide and the other trace gases in greenhouse calculations. Nevertheless, the warming effect of these other gases is partly exercised by the increase in atmospheric water vapor it brings about.

The natural greenhouse effect actually raises global surface temperatures by 33°C above what they otherwise would be — and hence makes the planet habitable. We depend for our existence on an effect we have taught ourselves to fear!

The real threat comes, not from this benign process, but from the human-induced rise in concentration of the greenhouse gases, currently in progress at about one per cent per annum, in terms of effective heating power. Figure 2-2 shows some of these increases. In the case of carbon dioxide, human interference is adding at least six and probably eight billion tons of elemental carbon to the atmosphere every year, of which about 3.4 billion remain there — an

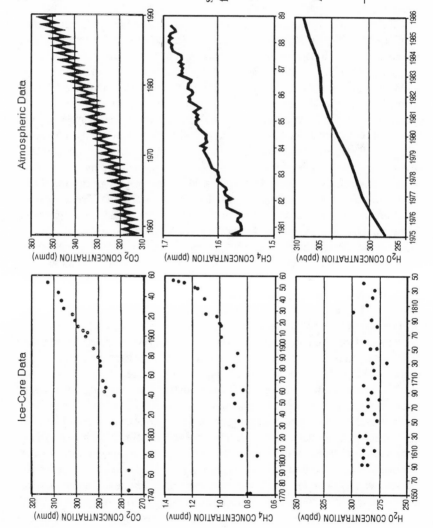

Fig. 2-2. Rises in concentration of three greenhouse gases, as revealed by air samples trapped in glacial ice, on left, and by recent measurement, on right. The saw-like appearance of the carbon dioxide curve (from Mauna Loa, Hawaii) is due to seasonal changes arising from the annual cycle of photosynthesis, which absorbs carbon dioxide, and respiration, which releases it. *Top curves: carbon dioxide (CO_2). Middle curves: methane (CH_4). Bottom curves: nitrous oxide (N_2O).*

Source: The State of Canada's Environment, Environment Canada, 1991.

annual increase of 0.5 percent. Methane and nitrous oxide are also increasing, possibly because of our activities, and the rising concentration of chlorofluorocarbons and other synthetic gases comes wholly from human agencies. The net effect, therefore, is that human action seems responsible for raising temperatures above those due to the natural greenhouse effect, at a rate that might prove damaging to living communities.

This addition, rapid by comparison with natural processes, is best called *the augmented greenhouse effect*.[4] Its consequences for world climate have been intensively studied by IPCC (1990, 1992). The predictions depend on estimates of the future rates of greenhouse gas release and accumulation (see, in particular, IPCC 1992 and Wigley and Raper 1992), and on simulation models of the consequent behavior of the atmosphere and ocean. These general circulation models (GCMs) call for the use of the most advanced supercomputers, and vast amounts of data and skill. The effort involved is internationally coordinated by the World Meteorological Organization (WMO) and the International Council of Scientific Unions (ICSU), in which most countries participate.

These models predict that a doubled greenhouse gas concentration (weighted by the relative effectiveness of the gases in producing a warming) should lead at equilibrium to a rise in global annual mean surface air temperature of between 1.5°C and 4.5°C. Since the date of such a doubling is highly uncertain, IPCC tried to specify ranges of probable temperatures by the year 2070. They suggested a rise of temperature between 1.6°C and 3.5°C (best guess 2.4°C) by that date. The predictions also imply that the earth's surface should already have warmed up by more than has been observed (i.e., more than the 0.5°C reported since 1910). If the observed warming has been due to the augmented greenhouse effect, then the result has been smaller than could be expected; climate seems to have responded conservatively to the new influence.[5]

A rise of such magnitude — more rapid than most changes inferred from the past 10,000 years of climatic history (which we know in some detail) — implies major impacts on sea-level, on ecosystems, and on crops. Global mean sea-level is thought to have risen by ten to twenty cm in the past century, and will probably rise further; a recent estimate is of forty-eight cm (Wigley and Raper 1992 — best guess) by the year 2100, considerably less than many speculative estimates, and with a wide range of uncertainty. The rise will come from melting land ice, and from expansion of the warming ocean water column.

There are many skeptics who question the above estimates. Some go so far as to doubt whether any measurable warming should yet have occurred, and whether any future warming is likely beyond a very small effect. These critics rely on a variety of arguments. The most important critics are those who believe that the immense heat capacity of the ocean should be able to absorb much of the added heating. Recent atmosphere-ocean models take this into account.

They introduce the greenhouse warming at a reasonable pace, and do indeed predict warmings of only about sixty percent of the equilibrium values cited by the year 2070. Other critics maintain that sulfate aerosols introduced into cloud systems, chiefly due to industrial pollution in the northern hemisphere, might induce a cooling that would partially or completely offset the greenhouse warming (Kaufman and Chou 1993; Kiehl and Briegleb 1993). Still others argue that the models' acknowledged failure adequately to treat cloud and precipitation renders the predicted warming implausible.

Nevertheless, there is a majority among the best qualified observers, who maintain (1) that the small observed warming since 1910 is real, and will continue; and (2) that the causal mechanism is the augmented greenhouse effect. These views carried the day at UNCED, leading to the signing of the Climate Convention, which called for drastic measures to slow the release of greenhouse gases worldwide.

THE OZONE PROBLEM

Anxiety about possible threats to the earth's ozone layer goes back to the early 1970s. Ozone is created by the breakup by ultra-violet radiation of two-atom oxygen molecules (O_2) in the stratosphere (above about thirty km) and subsequent recombination as three-atom ozone (O_3). The process shields the earth's surface from the more powerful forms of ultraviolet, which attack genetic materials in the human skin, and also in certain green plants.

In nature, the creation of such ozone is balanced by natural processes of dissociation, the most important of which depends on the upward diffusion of nitrous oxide (N_2O) from the earth's surface. In the early 1970s, however, it was proposed that active oxides of nitrogen from jet aircraft exhaust, or chlorine released from synthetic polluting gases, notably the chlorofluorocarbons, might also penetrate the stratosphere — and thereby reduce ozone concentrations in the protective layer.

Subsequently, it has become clear that chlorine is the chief agent of added ozone depletion. There is continuing argument as to the relative roles of volcanic sources and chemical pollutants for the observed concentrations of chlorine, chlorine oxide, and hydrochloric acid in the ozone layer (see, for example, Taubes 1993; Rodriguez 1993; and in particular Singer 1993, and Rowland 1993). What is unquestioned is that unexpectedly low values of ozone have recently been experienced worldwide. The eruption of Mt. Pinatubo in 1991 seems to have been responsible for record low ozone in 1992 (Gleason et al. 1993; Kerr 1993). Together with the "ozone hole" observed each spring over the margin of the Antarctic, and with a general downward trend of ozone since 1988, these low values have renewed fears that serious damage to the ozone layer is now unavoidable;[6] even the phasing-out of chlorofluorocarbon manufacture by 1996, as required by the revised Montreal Protocol, will not prevent such damage, if the models are correct.

The ozone problem is part of a larger phenomenon, as is the greenhouse effect. The chemical balance of the atmosphere is being upset by the introduction of alien chemical species, such as the CFCs, or by increased flows of greenhouse gases into the atmosphere. The most active agents have long atmospheric lifetimes (true of those that are not readily washed out by rain). Such gases are carried world-wide by the winds, and produce global effects on climate, the biota, and human well-being. The atmosphere is in many ways self-cleansing; but removal of the more unwelcome species is bound to be slow — too slow, in fact, for us to avoid the consequences of their increase in the atmosphere. We created this problem for ourselves; and it will not be easy to undo the damage to which the atmosphere has already been committed by our actions.

THE FATE OF GLOBAL ECOSYSTEMS

If we now ask the question: "what will climatic change do to the world's ecosystems?" we encounter a difficulty: that direct human impact has usually obscured any influence of current climatic change. The world's natural forests, at least a third of which have vanished, and at least another third of which have been greatly changed, have been cut down, burned, or drastically altered by humankind. Even in the dry scrub and savannas of the African Sahel, where the great desiccation of the 1970s and 1980s was accompanied by the spread of desert surfaces — desertification — destructive human use of the land under the stress of drought caused much of the damage. Climatic change within the past century, though it has certainly affected many of the world's ecosystems, has done so in subtle ways that can be identified only by careful study.

There is a long literature dealing with forest clearance by human societies that were seeking to establish farm economies, or to find timber for construction, fuel, or charcoal production. Ever since the beginnings of agriculture, this assault has been in progress, while subtler but no less profound change has occurred in natural grasslands — prairie, steppe, and savanna. Europe, in particular, has little left of its original forests and grasslands. The well-wooded landscapes of Britain, France, central and eastern Europe owe their appearance to forest regrowth or reforestation. Exotic tree species abound as proof of the influence of humankind. China and India show little trace of their once abundant forests, and growing human numbers have ensured that there has been no chance to rebuild. Every square meter of fertile land has been needed to feed more and more people.

The world's remaining stands are chiefly evergreen tropical rain forests, or dry forests, and considerable areas of the largely coniferous Boreal Forest. Large-scale replanting has restored many areas of mid-latitude forest, for example in central Europe and the eastern United States, so that in those areas the extent of wooded land has actually increased in this century — though in Europe considerable areas have been damaged afresh by acid deposition.

Although there have been many studies investigating individual cases of supposed impact of changing climate on ecosystems, no global synthesis has been attempted. Instead, ecologists have concentrated on (1) the aggregate human impact in specific areas, chiefly on forests; and (2) the probable effect of *future* climatic change. The IPCC reviews, for example, barely mention past human impact (Melillo et al. 1990).

Nevertheless, there have been attempts to synthesize impacts on key ecosystems. The surviving tropical rain forests, for example, have been surveyed as far as possible, and there is widespread anxiety at the rate of their destruction under the influence of slash-and-burn cultivation, clearance of land for pastoral farming, and exploitation of timber for export. Norman Myers (1992, 1993) has estimated that there are fourteen main theaters of destruction. He calculated that in 1991 148,000 square kilometers of forest were being destroyed annually, or 1.97 percent of the surviving stock. If the forest is rapidly replaced by renewed growth, as in slash-and-burn cultivation, the net transfer of carbon to the atmosphere is restricted. But replacement of forest by pasture represents a large upward carbon transfer. All forest clearance tends to augment atmospheric carbon content; the oxidation of soil humus (abundant only in middle and high latitudes) and litter may be responsible for the annual transfer of two billion tons of carbon to the atmosphere — as compared with fossil fuel burning now approaching six billion tons.

In many ways, the key question is the probable impact of global warming on biological production, i.e., on net synthesis of carbon-rich living tissues by the earth's ecosystems. Work at the Ecosystems Center, at the Woods Hole Marine Biological Laboratory, has allowed calculation of the probable response of world biomes (i.e., living communities) to the effects of doubled carbon dioxide and the associated warming, as depicted by four general circulation models. The results suggest increases in net production of between twenty and twenty-six per cent in all biomes — i.e., a significant invigoration of biological productivity. This will arise from carbon dioxide fertilization in tropical and dry temperate areas, and from warmth-induced increase of nitrogen availability in moist mid-latitude areas and high latitudes. The effect is not spatially uniform, however; in some regions increased cloudiness or decreased precipitation may actually lead to losses in production. Furthermore, the terrestrial ecosystem model used deals with the biomes as if they remained anchored in their present positions. In reality, there is likely to be a selective migration of species poleward, probably accompanied by severe stress for many present plants and animals. The authors assert that their main purpose was to develop a model to investigate "the potential effects of climatic change on biospheric functions in a quantitative and geographically specific way" (Melillo et al. 1993, p. 239). They have made a very good start.

But it is wise to be cautious about all such predictions. Notions that carbon dioxide fertilization will benefit terrestrial vegetation, or that precipitation losses in continental interiors will threaten food production, have little usefulness unless tied to specific times and places. Until atmospheric scientists, foresters, ecologists, and agricultural scientists have fitted their models together in a convincing way, the rest of us should reserve judgment. In any case, the effect of climatic change will still be dwarfed by the direct impact of humanity for some decades, if not longer.

CONCLUSION

I have not done proper justice to the extent to which the planet Earth's surface and biosphere are now being changed, chiefly by human action. My choice of subject has been colored by scientific interests and personal background. Others would have made different choices. But chiefly my account has been affected by two emotions. One is anger at the role of my own species in this assault on nature. And the other is a sense of urgency, coupled with a feeling of impotence at the size of the challenge facing us all.

Obviously, my account of the science is incomplete; an entire encyclopedia could not cover all that is relevant — and nearly everything remains to be done. Science is a system of progressive approximation to reality — a reality that evolves with time, the knowledge of which sometimes seems to recede. The scientific community is at work as never before, with instruments, vehicles, and methodologies barely conceived two decades ago. I cannot promise that this effort — which is uniquely international — will give clear enough answers to allow us to take remedial measures. I can only confirm that the Global Change movement, and its relatives, will not relax their efforts.

I repeat my profoundly felt view that this issue is moral, not merely at root, but in most of its substance. The facts can be objectively set out, and solutions devised that are potentially effective (at least, so we hope). None of this will solve our problems unless it is coupled with a rising conviction, among all peoples, that the planet must be protected against human follies. As yet, we are not even unanimous that they *are* follies. Our various backgrounds, political, economic, and religious, have so far kept us apart. Above all other requirements, in my own litany, is the need to control our fecundity. Increases in human numbers, with the related increases in economic product, and in world trade — ultimately we shall have to see the future in terms not of increase, but of stability. As yet, we are nowhere near that condition for survival.

NOTES

1. We distinguish between atmospheric composition and physical properties, on the one hand, and characteristic atmospheric behavior, which is climate, on the other. A similar distinction can be made in ocean science. Hitherto, distinct professional communities have worked separately on the two categories. Fear of global change has brought them together. The World Climate Programme, a long established effort, involves both domains.

2. The standardization and collation of observations is highly developed in the atmospheric sciences. The World Meteorological Organization, a UN agency, has recognized several world data centers, and most countries (Canada included) have national archives. The volume of data has multiplied greatly since the beginning of satellite observation. The inventory of ocean observations is smaller, but growing fast.

3. Nitrous oxide, N_2O, is released from the soil as the result of the decay of dead plant and animal tissues, and from certain industrial processes. It is inert until broken down in the stratosphere. It should not be confused with the various oxides of odd nitrogen, called collectively NO_x, which are chemically active pollutants.

4. The more familiar *enhanced* greenhouse effect is obviously ambiguous, since "enhanced" can imply improvement as well as enlargement.

5. I have treated these model estimates more fully in Hare 1993, pp. 17–20.

6. Between May and August 1993, total ozone above Canadian cities was between two and eleven percent below pre-1980 values. Montréal, Halifax, Toronto, Edmonton, and Vancouver were all in the range seven to nine percent below. Winnipeg, which had a very cloudy, wet summer, was only two percent below pre-1980 values (J. Kerr 1993).

BIBLIOGRAPHY

Angell, J. K. 1988. Variations and trends in tropospheric and stratospheric global temperatures, 1958–87. *Journal of Climate* 1: 1296–1313.

Angell, J. K. 1991. Stratospheric temperature change as a function of height and sunspot number during 1972–89 based on rocketsonde and radiosonde data. *Journal of Climate* 4: 1170–80.

Dansgaard, W., S. J. Johnsen, H. B. Klausen, D. Dahl-Jensen, N. S. Gunderstrup, C. V. Hammer, C. S. Hvidberg, J. P. Steffensen, A. E. Sveinbjörnsdottir, J. Jouzel, and G. Bond 1993. Evidence for general instability of past climate from a 250-kyr ice-core record. *Nature* 364: 218–20.

Gleason, J. F., P. K. Bartia, J. R. Herman, R. McPeters, P. Newman, R. S. Stolarski, L. Flynn, G. Labow, D. Larko, C. Seftor, C. Wellemeyer, W. D. Komhyr, A. J. Miller, and W. Planet 1993. Record low global ozone in 1992. *Science* 260: 523–25.

Gullett, D. W., and W. R. Skinner 1992. *The state of Canada's climate: temperature change in Canada 1895–1991*. State of the Environment Report No. 92–2. Ottawa: Environment-Canada.

Hare, F. K. 1993. The challenge. In *Ethics and climate change: the greenhouse effect*, eds. H. G. Coward and T. Hurka. Waterloo, Ont.: Wilfrid Laurier University Press.

Intergovernmental Panel on Climate Change (IPCC) 1990. *Climate change: the IPCC scientific assessment*. Cambridge: Cambridge University Press.

Intergovernmental Panel on Climate Change (IPCC) 1992. *Climate change 1992: the supplementary report to the IPCC Scientific Assessment*. Edited by J. T. Houghton, B. A. Callander and S. K. Varney. Cambridge: Cambridge University Press.

Jouzel, J., N. I. Barkov, J. M. Barnola, M. Bender, J. Chappelaz, C. Genthon, V. M. Kotlyakov, V. Lipenkov, C. Lorius, J. R. Petit, D. Raynaud, G. Raisbeck, C. Ritz, T. Sowers, M. Stievenard, F. Yiou, and P. Yiou 1993. Extending the Vostock ice-core record of palaeoclimate to the penultimate glacial period. *Nature* 364: 407–12.

Kaufman, Y. J. and Ming-Dah Chou 1993. Model simulations of the competing climatic effects of SO_2 and CO_2. *Journal of Climate* 6: 1241–52.

Kerr, R. A. 1993. Ozone takes a nose dive after the eruption of Mt. Pinatubo. *Science* 60: 490–91.

Kerr, J. 1993. Largest summertime ozone depletions ever noted. *Climatic Perspectives* 15: 9.

Kiehl, J. T., and B. P. Briegleb 1993. The relative roles of sulfate aerosols and greenhouse gases in climate forcing. *Science* 260: 311–14.

Melillo, J. M., T. G. Callaghan, F. I. Woodward, E. Salati, and S. K. Sinha 1990. Effects on ecosystems, in IPCC 1990 *vid. sup.*

Melillo, J. M., A. D. McGuire, D. W. Kicklighter, B. Moore III, C. J. Vorosmarty, and A. L. Schloss 1993. Global climate change and terrestrial net primary production. *Nature* 363: 234–40.

Myers, N. 1992. *Future operational monitoring of tropical forests: an alert strategy*. Ispra, Italy: Joint Research Centre, ISPRA Establishment.

Myers, N. 1993. Tropical forests: the main deforestation fronts. *Environmental Conservation* 20: 9–16.

Rodriguez, J. M. 1993. Probing stratospheric ozone. *Science* 261: 1128–29.

Rowland, R. S. 1993. Response to S. F. Singer letter, see *Science* 261: 1102–3.

Singer, S. F. 1993. Ozone depletion theory. *Science* 261: 1101–2.

Taubes, G. 1993. The ozone backlash. *Science* 260: 1580–83.

Wigley, T. M. L., and S. C. B. Raper 1992. Implications for climate and sea level of revised IPCC emissions scenarios. *Nature* 357: 293–300.

World Meteorological Organization 1993. In *World Climate News* no. 2, Geneva.

3

The Human Context

ANNE WHYTE

WHAT IS THE POPULATION-ENVIRONMENT PROBLEM?

Simply stated, human populations are the prime cause of environmental stress. The planet's capacity to meet human demands for natural resources, and equally, its ability to absorb the wastes produced by human activities, is under attack. In some parts of the world, the battle has been lost, at least temporarily, as natural systems break down. In many areas there are signs of stress, as fish populations decline, deserts expand, ground water becomes contaminated with agricultural chemicals, and forests do not regenerate. The signs of stress are evident locally, as soils become eroded and birds disappear. But more and more, local stress has escalated to become planetary stress, and "global change" has become part of our vocabulary. The sense of crisis has deepened, as the scale of environmental change has become apparent, and the understanding is growing that the causes are not easily "fixed," for they lie deep within human desires and the way that societies function. When we look at the "environmental crisis," we see our own human reflection; our lifestyles, the existence of great wealth and great poverty, and our ever-increasing numbers.

Some Key Population-Environment Linkages

We have become lulled over the past few decades into believing that the earth's resources were not finite, but could be expanded to meet growing demands,

Table 3-1. Some Critical Population-Environment Links

ENDANGERED ENVIRONMENTS

FROM RESOURCE DEMAND	FROM WASTE PRODUCTION
• Tropical forests	• Atmosphere
• Arid lands	• Coastal waters
• Fragile highlands	• Freshwater rivers, lakes
• Coastal lowlands	• Boreal forests
• Fishing zones	• Agricultural land
• Freshwater	
• Soils	
• Urban areas	

• Loss of biological diversity

MOST VULNERABLE GROUPS

• Environmental refugees
• Poor households
• Women and children
• Landless rural households
• Urban squatters
• Small landowners (< 1 hectare)
• Fishing communities

through new resource discoveries and new technologies. For the past fifty years or so, this has been achieved. But the situation has largely changed in the last decade. Globally, food production is not increasing. The slowdown is occurring in some of the world's most productive land and most bountiful waters. Water shortages are increasingly constraining development; agricultural land is being lost more rapidly than new land is being brought under cultivation. It is estimated that current rates of extinction for plants and animals are approximately one thousand times more rapid than recent historical values. In other words, current development patterns are reaching the limits that the earth's natural systems can sustain. In some cases, limits are exceeded, and irreversible environmental damage ensues.

The critical zones where population and environment are in a downward spiral are to be found in all parts of the globe: many, however, are in the South, where poverty acts as an intervening negative force (table 3-1). Land resources are under pressure where poor families live on smaller and smaller farms. Data from fifty-seven developing countries show that nearly half the farms are less than one hectare. In Kenya, the average size of farms has halved in the last thirty years, as the population has doubled. Smaller farms means more movement into marginal lands, whether they are the steeper, poorer slopes in highland areas, the drier zones in drylands, or the uncleared lands in forests. Population growth leading to in-migration is estimated to be responsible for eighty percent of recent deforestation in the tropics (UNFPA, 1991). Behind these alarming statistics are more depressing ones about social inequity: in Brazil, for example, five percent of farmers own seventy percent of the grazing land, while seventy percent of farmers cultivate five percent of the available arable land. At a time when we need to double the land under cultivation in order to feed the world's population in 2025, agricultural land is contracting rather than expanding.

Pressure on land means loss of soil: globally, this means a loss every year of some 26 billion tons of valuable top soil. In the words of Jean-Marie Sawadogo, a farmer in Burkino Faso who lost half his land to the desert:

> In my father's time, millet filled all the granaries and the soil was deeper than your body before you reached rock. Now we have to buy food in all but the wettest years, and the soil is no deeper than my hand. (Camp 1989)

Water is another basic resource that is being strained at the limits by the demands of human populations. In eighty-eight developing countries, representing forty percent of the world's population, water deficits are already seriously constraining development. The available fresh water per capita has shrunk from 33,300 cubic meters in 1850 to 8,500 cubic meters in 1991. In countries with rapidly growing populations, such as Kenya, water scarcity is reaching a critical point. Within 10–20 years from now, Kenya's water supply per capita will be half of what it is today; Nigeria's will decline by 42 percent and Egypt's supply will be down by 33 percent (UNESCO 1992).

The planet's natural systems provide vital services to human populations: they are the source of basic human needs for food, water, energy, and shelter. They maintain the necessary genetic biodiversity that sustains life and enables increasing productivity. They absorb wastes and provide basic recycling and renewal of nutrients, chemicals, and natural resources. All of these "services" are now under stress. But we risk a further loss if we continue to degrade our natural environment. These are the spiritual and cultural resources that the natural world provides to our societies. Already, fear of further loss of our natural world is impoverishing our spirituality, our hopes for the future, and our view of ourselves.

Table 3-2. Global Population Growth

PAST	
• First several million years	less than 5 million
• 8000 B.C.–0 A.D. (8,000 yrs)	250 million
• 0 A.D.–1800 A.D. (1,800 yrs)	1 billion
• 1800–1930 (130 yrs)	2 billion
• 1930–1960 (30 yrs)	3 billion
• 1961–1975 (14 yrs)	4 billion
• 1975–1987 (12 yrs)	5 billion
PRESENT	
• 10 August 1993	5.578 billion
FUTURE	
• 2000	8.5 billion
• 2025	10 billion
• 2150	11.6 billion levelling off

A Question of Numbers: Yesterday, Today, and Tomorrow

For the first several million years of human development, the population of *homo sapiens* remained at fewer than five million people world-wide. Mexico City has more than twenty million inhabitants today. Between 8,000 years B.P. and the birth of Christ, the world's population grew to some 250 million (about the present population of the U.S.A.), and there is evidence of local environmental stress occurring in places like Mesopotamia, where salination of soils was caused by excessive irrigation. From that time until 1800, the world's population reached its first billion, and the rest, as they say, is history (table 3-2). Within 130 years (1800–1930) the first billion became two billion, with most of the growth taking place in Europe as it led the world in the Industrial Revolution. North America became a release valve for this population pressure, as the American "frontier" absorbed more than fifteen percent of European population growth through migration, with consequent devastation for the American Aboriginal peoples.

Today, the world's population is over five and a half billion with a predicted population within ten years of some seven to eight billion. "Middle of the road" estimates see 11.6 billion population by 2150, before some leveling-off occurs. We know that our present 5.6 billion population is causing environmental stress that, historically, is unprecedented in scale. It is difficult to countenance a near-future world with ten billion people, even for those with the greatest faith in technological progress.

There are additional reasons to view present population growth with concern; the growth is unprecedented in other ways. More than 85 percent of current population growth is in the world's poor countries of Africa (3.0 percent annual population growth), Latin America (2.1 percent), and Asia (1.9 percent). The populations of these countries are getting younger, and thus are building in an even greater population "time bomb" (UNFPA 1993). In contrast, the populations of the industrialized countries of Europe, North America, Japan, and Australia have an aging population and negative growth rates.

Second, the current growth rates experienced in some countries of three percent per annum or greater, have *never been experienced before*. These growth rates are about twice that of Europe in the Industrial Revolution. Third, population growth (often combined with local resource depletion and poverty) has historically led to out-migration. For Europe in the last century, it was to North America. Today, the scale and diversity of human migrations is unprecedented, but the range of potential destinations to relieve this population pressure is limited, as wealthier countries close their doors to immigrants and refugees from poor countries ever more securely.

Another new characteristic of today's population growth is that it is increasingly *concentrated in urban environmental "hot spots,"* as cities in developing countries attract the rural poor to add to their own rapid growth rates. In 1950, seven out of ten of the largest cities were in the North; today eight out of ten are in the South. The scale of these "megacities" is also a new and alarming feature. In the 1950s, the ten largest cities in the world all had fewer than fifteen million inhabitants; today, they are all larger than fifteen million. Megacities such as Mexico City (population 20–25 million) create environmental stresses of a new order of magnitude on their local ecosystems. Uneven population distribution, even in a sparsely populated country such as Canada, can cause locally severe environmental problems: 90 percent of the 26.5 million Canadians are concentrated in 8.5 percent of the land area. Local population densities in southern Canada reach more than one thousand persons per square kilometer, compared to an average density of 2.6 persons per square kilometer averaged out over the whole country (Statistics Canada 1991).

Beyond the Numbers: A Question of Lifestyles

Enormous disparities between the developed countries and those in the developing world are seen in the lifestyles of their citizens. Between North and South, there lies a great "consumption divide." The epitome of the modern "consumer society" is North America. It has been estimated that, through resource consumption (especially energy), consumerism, and recreation, each person in the U.S.A. exerts twice the environmental impact of their counterpart in the

Table 3-3. North-South Consumption of Selected Items

| ITEM | SHARE (percent) | |
	NORTH	SOUTH
Meat	64	36
Cereals	48	52
Round wood	46	54
Paper, etc.	81	19
Fertilizers	60	40
Iron and steel	80	20
Cars	92	8
Electricity	81	19
CO_2 emissions	70	30

Source: Parikh *et al.*, 1991.

United Kingdom or in Australia; fifty times that of a citizen of India or China, and almost three hundred times that of a person in Uganda or Laos. This leads Norman Myers (1992) to ask "Can the world afford the U.S.A. and its population of 250 million people?"

Behind such anecdotal comparisons lie major differences in consumption patterns between developed and developing countries (table 3-3). Developing countries, with three-quarters of the world's population, consume only 19 percent of the electricity, 20 percent of the iron and steel, 36 percent of the meat, and own only 8 percent of the world's cars. The developed countries, for their part, have less than one-quarter of the world's population, and consume about 65 percent of the food calories. Similarly, industrial countries are major producers of waste through industrial production, agriculture, transportation, and consumer behavior. The North creates more waste, in total and per capita, and spreads its waste around the globe through the atmosphere, the waterways and oceans, and in landfill sites and waste dumps within and beyond their own borders. Developed countries produce seventy percent of the carbon dioxide emissions that are responsible for climate change.

The high-consumption lifestyles of rich countries also demand a wide variety of foodstuffs and products, which are available at any time of the year. Their wealth means that they can command a "shadow ecology" many times larger than their own food-producing areas, by drawing in food and other resources from other countries (Myers 1992). The production systems of poorer countries become drawn into this global economy in order to earn export dollars, and traditional sustainable agricultural systems providing nutritious, but unfashionable, staple food crops are transformed into unsustainable cash crops such as tobacco, cattle, and cotton.

The excessively wasteful consumption characteristic of the North is a relatively recent phenomenon. Solid waste in the U.S.A. has doubled within the last thirty years; and many of us can recall a time when consumer packaging was a fraction of the plastic "display-pak" of today's supermarkets. Annual global emissions of carbon dioxide have increased ten times this century, and those of sulfur dioxide (a major air pollutant) have increased nearly 450 percent. These are indicative of a significant increase in industrial activity on the planet (Speth 1991).

One of the chief driving forces of these global changes is technological development. Nowhere is this clearer than in the case of synthetic chemicals. In the past fifty years, tens of thousands of new synthetic chemicals have been created by human ingenuity: everything from plastics, industrial chemicals, agricultural fertilizers and pesticides, detergents, food additives, and pharmaceutical drugs. Of the 70,000 chemicals traded around the world today, as many as 35,000 are classified by the United States Environmental Protection Agency and by the OECD as definitely or potentially harmful to human health. Many of these will also be harmful to the environment.

These global statistics of increasing consumption and waste production conceal the major inequities that exist between the rich consumers, who are largely living in the North, and the poor, who are largely living in the South. Per capita consumption of domestic water and energy among the poor of developing countries is well below that needed to achieve minimal acceptable quality of life. There is a huge deficit in consumption patterns in many developing countries: essentially, they need to be granted resource-consumption "space" to enable their populations to catch up. There are also major differences in per capita energy use among developing countries. All developing countries consume only 23 percent of commercial energy (whereas they account for 85 percent of biomass fuel in the form of wood and charcoal); but while China accounts for almost half of that 23 percent, the 50 countries of Africa consume less than 3 percent (Kats 1992).

Increasing use of natural resources, while necessary to raise the standard of living in developing countries, will increase locally and globally the stress on the earth's natural systems. This stress is exacerbated, especially in the case of energy production, by the use of outdated "dirty" production technology together with poor pollution regulatory systems, which are all that developing countries can afford, or are provided with through international assistance. It is thus in the interests of both North and South that developing countries be provided with special access to the best available technology. Increasingly, this problem is recognized in international agreements, such as the Convention on Climate Change (1992) and the Montreal Protocol on Substances that Deplete the Ozone Layer (1987, 1990). The provision of financial resources to developing countries lags far behind the international recognition of the problems as affecting all countries, and constituting a shared responsibility.

Indeed, the 1992 United Nations Conference on Environment and Development (the Earth Summit) underscored the political recognition of the international agenda of global environmental issues. High on this agenda are climate change through greenhouse gas emissions, deforestation, ocean pollution and overfishing, desertification, and the loss of biodiversity. Less talked about, but nonetheless key, ingredients are poverty, population, social structure, and global economic relations. What the Earth Summit did achieve was to gain political acknowledgment that global environmental change is real and urgent and inextricable from social and economic development.

ENVIRONMENTAL PROBLEMS HAVE A HUMAN FACE

That the causes of global change lie largely in human activity that results in excessive waste production and pollution is clear, despite the prevarication of many governments and individuals. The "victims" of these environmental problems who become unemployed or ill, or die prematurely, are often "statistical," in that the links between cause and effect are understood in a general way with many intervening variables, rather than scientifically verifiable for specific cases. But in many developing countries, the human suffering caused by resource scarcity, population pressure, and poverty has a human face; we see it in environmental refugees, the landless rural poor, the urban squatters that make up an increasing proportion of third world cities, and the women and children of the poorest families everywhere.

There is consistent evidence that rapid population growth, and the related environmental degradation, can be reduced by four key interventions:

1. Creating income security and a rising standard of living;

2. Reducing child deaths;

3. Narrowing the gender gap by improving the lot of women;

4. Making family planning choices available.

Any one of these interventions has some beneficial effect, but to achieve significant success, they need to occur, or be introduced, together.

As family incomes rise, and people adopt more urban lifestyles, including employment and education outside of the home, birth rates decline. This is observed in all parts of the world, and among immigrant populations as they adapt to their new social and economic environment. One key element in this transformation is that the value of children to parents changes. Children are treasured for the emotional joy that they bring to a family; they also assure the biological continuity of the parents — they are our stake in the future. In many cultures, children (especially sons) play a special role in performing rituals for the parents when they die. Without children, one's spiritual "afterlife" or "place in heaven" is at risk. Children also contribute to the labor resources of the traditional household; as they grow, they can take increasing responsibility for household tasks, or work on the farm or in the family business, and eventually can expect to take over from the parents the major role of family providers. Children thus contribute economically to the family from an early age on a sliding scale, and eventually will give the parents security in their old age, when they are no longer able to work for themselves.

Children also incur costs for parents. Major costs include housing, food, energy, clothing, education, and child care in sickness and in health. In poor rural societies, the economic contribution of children outweighs the direct costs. In modernizing urban societies, the cash costs of providing such things as child care, education, and housing in raising children generally outweigh their direct economic contribution to the family. Expectations that children will provide for their parents in old age have also been eroded, as social mobility leads to dispersed and fragmented families, and the state has intervened with social support programs. Parents therefore desire fewer children.

The "need" to produce large numbers of children has also been dramatically altered where child mortality has been reduced. When child death rates are high, parents compensate by having more children than they might desire, as an insurance against the loss of some children through premature death. This insurance factor is compounded by gender preferences for sons or daughters. The emotional loss of a child also prompts parents to "replace" that loss by having another child, and this replacement is aided biologically by the sudden cessation of breast-feeding, which no longer acts to suppress ovulation. No country has managed to reduce fertility without first reducing infant mortality.

Improving the lot of women has been shown to be the most consistent variable in reducing the number of children born, and in enhancing each child's chances of survival beyond infancy. In particular, the education of girls and women appears to be one of the best ways out of the environment-population downward spiral. The survival chances of a child whose mother has four or more years of primary education is significantly greater than those of a child whose mother has never been to school (UNICEF 1991). If women are confident that their children will survive, they will have fewer births. Education is a key component in the social progress of women. When women are educated, they are more likely to have higher status in the family and in society, and be empowered to make their own decisions. They also need access to economic resources and to health care, if the investment in their education is to be realized in a greater contribution to society.

The fourth key element in reducing unwanted births is the availability of family planning education and services. While birth rates will eventually fall if child deaths are reduced, the time lag between the two is considerably shortened if family planning choices are known and are available. In the last thirty years, contraceptive use has risen from ten percent to fifty percent of families in developing countries, with China accounting for much of this gain. The availability of more reliable family planning has meant that while it took the United States 58 years to reduce average family size from 6.5 to 3.5, it has taken Indonesia only 28 years, Colombia only 15 years, and China, with a more aggressive approach, only 7 years. This reduced time lag between infant death rates and birth rates has meant about seventy million fewer births per year in developing countries (Catley-Carson 1993).

Better social policies are therefore better environmental policies. In developing countries, greater confidence is a key thread linking income security and a better standard of living, especially for women, to fewer children being born, but each surviving longer, and, consequently, smaller families. This means that even as per capita consumption increases, as it should for much of the developing world, the total burden of population on natural resources will be less. Fewer children among poor families also means less migration to cities and to wealthier countries. Today, with few employment opportunities for young women in rural areas, and increasingly cash-based economies, migration of young girls can be part of a household's strategy to survive. In central Mexico, for example, fifty-two percent of the daughters of large but landless families had migrated, compared to only thirty percent of those families with some land (UNFPA 1993). These migrant daughters are important sources of income for poor families, and are more reliable than migrant sons.

In most countries, especially those in the South, current social investment significantly favors men (table 3-4). This is true of national investments in education and health care, as well as family disparities in access to resources and nutrition. Younger daughters are the least likely to eat well, to go to school, and to inherit wealth. Yet we have seen that the gains in reducing child deaths and population pressure on the environment are greatest when families and societies invest more in their women. The human face that suffers most from environmental stress is female. Likewise, a key to solving the poverty-population-environment nexus is to raise the status of women.

Table 3-4.   Gender Disparities in the Human Development Index, Selected Countries, 1992

COUNTRY	WOMEN'S HDI AS A SHARE OF MEN'S (percent)
Sweden	96
Finland	94
France	92
Paraguay	88
USA	86
Canada	85
United Kingdom	85
Italy	83
Portugal	83
Sri Lanka	79
Philippines	78
Japan	77
Ireland	74
Costa Rica	70
Swaziland	68
Korea	65
Kenya	58

Source: United Nations Development Programme, *Human Development Report 1992* (New York: Oxford University Press, 1992).

RELIGIONS: PAST ROLES AND FUTURE RESPONSIBILITIES

Religion and science have much in common: one attribute they share is that each seeks to provide explanatory frameworks for understanding the relationships between individual human beings and the larger community, and between people and the natural world. Commonly, the explanatory framework they provide for our relationship with the environment shares many features with the explanations they give for our relationship with society. It is these broad explanatory frameworks, be they called myths or theory; parables or models; "revealed truth" or "objective truth"; that provide their adherents with the basis for making judgments about the present, choices for the future, and rationalizations (and acceptance) of the past. Religion and science frame the way that we view the environment, and influence the ways that we act upon it. They also bear responsibility for our attitudes to one another; the rich and the poor, adults and children, men and women. These two sets of values are central to the relationships between poverty, population, and environment.

Given the centrality of religion, and more recently science, in guiding the relationship between population and environment, religious leaders have been generally reticent in examining it. Some aspects of religious influence on development, such as the special role played by Christian missionaries in the European colonization of the countries of Africa, Asia, and Latin America, have been almost "off-limits" for religious reflection. Yet there is evidence that these missionaries helped to destroy traditional sustainable production systems by undermining indigenous reverence for nature; by supporting concepts of individual ownership to replace long-standing common property regimes; by denigrating traditional spirituality and indigenous environmental knowledge (Sihanya 1991). By providing girls with different, "lady-like" education and skills, missionaries also underscored the lower status of women (Carroll 1983).

The influence of religion and science on the relationship between population and environment can be considered under six broad categories:

1. Values relating to population issues;

2. Values relating to the natural environment;

3. Teachings on justice and equity;

4. Attitudes towards the future;

5. Value for speaking out, for "witness";

6. Emphasis on individual responsibility.

There is often a difference between the original fundamental philosophy and inner truth of a religion, especially as taught by its early leaders, and its later codification in religious institutions, rituals and customs. Both influence the attitudes and behavior of their followers, but especially powerful are religious customs and canons, which are interpreted as more relevant, and are often more vigorously promoted by religious institutions, than the original spiritual truths.

Religious values relating to population issues that affect environmental stress include the status and role of women; the purpose and meaning of marriage; attitudes toward sexual intercourse and procreation; attitudes toward family planning generally, and abortion specifically; and the spiritual, biological, social, and economic value placed on children and on the family. Another important set of "population" values are attitudes toward health and disease, and the explanations that are offered by a faith for illness and premature death.

It is instinctive to ask "Why him?" "Why me?" when faced with death or disaster. The explanation provided by religion, whether in terms of moral retribution, individual responsibility, blind chance, or fate, influences people's future behavior and attitudes.

Religious values relating to the natural environment have profoundly influenced the course of the present crisis of global change. The degree to which religion affirms that people are inseparable from the natural world or can maintain a certain degree of independence and difference from the rest of creation is fundamental. Judaic-Christian theology has developed the concept of human "stewardship" of the natural world, which has been blamed for some of the more negative impacts of western development models on the environment. Another dimension of religious "environmental teaching" is the relative weight given to the intrinsic value of the natural world, especially other species, compared to the utilitarian value of natural and biological resources to human societies.

Our view of the natural world influences the degree to which we are prepared to transform it for our own ends, to engineer our own concrete habitats, to reverse the flow of rivers, and to "make the desert bloom." A society's confidence in technology or fear of innovation has been often underwritten by religion. Technology and human organization have wrought great changes on the face of the earth, and religions have influenced the progress of both.

Justice and equity issues are integral to the causes of and solutions for the environmental crisis that faces us today. Population and environment problems cannot be dissociated from poverty and inequity at all levels; within the family, within the community, between countries, between the North and the South, and between generations. The Brundtland Commission (1987) focused attention on intergenerational equity as fundamental to sustainable development. Too many societies, especially the most advanced technologically, are living not only off the interest of environmental resources, but are also eating into the capital that should be transferred, intact, to future generations. How religious teachings explain the great inequities seen in the world today is relevant to how they can help solve the problems of population and environment.

Attitudes towards the future profoundly affect human behavior. Whether it is in the hope of future reward (either of a spiritual or economic nature) for present actions, or fear of retribution, the future plays a role in our present. For many, the environmental crisis, combined with global economic and social transformations in North and South, and continuing poverty for the majority of the world's population, has undermined their faith in the future. This is especially true for younger people who are aware of the global scale of environmental change, and who have seen the fragility of the planet as viewed from outer space. What does a religion teach about the future? Does it provide hope and reason for continued effort? Does it provide a coherent or a fragmented explanation for what is happening? Does it even address the environmental crisis as a matter for religious attention?

The importance accorded "witness," or speaking out, varies greatly between religions, especially on matters regarded as beyond the domain of religion. In Western societies, some Christian denominations appear to behave as though they exist in an intellectual and moral "ghetto," lacking confidence in their moral authority to speak out on major social issues, including environmental pollution and destruction. Scientists have suffered a similar reluctance to speak out against governments or organizations. Except for a few "whistle-blowers," most scientists think that their prior allegiance is to science rather than to society. Yet surely both religions and science share responsibility as key influences on human behavior and have a moral obligation to bear witness against consumerism, profligate energy consumption, major schemes and policies that will damage the environment, and unfair practices between rich and poor countries.

The value placed on individual responsibility versus individualism by a religion also influences how people will behave in their use of the earth's resources. The teaching of individualism encourages a selfish approach to life, in which the desires of the individual come before the good of the community. As often as not, such attitudes are congruent with resource waste and consumerism. Individual responsibility for global change means that people must believe that personal change leads to system change; that changes in their own lifestyle can lead to bigger changes, and that they can be influences for good. Religious institutions and congregations have been somewhat remiss in looking to how they can make changes in themselves, and in their own use of the world's resources, in order "to make a difference," and to influence others with a stronger moral authority.

The Parliament of the World's Religions, held in Chicago in 1993, identified environmental issues as fundamentally spiritual in nature, as the need "to discover who we humans are, how we are to relate to each other and to the whole community of life, and what we are to do, individually and collectively, here on Earth" (Barney 1993). The Parliament asked a number of questions of spiritual leaders. They included:

- "What does your faith tradition teach about the proper relationship between the human species and all other species? Can the concepts of justice, unity and peace be extended beyond the human community to the whole community of life?"
- "How are the needs and wants of humans to be weighed relative to the survival of other forms of life?"
- "How do the fertility stories of your faith relate to its teachings on human procreation? What norms are to be applied to the stew-

ardship of the gift of human fertility? What cultural practices and technologies are appropriate for individuals to employ in regulating their own fertility?"

- "What are the traditional teachings — and the range of other opinions — within your faith on the meaning of "progress" and how it is to be achieved? What dreams and hopes does your tradition inspire in young people? What does your faith tradition offer as a vision for the future of the Earth?"
- "What does your faith tradition have to say about consumerism, about the manipulation and stimulation of desire, about advertising?"
- "In your tradition, how long ago were the roles and rights, and responsibilities of men and women defined? What role did women have in the defining? What are the current teachings of your tradition about the role, rights and responsibilities of women and men?"
- "How does your tradition respond to the revelation from the past 1,500 years of meditation on Earth and its origins — a revelation we usually call "science?" How will the disciplines of religious and scientific inquiry relate to each other in the future? Can science provide new understanding of the primary, original source of religions insight — the universe itself?"

CHALLENGES FOR PUBLIC POLICY

Public policies for population and environment present two of the greatest challenges to governments. Many governments shy away from population issues, especially in policies that are directed to fertility reduction. International aid to population issues is less than 1.5% of total international assistance. Governments in both the North and South have been discouraged from being proactive in population policies, because of lack of public support, and sometimes outright opposition from religious and other groups. Support for environmental policies, especially those which advocate less consumerism, can be equally polarized when jobs close to home appear to be at stake.

Population policies require that governments become involved in areas of decision making that are usually regarded as private and individual: choices about having children; choices about where to live; choices about sexual and family relations. This perceived intrusion into private decision making has led governments to shy away from any accusation of limiting individual freedom, *by promoting population policies as integral to economic development.* In this approach, the present governments of the South have only to point to the recent historical development of the North, where standards of living went up as fertility went down.

Economic development as the solution to the problem of overpopulation is an oversimplification. It ignores both the great human costs incurred in the North as fertility declined (including the separation of families through migration and the large number of poor women entering the industrial work force), and the fact that the fertility decline took place over the course of half a century or more — a time frame which is not available today. Promotion of population control as a means of modernization also holds the promise of Western-style consumerism as the reward. This approach also puts population policies in head-on collision with environmental policies.

The real challenge for public policy is to frame population policies within environmental, cultural, and spiritual goals. This means that private choices must be brought into line with the public good. In other words, policies dealing with population and environment will succeed insofar as they are rooted in public education and public participation. They cannot be effectively imposed through regulation. People will support policies that require a change in their own lifestyles and personal choices if, and only if, they agree personally with the goals of the policies and can see equity and effectiveness in the way that they are applied. This is why sustainable development policies (which is essentially what we are discussing) are potentially revolutionary. They demand a new covenant between governments and citizens.

Sustainable development requires individual citizens, especially those who "have more," to voluntarily reduce their consumption of resources and adopt more modest lifestyles for the benefit of those who "have less." Any new covenant between people and democratically elected governments will succeed toward sustainable development only insofar as it can embody trust, goodwill, and a sense of fairness between all parties, because, ultimately, private choices, even in the public interest, cannot be regulated except under the most severe regimes, but have to be voluntarily undertaken.

Another challenge for public policy makers is to go beyond the national interest, as traditionally defined, and to champion policies that see the national interest as a component of the global interest. Nowhere is this need for a global perspective greater than in the areas of population growth, resource consumption, and waste production; that is, population and environment. Parallel with this need for more global horizons is the need for better understanding of the interconnectedness of all policies. Transportation policy, education policy, agricultural policy, and especially energy policy, are not discrete policy fields; they are all policies for population and environment, for sustainable development.

One of the disturbing trends of the past decade has been toward more inward-looking political agendas in many industrialized, high-consuming countries. The "peace dividend" is being used to shore up consumerism in the North. Political support for international assistance is waning, and consumer support to pay fairer prices for commodities purchased from developing countries is even further away. The call at the Earth Summit for new and innovative additional financing for sustainable development paths in the South has gone largely unheeded. Proposals for debt relief, new financing for "clean technology" transfers, or charges to be made for the use of the "global commons" such as the atmosphere and oceans, have not resulted in substantial initiatives (Holmberg 1992). Aggregate net financial transfers to developing countries have declined from an average of $46 billion in 1980–82 to $3 billion in 1989 (OECD 1990). In short, we are far from a new covenant for sustainable development in our own countries.

THE WAY AHEAD

One of the ways ahead that holds promise is to find common ground between religion, science, and public policy. For too long, these spheres of influence have talked within their own houses, as solitudes. There has been a recent resurgence of interest among some faiths in the Creation, and our present and future environment (Brooks 1990, Vischer 1991, Hallman 1989, The Greenhouse Crisis Foundation 1990, Presbyterian Eco-Justice Task Force 1989). Congregations are considering their own environmental impact and are changing their individual and community habits.

One important initiative has been the *"Mission to Washington": The Joint Appeal by Religion and Science for the Environment,* which brought religious leaders representing 330,000 congregations in the USA and some fifty scientists together in the US Senate on 12 May 1992, to find common cause in urging the US Government to better protect the global environment and to recognize the environmental impacts of consumerism and population growth (Congressional Record 13 May 1992). The Declaration, which was signed by leaders of many different faiths and by scientists (including myself), includes the following words:

> We are people of faith and of science who, for centuries, often have traveled different roads. In a time of environmental crisis, we find these roads converging. As this meeting symbolizes, our two ancient, sometimes antagonistic, traditions now reach out to one another in a common endeavor to preserve the home we share.
>
> We believe that science and religion, working together, have an essential contribution to make toward any significant mitigation and resolution of the world environmental crisis. What good are the most

fervent moral imperatives if we do not understand the dangers and how to avoid them? What good is all the data in the world without a steadfast moral compass?

Differences of perspective remain among us. We do not have to agree on how the natural world was made to be willing to work together to preserve it.

BIBLIOGRAPHY

Barney, G. O. 1993. *Global 2000 Revisited: What shall we do?* Summary Report on the critical issues of the 21st century prepared for the Parliament of the World's Religions, Chicago, 28 August–4 September 1993.

Brooks, D. B. 1990. *Judaism and Ecology.* Ottawa.

Brundtland Commission 1987. *Our Common Future: World Commission on Environment and Development.* New York: Oxford University Press.

Camp, S. L. 1989. *Population Pressure, Poverty and the Environment.* Washington, D.C.: Population Crisis Committee.

Carroll, T. F. 1983. *Women, Religion and Development in the Third World.* New York: Praeger.

Catley-Carson, M. 1993. *Explosions, Eclipses, and Escapes: Charting a Course on Global Population Issues.* Population Council, New York.

Greenhouse Crisis Foundation 1990. *101 Ways to Help Save the Earth.* New York: National Council of Churches of Christ.

Hallman, D. G. 1989. *Caring for Creation.* Winfield, Canada: Wood Lake Books.

Holmberg, J. 1992. "Financing Sustainable Development." In *Policies for a Small Planet,* edited by J. Holmberg. London: Earthscan Publications, Ltd.

Kats, G. 1992, "Achieving Sustainability in Energy Use in Developing Countries." In *Policies for a Small Planet,* edited by J. Holmberg. Earthscan Publications, Ltd.

Myers, N. 1992. A population policy for the North? *People and the Planet* 1(3), p. 31.

Parikh, J. et al. 1991. *Consumption Patterns — The Driving Force of Environmental Stress.* Bombay: Indira Ghandi Institute of Development Research.

Presbyterian Eco-Justice Task Force 1989. *Keeping and Healing the Creation.* Louisville, Ky.: Committee on Social Witness Policy, Presbyterian Church.

Sihanya, B. M. 1991. *Environmental Ethics.* Policy Outlook Paper. Nairobi: African Centre for Technology Studies.

Speth, J. G. 1991. *Environmentally Unsustainable Consumption Patterns: Is There a Way Out?* Washington, D.C.: World Resources Institute.

Statistics Canada 1991. *Human Activity and the Environment 1991.* Ottawa: Statistics Canada.

UNDP 1993. *Human Development Report 1993.* New York: Oxford University Press.

UNFPA 1991. *Population and the Environment: The Challenges Ahead.* New York: United Nations Population Fund.

UNFPA 1993. *The State of World Population 1993*. New York: United Nations Population Fund.

UNICEF 1991. *The State of the World's Children 1991*. New York: Oxford University Press.

United States 1992. *Congressional Record: Proceeding and Debates of the 102nd Congress, second session,* Vol 138, no. 66, 13 May 1992, Washington, D.C.

Vischer, L. 1991. *The Churches' Role in Protecting the Earth's Atmosphere;* Report of an Ecumenical Consultation of Churches in Northern Industrialized Countries. Gwatt, Switzerland, 13–18 January 1991.

II

Religious Responses

4

Aboriginal Spirituality, Population,
and the Environment

DAISY SEWID-SMITH

Population control has become a real dilemma worldwide. As the population increases, there are more and more demands on the world's resources — resources that are now rapidly being depleted. Some of the nations of the world are considering numerous ways of controlling their populations. This is not an easy task for many of them, because their population policies derive from religious doctrines that encourage procreation. The Aboriginal nations do not have the population pressure that the rest of the world faces, because circumstances never gave them the opportunity to increase in numbers, for several reasons. Until quite recently, the Aboriginals have been in danger of becoming extinct, and that is the reason why they were referred to as the "vanishing race." The Aboriginal Nations cannot possibly fathom the population problems facing China or India because every inch of those countries is being utilized. In Canada we see vast areas of unused lands, lands that the Aboriginal Nations are still negotiating for in Land Claims issues. The main concern of the Aboriginal Nations over the years has been to settle land claims issues and preserve the race, so that they would no longer be a "vanishing race."

POPULATION PRIOR TO EUROPEAN CONTACT

The population figures for the Aboriginal people prior to contact are not really known. The figures that are now being quoted are estimates from the Hudson's Bay Company, a missionary, or from some government official. Their

reliability is always open to question, because most Aboriginals were no-
madic. They would move from one location to another while preparing food
for the winter, so they never stayed in one area long enough to be counted. The
accuracy of these figures is also questioned by Wilson Duff, in *The Indian
History of British Columbia.*

> We would very much like to know how many Indians there were
> in the 1770s before the first effects of European contact began to be felt,
> but unfortunately it is not possible with the information now avail-
> able to make accurate estimates for any time earlier than 1835. About
> that time the traders of the Hudson's Bay Company were instructed to
> make censuses of the tribes with which they were in contact, and sev-
> eral of the resulting counts are available for sections of British Co-
> lumbia. (Duff 1965, 38)

However, the estimates given by the Hudson's Bay Company differ from
what the Aboriginal people estimated their own population to be prior to contact. The Hudson's Bay Company came into our territory (Kwagiutl) in 1845.
They built a fort at Fort Rupert. At that time, my nation consisted of eighteen
tribal groups. The total population given for my nation as a whole in 1835 was
10,700 (Duff 1965, 39). Many times, my grandmother and great-grandmother
talked about the population of my own tribal group (Mamalilikalla) as being so
large that they did not know each other. If you average out the estimated population of 10,700, the eighteen tribal groups would have a population of approximately 600 for each tribe. The population of my mother's tribal group
(Nimpkish) was approximately 800 people in the early 1960s. Everyone knew
each other. The population was aware of every birth and death in the tribal
group. The total population given for the nine Aboriginal Nations in British
Columbia, including my own tribal group, was 70,000. Apparently, Wilson
Duff also questioned this figure, for he comments that "the population in aboriginal times must have been considerably larger than 70,000." He goes on to
say:

> Other writers have been bold enough to guess at what the pre-
> contact population of the Province may have been. Hill-Tout (1907, p.
> 28) set it at 125,000 or more. The best estimates are those of James
> Mooney, who attempted to establish the population in 1780 of all
> North American tribes (Mooney 1928); his estimates for those with-
> in British Columbia give a total of 86,000. All that can be said with con-
> fidence is that the aboriginal population must have been at least 80,000
> and probably somewhat more." (Duff 1965, 39)

POPULATION AFTER EUROPEAN CONTACT

The arrival of the first Europeans was not for the purpose of immigration from their respective countries but for the sole purpose of exploiting our resources. This was done with very little regard for the Aboriginal people's welfare. The first to arrive in the northwest in 1741 were the Russians. In 1774, Spain ordered Juan Perez to sail from Mexico to explore the coastline and to open trade with the Aboriginal Nations. He arrived at the Queen Charlotte Islands and later came south to Nootka on the west coast of Vancouver Island. Juan Perez only stayed for a few days, but, in 1775, two ships arrived on the coast from Spain under Commander Bodegay Quadra. It was at this time that Bodegay Quadra took possession of our lands for Spain. He later established a settlement at Nootka in 1789. In 1775, the year Spain arrived on the coast, the first major smallpox epidemic ravaged the Aboriginal Nations. In 1778, the English, under Captain James Cook, arrived in Nootka. There was a confrontation between Spain and England over ownership of the Nootka territories. Spain finally conceded in 1793 and turned the Nootka territories over to England. The two English ships, the *Resolution* and the *Discovery,* sailed for China with a large cargo of furs. Exorbitant prices were paid for the furs by China, and the demand for these furs in the Orient was limitless. The news of this spread like wild fire all over Europe. In 1785, ships from other countries arrived on the coast, bringing with them diseases that would ravage the Aboriginal Nations. The smallpox epidemics are still talked about by the Aboriginal Nations today, because there was and still is a hint that the smallpox contaminations of the Aboriginal Nations were not an accident.

> A visitor to the fort in 1845, commenting on this epidemic, noted that its ravages had been "more against the families of the Chiefs, than among the inferior class. (Dunn 1845, 410; Duff 1965, 42)

There were two more major smallpox epidemics in British Columbia, one in 1848 and the other in 1862. The 1862 epidemic started in Victoria when a white man with smallpox arrived from San Francisco. Many of the First Nations would visit the city of Victoria every year. They would camp on the outskirts of the settlement. It was not long after the arrival of the American from San Francisco that the smallpox epidemic reached the Aboriginal camp. The Aboriginal people were driven out of the camp and the settlement. The dead bodies of Aboriginal people could be seen all along the British Columbia coastline:

> Before long, despite dire warnings in the *Colonist,* the disease reached the camp of the Indians, and they began to die in fearful numbers. Alarmed,

the authorities burned the camps and forced the Indians to leave. They started up the coast for home, taking the disease with them, leaving the infection at every place they touched. The epidemic spread like a forest fire up the coast and into the interior. (Duff 1965, 42)

The smallpox epidemic of 1862 was the most painful and devastating of all the diseases that plagued the Aboriginal Nations. Our populations plummeted.

Several causes contributed to the tragic decline which followed the arrival of the Europeans. The most destructive was the introduction of diseases which were long familiar and no longer fatal to Europeans, but new and lethal to the Indians, who had inherited little or no resistance to them. And of these the worst was smallpox. (Duff 1965, 40)

Other diseases were to cause further population decline. There was a measles outbreak in 1848–1868. Venereal disease, influenza, alcoholism, and tuberculosis contributed to further population decline. It has been estimated that there were approximately 70,000 Aboriginals in British Columbia in 1835, and by 1885 it had dropped to 28,000. There are other reasons for the decline in the populations of the Aboriginal Nations, but they are too painful to mention. By 1963, we had increased to 40,800. The latest population figures are again open to question. The government of Canada only considers those who are "registered" as being Native Indians. This includes white women who had "become Native Indians" by marriage. Native women who married unregistered Aboriginals or non-native men were no longer natives in the eyes of the Canadian government. Bill C-31 rectified many of these unjust laws, but there are still Aboriginals who are not registered; therefore, they are not considered Native Indians. The laws against Native women were devastating to the Aboriginal Nations of the coast because women had had equal ranking with the men. There was no need for a feminist stand. Women held powerful positions in our Nations. Women had seats in Council, seats in our government, they became medicine women, and women of great wisdom were sought when advice was required. Many Europeans were horrified that women were permitted to hold such positions. The demoralization of some of the women did not happen in our Nations until European contact.

LAND BASE

Aboriginal people were put on reservations that were allocated to them by the federal government. The coast tribes were given a maximum of twenty acres per family because they were not farmers. According to the powers that be, "they did not need much land." In the interior and in other provinces, each family was given 160 acres, or one square mile per family. On this 160 acres they were expected to settle and establish farms. No consideration was given to future population growth. To even hint that the Native people are building their population as a strategy to try to force the government to provide more land is ludicrous. One can make the same remark of Israel, that they are building their population as a strategy to try to force the United Nations to provide more land for them. For me to make such a remark, knowing their history, would be very insensitive and unwise. The Canadian government has a legal obligation that they have not fulfilled and they know this. If this was not the case, the land claims issues would not be lingering in the courts. After the Aboriginals were put on reserves, they were told that they were not an "entity." That they were now "wards of the government." They were considered a minor in need of a guardian, and the Federal government became that guardian. As the guardian, the Federal government handed the lands and resources over to the Provinces, except for the reserve lands which remained under Federal jurisdiction. The Aboriginals no longer had any control over resource consumption or the conservation of these resources. The consumption machines have been prevented from swallowing up more of the natural resources by land claims issues. It has not stopped them, but it has slowed them down. The Aboriginal Nations are still considered "wards of the government" today. The laws that govern them on the reserves are not the laws of Canada but a special law called the "Indian Act." This law was drawn up for the Aboriginal by their guardian, the Federal Government of Canada.

BIRTH CONTROL AND POPULATION CONTROL

Prior to contact, the Kwagiutl practiced sexual abstinence. Men and women who were engaged in a spiritual quest were required to abstain from sexual activity. Warriors and hunters also had to practice abstinence. The length of abstinence varied. It could be four days, four weeks, four months, or four years. Whenever a child was born it was considered a blessing. If a child reached the anniversary of his birth, it was a miracle. In fact, children never received a proper name until the age of ten months. At the age of ten months, they were considered out of danger. After European contact, birth control was not a problem, because many of the Aboriginals were rendered infertile by the diseases that ravaged the Nations. The Aboriginal population continued to decrease. In 1929, the Aboriginal population of British Columbia was estimated at 22,605. The rate of population growth for the Aboriginal Nations was very slow. In 1963, the population grew to 40,800 because of healthier living conditions and better medical care. The total population of the Aboriginal Nations today is just as confusing as those estimated shortly after European contact. The population of the Aboriginal Nations has increased drastically in the past few years, but it has not been because of procreation. Bill C-31 has made it possible for unregistered off-reserve Aboriginals to be registered, and they are now considered "Native Indians." These registrations are still going on today, so to estimate the present population would be impossible. Birth control is practiced by many Aboriginals today by choice. The ideal family now is two or four children, instead of the ten or twelve of thirty years ago.

ABORIGINAL SPIRITUALITY

The information I share in this chapter is from my own personal knowledge of my own people, the Kwagiutl Nation, who live on the northwest coast of British Columbia — especially pertaining to Aboriginal spirituality. Although there is some similarity among the various tribal groups in North America, there are also some distinct differences. Aboriginal spirituality, for one. Aboriginal spirituality can mean many things to many people: meditating; beating a drum; burning sweet grass; going to sweat lodges; or singing sacred songs. All these are mere rituals or expressions of the religions of the respective tribes in North America. However, Aboriginal spirituality was more than a ritual. It was a daily communion and encounter with what we call the Supernatural world that changed you from within. Good spirits were to be sought and bad spirits were to be shunned. There was never any question about the existence of a world or agencies beyond the known forces of nature, nor that of a deity that ruled life and the universe. The Supernatural was a force that went beyond human understanding, but if one was able to link with these forces, it brought certain abilities. Abilities that homo sapiens was unable to accomplish independently. An individual who was able to link with these supernatural forces or world was considered blessed with good fortune. If they acquired a supernatural gift, such as a song, chant, dance, or supernatural powers, it was referred to as a gift resulting from good fortune. These encounters with the Supernatural were very much desired, and the Kwagiutl believed that the secular and supernatural were only divided by a thin veil and one only had to walk through it. To be fortunate enough to be invited into the supernatural world was wonderful, but to be invited to the upper world was the ultimate experience, and one looked forward to the upper world after one's death. One would stay in the upper world until one was ready to be reborn into one's family unit once again.

The great forests of the Pacific coast were considered to be the favorite sojourn for these supernatural forces. To seek this supernatural force one had to go into the forest for several months. One had to bathe four times daily in a river or lake. After each bath one was required to rub oneself with hemlock branches and meditate. This was to prepare the physical body as well as the mind to receive the supernatural force. It was through such encounters that the Kwagiutl people learned that one must have respect for the environment and all life form on this planet. They were taught to express gratitude to all species of life for giving up their own lives so homo sapiens could live. When a Kwagiutl hunter killed a bear he would give praise to the bear for his sacrifice by saying:

> "Greetings friend that we have met, only to destroy you my friend. Apparently the creator created you so that I could hunt you to feed myself and my wife, my friend." (Boas 1934, 186)

When he went looking for a young hemlock tree for his land otter trap, and he found the tree, he acknowledged it before he cut it down by saying:

> "Thank you my friend that I have found you, for I have come to ask you for your assistance, my friend. I would like you to work for me and be an instrument to kill the intelligent land otter when he enters my trap. You must be careful to help one another, you and the deadfall. Do not let the otter escape and be sure he dies instantly (not to suffer)." (Boas 1934, 193)

When a fisherman caught salmon he would also acknowledge the salmon's sacrifice. When the fisherman brought home the salmon to his wife, she would not cut the fish until she also acknowledged the sacrifice the salmon had made for her and her family, by saying:

> "Come salmon, supernatural one. For you have come to save my husband and I, so that we may not starve. You who prolong life. I ask you to protect us so no harm may befall us. You woman of wealth. We will meet again next year great supernatural one." (Boas 1934, 200)

These practices may seem foolish to modern man, but these daily acknowledgments seemed to remind the Kwagiutl that they were not the only important species on this planet. They had a daily reminder that other species had to sacrifice their lives so that they might live. It also helped to remind them that one must live within certain boundaries; otherwise, one must pay the consequences. In our society we have social boundaries enforced by our laws. We all know that if these boundaries did not exist we would have anarchy. Man is the only species on this planet that seems to need laws to keep him within his own boundaries.

Judging from the way homo sapiens has treated the environment, it is not surprising that the Kwagiutl believed that every life form except for homo sapiens possessed supernatural powers from birth. It was not always like this. Our first ancestors, it is said, possessed these powers, but the later generations lost them because they became too humanistic. To be able to reclaim these qualities, humans have to purify themselves physically and mentally, before they may be gifted with such powers. The Kwagiutl believe that children possess spirituality at birth and retain this quality until they become humanistic, at the age of five or six. If they are able to retain these qualities when they reach adulthood, they will also receive the powers that humans do not normally possess. These are the men and women of wisdom. They must guard themselves against humanistic qualities such as pride, hate, envy, and jealousy, or they will lose whatever powers they have.

To tamper with the environment was considered disastrous by the Kwagiutl people. Everything had to be balanced. Daring to break the laws of nature was inviting anger from the supernatural realm. They would always be warned to cease what they were doing or pay the consequences. This warning always came by way of a dream. The dream world was considered a vehicle of communication between the secular and the supernatural.

The Kwagiutl people had no regard for materialism, but valued the spiritual aspects of life. They lived off the land and stored only what was required for the winter. They had industries, but again they supplied only what would be required for the winter months. They believed that every living thing had a soul and a purpose for being on this planet, and even mountains and certain rocks had some spiritual significance because some supernatural being had appeared to them at that spot. Every living thing including vegetation had to be respected and shown appreciation of worth, honor, and esteem. They were created for the benefit of homo sapiens but they were never to be abused.

The Kwagiutl people could not separate themselves from their environment, because it was this very environment that dictated how they would live out their lives, and how and when life would end. Their doctrine and religion encompassed their environment. They considered the environment totally entwined with their physical and spiritual being; therefore it affected the moral and spiritual part of themselves as related to their Creator. Their daily encounter with the environment filled them with awe and admiration for the Creator, drawing them ever closer to him. Some of the Kwagiutl believed that the physical being of their Creator was the Sun, because the Sun was the energy that made everything come to life.

Many Aboriginal people converted to Christianity because they saw a parallel between Christianity and their own beliefs. Christianity believes in a supernatural God, a supernatural world, supernatural powers, and an upper world that you go to after death, called heaven. Christianity also teaches that one must take care of the many gifts of the Creator Jehovah, and that includes this planet we call earth.

The Aboriginal perspective on resource consumption and the environment is not an easy subject to discuss in the world communities today, because our perspective, it seems, is contrary to world view. This is clearly evident in the position that the world has placed the environment with regard to laws and statutes. A majority of the Aboriginal peoples still place the environment at the pinnacle of importance because it has special relevance in maintaining the life form on this planet. They are clearly aware of the fact that if our environment ceases to exist, all life forms, including homo sapiens, will become extinct. The second order of importance to the Aboriginal is that of conservation. The Aboriginal people believed and still believe that all life must be in a state of equilibrium. To cause an imbalance in nature invites an environmental disaster and, ultimately, it will be homo sapiens who will experience the adverse effects of their own stupidity.

The third order of importance is that of industry and consumption. However, the rest of the world seems to place the environment as having the least amount of importance, and industry and consumption are considered the most significant of the three. Placing industry and consumption before the environment is incomprehensible to the Aboriginal mind. How can humankind and its industries expect to survive after destroying the environment?

We have arrogantly unbalanced the scales of nature. There will no longer be a dream of warning, for we are now more concerned about the material rather than the spiritual. Materialism is considered the norm, and being spiritual is now considered foolish. Are we now prepared to face the consequences for our greed and foolishness? Or do the humans really believe they are immortal?

The Aboriginal Nations are not perfect by any means. We make grave errors just like anyone else. Unfortunately, many Aboriginals are now very materialistic, and they have left the "ancient ways." Perhaps there is something in the "ancient ways" that will help modern man rethink his position on this planet. This planet was created for humankind, but it was also created for all other living species.

BIBLIOGRAPHY

Boas, Franz 1930. *Religion of the Kwagiutl Indians,* Vol. X (Kwakwala text). New York: Columbia University Press.

Duff, Wilson 1965. *The Indian History of British Columbia,* Vol. I: The Impact of the White Man. Victoria, Provincial Museum.

5

Judaism, Population, and the Environment

SHARON JOSEPH LEVY

THE CHILD

Most of us who live in the Western world take for granted the blessing of our basic necessities and the availability of excess to satisfy our desires. Ask a young child where bread comes from and the response will probably be "the grocery store" or "bakery." Ask again where water comes from and you'll probably be told "the tap." Should you ask what meat originally was, be prepared for the child to consider becoming vegetarian after you explain that it is not the stuff on the styrofoam tray, covered with plastic wrap!

When told to finish the food on their plates because throwing away food is wasteful, the child doesn't understand. There is more in the store and there are so many stores, all with everything they could ever think they need or desire. If we try the approach of "there are children starving in . . ." he/she will want to know either what their eating has to do with those faceless, nameless children, or if, perhaps, they can package it up and send it to them.

What about the things we get rid of? Where do they go? The child will tell you "the garbage truck," "the air," "the toilet."

If the weather should get too hot or too cold, we adjust the thermostat. If the room is too dark, we put on the light. When there is a blackout, the child may wonder why there is no electricity and where it comes from. He/she probably will want to know when their T.V. show will come back on, or why the computer is "down."

Children see the newest and latest toys as things that are wanted, indeed, needed. Extracurricular activities are imperative. If they do not get what they want, we are "not being fair."

For a short while, the child ponders life itself. Who am I? Why am I here? What should I do in life that will be meaningful? Why does the world exist? Is there a purpose to life? Then life happens and these most significant questions fade into the background of friends, activities, school, careers, business, and family.

We are not that different from the young child. Many of us have come to be satisfied with this simplistic level of understanding and relating. Rarely do we take time to reflect upon how our own personal attitudes, behaviors, and actions impact on ourselves, society, and the world at large.[1] How often do we stop to consider our moral and ethical obligations and not just our presumed rights? Our actions are presumptuous, our relationships assumed.

Many of us are not sure if we should change, or why. Most of the environmental problems that are spoken of on a global scale are unseen by us in our daily lives. It's hard enough for us to change a personal habit when we are aware of it. We think that these problems are just too big, too distant, and too impersonal. Most importantly, we feel that even if we can make a change, it really will not make a difference in the long run. We're damned anyway, so we might as well enjoy ourselves.

Judaism's approach to the issues of consumption and population growth addresses our attitudes, behaviors, and actions. In this chapter, we will explore what Jewish sources have to teach us about wants and needs, about appreciation, about satisfaction and wealth, about our responsibility to each other and the world, about how we should relate, about our ability to change, and about defining who we are as human beings. We will discover that these teachings are grounded in action, that is, *Halakha,* the Jewish code of law that impacts upon every aspect of daily life. These values are not left as abstract, lofty ideals but actualized in normative, divinely sanctified behavior. We will preface that discussion with remarks regarding the unique predicament confronting the Jewish people, which inevitably impacts upon Judaism's attitude toward its own role in population control.

THE JEWISH POPULATION

During our enslavement in Egypt, there was a decree that all baby boys were to be killed.[2] Amram, a grandson of Levi and a leader of the people, believed that it was therefore useless to have children at all. He proceeded to separate from his wife, and the rest of the people followed his lead. His daughter Miriam pointed out to him that in so doing he was imposing a far more severe decree than did Pharaoh, for Pharaoh had only decreed that the boys should be put to

Table 5-1.

YEAR	TOTAL WORLD JEWISH POPULATION (ROUGH ESTIMATES)[11]	TOTAL WORLD POPULATION (ROUGH ESTIMATES)[12]
48	8,000,000	250,000,000 - 300,000,000
70	*no statistics available — rapid decline*	— — —
End of 12th C.	1,000,000–2,000,000	— — —
1650	— — —	500,000,000
1820	3,281,000	1,171,000,000
1880	7,700,000	— — —
1900	10,602,500	1,608,000,000
1939	16,724,000–18,000,000	2,296,000,000
1948	11,373,000	2,516,000,000
1967	13,837,500	3,419,420,000
1985	13,000,000	4,856,488,000
1990	12, 849,500	5,295,111,000
2000 *(projections)*	12,400,000	6,166,468,000
2010 *(projections)*	12,000,000	7,026,887,000

death, whereas he was preventing even girls from being born. Amram accepted Miriam's words and returned to his wife, the rest of the people following his lead.[3] Amram and Yocheved had a son named Moses.[4]

Later, during the era of the destruction of the Second Temple in Jerusalem (70 C.E.), there was a discussion among the rabbis whether or not to enact population control measures. The concern was that children were being created who would be persecuted and prevented from observing the laws of the Torah. Looking at table 5-1, one can see that these fears were well founded. Later rabbinic authorities disagree whether the discussion had been one of an outright ban, actually abolishing the *mitzva* of "be fruitful and multiply," or rather modifying the *mitzva*, allowing for replacement but suspending the behavior of *La' erev al tanach yadecha*,[5] which encourages families to have more than two children.[6] In fact, no decree was ever enacted, for the rabbis felt that it was virtually impossible for the public to adhere to such a severe ban.

Through the worst moments in our history, there has never been any prohibition against having a family of any size.[7] Indeed, world Jewry did not grow the way one not versed in Jewish history might imagine. It has been estimated that a people this ancient, living continuously in its own homeland without ever being exiled, would number one billion people.[8] For as an ancient people, uprooted from our homeland two thousand years ago, our survival throughout generations of persecution, expulsion, exile, homelessness, libel, torture, pogroms, rape, infanticide, murder, forced abortion, forced sterilization, forced medical experimentation, and enslavement is indeed testimony to the strength of the Jewish family, led by dedicated men and women,[9] adhering to the precepts of the *Torah*.

During World War II, world Jewry's population was devastated by the loss of one-third of our people and the destruction of thousands of communities. In 1939, at the beginning of the war, we had a total population of approximately 16,724,000 people. Today our population is approximately twelve and a half million people, less than one quarter of one percent of the total world population. There are presently six times more people born in the world annually than our total population. Our low birthrate is a reflection of the birthrate of the society at large in which the majority of the Jewish population lives. We have not achieved replacement levels and projections are for the Jewish population to continue to dwindle, decreasing eight percent over the next sixteen years.[10]

Therefore, for the Jewish community the issue of self-imposed population control is extraneous and absurd. It has been inflicted upon us for so many centuries that we will continue to suffer from its effects well into the twenty-first century.

As a point of interest, birth control for Jews centers around the issue of maternal health. There are situations in which certain contraceptives would be permissible. Abortion is not considered a form of birth control. Only in cases of maternal health is it deemed permissible.[13, 14] Each situation is dealt with independently.

Having demonstrated that the issue of population control vis-à-vis the Jewish community is extraneous, let us move on to the discussion of world population growth and of consumption.

WORLD POPULATION AND CONSUMPTION PATTERNS

Growth Rate

Throughout much of human history, it took approximately 1,000 years each time for the world's population to double. Human numbers were relatively small and technology was innocuous. Our impact on the ecology of the world was usually localized, and the earth had time to heal itself.

As time went on, the number fell to 700 years between doubling. Between the years 1650–1815, a period of only 165 years, the world population not only

Table 5-2.

	POPULATION	% OF WORLD POPULATION	RATE OF GROWTH
Developed countries	1,188,590,000	22.4%	0.53%
Developing countries	3,680,792,000	69.5%	2.00%
Third world countries	429,069,000	8.1%	2.75%
World Population	5,298,451,000	100.0%	1.73%

doubled but passed the one billion level.[15] During this period, the growth rate was four tenths of one percent a year. This era also saw the dawn of the Industrial Age. By 1920, after a passage of only 105 years, the world's population had once again doubled. The growth rate was now above one percent. CFCs and leaded gasoline arrived on the scene. Between 1940 and 1950 the world population growth rate was 1.3 percent per year. By 1970 the world population growth rate had peaked at 2.2 percent.[16] We had landed on the moon. By 1974, the world's population had doubled to four billion people. This time, only fifty-four years had passed since the last doubling. Since then, there has been a steady decrease in the annual growth rate.

The rate is going down, but the absolute number of people is going up. We now live in an age of technology and information. There are today over five and a half billion people on Earth. At the present growth rate, there will be 85–90 million people born each year for the next thirty-five years. Demographers project that at the present decreasing rate of growth, the world's population will reach eight billion sometime around 2020 and stabilize between ten and fourteen billion people in the following one hundred years.

What factors have contributed to this continual decrease in the population growth rate? The projected decreased rate of growth is attributed to development, as well as to the availability of health care, family planning services, job training, education, and women's education in particular.[17] Yet, in comparing whether distributing birth control or educating a given population was more effective, education, which in turn leads to increased self-sufficiency, was found to be far more effective.[18] This is most significant.

How is the birth rate reflected in the populations of the world?[19] The developing countries noted in table 5-2 include, but are not limited, to Africa, China, and India, the three most populous regions on Earth. This, too, is of significance.

Table 5-3.

GOODS	INDUSTRIAL COUNTRIES' SHARE OF WORLD CONSUMPTION (PERCENT)	CONSUMPTION GAP BETWEEN INDUSTRIAL AND DEVELOPING COUNTRIES (RATIO OF PER CAPITA CONSUMPTION RATES)
Aluminum	86	19
Chemicals	86	18
Paper	81	14
Iron and Steel	80	13
Timber	76	10
Energy	75	10
Meat	61	6
Fertilizers	60	5
Cement	52	3
Fish	49	3
Grain	48	3
Fresh Water	42	3

Appetite

The facts regarding current consumption patterns support the thesis that the issue confronting us is one of attitude. Who is using what? Are the limited resources of our planet being equitably shared? For what purposes are these limited resources being used? Are we using our resources wisely and compassionately? We find that less than one-quarter of the world's population is responsible for consuming between 40 and 86 percent of the various major resources on earth. Table 5-3 gives us an understanding of the degree of imbalanced use that exists.[20]

Not only do the "developed" countries use a grossly disproportionate amount of the world's resources, we do so without minding how they are used, who is affected by our imbalanced use, or what effects we have on the Earth. We do not yet comprehend that our numbers have increased, and that the impact of our lifestyle and technology is beyond our ken. Not to minimize the significance of over eighty million people born each year for the next thirty-five years, but environmental degradation is more a consequence of lifestyle and waste than it is of sheer numbers. Given the present rate of consumption, the two million children born annually in the United States alone would "consume as much of the world's resources and pollute the atmosphere as would (forty) to two hundred million 'Third World' children." Most individuals living in industrialized countries impact the world twenty to one hundred times more than do persons living in a "developing" country. If one is wealthy (and wasteful) the impact is a thousandfold.[21]

The question at hand is one of how we relate to the world and to our fellow human beings, more than it is a question of birth control. When we behave the way we ought to, when shelter, food, water, education, and health care are made available, the birth rate falls naturally. We see this, as a fact, in "developed" countries and in "developing" countries where these basics have been made available. Should we change the way we relate to each other, as well as to the world and how we actually use and care for it, then it too would be healed.

Be Fruitful and Multiply

The first injunction given to people is to procreate:

> God created the human being [Adam][22] in God's own image, In the image of God did [God] create Adam, male and female [God] made them. God blessed them and God said to them: *Be fruitful and multiply and fill the earth and subdue it.*[23]

We are to fill the earth with our species. Interestingly, an almost identical injunction is given to the birds of the sky and the fish of the seas.[24] There is one major difference. With regards to the fish and the birds, the need to procreate is inbred. With people, procreation is a blessing and a directive: "God said to them." The communication is direct. Human beings are not simply animals doing what comes naturally. We have divine directive, and we can exercise self-control.[25]

There is an interesting account, given over 1500 years ago in the *Talmud*,[26] which states that the original Adam was created as a composite male and female being. Later, God separated Adam into two beings, male and female. "Therefore," the *Torah* says,[27] "a man should leave his mother and father and cleave off to his wife and they should be one flesh."

The body is seen as a sacred vessel.[28] Marital relationships are seen by the Torah as part of the original design of creation. Marital relations are permitted, nay, essential, even if the couple is unable to have children. They have the potential to be sacred, harmonizing that which was meant to be together.[29] Marriage is so important, both for the man and the woman, and for the purpose of having children, that in a case of extreme need, even a *Torah* may be sold to enable the marriage to take place.[30] Children are valued not as an outcome of physical weakness, but as a gift, entrusted to us by God.[31]

Bnai Noach — The Children of Noah

Within a *Torah* perspective, there exists a framework of ethical and moral laws for those who are not Jewish. These laws, known as the *Seven Mitzvot of Bnai Noach*,[32] or Noachide Laws, enjoin humanity to follow basic Divine rules. These laws are based upon the belief that one need not be Jewish to have a relationship with God.

The intention of the commandment "be fruitful and multiply" was to perpetuate the human race, not simply to have enough children for replacement value. Certainly "being fruitful" alone, without "multiplying" would never have populated the earth.[33]

There is another principle that is considered when discussing population control and it is known as *lo tohu bera' a, lashevet yetzara*. In the book of Isaiah we read:[34]

So says the Lord, Creator of the Heavens: [God] is God, [God] fashioned the earth and made it. [God] established it. [God] did not create it to be a wasteland. *[God] fashioned it so that it would be inhabited [lashevet yetzara].*

God created the world to be inhabited. If indeed this directive has been, or is on the verge of being, fulfilled, then the goal stated by Isaiah would have been achieved and the moral duty may no longer apply. If every effort has been made to bring self-sufficiency[35] to a population and it is still experiencing excessive growth, then, under such circumstances, certain forms of birth control may be permissible for a population following the Noachide Laws.[36] Abortion, under Noachide Law, is permitted only under dire medical circumstances[37] and is not acceptable as a means of birth control.[38] Adopting a child is considered moral conduct of the highest order.[39]

Once we have actually brought our children into this world, our responsibilities have just begun. By the very act of bringing a human being into this world, we have incurred the obligation to create a *humane* being. Saadiah Gaon, the rabbinic leader of Diaspora Jewry, based in Sura, Babylonia (present day Iraq) in the early 10th century, said as follows:[40]

Others, again, are of the opinion that [people] ought to dedicate themselves to the begetting of children. . . . Now I considered this allegation on their part carefully and I noted that it was correct so far as those children whom the Creator grants to His servant in accordance with His wish. The mistake of the advocates of this theory lies in their requirement that one pay attention to this matter alone, to the exclusion of everything else.

I say, however: Of what benefit are children to a person if he is unable to provide for their sustenance, covering or shelter? And what is the good of raising them if it will not be productive of wisdom and knowledge on their part? And of what use are the pity and sympathy lavished upon them in the absence of these factors unless it be to add to the heartache of the parents?

Humanity's relationship to God, according to Judaism, is a reflection of our actions to other humans, starting with those God has entrusted to our care, and to the world at large. Whereas it is our Divine duty to procreate, our relationship to God is not simply a reflection of the number of children we have. Given the present world population, this approach leaves open the invitation to encourage attitudes and actions that result in natural population control. As stated earlier,[41] the question at hand is one of how we relate to the world and to our fellow human beings more than it is a question of birth control.

DIRECTION

Many contemporary thinkers,[42] coming from different disciplines, insist that above and beyond necessary changes in technology or new government legislation, the most important change we can make to help the world at large is a change in ourselves. What is necessary is a change in the way we, as human beings, relate to the world. This, they say, is the change that is going to have the greatest impact on life on this planet:

> I am convinced that such a quasi-religious movement, one concerned with the need to change the values that now govern much of human activity, is essential to the persistence of our civilization.[43]

In this next section we will highlight a number of ways in which Judaism addresses humanity's relationship to the world and how Judaism works to create those very attitudes that would reconcile the dual issues of population and consumption.

PERSPECTIVE

The earth and everything in it belongs to God,[44] the Creator of the universe[45] and the God of history.[46] Abraham recognized that there was a harmonious and meaningful design in the world, and that there was One unifying force that brought everything, including people, into existence.[47] This harmonizing force gives purpose to existence. Nature in and of itself is not divine and is never the object of worship. There are no intermediaries between us and God.[48] Everything has been created for a purpose[49] and God's will is manifest in everything.[50] There have been different philosophies throughout Jewish history as to *why* God created the world but there seems to be unanimity in viewing the act of creation as one of love and giving, many viewing this as the purpose of creation itself.[51]

There exists, as well, the discussion in Jewish thought as to whether or not the universe was created specifically for people or if it has an existence separate from us.[52] Again, there is debate regarding whether God is to be found within nature, or is separate from nature but still its Creator. There are, interestingly, thinkers on both sides of these discussions.[53] There is no question, however, that people are responsible and accountable for God's world.[54]

The *Torah* is a way of life. The word itself has the meaning of "way," "show" and "guide." In its primary definition, *Torah* refers to the Five Books of Moses. In a broader sense, *Torah* refers to the entire body of Jewish teachings. The *Torah* is said to be the blueprint by which God created the world.[55] It provides us with a functional framework within which we can actualize a humble relationship with God, creation, humanity, and ourselves. To live by it is to be in tune with the way the world works. God tells us the outcomes of living in harmony or in dissonance with the design of creation.[56] By living a just and caring life, according to the *Torah*, we make the world a better place. By living according to our own deities, we are out of sync with the way the world works and we bring about its destruction.[57] Never before in human history has this idea been so universally manifested. In our age of information we even have a term for it: "garbage in — garbage out." That's how the system was built to work. We are dependent upon the world. The world is dependent upon us. The *Torah* is our user's manual.

The *Torah* is interested in creating both righteous individuals, and just, caring communities. The *Torah* addresses all human needs and relationships, by providing them a structure whose boundaries are rendered by *mitzvot* (commandments/directives) and *halakha* (understood as law, but, literally, "paths on which to walk"). Food, clothes, speech, education, visiting and caring for the sick, hospitality, sexual relations, marriage, divorce, death, agriculture, safety, zoning, pollution, waste, business, prayer, and study are examples of matters with which the *Torah* deals. Lofty ideals are always actualized in the realities of life.

APPRECIATION

A prerequisite to being responsible and caring is being aware. Awareness, in Jewish life, is heightened through appreciating that which is. In Judaism this is known as *hakarat hatov,* acknowledging goodness. We must be grateful for, and caring toward, everything from the inanimate,[58] to even a small kindness of another,[59] to our parents,[60] to the beneficence that is God's creation.[61] In fact, being an ungrateful and unappreciative person leads one to deny God.[62] Conversely, being an appreciative person can lead one to recognize God.

One practical way we translate this abstract idea into reality is through the *brakha.* There are *brakhot* that are expressions of praise and *brakhot* that are expressions of thanks for the enjoyment of the pleasures of life. *Brakhot* help us recognize the reality of the blessings that exist. *Brakhot* create an awareness in us not to take life for granted. We recognize the One God as the source of the blessings and the challenges[63] in our lives.[64]

The most widely known are the *brakhot* we say before and after eating bread.[65] There are, as well, *brakhot* to say before and after eating anything, whether it is a glass of water, a snack or a full meal. *Brakhot* are not limited to the sense of taste. We appreciate God upon smelling[66] fragrant oils and herbs, flowers, shrubs, trees, and fruit. We appreciate God through the sights we see, such as rainbows,[67] oceans, trees in bloom,[68] and electric storms. We appreciate God for things that we hear, such as thunderstorms, or good or bad occurrences.[69] We thank God for sharing God's wisdom with humanity.[70]

When we say a *brakha,* not only are we appreciating God but we are recognizing that the source of everything is the One God.[71] If we should partake of something without a *brakha* it is considered as though we were stealing, for we are taking that which is not ours.[72] We have no inherent right to anything, for everything is God's. The *brakhot* help create an awareness in us that life has purpose, that everything and every moment are blessings to be enjoyed and cherished, and that nothing is to be taken for granted.

Consider what defines a person as being good. The following passage expresses one classical Jewish perspective on the question:

> An evil person is considered as dead, for they see the sun shining and do not praise the Creator of light, they see the sun setting and do not praise the Creator who brings on the evening, they eat and drink and offer no praise. But the righteous recite a blessing on every single thing that they eat, drink, see or hear.[73]

What an incredible statement! We don't have to be aggressively bad in order to be not good. A lack of awareness, of appreciation, of articulation, makes us "dead." *Brakhot* come to infuse the mundane moments of our lives with awareness, appreciation, and articulation of the gift that life is. To borrow a term,[74] a *brakha* is a one-minute *mitzva*, a moment of spiritual elevation, injected on a regular basis into our day to day lives. We recognize the beauty, wisdom, intricacy, and interdependence of all of nature, not simply as things that we may consume or manipulate but as the profound gifts that they are.

We thank God for our lives. We recognize the ephemeral nature of our existence and we daily, in our bedtime prayers, assign our souls back to God. Although we do anticipate waking in the morning, we don't expect[75] to, and when we do, we thank God for the compassion shown us and we place our trust in God.[76] We are to take nothing for granted. We are to be grateful to God for every single breath we take.[77]

AWARENESS

Another way Judaism helps us perceive and actualize ourselves as the humble guardians[78] we are meant to be is through the *Shabbat*, one of the cornerstones of the *Torah*[79] and of the Jewish people, and one of the most often misunderstood practices of Judaism. Someone who "guards" *Shabbat* does not turn on lights, use the phone, write, cook, or drive on *Shabbat*. They do not do any laundry, sewing, housework, homework, gardening, or repair work. They don't "go out." No work, no shopping, no recreation, no entertainment. Many people think that these practices are archaic and restrictive. What "work" is involved in flipping on a light switch? Why ever limit oneself in such a way but especially on our "day off"?

Some people, in society at large, devote time to prayer and worship. Most people though, who have two days off from work, use this time to "catch up," be it on groceries, housework, or projects. We also use it to entertain and distract ourselves, each of us in our own way. If we should have nothing to do, we try to figure out how we're going to "kill some time." We might rent some videos, or spend hours watching T.V. and snacking. We might even put in another few hours of work. Is this why we want to live a longer and better life? Do our work, our play, and our possessions define who we are? Do they give our life meaning? Do they help us live in harmony with the world?

Shabbat addresses these questions. *Shabbat* is first mentioned as the final act of creation. We will deal with this in a moment, but first let's take a look at a later part of history for a fuller understanding of the meaning of *Shabbat*. During the years of our slavery in Egypt, the Jewish people were afraid of losing their cohesiveness as a people. Moses went to Pharaoh and counseled him that working his slaves seven days a week would kill them, and that they needed a day of rest. With great self-interest, Pharaoh understood the wisdom of this advice. He would maintain his work force and it would be more productive. Upon Moses' suggestion, Pharaoh instituted a day of physical rest on the seventh day, the *Shabbat*.[80] We call this aspect of *Shabbat Shabbat "Mitzrayim,"* the *Shabbat* of Egypt. It is this aspect of *Shabbat* that is at the heart of the modern weekend.

It behooves us to look at history itself for perspective when we are looking for a Jewish attitude to the topic at hand. At the heart of the discussion on population and consumption is the question of how, in our increasingly growing and interdependent world, are we or are we not going to care and going to share. Who is entitled to what? Who determines the answers? Do we have an interest in other countries and in other people only in regard to our own economic gain? Do we, in our heart of hearts, really care about other people? Do we care enough that we would want for them what we want for ourselves?[81] Would we want for ourselves what we accept for them? Would we support birth control efforts but not forge ahead with bringing justice to those in need? Would we be willing to modify our lifestyles for their sake and the sake of the world itself?

As a people, we are enjoined to remember that we were slaves in Egypt. We know the soul of the downtrodden. We can and must empathize, for we have experienced subjugation. Time and time again, we are enjoined[82] to remember those less fortunate "for you know the heart of the stranger, for you were strangers in the land of Egypt."[83] Sensitivity to the anguish and plight of others is seared into our consciousness. Every week, through the celebration of *Shabbat,* and every day in our prayers,[84] we connect with that experience. We remember that the God of history, who has saved us from slavery and destruction, demands that we be forever vigilant regarding our behavior to all, especially those in need.

On *Shabbat* we acknowledge that no human being is more important than any other. Each human being is precious because they have been created in the image of the Divine.[85] Each human being, regardless of sex, color, religion or economic standing has equal standing in the eyes of God. This idea of the universality and equality of humanity is expressed beautifully in the following two sources:

> God formed Adam[85] out of dust from all over the world: yellow clay, white sand, black loam and red soil. Therefore, the earth cannot say to any race or color of people that they do not belong here since this soil is not their home.[87]

> Adam was created as the common ancestor of all people, for the sake of peace of humanity, so that one should not say to another, "My ancestor was better than yours."[88]

Shabbat regularly reminds us that God is the only true master. In reality, we can be no one's boss. God created all of us. We are all answerable to God. We have no right to subjugate anyone. Servants[89] too "will be able to rest (on *Shabbat*) just as (we) do. . . . It is for this reason that God . . . has commanded (us) to keep the *Shabbat*."[90] *Shabbat* helps us realize the equality of all people. There is no difference between master and servant, between rich and poor. We can be no one's slave. We can make no one our slave.

Shabbat is the final act of creation. We read in Genesis[91] that on the seventh day,[92] God "rested" from all the "work" that (God) had done. The English translations of "rest" for the word *shavat* and "work" for *melacha* are problematic. A basic principle of Judaism is that God does not tire nor sleep,[93] so "rest" cannot be a valid interpretation. The act of creation was not an exertion in any physical sense, as the universe was created by the "word" of God.[94] So then, what was it that God was doing?

Over 1,500 years ago, the *Midrash*[95] gave the following answer:

"God completed on the seventh day"[96] What was created therein? Tranquility, quietness, peace and calm. . . . As long as the hands of their Master were working on them, they went on expanding. When the hands of their Master rested, rest was afforded to them. . . .

Thus, according to this explanation, God's "rest" was, in fact, the final act of creation, without which creation itself would have been wanting. God did not need to go on creating and the world did not need to go on expanding. Built right into the mechanism of creation is "tranquility, quietness, peace and calm," a touch of the Divine harmony. *Shabbat* is the time in our lives when we can get rid of the "background noise." Through the celebration of *Shabbat*, we tap into this energy of creation and allow it to be released into the universe and into ourselves.[97]

This will help us further understand the notion of "work" from which we are to "rest." Work of a creative nature is what the *Torah* has proscribed.[98] Strenuous labor, although not in the spirit of *Shabbat* and not permitted, is not the sole intention. We are limited from applying our uniquely human creative touch to the world one day a week, a seventh of our lives.

The *Talmud*[99] elucidates this idea further:

When we observe *Shabbat*, we refrain from interfering or making any permanent change in the order of creation.

The ability to exercise self-control is a uniquely human trait,[100] and a Divine attribute. No other known being in the universe demonstrates this ability.

By not doing any *melacha* ("work") we suspend our creative interference in the natural order of the world. This is indeed *Imitatio Dei,* emulating God.[101] God restricted God's own creative ability, so as not to overwhelm creation. We, too, can choose not to overwhelm creation with what we do. Our partnership[102] with God in the creation of the world takes on a new dimension on *Shabbat.* When we restrict our creative abilities on *Shabbat,* we acknowledge both our uniqueness and our limitation. *Shabbat* is the forum that God has given us in order to actualize this realization.

The influence of *Shabbat* is not restricted to one day a week, and its influence guides us throughout the work week.[103] The following passage is the basis for the notion of "stewardship":

> The Lord God took [the] Adam and placed [Adam] in the Garden of Eden to work it and guard it.[104]

The *Midrash*[105] gives a fascinating explanation of this verse:

> "Work" *[l'ovda]* means "six days you shall work."[106] "Guard" *[u-l'shomra]* means keep/guard the *Shabbat.*[107]

We guard the Garden by keeping *Shabbat*! We have been entrusted to be "partners in the creation of the world,"[108] working to make this world a place of caring and kindness. God has given us everything that we need in order to attain this goal. We have not been given the world to exploit as we see fit. On *Shabbat,* we are reminded that we are not the master but simply a guard, a caretaker. Our weekday endeavors take on a most humble dimension through this realization.[109] When we actualize in deed the belief that God is the Creator, then our "stewardship" takes on its intended dimension. We are guarding someone else's possession.[110] We are accountable[111] and responsible.[112]

The world is ours to take care of. Through *Shabbat,* we understand that the world continues to exist without our interference. We take our place simply as one of God's creation. We join together, in harmony, with the sky, the land, the seas, the animals of the waters and of the land, the planets, stars and galaxies[113] in recognizing[114] God as the Life[115] and Strength[116] of the universe. On *Shabbat,* we are at one with creation, of which we are a part. This idea is reflected in the following *Aggadah:*

> All the creatures saw [Adam] and became afraid of him, thinking that [Adam] was their Creator. . . . Adam said to them, "Why are you bowing before me?! Come, I and you, let us go and adorn in majesty and might, and acclaim as Ruler over us the One who created us."[117, 118]

We call this aspect of *Shabbat* "*Shabbat Breisheet,*" the Shabbat of Creation. It is this aspect of *Shabbat* that is at the heart of the idea of stewardship.

When *Shabbat* begins, we are told, we are to possess an awareness that we are where we need to be in life. *Shabbat* is our goal, and we have arrived. When *Shabbat* comes, peace comes.[119] We are to perceive all our unfinished business as finished,[120] for there is nothing left for us to do. No more phone calls. No more shopping. No more housework. No more places to go. Nowhere else to be and no more things to get. There is nothing waiting to be done. There is nothing that I need. We do not even talk about money matters, business, or our weekday plans.[121] We are more than our habits and lifestyles. We need not be slaves to them.[122] They need not determine who we are. We experience a taste of the spirituality that is within each one of us.[123] We are at peace. We are free.

We not only observe *Shabbat* through what we don't do; we celebrate *Shabbat* through what we do.[124] *Shabbat* is a time to study, read, pray, reflect, evaluate, take a walk, be with oneself, reconnect with one's family, one's wife, one's husband, and one's children, if one is so blessed. *Shabbat* is a time for heightening our awareness through the study of *Torah*.[125] With nowhere to go and nothing to do, it is the opportune time to get reacquainted with ourselves and the world around us. The table is set with a white tablecloth. Two candles are lit, to remind us to both celebrate and remember *Shabbat*, and to bring peace[126] into the home.

We celebrate *Shabbat* with *kiddush* and *challa*. The *kiddush* is said prior to each of the two festive *Shabbat* meals. In it, we recognize God as both the Creator of the world and as the God who took us from slavery to freedom. We begin both meals with two whole loaves of *challa,* bread, as a reminder of the manna[127] through which God sustained us in the desert. The manna is a constant reminder to us that all our sustenance, all we truly need, comes from God. The manna also reminds us that we must equally and fairly distribute our God-given resources. Greed and manna cannot coexist. On *Shabbat*, we recognize God as the Creator, the Provider, the Redeemer, and the Healer. We recognize God as the source of tranquility, peace, and harmony.

APPLICATION

The problem of consumption in our day and age is not a new problem in the world. The magnitude of the impact that consumption is having is what is new. Lack of appreciation, lack of awareness, waste, want, and hatred[128] are all factors that impact on how we relate to the world and how we use it. A life of caring and giving, exhorted by men and women of moral and ethical stature throughout human history, now needs to become the norm for life to go on as we know it.

Are we bothered when we waste? Are we bothered by how much we waste? Do we consider the forests that have been ravaged and the ecosystems that have been destroyed[129] so that we can read the sports, lifestyles, or comics in the daily newspaper? Do we even know or care how our heavily meat-centered diet affects the animals that we eat or the planet as a whole? Do we think that there is an unending supply of aluminum when we throw yet another can[130] into the recycling box? Is recycling itself effective? Is less really being taken from the earth or have we just created a new industry?

Commenting on the prohibition against "waste," the *Sefer ha-Hinnukh* says:[131]

> The purpose of the *mitzva* is to train our souls to love good and that which is creative and useful and to refrain from all that which is destructive. The way of the righteous and of people of good deeds is to love peace, take pleasure in the welfare of their fellow human being and draw them closer to the *Torah. They would not destroy even a mustard seed.* They are grieved and oppressed at the sight of destruction. If they could save anything from being destroyed they would do so with all their power. The wicked are not so. They are happy in destroying the world.

We are to train ourselves to be such caring[132] people that even something so seemingly insignificant as wasting a mustard seed should bother us! Imagine planning one's shopping, one's cooking, and one's eating with this in mind![133] What would happen to impulse purchases, overpackaging, and to the garbage problem? Would we be decimating the forests of the world if we approached life with this attitude?

The above comment is made regarding the *mitzva* in the *Torah* "not to waste," *bal tashkhit.*[134] The prime case that is stated in the *Torah* refers to not cutting down fruit-bearing trees. The classical understanding of this verse was that this was to apply to all acts of wanton destruction, for example:

> Rabbi Zutra said: "One who covers an oil lamp or uncovers a naphta lamp, infringes the prohibition of wasteful destruction since these acts cause the lamp to burn with unnecessary speed."[135]

Imagine applying this principle of caring for God's world to our energy resources. Would our economy be so dependent on oil? Would we need to build new nuclear facilities to compensate for our wasteful habits? Would we help decrease pollution and global warming?

Maimonides, in the 12th century, stated:

this is the case not only with trees. Whoever breaks utensils, tears garments, demolishes a building, stops up a well and willfully destroys food violates the prohibition of "you shall not destroy."[136]

What Maimonides has brought to our understanding of the *mitzva* "not to waste" is that even things that are made by people, as opposed to natural resources, cannot be wasted. Rabbi Hirsch, living during the nineteenth century in Germany, said that

> [We are not to regard] things as though possession was their whole purpose rather than means. . . . We must regard things as God's property and use them with a sense of responsibility for wise human purposes. [We are to] destroy nothing.

Rabbi Hirsch explains "destroy" as using more things (or using things of greater value) than is necessary to attain one's aim.[137] Imagine approaching the issue of packaging and waste disposal with this as the guiding principle.

Our economic needs and environmental responsibilities need to be balanced with the concept of *yishuv ha-olam,* settling the world.[138] Human needs, as well as environmental considerations, must be considered. The livelihoods of individuals and of communities must be weighed in any discussion of conflict. Each case of contention is settled in a *halakhic* manner, taking all aspects into consideration.[139]

TEACHING BY EXAMPLE

Maimonides certainly would have had much to say[140] about our throwaway society, with its built-in obsolescence and lack of satisfaction. From cans to computers to cars, we are pressured into believing that what was perfectly fine yesterday is just not good enough today, not satisfying enough, not prestigious nor popular enough — even if it's made out of recycled parts!

We read in the *Torah*:[141]

> Because you did not serve God with happiness and with good-heartedness, [at a time when you had[142]] plenty . . .

Later sources explain that contentment and sharing are prerequisites to happiness and goodheartedness. Serving God with happiness can be achieved through learning to be "content with whatever we have."[143] Is the rich person happy if they don't satisfy their appetites?[144] Is the person of simple means happy if they are constantly wanting what they don't have? We intellectually know that this is not true. Yet mottoes such as "shop till you drop" and "he who dies with the most toys wins" are accurate reflections of our society at large. We must learn not to confuse what we have with who we are. We need to learn to be content with whatever we are blessed with. We need to teach this to our children by what we do.

The *Torah* teaches us that wealth, like any other blessing, must be utilized in the service of the Creator.[145] Wealth has the potential to be life-giving and ennobling.[146] Maimonides states[147] that:

the main design in [the acquisition of wealth] should be to expend it for noble purposes and for the maintenance of the body and the preservation of life so that its owner may obtain a knowledge of God insofar as that is [granted] unto human beings

We also find[148] that:

riches enable one to perform suitable and desirable deeds through which one will find "grace and favor in the sight of God and human beings"[149] . . . Riches were created only so that one could fulfill the commandments. . . . Riches are a crown and an honor for the wise, for such persons will use them in a way that will bring honor to themselves and to others. This is the exact opposite of the wealthy fool, who, upon becoming rich, uses wealth for foolishness. . . . Because of wealth, one may want to oppress others.

Ezekiel[150] warns us that the reason Sodom[151] was destroyed was not that it was wealthy, but rather that in its abundant prosperity, the people of Sodom did not share with the poor and the destitute. Their wealth was self-serving.[152] Their love of wealth was greater than the love of their fellow human beings. This was the cause of their ruin.

[There are situations where] the Blessed Holy One gives a person wealth but they do not share it with poor people. With this same [allocation] another person would have been able to sustain a thousand people and they have not been good to us. The poor people come before God and say: "You have given this person sufficient wealth to sustain a thousand people and they have not done good with us!" [God] will [judge] the wealthy as if they have stolen from numerous poor people, saying: "I have given you abundance so that you may give to those in need to the extent of your means and you have not given. I will punish you as if you have stolen and as if you have denied having in your possession something that I entrusted to you. I have given abundance into your hands so that you may distribute it to those in need and you have appropriated the abundance for yourself."[153]

We need to realize that wealth is a tool, indeed a blessing, that can be used to enhance life on earth for the better. We need to learn to share that with which we have been blessed. We need to teach this to our children by what we do.

Greed, wanting more than one ought to, and envy, being jealous of what another has, have been with us since the beginning of time. They are said to "remove a person from this world."[154] The *Midrash* ascribes the murder of Abel by Cain to greed and envy.[155] It also sees in the generation of the flood a hideous type of greed, one that was so subtle that it was not able to be tried in a court of law.[156] So destructive is not being satisfied with what one has, that the last of the *aseret ha-Dibrot,* the Ten Commandments, directs us "not to long for . . . anything that belongs to your friend."[157] We need to teach this to our children by what we do.

Rabbi Akiva, the famed rabbi of Israel during the first and second centuries, teaches us that we must live within our means. He lived most of his life in poverty, and taught that even *Shabbat,* the focal point of Jewish life, should be modestly celebrated in food, drink, and dress, rather than be celebrated elaborately if it means being beholden to others.[158] Rashi, the great *Torah* commentator of eleventh-century France, tells us to[159] "teach our families the ways of proper living — to be satisfied with simple foods." Certainly, learning to live within our means, not on credit, would have benefits not only for us as individuals but for the society as a whole, one of which is lessening the burden we are placing on limited resources. We need to teach this to our children by what we do.

During the Middle Ages, numerous Jewish communities imposed sumptuary laws, enactments *(takkanot)* limiting the amount that was allowed to be spent at weddings and other festive occasions. The purpose of these laws was to lessen the financial strain on the individual, protect the poor from embarrassment, and protect the community as a whole.[160] Nowadays, a number of Hasidic communities have enacted their own *takkanot.* Communities, synagogues, organizations, schools, and individuals are implementing educational programs and action ideas, applying *Torah* principles to our present situation.[161]

Tzedek, Tzedek *You Shall Pursue*[162]

A World of Hesed *Shall be Built*[163]

We live in a time of unparalleled abundance, technology, information, and communication. Our knowledge and abilities are unique among all of known creation. To what end are we becoming more comfortable, more informed, more connected? We have no excuse for living in ignorant arrogance and inaction. What is it all for? As we read this, there is a person dying for lack of adequate food, shelter, water or health care. What do we do? Most of us don't do a thing. We don't realize or care how important and precious one person is.

The texts on justice are numerous.[164] Justice, *tzedek,* is a cornerstone and a hallmark[165] of Judaism. Justice is divinely mandated. Justice is to be pursued, for all people. We must strive[166] to help those who are the weakest and most unprotected in society. We must never be content or complacent with regard to another's situation of need and despair.

Tzedaka. We could call it charity but it is not. *Tzedaka* is derived from the concept of *tzedek,* justice. Everyone, even one who lives off of *tzedaka,* is obliged to give *tzedaka.*[167] If someone should refuse to give *tzedaka* or if they give less than they can afford, the Rabbinic courts can coerce them into giving.[168] *Tzedaka* establishes just, habitual, regular giving. *Tzedaka* is considered equal to all the commandments of the *Torah.*[169]

Hesed goes beyond *tzedaka,* yet they must coexist. *Hesed* is loving kindness. This is the personal-touch part of doing for another. It does not require money, only devotion.[170] *Hesed* is altruistic, hands-on, giving. The purpose "of the laws of the *Torah* . . . are to promote compassion, *hesed* and peace in the world."[171] The *Torah* itself begins and ends with acts of *hesed.* These are like bookends holding up, defining, the *Torah.* We are to imitate God in God's ways of *hesed.* God clothes the naked, visits the sick, comforts the mourners, and buries the dead. We are to do likewise.[172] This is to be the organizing principle of our lives.[173] Our relationship to God is defined by our relationship towards our fellow human beings and the world itself.[174] We must constantly strive to make the world a better place.

The highest form of *tzedaka* is to give a person the opportunity to be self-sufficient.[175] In countries where justice, *tzedek,* and kindness, *hesed,*[176] are being implemented, where education and job training are provided to help give people independence and dignity, birth rates naturally fall.[177] By doing what we ought to be doing, not only is righteousness and kindness done but the population's growth rate is decreased, as is the environmental impact that accompanies poverty and population growth. God built the system to respond to *tzedaka* and *hesed.*

How are *Shabbat* and *tzedaka* and *hesed* related? The following passage,[178] read on Yom Kippur, the day known as the *Shabbat* of *Shabbats,* gives us a clear answer:[179]

This is the fast of My choice: to loosen the chains of wickedness . . . to share your bread with the hungry, to bring the poor to your house, to cover the naked. . . . If you remove the pointed finger and speaking of iniquity . . . you shall be a spring of water. . . .

If you restrain your foot on shabbat from pursuing business . . . and call the *Shabbat* delight, the sanctified day of God honorable, and shall honor it, not doing your own things . . . nor speaking of vain matters, then shall you delight yourself in Hashem.

The first part speaks of social justice. The second part speaks of *Shabbat*. The two seem to be disconnected or, at best, present social justice is a prerequisite for a future time of harmony. In fact there is a much deeper connection. *Shabbat*, as was presented above, is a day when we recognize our humble position within God's creation and our obligations in God's world. By "not doing our own things" on *Shabbat*, we are creating in ourselves the awareness of who we are and what we ought to be doing. By not interacting with the world one day a week, we are reminded *how* to interact with the world during the other six days. It is, indeed, "a day of delight," a day of enjoyment. The harmony that seems like a distant dream is in fact within our ability to actualize.

RESPONSIBILITY, TRUST, AND CHOOSING TO CHANGE

Even in the best of times, we are obliged to leave the world a better place for our children.[180] This idea was expressed quite beautifully when God took Adam[181] on a walk through the garden:

God created Adam and led Adam through the trees of the garden. "See my works, how fine and excellent they are. Know that all I have created is for your benefit. Reflect upon this and do not destroy my world for if you do, no one will fix it after you."[182]

This task, especially in today's day and age, seems to be overwhelming. We are taught:[183]

It is not for you to complete the work but neither are you free to desist from it.

We are not allowed to perceive our own situation as so futile that we give up. Regardless of whether or not we live to see the outcome of the changes we make, we must reset[184] the course we are on, and reorganize the principles by which we interact with the world. No situation is ever so futile that we must lose hope. As Jews, we are living proof of that statement. We believe that we must do what we are obliged to do. We trust that God will take care of the rest.[185]

[The earth] cried before its Creator: Sovereign of all worlds! I have not the power to feed all of humanity. The Blessed Holy One replied: I and you together will feed humanity.[186]

Our generation is indeed unique. All the realities of history, technology, demographics, and environmental degradation have converged. We have enhanced the lives of billions of people, but at a great cost. We can now harness our dreams, talents, and imagination to humbly redirect the course of both human history and of nature. The two go hand in hand. We can either heal the world or let it spiral into self-destruction. It is up to us as human beings. We have brought it to this moment. It is up to us to "fix the world."[187]

Interestingly, it is in fact the unprecedented population growth and the inventions of human hands that are forcing us to deal with each other and with the world at large. Never before have the daily choices that individuals have made had such a cumulative effect on others or on the world as a whole. Now, with more people on the face of the earth than at any time in previous history, each individual's actions are more paramount then ever and each individual *must* be compassionately regarded.

We must change the way we perceive our relationships. We define ourselves as a consumer society, and you and I are the consumers. This perception is certainly not conducive to building a caring, sharing, and just society. We, unique among all of God's creation, have the ability to choose and to change. Maimonides articulates this point:

> Behold, this species of [people] has become unique in the world, and there is no other species in this respect, that [we] by ourselves, with [our] own thoughts and intellect, shall know [to discern] between good and evil, and [we] can do whatever we desire. Nor is there anyone to prevent [us] from doing good or evil.[188]
>
> This matter is a great fundamental principle, and it is a pillar of *Torah* and *mitzvot*. . . . This means that the choice is in [our] hands, and that any act that an individual may wish to perform, in the entire range of human behavior, [one] can perform, whether good or evil. . . . This means that the Creator does not compel individuals, nor decree upon them that they do either good or evil. Rather, everything is given over to [us] [to choose].[189]

This certainly is not a description of a "consumer." We are also not simply "an intelligent being," a *homo sapiens*. Other beings are intelligent as well. Would we be in the situation we are if we weren't filled with such haughtiness? We are taught that people were created last in the order of creation so that if we get too filled with ourselves, we can be humbled by realizing that bugs were here before us.[190] Maybe it is time for a new definition of who we are, a definition that would encompass both our physical reality and our spiritual potential.

While writing this chapter, I came across a book wherein this had already been done.[191] *Homo spiritus* — we are both similar to, and, I believe this is hard for people to say, different from, the animal kingdom. We, in our day and age, are looking to redefine our relationship to the world, moving away from a persona-centered to a geo-centered way of relating. I believe that this hierarchy has its own set of unjust problems inherent in it.[192] The desire for a new definition is positive. I would submit that, in defining who we are and what we ought to be doing, we mute the voice that tells us that we are no different from other living organisms. We are. What ought to define us is much more sublime. We are to have humble self-awareness. We can choose to change.[193] We can choose to realize that *we* are *the* only creation that can make this world a place of justice, caring, and kindness. We can choose to be "partners in creation." We can choose to become the beings God wants us to be.[194] We were created last in the order of creation[195] in order to "work it and guard it." We must take care of God's gift. No other life form can. This is *our* job.[196]

CONCLUSION

The issues of population growth and consumption, with their concomitant environmental, social, and ethical problems, must be jointly addressed. To address one without the other would not only be senseless, it would be morally objectionable. Worthy of special regard is the *Torah*'s attitude toward population growth as it relates to *Bnai Noach*. Essential to the discussion is the necessity to redirect and redefine the underlying values that govern our society's attitudes, behaviors and relationships. *Shabbat, brakhot, bal tashkit, tzedek* and *chesed,* can guide[197] us to become the *homo spiritus* we have the responsibility and the choice to be.

NOTES

1. See Anita Gordon and David Suzuki, *It's A Matter of Survival* (Toronto: Stoddart Publishing Co., 1990); Lester R. Brown, Christopher Flavin and Sandra Postel, *Saving the Planet: How to Shape an Environmentally Sustainable Global Economy* (New York and London: W. W. Norton and Co., 1991).

2. Exodus 1:15–22.

3. *Talmud Babylonian* (herein cited as *TB*), *Sotah* 12a; TB, *Bava Batra* 199b; *Rashi,* Exodus 2:1.

4. Exodus 2:2.

5. Based on Ecclesiastes 11:6 "In the morning you should plant your seed and in the evening, as well, you should continue to do the same." With thanks to Norma Joseph (no relationship) for recommending that I do this paper.

6. *TB, Bava Batra* 60b; *Pnai Shlomo,* ad. loc.; *TB, Yevamot* 90b; *Taz, Shulhan Arukh, Orah Hayyim,* end of 588; *Biur ha-Gra* to *Shulhan Arukh, Even ha'Ezer,* Chapter 1, Section 10; See Rabbi Herschel Schachter, Halachic Aspects of Family Planning in *Halacha and Contemporary Society,* ed. Rabbi A. Cohen (New York: Ktav, 1983) pp. 15–17.

7. In order for the Jewish woman to be protected from potential risks arising from pregnancy, birth control was permissible during the Holocaust. See Rabbi Ephraim Oshry, *mi-Ma'amakim (Responsa from the Depths)* (New York: Self-published, 1959), Responsum 18 and 20, See Irving J. Rosenbaum, *The Holocaust and Halakhah* (New York: Ktav,1976) pp. 40–44.

8. In conversation with Dr. Leo Davids, Associate Professor of Sociology, Chairperson of the Department in Atkinson College of York University, Toronto. With thanks for your help in this section. See Deuteronomy 7:7, wherein the relationship between God and the Jewish people is not based on size.

9. Of interest to note, especially in this context, is that a person's "Jewishness" is defined by matrilineal descent, a testimony to the influence of Jewish women in relationship to the survival of the people as a whole.

10. Professor Roberto Bachi, The Demographic Evolution of World Jewry in Modern Times: Expansion and Decline, *1980 Zionist Yearbook,* American Jewish Committee (Philadelphia: Jewish Publication Society, 1980); U.O. Schmelz, *Aging of World Jewry,* (Jerusalem: Institute of Contemporary Studies, 1984). Also Dr. Leo Davids, *Reflections on Canadian Jewry, 1991* (Unpublished manuscript, February 1994). Dr. Davids observes that there "is a substantial increase of (Canadian) Jews aged 0–14 in the period from 1981 to 1991 . . . . The best hypothesis I can suggest is that we are beginning to see a real impact on the child population by the considerably higher birth rate that everybody knows is to be found among Orthodox and Ultra-Orthodox Jews."

11. Encyclopedia Judaica, Volume 5. *Demography* by U.O. Shmelz; *World Jewish Population in the 1980's: A Short Outline.* U.O. Schmelz. The Institute of Contemporary Jewry, The Hebrew University of Jerusalem, Israel, 1987; *World Jewish Population, 1991,* pp. 423–45. With thanks to Michele Anish, Blaustein Library, American Jewish Congress, New York.

12. U.S. Bureau of the Census, International Data Base, November 1993, *Counting People,* p. 28.

13. See Schachter, *Halachic Aspects of Family Planning* for a full discussion of the issue.

14. From a metaphysical approach we find the following statement (*TB, Yevamot* 62a): The son of David [the Messiah] will not come until all the souls in the *guf* [*"spiritual body"*] have been born; See Yehuda HaHasid, *Sefer Hasidim* (Warsaw, 1879), Para. 500.

15. Hyman Alterman, *Counting People: The Census in History* (New York: Harcourt, Brace and World. 1969), pp. 325–28.

16. Edward Stockwell and H.T. Groat, *World Population: An Introduction to Demography* (New York: Franklin Watts, 1884), pp. 26–32.

17. *The P.P.E. (Poverty, Population, and Environment) Spiral in the State of the World's Children, 1994* (New York: UNICEF, 1994); *The Human Development Report, 1994* (New York: United Nations Development Program, 1994). Thanks to Aaron Sacks, Worldwatch Institute, Washington, D.C.

18. As reported by Reuters, Limited. Tuesday, 19 April 1994, The Gazette, Montreal, Dateline: United Nations, Headline: *To fight overpopulation, educate women.* Professor Amartya Sen, a Harvard economics professor told the U.N.'s Eminent Citizens Committee for Cairo '94 that "in countries where women are educated, where there is an emphasis on female education, the birth rate drops . . . the more educated the population, especially the female population, the lower the birthrate." Pakistan's former planning minister, Mahbub ul-Haq, told Prof. Sen that he "wished he had used the $25 million in U.S. foreign aid to educate women instead of spending it on distributing condoms . . . . When we began the birthrate was 3 percent. When we went back to see how the program was doing we found the birthrate had increased to 3.2 percent. I wish I'd spent the money on educating women. Only 6 percent of the women in rural areas were literate." With thanks to Faye Abrams, Coordinator, Industrial and Business Information Service, University of Waterloo, Ontario.

19. *World Population Prospects, 1988,* Population Studies No. 106. Department of International, Economic and Social Affairs, United Nations, New York, 1989. If the growth rate of the developed countries continues, their population would double in 132 years. If the growth rate of developing countries continues, their population would double in 35 years. If the growth rate of the third world countries continues, their population would double in 26 years.

20. Alan During, *How Much is Enough? The Consumer Society and the Future of the Earth* (New York: W. W. Norton and Co., 1992), p. 50, Worldwatch Environmental Alert Series.

21. Gordon and Suzuki, p. 104. See below 153.

22. Adam, herein and as is so often the case in Jewish texts, refers to the first being. Adam is the archetype of every human being. See also Genesis 5:2 "Male and female [did God] create them . . . . [God] called *them* Adam." Adam means earth (Genesis 2:7). See *TB, Sotah* 5a.

23. Genesis 1:27–28.

24. Ibid., 1:22.

25. This pattern is repeated after the flood. See also Genesis 8:17, 9:1, 9:7; *Abarbanel,* Genesis 1:28. *Genesis Rabbah* 8:11.

26. *TB, Berakhot* 61a; *TB, Eruvin* 18a; *Genesis Rabbah* 8:1; *Rashi,* Genesis 2:21.

27. Genesis 2:24.

28. Ibid., 2:7; *Leviticus Rabbah* 34:3; *Abraham ibn Ezra,* Exodus 25:40.

29. *TB, Yevamot* 63a; *Tosefta,* ibid., 8:4; *TB, Yoma* 54a; *Genesis Rabbah* 8:9; ibid., 34:14.

30. *Shulhan Arukh, Even ha' Ezer,* 1; See *Song of Songs Rabbah* 1, s.v. "Draw me, we will run after thee," 1: Children are the surety that enabled us to receive the Torah;

TB, Yevamot 62b. During the 19th century, in the Carpathian Mountains town of Bilke, my great-great-grandfather, Shmuel Tzvi Weiss, a "h, tragically drowned while on his way to visit his relative, the Spinka Rebbe. Subsequently, his family had to sell the *Torah* he had spent three years writing. I am named after my grandfather, Shmuel Tzvi Joseph, who was named after him.

31. *Midrash Proverbs* 31:1; *Job* 1:21; *TB, Kiddushin* 30b: *Niddah* 31a; *Ecclesiastes Rabbah* 5:10.

32. Bnai Noach means Children of Noah. See David Novak, *The Image of the Non-Jew in Judaism: An Historical and Constructive Study of the Noahide Laws,* Toronto Studies in Theology, Vol. 14 (New York and Toronto: The Edwin Mellen Press, 1983).

33. Moses Maimonides, *Mishneh Torah* (Jerusalem: Jerusalem Publishers, 1970), *Hilkhot Melakhim* 10:7, *Mishneh le-Melekh,* ad. loc.; See the *Maharsha* on *TB, Sanhedrin* 59b, *Avnei Nezer (Even ha' Ezer,* 79). For a full discussion see *Halachic Aspects of Family Planning,* pp. 3–30.

34. Isaiah 45:18.

35. See 17 above.

36. With special thanks to HaRav Moshe Tendler for reading this paper and allowing his name to be associated with it. See Rabbi Dr. Moshe D. Tendler, Population Control — the Jewish View, in *Challenge: Torah Views on Science and Its Problems,* ed. Aryeh Carmel and Cyril Domb (London and Jerusalem, 1976), pp. 462–71; *Tosafot, TB, Sanhedrin,* op.cit.

37. *TB, Sanhedrin* 59a; Ibid., *Tosafot* s.v. "leyka." See Novak, *Image of the Non-Jew,* p. 186.

38. *TB, Sotah* 12a; *Tosafot,* TB, *Ta'anit* 11a, s.v. "It is not permitted for one to engage in sexual relations during years of famine." Yocheved, Levi's daughter and later to become Moses' mother, was herself born while her family was migrating to Egypt. The reason that they were going to Egypt in the first place was because it was a famine. This would mean that her parents did have relations during a time of famine. From this we could deduce that relations are not forbidden but for the one who would take on this additional measure of piety. Joseph did not engage in marital relations but other people (like his brother Levi) did.

39. *TB, Sanhedrin* 19b; *TB, Megillah* 13a.

40. Saadia Gaon, *The Book of Beliefs and Opinions,* Samuel Rosenblatt, trans. (New Haven: Yale University Press, 1951), p. 381. Much thanks to Mr. Ronnie Finegold, Jewish Public Library, Montreal, Quebec for all his help.

41. See above 17 and 18.

42. Paul Ehrlich, *The Population Explosion* (New York: Simon and Schuster, 1990); Erich Fromm, *To Have or To Be?* (New York: Bantam Books, 1982); Jeremy Rifkin, *Entropy Into the Greenhouse World* (New York: Bantam; 1989); David Suzuki, *Inventing the Future: Reflections on Science, Technology and Nature* (Toronto: Stoddart, 1989).

43. Paul Ehrlich, *The Machinery of Nature* (New York: Simon and Schuster, 1986), p. 17.

44. Psalms 24:1.

45. Genesis 1:1; *Nachmanides* (13th century) ad. loc.; Maimonides, *Mishneh Torah, Hilkhot Teshuvah* 3:7.

46. Exodus 20:2; Deuteronomy 5:6.

47. *Genesis Rabbah* 39:1; Maimonides, *Mishneh Torah, Hilkhot Avodat Kokhavim* 1:3.

48. Exodus 20:3–4; Maimonides, op. cit.., 1:1; *Midrash Hagadol* on Genesis 11:28.

49. *TB, Shabbat* 77b: "Of all that the blessed Holy One created in [God's] world, [God] created nothing in vain."; *Genesis Rabbah* 8:6; ibid. 10:6; "The son of Sira said: Hashem caused drugs to spring forth from the earth — with them the physician heals the wound and the pharmacist compounds their preparations."

50. *Genesis Rabbah* 10:7: "Even those things which you may regard as superfluous to creation . . . such as fleas, gnats and flies are included in the creation and Hashem's purpose is carried out through everything, even through a snake, a scorpion, a gnat and a frog."; *TB, Shabbat* 77b.

51. Psalms 89:3; ibid., 104:31; *TB, Hullin* 60a; Moses Maimonides,*The Guide for the Perplexed,* trans. Shlomo Pines (Chicago and London: University of Chicago Press, 1963, 1969) Part 3, Chapter 25. See below 163.

52. Saadia Gaon, *Beliefs and Opinions,* pp. 38–86; Maimonides, *Guide,* Part 3, Chapter 13.

53. The ways of God are truly a mystery, beyond human comprehension. See Job 38:1–41; 39:1–30; 40:1–32; 41:1–26.

54. *TB, Avot* 3:1.

55. *Genesis Rabbah* 1:1; Proverbs 8:22; Judah Halevi, *Kuzari* (New York: Schocken Books, 1964), 3:73, p. 196.

56. Deuteronomy 11:13–17.

57. God has warned us that we must be the guardians and not play God. Leviticus 19:19; *Sifra,* ad loc.; *TB, Kiddushin* 39a and *Talmud Jerusalem* (herein cited as *TJ*), *Kilayim* 1:7: "You shall keep my laws — the laws I engraved in my world."; Maimonides, *Mishneh Torah, Hilkhot Melakhim* 10:6: Cross-breeding of animals is prohibited under the Noachide Laws; *Pirke de Rabbi Eliezer* (New York: Hermon Press, 1970), Chapter 34, p. 254 "When people cut down the wood of the tree which yields fruit, its cry goes from one end of the world to the other and its voice is not heard."

58. *Rashi,* Exodus 7:19 and 8:1, 12; *Rashi,* Exodus 20:23; *Exodus Rabbah* 9:10;10:7; *TB, Bava Kamma* 92b.

59. *Avot de Rabbe Natan* 41; *Tanna de-Vei Eliyahu* 18.

60. Ascribed to Rabbi Aaron haLevi of Barcelona, *Sefer ha-Hinnukh* (Jerusalem: Eshkol, 1962), Mitzva 33: "A person should realize that their mother and father are the cause of their being in the world, and therefore it is truly proper that they give them all the honor and do them all the service that they can."; Rabbi Avraham Danzig, *Hayyei Adam* (Jerusalem:Shilo), Laws of Honoring Parents, 67:2, p. 129. ". . . those who speak falsehood, they say no gratitude is owed parents, for their immediate motive was self-gratification and the child was merely created incidentally. Now that with the child born, the God made the nature of the parents such that they would raise him, as indeed all animals who raise their young without the young being grateful for

this . . . concerning such opinions our sages say, "whoever is ungrateful towards another will come to be ungrateful to God." Special thanks to my husband, Rabbi David J. Levy, LL.D. To my parents, Zelig and Bernice Joseph, this paper is a tribute to you. To my mother-in-law, Dr Edith Rechter-Levy, for your encouragement. To my brother, Lawrence Joseph, without whom this paper would not have happened. Thank you.

61. See *Rashi,* Genesis 2:5.

62. *Exodus Rabbah* 1:8; See Rabbi E.L. Dessler, *Michtav Me'Eliyahu* (Jerusalem: Committee for Publication of the writings of Rabbi E.L. Dessler, 1978) Volume 3, pp. 85–104.

63. *Lamentations* 3:38: "Out of the mouth of the most High do not both good and bad come?!"; Isaiah 45:7; *TB, Berakhot* 60b, "Whatever God does is for the best"; *TB, Ta'anit* 21a, "This too is for good." These words were forever on my grandmother, Chaya (Miller) Hartogson's, lips.

64. *TB, Berakhot* 9:1; Ibid 54a.

65. Deuteronomy 8:10.

66. *TB, Berakhot* 43b.

67. Ibid., 59a.

68. Ibid., 43b.

69. Maimonides, *Mishneh Torah, Hilkhot Berakhot* 10:3–4.

70. *TB, Berakhot* 58a.

71. *Tosefta, TB, Berakhot* 4:1; Maimonides, *op. cit.* 1:1–4.

72. *TB, Berakhot* 35a and b.

73. *Tanhuma, (ve-Zot) HaBeracha,* 7.

74. Kenneth Blanchard, Patricia Zigarmi, Drea Zigarmi, *Leadership and the One Minute Manager* (New York: William Morrow and Company, 1985).

75. End of Adon Olam prayer; *Midrash Shoher Tov* (Jerusalem: Midrash, 1960) 25; On the topic of expectation, *Rashi* comments on Deuteronomy 18:13, "Be whole-hearted with the Lord your God": "Walk with God in whole-heartedness and depend upon God and do not seek into the future. Rather whatever occurs to you, accept with whole-heartedness and then you will be with God and God's portion." See above 63.

76. *Midrash Tehillim* 25; Lamentations 3:23; *Tikun Tefilla* in *Sidur Otzar HaTefillot* (New York: Friedman Publishing); Vol. 1, p.120. *TB, Berakhot* 60a.

77. *Genesis Rabbah* 14:9; Psalms 150:6. I thank my teacher, Rav Ephraim Oratz, for teaching me this source.

78. Genesis 2:15. I thank my teacher Mrs. Miriam Hauer for encouraging the development of the section on Shabbat.

79. *Exodus Rabbah* 25; *TJ, Nedarim* 3:9: Shabbat is equal to all the commandments of the Torah.

80. Exodus 2:11; *Exodus Rabbah* 1:28; ibid., 5:18.

81. *Sefer ha-Hinnukh,* Mitzva 243; Leviticus 19:18: ". . . Love your neighbor as yourself, I am God."

82. Exodus 22:20; Leviticus 19:33–34; Deuteronomy 10:19.

83. Exodus 23:9.

84. As part of the daily recitation of Shma, the declaration of the unity of God. See Numbers 15:41.

85. Genesis 1:27; ibid., 2:7; ibid., 5:1–2; *TB, Avot* 3:18, "precious are people for they have been created in the image of God."

86. See 22 above.

86. See 22 above.

87. *Yalkut Shimoni* (New York: Pardes, 1944), Volume 1, *Breisheet* 1:13; *Pirke de Rabbi Eliezer*, Chapter 11, p. 76–77. See also *Rashi*, Genesis 2,7 s.v. "dust from the earth."

88. *Sanhedrin* 37a.

89. Slavery was in ancient times, and in some places is still today, the norm. The Rabbis enacted measures to help alleviate the severity of the servitude. *TB, Kiddushin* 20a states: The slave should eat and drink with you, so that you don't eat clean bread and [the slave] moldy bread, so that you don't drink old wine and [the slave] new wine, so that you don't sleep on soft feathers and [the slave] on straw. It is said, "Whoever buys a . . . slave for themselves, is as if they have purchased a master for themselves."

90. Based on Deuteronomy 5:14–15. This text is the second repetition of the Ten Statements (Commandments). See Exodus 20:8–11.

91. Genesis 2:1–3.

92. Creation in 7 days as literal or allegorical: *Genesis Rabbah* 3:7; *Rashi* and *Nachmanides,* Genesis 1:1; See Israel Weinstock, *Bema'aglei Hanigleh Vehanistar* (Jerusalem, Mossad Harav Kook, 1969), pp. 190–206.

93. Psalms 121:4, "Behold the God of Israel does not tire nor sleep"; Isaiah 40:28, "Do you not know? Have you not heard? The Lord, The everlasting God, Creator of the whole world, grows neither weary nor faint . . . ."

94. Genesis 1:3; *Nachmanadies* ad. loc.; *Rashi,* Genesis 2:4; Psalms 33:6,9; *Genesis Rabbah* 4:7, 12:10, "Not with work nor effort did God create the universe, but with a mere word."; *TB, Menahot* 29b; Maimonides, *Guide,* Part1: Chapter 66; Jeremiah 10:12, "[God] made the earth with [God's] power, founded the world with [God's] wisdom, and stretched out the skies with [God's] understanding."

95. *Genesis Rabbah* 10:9; *Rashi,* Genesis 2:2; *Siftei Hakhamim* 80 and 90 on *Rashi* ad loc. With thanks to Rabbi Dr. C. Grysman.; *Rashi, TB, Megillah* 9a, s.v. "and [God] completed"; *Ecclesiastes Rabbah* 4: s.v. "better a handful with quietness."

96. Genesis 2:2.

97. Dessler, *Michtav,* Volume 2, Shabbat section; Proverbs 14:30, "A tranquil, healing heart gives life to the flesh, but envy brings rotting of the bones."

98. *TB, Bezah* 13b; *Yalkut Shimoni,* Volume 1, Vayakhel 35.

99. *TB, Shabbat* 102b.

100. To be differentiated from the survival instinct, which animals obviously possess.

101. Deuteronomy 28:9: "and walk in [God's] ways"; Proverbs 3:6 : "know [God] in all your ways"; *Sefer ha-Hinnukh,* Mitzva 611; *Hayyei Adam, Laws of Blessings and Prayers,* 1:1.

102. *TB, Shabbat* 10a; *Genesis Rabbah* 11:8.

103. *Arukh HaShulkhan, Orah Hayyim* 242:1; Eliyahu de Vidas, *Reshit Hokhmah* (Jerusalem: Or ha-Musar, 1984), The Gate of Holiness, Chapter 2: "When the Torah com-

mands 'you shall be Holy because I am holy,' this means that we should make the spirituality that is Shabbat extend to everyday living and we should sanctify ourselves in our actions and in our thoughts." *Hayyei Adam, Laws of Shabbat,* 1:1, p.138: . . . So, too, when we count the days of the week, we do so with reference to Shabbat — "the first day with regard to *Shabbat*" (in contrast to Sunday), "the second day with regard to Shabbat" (in contrast to Monday) and so on because the sanctity of Shabbat continues to everyday. (Shabbat) is the hub from which all the days of the week are nurtured. The first, second and third days are referred to with regard to the previous Shabbat from which they draw their sanctity and the fourth, fifth and sixth days are referred to with regard to the coming Shabbat from which they draw their sanctity. See *Michtav Me'Eliyahu, op. cit.* Rabbi Zalman Sorotzkin, *Insights in the Torah (Bereishis) (Oznayim la- Torah)* (New York: Mesorah Publications, 1991), Genesis 1:131: This is the secret of the Holy Shabbat. On that day we should judge everything we have done to serve God during the week, and we should make amends wherever necessary, until we can say honestly, "Behold, it was very good!"

104. Genesis 2:15.

105. *Genesis Rabbah* 16:5; See also *Pirke de Rabbi Eliezer,* chapter 12, p. 85.

106. Exodus 20:9.

107. Deuteronomy 5:12.

108. See above 102.

109. *Sforno* on Exodus 20:8.

110. It is interesting to note the halakha that we do not give gifts on Shabbat, as a testimony that nothing is ours to give or to receive, as all is God's.; See Rabbi Yehoshua Y. Neuwirth, *Shemirat Shabbat Kehilkhata* (Jerusalem: Moriah, 1979), Chapter 29:29.

111. *TB, Avot* 3:1.

112. *Ecclesiastes Rabbah* 7:28.

113. Freely translated from the *Shabbat* song Menucha v'Simkha (Peace and Happiness).

114. See *Mekhilta* to Exodus 20:16: Shabbat as witness to creation; Maimonides, *Guide,* Part 1, Chapter 44.

115. God is also known as Hai ha-Olamim — the Life of the Worlds.; See also *Nishmat kol hai* in the Shabbat morning prayers; the *Akdamut* prayer of Shavuot; *Perek Shirah.*

116. Deuteronomy 32:4: God is also known as Tzur — a Rock (of Strength).

117. *Pirke de Rabbi Eliezer* Chapter11, pp. 79–80.

118. Deuteronomy 5:14. Interestingly, the mitzva of Shabbat observance includes allowing our (work) animals to rest.

119. See 95 above.

120. *Rashi,* Exodus 20:9.

121. Isaiah 58:13; *TB, Shabbat* 113a, b.

122. *TB, Avot* 4:1, "Who is strong? One who conquers one's desires."

123. *TB, Berakhot* 57b; *TB, Bezah* 16a.

124. See Lori Palatnik, *Friday Night and Beyond: The Shabbat Experience Step-by-Step* (New Jersey: Jason Aaronson, 1994).

125. *Siftei Hakhamim* 80 on *Rashi*, Genesis 2:2; *TB, Peah* 1:1; *TB, Kiddushin* 40b; *TB, Shabbat* 127a; *Yalkut Shimoni, op. cit.*

126. *TB, Shabbat* 25a; *Yalkut Shimoni*, Volume 1, Behaalotecha 8.

127. Exodus 16:14–27.

128. Genesis 6:11–12; ibid., 19; *Genesis Rabbah* 49:6; *TB, Sanhedrin* 108b; ibid., 109a, *Pirke de Rabbi Eliezer*, Chapter 25; Deuteronomy 32:15; Isaiah 5:8; 32:11; Jeremiah 2:34; 5:28; Ezekiel 16:49,50; 22:29; Amos 6; Micah 2:2.

129. Regarding taking care not to cause the extinction of any species, see Deuteronomy 22:6–7; *Sefer ha-Hinnukh*, Mitzva 545; *TB, Sanhedrin op. cit.;* "The raven said to Noah: 'You must hate me, for you did not choose from the species of which there are seven but from a species of which there are only two. If the powers of the sun or of the cold overwhelm me, would not the world be lacking a species?'"

130. *TB, Arakhin* 24a; *TB, Hullin* 91a.

131. *Sefer ha-Hinnukh*, Mitzva Number 529.

132. *Rashi*, Exodus 20:23 comments regarding the priest having to take modest steps on the altar steps, "Because of the steps [of the altar] you need to widen your paces and this is close to nakedness. If [we must take care regarding these] stones which are inanimate and have no understanding of shame, how much more so our fellow human being, who is [created] in the image of God and is sensitive to shame."

133. *TB, Eruvin* 64b; *Shulhan Arukh, Orah Hayyim* 180:4: "One who finds food on the road is not permitted to pass by and leave it there."

134. *Sifri* on Deuteronomy 20:19–20.

135. *TB, Shabbat* 67b.

136. Maimonides, *Mishneh Torah, Hilkhot Melakhim*, 6:8.

137. Rabbi Samson Raphael Hirsch, *Horeb*, Dayan Dr. Grunfeld, trans. (London: Soncino, 1962), Volume 2, chapter 56, p. 280.

138. *TB, Tamid* 29a; *Encyclopedia Talmudit*, 2:226; *She'ilat Ya'avetz*, Part 1, Responsa 76.

139. Dr. Meir Tamari, *In the Marketplace: Jewish Business Ethics* (New York:Feldheim/Targum, 1991), pp. 128–46.

140. Maimonides, *Guide*, Part 3, Chapter 12–14: Many of our difficulties are due to our desire for the superfluous. When we seek unnecessary things, we have difficulty in finding even that which is truly necessary. The soul, when accustomed to superfluous things, acquires a strong habit of desire. This desire is without limit, for what is unnecessary is without end.; *TB, Berakhot* 32a; *Tosefta, TB, Sotah* 3:6; *TB, Sanhedrin* 108a; *Genesis Rabbah* 26:5; ibid. 28:6.

141. Deuteronomy 28:47.

142. According to *Rashi's* explanation to Deuteronomy 28:47.

143. Psalms 100:2; *TB, Avot* 4:1, "Who is wealthy? One who is content with what they have."; See Yehiel ben Yekutiel, *Sefer Ma'alot ha-Middot* (Jerusalem: Eshkol, 1968), pp. 266–88.

144. *Ecclesiastes Rabbah* 1:34; 3:12 "No person dies with half their desires fulfilled."; *TB, Avot* 2:8: "The more possessions — the more worry."

145. Deuteronomy 6:5; *Rashi*, ad. loc.; 1 Chronicles 29:12,14; *TB, Avot* 3:7.

146. See *TB, Berakhot* 16b; Genesis 24:1; *Abraham ibn Ezra*, ad. loc.

147. Moses Maimonides, *The Eight Chapters of Maimonides on Ethics*, Joseph I. Gorfinkle, trans. (New York: Columbia University Press, 1912), chapter 5, p. 70.

148. Bahya ben Asher, *Kad ha-Kemach* (Lwow, 1892), pp. 28a–30a; *Tanhuma, Naso* 28.

149. Proverbs 3:4.

150. Ezekiel 16:49–50.

151. See Genesis 19.

152. See *TJ, Yoma* 4,6.

153. *Sefer Hasidim*, para. 415; *Exodus Rabbah* 31:3: There is an ever rotating wheel in this world. One who is rich today, may be poor tomorrow. One who is poor today, may be rich tomorrow.

154. *TB, Avot* 4:28.

155. *Genesis Rabbah* 22:7. I thank my teacher, Professor Nechama Leibowitz for teaching me this source.

156. Genesis 6:11–13; *Rashi*, Genesis 6:13; *TB, Sanhedrin* 108a; *TJ, Bava Mezia* 4:2.

157. Exodus 20:14; Deuteronomy 5:21.

158. *TB, Shabbat* 118a; *TB, Pesahim* 112b; *TB, Avot* 2:14.

159. *Rashi, TB, Hullin* 84a; This approach is to be balanced with enjoying the world God has blessed us with. *TB, Sukkah* 28b: "It is like one who, when offered a gift, takes and throws it back at his friend's face."; *TJ, Kiddushin* 4: "Every person will have to give an accounting for every [permissible] enjoyment that they denied themselves."

160. Rabbi Israel Schepansky, *"Hatakanot B'Yisrael"* (Jerusalem: Mossad HaRav Kook, 1993).

161. I would like to thank Dr. Elisheva Kaufman for her presentation of this topic at the conference.

162. Deuteronomy 16:20.

163. Psalms 89:3; See above 51.

164. Exodus 21:21–26; ibid., 22:20–21; Deuteronomy 16:20; Isaiah 1:17,27; ibid., 5:16; Psalms 82:3; Proverbs 21:3; Micah 6:8; Hosea 2:21–22.

165. Maimonides, *Mishneh Torah, Hilkhot Matnot Aniyim* 9:3.

166. *Genesis Rabbah* 9:9; *Midrash Tehillim* 36:4; *TB, Makkot* 23b; *TB, Yoma* 69b; Maimonides, *Guide*, Part 3, Chapter 26.

167. *Shulhan Arukh, Yoreh De'ah*, 248:1.

168. Maimonides, ibid., 7:10.

169. *TB, Bava Batra* 9a.

170. Maimonides, *Mishneh Torah, Hilkhot Avadim* 9:8.

171. Ibid., *Hilchot Shabbat* 2:3; *TB, Gittin* 59b.

172. *TB, Sotah* 14a; *Exodus Rabbah* 35:2: (The wood used for building the desert sanctuary was acacia wood.) Hashem was teaching people a lesson for all times that if a person wishes to build their home from wood of fruitbearing trees, it is said to them "Hashem who is master of everything, said to build the Mishkan [tabernacle] of wood from non-fruitbearing trees, how much more incumbent it is upon people [to take care in choosing wood for their homes]."

173. See 101 above

174. We have not dealt at all with tza'ar ba'alei haim (compassion to animals), vegetarianism, zoning laws, or safety laws.

175. Maimonides, *Mishneh Torah, Hilkhot Matnot Aniyin* 10:7–12; *TB, Shabbat* 63a: "It is better to lend to a poor person than to give him a handout, and best of all is to provide him with capital for business."

176. See Jeremiah 9:23; Proverbs 21:21.

177. See 17 above.

178. Isaiah 58:6–13.

179. Leviticus 16:31; ibid., 23:32.

180. *Tanhuma, Kedoshim* 8: The Blessed Holy One said to Israel: "Although you will find the land full of good things, you should not say, 'we will sit and not plant.' Rather, as others have planted for you, so must you plant for your children. A person should not say 'I am old. How many [more] years will I live. Why am I making an effort and toiling on others behalf? Tomorrow I will die'. . . . Therefore, a person should never cease from planting. Rather, above and beyond what one has found [in this world], [a person] should continue and plant — even if they should be old. The Blessed Holy One said to [the Children of] Israel: Learn from me. Just I am not in need [of planting yet I have planted] as is written in the Torah [Genesis 2:8]. And God planted a garden eastward in Eden.; *TB, Ta'anit* 23a; *Avot de Rabbe Natan* 31.

181. See 22 above.

182. *Ecclesiastes Rabbah, op. cit.*; Rabbi M. H. Luzzato, *Mesillat Yesharim* (Jerusalem: Eshkol, 1964), Chapter 1, p. 11.

183. *TB, Avot* 2:21.

184. Genesis 4:7.

185. It is interesting to note that previous predictions were not able to foresee or take into account such developments or events as the Industrial Revolution, mass transportation, electricity, birth control, the women's movement, the bomb, global warming, nuclear or solar energy. Obviously, each generation must do what it has to do, with the knowledge it has, to improve life on earth and not rely on miracles. See above 183.

186. *Pirke de Rabbi Eliezer*, Chapter 12, p. 86.

187. See above 114.

188. Maimonides, *Mishneh Torah, Hilkhot Teshuvah* 5:1.

189. Ibid., 5:3; *Job* 28:28; Saadia Gaon, *Belief and Opinions*, end of 4:1; See above 166.

190. *TB, Sanhedrin* 38a; *Genesis Rabbah* 8:1.

191. Abraham J. Twerski, M.D., *I'd Like to Call for Help, But I Don't Know the Number: The Search for Spirituality in Everyday Life* (New York: Pharos Books, 1991), pp. 9–15, 146–49.

192. See Rabbi Barry Freundel, The Earth is the Lord's, *Jewish Action* magazine, Summer 1990, pp. 22–26; Dennis Prager, Little Events that Changed My Thinking, *Ultimate Issues: A Quarterly Journal by Dennis Prager*, Volume 6, Number 3, July–Sept 1990.

193. Genesis 4: 7; *TJ, Makkot* 2:6; *Genesis Rabbah* 1:4; *Midrash Shoher Tov* 90; *Leviticus Rabbah* 10: "Cain went out from God" (Genesis 4:16) Rav Huna said in the

name of Rabbi Hanina the son of Isaac: He went out happy! When he departed from God he met Adam. Adam asked him what happened with your judgement? Cain answered: I did teshuva and [God] made peace with me. When Adam heard this he started hitting his own face [in amazement] saying; this is the power of teshuva /repentance and I did not know. In that hour Adam composed: "A Song for the Shabbat Day"! (Psalms 92:1).

194. *Sefer ha-Hinnukh,* e.g., Mitzva 16: Know that a person behaves according to their deeds. Their heart and all their thoughts always follow the actions that they regularly do, be they good or bad . . . . The emotions are drawn by actions.

195. See section above on Awareness (Shabbat); *TB, Sanhedrin, op. cit.*

196. See Rabbi Samson Raphael Hirsch, *The Pentateuch* (London: Isaac Levy Publisher, 1963), Genesis 1:28: ". . . dominion is no enslavement or degradation, rather the elevation of all earthly material elements into the service of God."

197. We offer, along with the three Rs of reduce, reuse and recycle, the four As of awareness, acceptance, actualization, and altruism.

6

A Christian Response
to the Population Apocalypse

CATHERINE KELLER

ACTIVELY AVOIDING THE POPULATION ISSUE

It is my ambiguous honor in this collection to represent a Christian perspective on the issue of population ecology. Fortunately, however, no one — neither the Pope nor I — can speak for "Christianity." Christianity is not one. Those who stress its unity today are usually those seeking to muster allegiance to an orthodox Christian core, which even in classical times existed only for those willing to assent to the conciliar consensus. That consensus, forged in the fires of the fourth-century church's fusion with the Constantinian empire, set the stage for the aggressive political impact of this particular religion upon the planet. The ensuing global force of Christendom accounts for the most powerful forces of pronatalism, i.e., of opposition to any effective birth control options and policies. At the same time, modern Christian — Western — cultures have been overwhelmingly responsible for the imposition throughout the planet of ecologically unsustainable patterns of development. It is not that, compared to other world religions, Christianity has the worst ideas for the environment and for women. Many of the most progressive ideas share Christian sources. But in its tradition of colonizing for Christ, it has also sanctified the ideological framework for the unprecedented aggressions of the modern Western circuits of political, economic, and cultural domination.

Nonetheless, the diversity of Christianity stubbornly persists. On the theological practices pertaining to the sustainability of the biosphere — as perhaps on every other issue of material force in the world today — Christians differ more among each other than from ideologically kindred members of other groups. For instance, those with conservative Christian commitments will share more on issues of population and birth control with conservative members of non-Christian faiths than they do with their own siblings in Christ, who, likewise, will find affinity with a variety of secular and non-Christian progressives.

This diversity, for all its frictions and marginalities, gives people like me — those Christians involved in a systematic critique of our religion's patriarchal colonialisms — space to work in. The fierce, if fragile, transmutations of Christianity's "mainstream" into a self-critical force for "Justice, Peace and the Integrity of Creation"[1] lends hope that the work may be worthwhile. From this emerging vantage point, concern for the planetary ecology cannot be separated from commitment to social justice, and will, I hope focus itself ever more sharply through the lens of women's critical inquiry. It is becoming a planetary truism that analysis of the forms of women's traditional subjugation may be the only viable starting point for an effective engagement of the question of overpopulation. Margaret Catley-Carlson, President of the Population Council, makes it clear that there can be no effective, let alone humane, approach to overpopulation that does not begin with the situations of women in poverty.[2] Only with the enhancement of female access to education, human rights, and paid work, and, at the same time, reduced infant mortality are there notable reductions anywhere in the rate of population growth. Patriarchy and overpopulation function as correlatives (which does not imply that population reduction solves sexism). It would seem that only a forthrightly feminist (a term loaded with the ambiguities of race, class, and national difference — I mean it as my own appropriate shorthand for the point of conjunction of womanist, *mujerista,* and any other terms preferred by non-white women to express the anti-sexist agenda) version of Christianity will be able to engage the interstructured social and ecological injustices that nest within the thorny issue of population growth.

I come to this discussion as a theologian, not as a population activist or expert. But I soon learned that while the environment has finally, almost "too late,"[3] gotten on the Christian progressive agenda, the issue of the population curve still has not. As I browsed through various journals, anthologies and ecotheological texts, I became aware of a veritable conspiracy of liberal silence. Among Northern ecumenical Protestant Christians — ethicists, feminists, ecospiritualists, liberation theologians, and justice activists — there seems to reign an unstated assumption that population is *never* worth highlighting.

The reasons are good and clear. The justice-centered Christians speaking on behalf of the worlds of the poor — the "third" and "fourth" worlds — make the irrefutable point, the point that stimulates the present discussion: *how can first world persons, who on the average consume at least thirty times as much as an average African or Asian or Latin American, instruct the "others" to reduce themselves?* Since it is the exploitation of the resources of the "third" world for the sake of the self-designated "first" and their client elites — not overpopulation–which deprives those populous "others" of the resources they need, focus on population control appears dangerously akin to the genocidal policies which seek to rid the world of the troubling, potentially revolutionary masses of the poor.[4] Moreover, cases of successful population reduction, such as Brazil, have not resulted in the reduction of poverty. These are the key objections to the very terms of the population debate heretofore, and they have rightly set the limits for any contemporary re-engagement of the issue.

Feminists come from another angle: rightly indignant about the misogynist means of much state-driven population reduction (such as involuntary sterilization of poor and dark women), and indeed the genocidal results increasingly possible (as in abortion of female fetuses in China), we also are loath to problematize population growth as such. Feminist ethicists have needed, moreover, to direct their birth-control energies to the relentless debate about abortion, with little left to spare.[5] We might expect to get some guidance from the writings of ecofeminists and ecotheologians. But while one delights here in the rediscovery of the intermeshed life of the creation, and in the evocation of the interdependence of human and creaturely life, the all too human problem of overpopulation — begging for scientific and social address — hardly enhances the desired naturalism.

We may add to this mix of silences the desire for strategic solidarity with progressive Roman Catholics, who usually have few qualms about artificial birth control but may draw the line at abortion, and therefore make unlikely partners in any attempt to disseminate a wide variety of birth control options. More importantly, if more vaguely, we cannot forget the residual Christian ambivalence about sex, the body, women's bodies in particular, and the fertility of the earth in general. And, theologically, we confront the lack of any prophetic-biblical resources comparable to those addressing oppression and poverty. All told, it is not hard to understand why the issue slides off the conference tables.[6] Indeed, I myself had never given it any steadfast attention until recently.

Yet to criticize the ways the population explosion can be misdescribed and misused for one-third world or masculinist or white self-interest is surely not reason enough to ignore or dismiss the issue. The fact of the Malthusian growth curve within the diminishing resource base does not go away while we focus on other critical struggles. One would rather hope that the critical concerns of feminists and liberationists would be the basis for a socio-ecological reinterpretation of the population problem — one based on the awareness that the poor, and especially poor women, will always suffer the most from the environmental effects of overpopulation; and that conversely, it is precisely the structures that maintain poverty and sexism that create overpopulation.

Let me suggest that we will only be able to overcome the rather formidable inhibitions to addressing the population explosion globally and ecumenically inasmuch as we move toward a discourse which can sustain multiple voices advocating multiple commitments, without retreating into the stale Western logic of "either" vs. "or," of "a or not-a." An alternative logic — indeed an eco-logic — which seeks to understand the "eco"nomy and "eco"logy as interrelated dimensions of our "ecu"menical accountability to each other and the earth must be ever more confidently articulated. Such a logic seeks to hold together multiple struggles simultaneously. In so doing, it moves so far from Western ways of knowing as to resemble faith rather than reason. Or rather, it resembles ecospirituality: it will recycle the often toxic complexities of the tradition through the criteria of the multiple voices of those who suffer. The task of the theologian in such a situation resembles that of a compost heap — what, amidst the wastes and the cliches of our overused tradition, can be recycled for life?

In the absence of a developed Christian alternative, it has been the Pope who *ipso facto* is left to speak for Christianity. The papal position seems to transcend the ambiguities bred of the multiple global voices. "Every sexual act must be open to the transmission of life."[7] "Life," in the broader papal discourse, has rich humanistic resonances, evoking all that vitalizes interpersonal existence and redeems it from modern depersonalizing alienation. But when it comes to sexuality, that vitality is here reduced, with an unflinching literalism, to the size of a fetus. "Morality," in the papal encyclical *Veritate Splendor* which soon followed, seems at moments to translate into the ecclesiastical supervision of Christian genitalia. "Life" thus becomes a pawn in the "pro-life" politics which have forged strange ecumenical links between conservative Catholics, formerly uninterested in ecumenism, and right-wing, traditionally anti-Catholic Protestants; and more recently, even with fundamentalist Muslims. For this reason, profeminist Protestants can no longer afford the luxury of polite ecumenical silence toward Rome. But at the same time, any demonizing reduction of Roman Catholicism to the papal denominator misses the mark.

It must be emphasized that even among the celibate male leadership of Roman Catholicism, there are important alternative voices. For instance, Sean McDonagh, SSC, head of the Columbian missioners, asks, "Is it really pro-life to ignore the warning of demographers and ecologists who predict that unbridled population growth will lead to severe hardship and an increase in the infant mortality rate for succeeding generations?"[8] McDonagh is an Irish priest who worked for twenty years in a mission in the Philippines, helping to develop a small indigenous community's economic and ecological potentialities under relatively rare, isolated, and protected circumstances. He demonstrates that, even with the most egalitarian policies, this community, Tablo, is faced, precisely because of its population growth, with irresistible temptations to overwork the land and harvest the forest, thus undermining the possibility of future stability and self-sustenance. He cites Fr. Mansmann, CP, (who has lived in the area for twenty-seven years): "the simple conclusion is that there cannot be a stable livelihood or sustainable community without population control." As to "natural family planning methods," these failed repeatedly even with the four assistants to the Roman Catholic clinic, leaving the women "disturbed and depressed by their third and succeeding pregnancies. . . . Is it pro-life to ignore the increase in population levels to such an extent that the living systems in particular regions are becoming so impoverished that they will never recover?"

Any Christian moralist elimination of reproductive choices not only mitigates against responsible birth control policy for those plentiful peoples who are at once Roman Catholic and poor; more insidiously, it strategically distracts from the attempt to raise morality from the level of sex to the level of prophetic social concern. In this way, the conservative sexual agenda helps to delegitimate that theological movement within Roman Catholicism that has evinced perhaps the greatest vitality in twentieth-century popular Christianity, that of the Base Christian Communities in which Liberation Theology is grounded. Among Protestants, it serves analogously to deflate our most transformative theological movement, that of feminism.

We who would hold Christianity to its prophetic potential must ask: how did this reductive, biologistic, anthropocentric, and patriarchal notion of "life" — this "life" to which every sexual act is to open itself — come about? Though most Protestants don't believe it and many Catholics don't practice it, it still functions as a kind of ghostly norm, haunting Christian sensibility and thus reinforcing the conspiracy of silence. So we must come to terms with the origins of pronatalism[9] in the scriptures, as the texts that in some way serve as sounding board for all Christians.

THE EMERGENCE OF PRONATALISM

Hebrew scripture offers as the first *mitzvoh* — both a commandment and a blessing — the injunction of Genesis 1:28: "Be fruitful and multiply and fill the earth. . . ." John Cobb once wryly called this the only commandment humankind has obeyed. The fertility refrain is soon picked up in the covenant with Abraham, which offers multiplication as the primary blessing. The covenant is, first and foremost, a deal for the continuation of the male line. In other words, the originating mythic moments of the relationship of God to "His" people are sealed with the promise of "seed." The most formative biblical stories equate divine blessing with natal abundance. In this way, at least as the texts retroactively tell the tale, the people of Israel could envision a long future as the horizon of their hope.

Certainly the Hebrew tradition confirms the patriarchal family arrangements characteristic of its place and time. But pronatalism as reinforcement of the population explosion is a Christian rather than a Hebrew problem. During the formative periods of Jewish history, the population tended to need expanding rather than contracting. The problem for us lies not so much in Hebrew intentions as in Christian expropriations.

But then, here lies a paradox. Hebrew scriptures emphasize fertility, but that never resulted in Jewish overpopulation. The reverse is true of Christianity. The New Testament *nowhere* picks up the theme of procreative abundance. From the vantage point of its own scripture, one is hard pressed to explain how Christianity resulted in any preoccupation with the literal "transmission of life." The gospels and the epistles are almost alarmingly devoid of natal interest. Jesus uses fertility and birth images, such as that of cursing the fig tree (Lk. 3:8), strictly as metaphors for spiritual flourishing. One can explain this absence in terms of the apocalyptic expectations of the period. If the world was expected to conclude its business within the generation, there was hardly any point to further fertility. "Blessed are those who are not with child," so that you may flee more easily "on that day,"[10] suggest similarly non-, if not anti-natalist sentiments.

Hope shrank down very close to the wire. Distant futures were a thing of the past. But much current scholarship disputes the now standard claim that Jesus himself was an apocalyptic prophet, expecting a literal end; his parables suggest a more subtle eschatology, an evocation of the "kingdom of God," or realm of sacred relations, already taking place within the human community (cf. Crossan). For Jesus, the apocalyptic sense of emergency may have been more a wakeup call to a new way of life. However literal were Jesus' own expectations of the end, he consistently withdraws energy from the project of literal procreation. Though the synoptic gospels paint a consistent picture of his unusual respect for children as models of that very realm, the figure of Jesus displays either indifference or contempt for the (patriarchal) family (cf. Lk. 14:26, etc.). While the Jesus constructed especially by Luke shows also a striking awareness of the personhood of women, he displays no interest whatsoever in women's "vocation" to motherhood.[11]

Indeed, early Christianity does not fail to note the shift and must struggle with this apparent contradiction between its own "old" and "new" testaments. Jerome regarded the commandment to multiply as valid only within the "old law": "What has that to do with us upon whom the ends of the ages are come?" The early tendencies toward celibacy still reflect the apocalyptic sense of crisis: the world is in a state of emergency, this is no time for business as usual. Having sex before secure birth control was more or less synonymous with having children, and neither Jesus nor his most committed male and female followers considered procreation a priority. Thus the roots of asceticism do not lie in the programs of self-control and mastery of lust; especially in their New Testament forms, they evince none of the moralizing distaste for the body's desires which would dominate later discourse.

Within four centuries, Christianity settled into institutional longevity. Because the "end of the world" did not come, the church contented itself to rule the world in the meantime. Business as usual was encouraged again. A strange power configuration emerged with the Constantinian collaboration: an elite of celibate males extracted from the multiplying masses reinforce the structure of the patriarchal family order, as the very building block of the state.[cf Augustine] Within these families, "marital chastity" was recommended then, as now, as the only moral alternative to reproductive intention. We witness then in orthodox Christianity the return to the *pater familias pattern of Hebrew scriptures* — the sociofamilial structure of patriarchy — *without* the healthier Hebrew earthiness. Rather, patriarchy is now accompanied by a new sexual guilt complex, which, as Foucault has analyzed, finally led not merely to repression but also to obsession: the post-tridentine Catholic as well as the Freudian forms of confessional constitute a continuous modern tradition of maximizing fertility, minimizing pleasure.

In this venue, the classical Christian heritage seems to have left us with the worst of both worlds. That is, the "old testament" patriarchal family, centered around procreative blessing, synthesized itself strangely with the "new testament" asceticism in its hellenized, hierarchical form. The Christian canonical doubling of the "testaments" — in Latin from the same root as "testes" — served in the fourth century to reinforce sexist pronatalist pieties with imperial power. The fertility and the servility of Christian women was no doubt useful for expansion of the territories of Christendom. Here lies the early history of today's duplicitous Christian testament of over-population and sexual denial.

A WAY FORWARD?

What is there, then, for Christianity to recycle in this complex history? Quite a bit, I would maintain, if only for the purposes of taking responsibility for the toxic effects of our own pollution through power. But even more, there remain the traditions that in this period are proving to be high-energy resources for "justice, peace and the integrity of creation."

First of all the Hebrew prophetic priority of justice must structure our discussion of population control: and specifically, the classical prophets addressed resource consumption from the vantage point of the poor. "If you pour yourself out for the hungry and satisfy the desire of the afflicted, then shall your light rise in the darkness. . . ." (Isaiah 58:10). These are persistent themes: the people cannot long flourish if resources are unjustly distributed. Furthermore, why not affirm the Hebrew sense of every child as a gift of God — once it is a child and not a fetus, a person and not just a potential person, that is? Hebrew scriptures never regard the fetus as equivalent to a human life.[12] Rather than continuing an outdated natalism aimed at beefing up the size of the "chosen people," may we not greet children as chosen persons? But then let us indeed choose them now and not receive them merely as a vaguely supernaturalized biological fate. This does not suggest some arrogation of divine prerogative to ourselves via the technology of birth control. Within the bio-social reality in which the justice possible in the face of diminishing resources demands a sustainable level of population, we do need a new spirituality of chosenness: of choosing persons and therefore not giving birth to more than we, as a world, as particular communities, and as individual families, are capable of both nourishing and cherishing. The desperate surplus populations of the two-thirds world, largely generated by the structural poverty produced by late capitalism, make it virtually impossible to cherish every child as blessing. The one-third world cannot legislate the population policies for the two-thirds world, however. A spirituality of chosen persons affirms that whichever children are already born, whether by choice or by economic and social necessity, deserve to be chosen, to be cherished as unique and precious beings. And, indeed, so many are born and will continue to be born, that the choice to have no children, if taken in the context of commitment to work for justice for all the children, may appear as precisely the way to affirm life and choose children! But this choice of minimal fertility, as we will see, may be more appropriate for one-third world parents who could ostensibly support more children, than for their poor-world counterparts.

So a revised Hebrew prophetic population policy, for Christians at least, would affirm every choice not to multiply the *quantity* of life, if it enhances the *quality* of life — and that is intended precisely not in the yuppie terms of selfish accumulation, in which adults want to guard their affluence and leisure for their own enjoyment; such choices constitute the very heart of the quantifiable lifestyle, the consumer inhumanity, which demands the surplus poverty-populations elsewhere. Quality of life in the Hebrew vision is about a shared abundance, a *shalom* — a metaphor of wholeness at once physical and material, just and loving — which unravels the power elites for the sake of the possible well-being of all, including "the nations." Not an otherworldly ascetic viewpoint, but one of all workers enjoying the fruits — quite literally, in Isaiah, the grapes — of their own labor, of all living long and celebrating life together. The "life" of our scriptures' God of Life is not comprised of a random quantitative increase in birth, but of the quality of loved life of persons within communities.

And what of Christian sources, steeped as they are in apocalyptic asceticism; can we recycle them as resources for the struggle for *shalom,* for the "realm of God"? Let me make a suggestion that may sound alien and even self-contradictory: let us consider a revised form of that early apocalyptic asceticism. Why not acknowledge the affinity between the first century C.E. and our own time, since an apocalyptic sense of emergency accurately characterizes both? (Cf. my forthcoming *Apocalypse Now and Then: A Feminist Approach to the End of the World,* Beacon Press.) In the former, faith was required; in the latter (or Latter Day!), only newspaper literacy. Population only names one of at least four horsemen of doom — the others might be named Economics, Militarism, and Environment. But they gallop together, this quartet, inextricable in their cumulative momentum of horror. Even without any literalist expectation of a particular and predictable termination — which Jesus seems not to have shared then with such followers as John of Patmos — it is hard to miss the contemporary global threat of doom. If many of us came of age under the sign of the nuclear Armageddon, it is at this moment preeminently an eco-apocalypse we fear. Salvation may lie in facing the apocalyptic threat, in letting it exhort us to "wake up," to raise consciousness, to "prepare," to rub away the numbness brought on either by too much pain or too much comfort. But the point is not to succumb to panic and its dualistic, demonizing ways, in which some others — as perhaps the "others" construed as overpopulating "our" planet — get blamed. Such spiritual awakening may be said to take the form of a "counterapocalypse" not unlike Jesus' own commonwealth of God. Its sense of urgency does not plan on ultimate doom but rather begins already in the present "communities of resistance and solidarity"[13] to experience the divine realm, i.e., that which for us may better translate as fullness of life, or as meaningful, sustainable, and lively livelihood.

As to the topic at hand, this means that, like the first century, the beginning of the next millennium is not a time in which procreation can be an overriding priority. Blessing for "the people" — now as in the experience of the primitive Christian community — will not come from enhanced fertility. The new Christian asceticism, like the original, does not concern sex per se but its fruits. The new asceticism will focus on abstinence from inappropriate childbearing rather than from sex. If sex, apart from its procreative uses, is safe, mutually voluntary, and linked to a communally responsible, egalitarian ethos, it simply does not deserve much further discipline by Christian social ethicists. This is by no means simply to reverse traditional dogma and to decry the choice to parent as immoral: on the contrary, it is only to discourage any parenting which is not based upon responsible choices, made within the framework of not just private but familial, communal, and global responsibility. And again, this is *not* to say that only those with adequate resources should parent; it might mean that they also choose to offer those surplus resources of energy, time, and wealth to the larger communal struggle. For at the heart of a new eco-asceticism lies not self-denial per se, but a lively choice to awaken desire to the needs of the larger earth-community, that is, to know oneself as a creature inextricably created in interdependency with all the other denizens of creation.

But this discussion needs to frame itself more specifically in terms of the larger eco-political context. In other words, the issue of the disproportionate resource consumption by poor and rich peoples — which any prophetic spirituality will address — must shape the terms of this proposed asceticism. The following formula seems revealing: *population x consumption x technology = environmental impact.*[14] In other words, given that the average U.S. citizen uses at least ten times the technology and ten times the resources of a poor "third world" dweller, each first world child will have at least twenty times the environmental impact of a poor world child. The discrepancy jumps to thirty times if the first world child is wealthy. (These statistics may be themselves already dated and vastly underestimated: one sometimes now hears the figure of a first world child using 80 times the resources of a poor child from the South.) If one calculates waste as well, the difference increases tenfold again. In other words, the child who will have the most is the one the world can least afford.

This is not to underestimate the impact of the population of poor nations upon their own environment. But there is simply no way for affluent denizens of the North, whose lifestyle preys upon just those beleaguered resources and populations of the South, to make any credible case for world-population control, in isolation from the larger context of our own resource use and environmental impact. This discrepancy between the theory and practice of population pundits makes one wonder if the conspiracy of progressive silences on population may not represent the more ethical posture. Indeed, only as we in the North begin in greater numbers to practice our own forms of eco-asceticism, thus reducing our disproportionate dependency upon resources and technology — and continuing to reduce our own populations to make space for the needs of the poor forced by Northern policies to migrate Northward — may we engage the population issue in good faith.

Silent deferral of the issue, however tempting, remains nonetheless an irresponsible luxury. Irrevocable damage to endless local ecologies is going on, now, as we threaten to surpass the carrying capacity of the earth. A counter-apocalyptic sense of urgency, without the apocalyptic self-righteousness and doomsday determinism characteristic of much population control rhetoric, is only appropriate. Hence the call to a reconsideration of Christian priorities, which *ipso facto* involves a global clientele, already commits us to a divestment of procreative piety. Except for any people who are the victims of attempted genocide, this means that ecumenical Christianity, where it has a voice, will actively advocate non-procreative options for fulfillment, precisely in order to realize the blessing of every child as chosen and as gift.

The eco-asceticism I am advocating will thus remain deeply Hebrew in its roots: it will not feel like the sort of virtue that comes from negation of pleasure. Rather, it will seek to maximize joy, including erotic joy, by heightening the awareness of our interdependence with each other and with all creatures. Thus I am advocating not a new ascetic of self-denial, even for the first world; such an appeal only works for those already denying. Beyond rhetorical pragmatics, it seems to me that the prophetic vision of *shalom* is sensuous in its relation to the world, and rarely prone to obsessions about private morality. A healthy sense of limits, sexual, economic, and procreative, grows from a rooted and nourishing sense of interrelatedness. What we need is a sensuous asceticism, enhancing the inexpensive joys of our senses — at the rhythm of day and night, the rising of sun and stars, the parade of seasons, the delight of fresh water, of wholesome food, the zest which arises from having enough, and in the Northern case, of not having too much. All of this works to support the reduction of one-third world consumption levels, with all of its joyless addictions to overindulgence and its corollary self-loathing. At the same time, the delights and demands of participation in larger communities, in voluntary groups, affinity networks, and alternative families, at once satisfy many needs traditionally met by reproduction within the nuclear family unit, and lend the framework in which abstinence from childbearing receives positive motivation. But such choices by many then also lend a communal support network for the care of children, those chosen responsibly as well as those deprived, abandoned, or abused.

As one can witness traces of this possibility all around, in North and South, let me further concretize what I mean by this "ascetic" choice. As to sexuality: moral issues are thus shifted from traditional genital piety to the network of relationships. This morality addresses not just the matter of population impact, but, first of all, the quality of relationship itself. Hence the community itself becomes a source of encouragement of egalitarian, loving bonds between sexual partners, and a source of shame for those who dominate and violate. As stated at the outset, the deconstruction of patriarchal power structures within the family is the necessary prerequisite for reproductive responsibility. Furthermore, let us not denigrate the ancient option of celibacy for anyone, ordained or not. Probably everyone should practice it sometime, to enhance their freedom and self-understanding. The celibate option in various situations, at different ages, must surely also be supported as not only helpful for population control but as potentially releasing generous energies into the larger network of relations.

Such counter-apocalyptic community building will derive inspiration from more ecocentric tribal cultures, as well as from Hebrew hopes for "jubilee" for all creation. It is also, for Christians, thoroughly Christian. The nodal point of connection, the "inter" of interdependence, is what Christians call Holy Spirit. The flesh of the interdependence is what Christians call "the Body of Christ," of which all are "members one of another" (1 Corinthians 12). This becomes liturgically embodied ("leitourgos" means "the work of the people") in some Christian ecclesial groupings, such as the Base Christian Communities of Latin America and the (still few and far between) liberation churches of the North — those marked by their commitment to social justice and their opening up of welcoming into their midst of singles, gays, lesbians, and other non-procreative units, as well as traditional and non-traditional families. The "Kingdom of God" does not wait for the space to be apocalyptically cleared by some forthcoming set of plagues, starvations, wars, and poisons. Its "God" symbolizes the creative force flowing through that interdependence, at least when its delicate potentials are attended to faithfully.

The ecumenical Christianity I advocate knows itself part of a larger network, vastly exceeding Christendom, organized religion, and finally humanity itself. It knows itself a part of a *green ecumenacy,* in which the ecological and economic resonances of the "ecumene," itself meaning originally "stewardship," become discernible. Thus, action for social *shalom* will refuse the anthropocentrism of the prophetic traditions, and, indeed, of all traditional ecumenism between "the great world religions" (all of whom are not only anthropocentric but androcentric). I suspect that the sensibilities of indigenous peoples to the inextricability of specific environments and specific communities must lead the way. This requires not a romanticism of "noble savages" but an ecumenism of the mind, and hence a pluralistic epistemology, a way of looking at problems such as population and resource consumption as expressions of our interdependence and thus as themselves interdependent and plurally conceived problems. Christians will have to work to overcome the monotheism of our minds, the tendency to look for single issues and single solutions, a habit which, because of the perpetual self-contradictions into which it leads, assures that we rarely and too late get to the action phase of *shalom.*

The multiplication we need today is not that of seed but of strategies, not of people but of perspectives; the blessing we need not that of a depleting growth but of a just sustainability; the asceticism we need not of self-denial but of communal flourishing; the ecumenism we need not of a unity of beliefs but of common actions.

NOTES

1. The theme of the ongoing World Council of Churches program.

2. Margaret Catley-Carlson. *Explosions, Eclipses and Escapes: Charting a Course on Global Population Issues,* The 1993 Paul Hoffman Lecture (7 June 1993), UN Development Program, New York.

3. Hence the title of John Cobb's warning to Christians, *Is It Too Late?* (Beverley Hills: Bruce, 1972).

4. Roger L. Shinn, *Forced Options: Social Decisions for the Twenty-First Century* (Cleveland: Pilgrim Press, 1991), pp. 85–105, addresses this tension head-on, and constitutes a significant exception therefore among mainstream Christian ethicists.

5. Beverly Harrison, *Our Right to Choose* (Boston: Beacon, 1983), does, however, perform an analysis of Christian pro-natalist tradition, which is just as relevant to the population as to the narrower abortion issue on which this book rightfully focuses.

6. Rosemary Ruether constitutes the exception to all of the above categories. Cf. especially *God and Gaia* (San Francisco: Harper, 1992).

7. Sean McDonagh, *The Greening of the Church* (New York: Orbis, 1990).

8. Pronatalism, meaning "pro-birth," is a polemical but useful term designating the belief that sexuality is to function primarily for purposes of reproduction, and that, therefore, artificial birth control impedes the divine will playing itself out in nature.

9. Matthew 24, Mark 13, Luke 21.

10. See Elizabeth Schussler Fiorenza, *In Memory of Her: A Feminist Theological Reconstruction of Christian Origins* (New York: Crossroad, 1984).

11. Michel Foucault, *History of Sexuality* (New York: Random House, 1980).

12. Cf. Ex. 21:22, where when a miscarriage is caused, the loss is treated as property damage (i.e., the injury to the woman is punished by payment of a fine to the husband) and not even as loss of a life.

13. Cf. Sharon Welch, *Communities of Resistance and Solidarity* (New York: Orbis, 1985).

14. Cf. Ehrlich and Holdren 73 *Human Ecology;* also in Rosemary Radford Ruether, *God and Gaia* (San Francisco: Harper, 1992).

7

Islam, Population, and the Environment: A Textual and Juristic View

NAWAL H. AMMAR

There are one billion or so Muslims who live in more than eighty-three countries. These Muslims live in all kinds of geographic locations. This religious community speaks numerous languages/dialects in their daily life, including Arabic, English, French, Hausa, Persian, Turkish, and Urdu. Muslims live in oil-rich countries such as the United Arab Emirates and Libya, while others live in poorer countries such as Somalia and Bangladesh. From amidst this plurality and diversity of Muslims, I have been asked to present *an* Islamic response to the environmental crisis that is threatening our humanity. The dilemma of providing *an* Islamic response brings forth with it questions such as: "Does my view represent the mainstream thinking in Islam?" or "Should I represent an interpretation of the texts?" Once these questions have been answered, other questions arise, such as: "How might this particular Islamic view become part of the mainstream?" or, if my interpretation is already in the mainstream, then: "How can we implement it?" Although these are very important questions, the problem with them is that the Islamic world is a diverse world, and within this diversity there are many mainstreams and many marginals. It is only justifiable to discuss the Islamic world as a homogeneous community insofar as Muslims adhere to a defined textual literature. Beyond such a unity, a discussion of an Islamic mainstream, or one Islamic view, is methodologically unsound and politically dangerous (Ammar 1993, 16). Any monolithic examination of the Islamic communities as only Islamic sounds like discussing American, Canadian, English, French, Russian, and Zambian reactions to the environmental crisis under the banner of Christianity.

Hence, in this chapter, I will address the laws and rules covered in the Islamic texts, and present commentaries on their interpretation as they pertain to the environmental crisis of today. The ground rule of evaluating the discussion that follows is, then, not whether the ideas presented fit within the mainstream, but whether the interpretations are close to the holy texts.

But even in the interpretations of the texts, it is not possible to attempt a comprehensive/mainstream description of the Muslim environmental ethical tradition, for at least two reasons. The first lies in the changing historical condition of Muslim communities. Although it is believed that the *Qur'an* represents the unchanged words of God, the Muslim communities' conscience is a changing one.

Hodgoson, in a three-volume history of the Islamic peoples, notes that:

> the Muslim conscience expresses itself differently in different phases of history as Muslims venture to respond to their understanding of God's purpose for humanity. The conscience necessarily operates within the limits and possibilities imposed by the specific situation. (quoted in McDonough 1984)

In fact, the Muslim world today is mostly not governed solely by Islamic principles. Many of the Islamic values and precepts have been influenced by Western culture, capitalist and communist politics, and industrial technology. Despite this situation, however, Islam is still a strong religious and spiritual force, but its contextual setting is different from that of six hundred years ago.

The second reason that restricts me from providing a comprehensive description of Islamic environmental ethics pertains to the theological nature of Islam. Although a Muslim is a person who has responded to the Qur'anic call to "declare that there is no god but Allah and Muhammad is his Prophet," at any point of history each individual Muslim wishing to respond appropriately to his or her awareness of God's guidance may do so. But it is not until the end (Judgment Day) that any evaluation of the appropriateness of the response/interpretation may be judged.

Hence, due to this uncertainty one cannot speak of a comprehensive or a final ethical interpretation.

THE ISLAMIC ETHICAL PARADIGM

Sources of Islam

The Islamic paradigm as it relates to the sacred and profane practices is based on ontological rather than epistimological principles. In essence, Islamic behavior and moral codes are patterned by the existence of the revelation that was later compiled in the form of the Book, the Holy *Qur'an*. The source of knowledge in the Holy *Qur'an* is a given, and is not subject to empirical or other testing procedures. The Muslims believe that the Holy *Qur'an* is the uncreated words of God. These words were revealed to the Prophet Muhammad in 610 A.D. and during a period of twenty-three years, with some chapters revealed entirely at one time, while others extended over many years. The revelations are divided into Meccan and Medina because of the place they were revealed. The Meccan revelations, generally, address more theological/religious injunctions, while the Medina revelations address social, political, economic, and environmental practices. Although the Prophet Muhammad organized the Book, the Holy *Qur'an* was not committed to writing until thirty years after his death.

Today, the *Qur'an* is divided into 114 structures, each of which is called *Surah*, section. The Surahs are of varying lengths; each is divided further into smaller verses called *Ayah*. The fact that the *Qur'an* represents the words of God forbids Muslims from varying its organization and using the *Qur'an* except in its Arabic origin. The revelation in Islam separated the "what" from the "how" (al-Faruqi and al-Faruqi 1986, 108). The what was God's injunctions, and the how was the domain of humans. The what is ultimate and absolute, while the human is changing and developing.

The *Qur'an* is the highest religious and most absolute source in Islam. There are, however, three other religious sources that guide the religion. These are the Prophet's Sayings, *Hadiths*, the Prophet's Actions, *Sunnah*, and the jurists decisions, *Sharia'h*.

Muslims are required to apply both the *Hadiths* and *Sunnah* in their personal and social life. The *Hadiths* began to be committed to writing fifty years after the death of the Prophet Muhammad. A large number of *Hadiths* were fabricated through the years. The struggle for succession provided the largest opportunity for such fabrication. As a result, a science of *Hadith (I'lm al-Hadith)* developed to distinguish between sound and false *Hadiths*. The science is based on verifying the historical retrieval of the narration, *Isnad*, and the content of the *Hadith*, *Matin*. Six anthologies were made between 815 and 870 A.D. Two of these collections, by Bukhari and Muslim, are actually known as the "two sheiks." They examined 600,000 *Hadiths* and found that 7225 were sound.

The Prophet's Actions, *Sunnah*, are not written, but are rather a tradition that is orally transmitted.

The *Sharia'h* is the form of law that covers the ever changing conditions and situations of human life. The science of *Usul of Fiqh* (the origins of thought) was developed in the eighth century to distinguish between the changeless and changing, and to develop a methodology out of the relevant principles of the

Qur'an, Hadith, and *Sunnah.* The changeless were those that were clear in their prescriptive texts. Such prescriptions were open to interpretation only in as far as their linguistic hermeneutics, and the mere clarification of their lexicographic meanings (al-Faruqi and al-Faruqi 1986, 267). Otherwise, these were universal prescriptions that eternally bind the Muslims.

The new laws *(Sharia'h),* that develop in the face of a changing society, were derived from the spirit of the prescriptive revelation on the basis of *Ijma'* and *Qiyas. Ijma'* consists of the agreement of all jurists in any given period on a matter of law. *Qiyas* consists of subsuming a new matter under an established law because of the equivalence of the causes underlying them. To the two above principles, seven others were added to guarantee the dynamism of the law with guarantees for the preeminence of these principles and values.[1]

The *Qur'an,* the *Hadith, Sunnah,* and the *Sharia'h* determine the parameters of knowledge and information in Islam. Hence, all ethical codes in Islam are based on foundations that are formulated and passed on by God directly or by analogy.

The Meaning of Ethics In Islam

The branch of philosophy that is concerned with human character and rules of behavior for a Muslim is not separate from the *Qur'an.* The *Qur'an* sets forth all that a Muslim needs to discern as ethical or unethical. Ethics according to the religious interpretations is a state of respect, *hay'a.* Respect is an outcome of socialization, both in the formal and informal sense. In Arabic those with *hay'a* have good ethical values and those without *hay'a* have no ethics (and not simply bad ethics). Islam strongly recommends that people be with *hay'a.* The road to *hay'a* is to practice good and prohibit evil. The Arabic word *al-m'aruf* (practice good deeds) has been mentioned in the *Qur'an* thirty-nine times (Izzi Dien 1992, 31). The Islamic ethical prescription does not limit its parameters with the expectation of good practice only. The Qur'anic injunction emphasizes the prohibition of evil as well (3:104) and considers ethical accounting, *hisba,* as a product of both the practice of good and the prevention of evil deeds (Izzi Dien 1992, 25–27).[2] One of the Prophet's *Hadiths* emphasizes this. He said: "Anyone who witnesses evil should remonstrate upon it by his hand, his mouth or his heart, the last is the weakest of faith" (Imam Ahmad, sahih).

Jurists have emphasized that Islamic ethical values prioritize the avoidance of evil over achieving good deeds. According to Islamic jurists, ethical values are either absolute, *qati',* or analogous, *Ijtihadi.* The absolute ethical values are guided by clear Qur'anic injunctions and require no human opinion, *ra'y.* The ethical values based on analogy are guidelines not clearly mentioned in the *Qur'an,* but jurists find them fulfilling the spirit of the *Qur'an.*

Ethical guidelines in Islam can be summed up by the answer that the Prophet's wife, A'isha, gave to the question: "What about Muhammad's ethical guidelines?" She replied: "His ethics are the whole *Qur'an*."

ISLAMIC VIEWS ABOUT THE ENVIRONMENTAL CRISIS AND POPULATION CONTROL

Discussing fertility control as a method of ameliorating the pressure on the earth's limited resources will lead many Muslims to disengage from this important discourse.

Fertility control *(Tahdid al Nasl)* is forbidden by the *Qur'an*. Human reproduction is viewed as being a sign of God's power and will. As a result, humans should not interfere in the natural cycle of fertility. One of the verses of the *Qur'an* states: "And we cause who we will to rest in the Wombs" (22:5).

The *Qur'an* does not only forbid the control of fertility, but encourages reproduction of children. The *Qur'an* says: "Money and Children are the decoration of life." The same theme about fertility can be found in the Prophet's sayings; he said: "An ugly woman who is fertile is a better wife than a beauty who is barren."

To control your fertility due to financial or material constraints is forbidden behavior in Islam. The *Qur'an* clearly states *"no soul shall have a burden laid on it greater than it can bear"* (2:233 *my emphasis*). The *Qur'an* also says: "Kill not your children for fear of want. . . . We will provide sustenance for them as well as for you. . . . Verily the Killing of them is a great sin" (17:31).

Although Islamic texts permit fertility control as a form of organizing one's family *(Tanzim* versus *Tahdid al-Nasl)*, the conditions are restrictive. Women can organize their fertility only when their health is at risk. They can use any method of fertility control that is not permanent or that does not interfere with the natural cycle of their hormones.

Abortion is encouraged as a means of fertility control, again if the mother's health is at risk. The embryo/fetus should be aborted prior to the 120th day of pregnancy, or else the family pays a punitive damage tax *(Diyah).*[3]

The discussion in Islam about fertility control is one about exceptional cases and temporary procedures. Otherwise, the texts encourage the expansion of the Muslim population. The Prophet, for example, said: "Consummate marriages, reproduce, for I will take pride [in your numbers] on Judgment Day."

As a result of the above view about fertility control in Islam, there is a need to initiate the cross-cultural, interfaith, cross-discipline discussion about the environment first with what is relevant in the perspective. Such an initial discussion must be a sensitive, inclusive discourse, which would allow one billion

Muslims to become engaged in the process of saving our environment. If we do not attempt to be inclusive and sensitive in the cross-cultural, interfaith discourse, our collaborative achievements will be reduced, and, in the case of our environmental crisis, such a reduction will be catastrophic. As a result, the remainder of this chapter will discuss the relevant Islamic textual prescriptions as they relate to preserving nature, the earth, and precious resources.

NATURE IN THE ISLAMIC TEXTS

Guidelines concerning nature and its resources are a very crucial part of the Islamic message. In the *Qur'an*, the protection of nature is based on the principle that God created the various components of the universe, and that all these components are ordered, and have purpose and function. The Qur'anic verse says: "Verily, all things have we created with measure" (54:49), and says: "Every thing to Him is measured" (13:8). To respect God means that you should respect His creation.

In a Sufi interpretation, God himself is seen as the ultimate environment (Nasr 1992, 89).[4] The verse in the *Qur'an* that says: "But to God belong all things in the heavens and on the earth, and He it is who encompasseth [Muhit] all things" (4:126). It is assumed that humans are immersed in a Divine environment, but are only unaware of the reality due to their own forgetfulness and negligence (Nasr 1992, 89). The *Qur'anic* injunction, "withersoever you turn there is the Face of God" (11:115), is often used to convey this message.

The divine environment in the Islamic paradigm is a manifestation of God's Almighty power (20:5). The *Qur'an* declares that God "created the heavens and the earth, and all that is between them in six days" (32:4). The Islamic notion of creation differs from the Judeo-Christian one in that God did not rest. "We created the heaven and the earth and all between them in six days nor did any sense of weariness touch us" (50:38).[5] This measured, divine universe was created by God not as a game. It was "coordinated and well adjusted and there is no disorder, discord, or incongruity" (67:3–4) for all to enjoy.

The *Qur'an* is not an anthropomorphic revelation. Some verses in the *Qur'an* address natural forms as well as human beings (1992:88). The revelation does not draw a demarcation between humans and nature. The unity, *tawheed*, between humans and nature is best explained in the common origin of life. The *Qur'anic* verse declares that "God created every animal out of water: of them there are some that creep on their bellies, others that walk on two legs and others on four" (24:25).

The unity between humans and nature is also exemplified in the *Qur'an* in terms of social structure. All that God created, he created as communities. The *Qur'an* says: "There is not an animal in the earth nor a flying creature on two wings but they are nations unto you. We have neglected nothing in the Book [of our decrees]. Then unto their lord they will be gathered" (6:38).

The unity between all the creatures of nature is also exemplified in the obedience of God. "Do you not see that all things bow down to Allah, all things in the heavens, and in the earth, the sun, the moon, the stars, the hills, the animals, and a great number of human kind?" (22:18).

Certain *Hadiths* also attest to the unity between humans and nature. It is reported that the Prophet said about the mountain Uhud, close to Mecca: "It is a mountain that loves us and we love it," and he also spoke to this mountain after an earthquake saying: "Be calm, Uhud." The Prophet is quoted to have said: "Some trees are as blessed as the Muslim, especially Palm." (quoted in Izzi Dien 1992, 29 as Bukhari, sahih).

All creatures are alike and equal in having been created from a common origin. Human beings, however, are the only creatures with special qualities:

> All creatures are alike . . . plants are superior to minerals in being able to absorb nourishment, to grow and feed, animals in addition to these powers have one or more of the five senses, and man, while of the animal kingdom in other respects and possessing all senses, also speaks and reasons. (Raisail II 153, quoted in M Rafiq and Mohd Ajmal 1989, 123)

Islam considers humans because of their special qualities as God's vice-regent *(al-Khalifah)* on earth. The Qur'anic injunction states that "I am setting on the earth a vice-regent" (2:30). The role of *Khalifah* is more like a manager's than a proprietor's, more like a beneficiary's than a disposer's (Bakader et al. 1983, 13). These managers, due to their special qualities of speech and reason, are capable of knowledge and distinction between good and evil. As a result, this well measured, ordered, and beautiful universe is given to humans as a trust — *ammanah* — which they accepted when they bore witness to God's lordship in the pre-eternal covenant — *al-Mithaq* — to which the *Qur'an* in the famous verse says: "Am I not your lord? They [That is the members of humanity] uttered yea we bear witness" (7:172). In another verse, the *Qur'an* explains further: "God offered his trust to heaven and earth and mountain, but they shied away in fear and rejected it, Humans only carried it" (33:72).

This covenant between God and humans is based on humans being God's servants, *Ibad Allah*, who obey him and respect his creation. In return, God makes nature and the earth subservient to them (22:65 and 67:15). All humans are thus entitled to the use of the earth equally without discrimination, abuse, corruption, or coercion. But this covenant leaves an element of free will as to how the humans will honor their covenant with God. The *Qur'an* relates the incident in which, when God declared that humans will be his vice-regent, the angels asked "Wilt thou place therein one who will do harm therein and will shed blood?" The *Qur'an* answers that humans can distinguish between good and evil (91:7–8), are capable of judging what is right and what is wrong (90:8–10), and that it is up to humans to control harm and bloodshed (79:40).

Hence, from the above discussion, one can argue that there is a basis for environmental ethics in Islam. Such ethics are based on the demand to treat nature with respect *(hay'a)*. It demands this respect because nature is the creation of God. In itself it is neither good or bad; its goodness is derived from its divine creation. For the Muslim, nature is not his/her possession, it is a trust that he/she should utilize and enjoy according to certain methods (al-Faruqi and al-Faruqi 1986, 322). The Prophet said: "on Doomsday, if anyone has a palm shoot in hand, he should plant it" (Bukhari, sahih).

Islamic ethical guidelines are not always clear, but with regard to some aspects of nature they are very precise. The following section describes some of the clear environmental ethical guidelines in Islam that most Islamic jurists agree on, especially as they pertain to natural resources.[6]

CLEAR GUIDELINES OF ENVIRONMENTAL ETHICS IN ISLAM

The Use of Natural Resources

It is clear from the above discussion that Islam has indigenous prescriptive guidelines about dealing with nature. These guidelines emphasize respect *(hay'a)* for nature. Such respect has no "ontological relationship between the creator and the creature" (al-Faruqi and al-Faruqi 1986, 323). But rather, the relationship is that of one creature, humans, acting as vice-regent. Although one can argue that because the vice-regent is human, the Islamic view is anthropomorphic, the *Qur'an* emphasizes that God tried to give this responsibility to other creatures, but they shied away. This entrusting of the earth to humans includes demands for respect as well as enjoyment and the utilization of its natural resources: "Eat of that which Allah has provided for you, and follow not in the footsteps of Satan" (6:143).

The *Qur'an* mentions natural resources on numerous occasions. Wind, animals, trees, the earth, the stars, mountains, birds, insects, clouds, seas, rivers, fruits, and minerals are among the many resources mentioned. Water, however, is the most important resource. The *Qur'an* states "Do not the unbelievers see that the heavens and the Earth were joined together (as one unit of creation, before we clove asunder? We made from water every living thing" (21:30).

Toward this trust of natural resources, there are five essential rules that Muslims need to follow to fulfill their moral obligation to God. The first includes:

The use of nature and its resources in a balanced, not excessive, manner. The *Qur'an* mentions very clearly its prescription of using nature in a balanced manner; it says: "Eat and drink, but waste not by indulging in excess, surely, God does not approve" (7:31).

Such a clear Qur'anic injunction is also supported by a variety of *Hadiths* by the Prophet. He set the standard of usage, also very clearly, by saying: The merit of utilization lies in the benefit it yields, in proportion to its harm.

The second rule is: *Treat nature and its resources with kindness.* Kindness to nature is a celebration of God's creation, The *Qur'an* states that Allah has prescribed kindness *(ihsan)* for everything, while the Prophet, on kindness to nature, related the following story:

> An Ant once stung one of the Prophets, who then proceeded to burn
> an entire colony of Ants. God in rebuke told him: thou has destroyed
> a whole nation that celebrates God's praise because an ant stung you.
> (Bukhari, sahih)

Islam, also in the spirit of kindness *(ihsan)*, discourages the killing of animals for mere sport. The Prophet said: "A sparrow killed just for entertainment would on the day of judgment complain to [God] against the person who did so just for fun," and: "Whosoever is kind to the creatures of God is kind to himself" (quoted Bakader 1983).

Muslim leaders and thinkers have historically been kind to nature and its resources. In his letter of recommendation, the first Muslim Caliph ordered his troops: "Do not cut down trees, do not abuse a river, do not harm animals, and be always kind and human to God's creation, even to your enemies."

The Prophet's cousin and the fourth Caliph, Ali Ibn Abi Talib, told a man who had dug canals and reclaimed abandoned land: "Partake of it with joy, so long as you are a benefactor, not a corruptor, a cultivator not a destroyer" (quoted in Llewellyn 1992, 89).

Islamic scholars such as 'Izz ad-Din Ibn Abd as-Salam even formulated an animal-rights statement in the thirteenth century, based on the stories and sayings of the Prophet.

The third rule concerning the use of nature and its resources is: *Do not Damage, abuse, or distort nature in any way.* The *Qur'an* is very clear on the issue of not damaging nature. It states: "Do not mischief on the earth after it hath been set in order." The word mischief in Arabic, *fasad,* means corruption, destruction, deterioration. There are ten things that the assumption of Abraham make forbidden: "They include taking part in hunting free wild animals which are edible; whether killing or injuring, and participating in any despoiling of trees or vegetation on the sacred territory, whether by cutting or plucking" (Iqbal 1977, 98).

The fourth rule in Islam regarding nature and its resources can be summarized as: *Share natural resources.* The *Qur'an* in relation to water use says: "And tell them the water is to be divided among them" (54:86). In Islam no one person owns nature. Humans are beneficiaries. But if, due to population pressure, some artificial boundary must be enforced, the sharing then must be regulated so as to ensure equal access and equal opportunity to all. All humans are entitled to the use of the Earth and its resources equally without discrimination, abuse, corruption, or coercion. The concept of sharing nature is also exemplified by the Prophet's saying: "People share three things: Water, pasture and fire" (Bukhari, sahih). A weaker *Hadith* emphasizes the sharing and caring among Muslims by having the Prophet note that "He who does not show concern for the interest and good of all Muslims is not a Muslim" (quoted in Bakader et al. 1983, 16).

The fifth important environmental rule is: *Conservation.* In the Islamic context, conservation includes preventing damage as well as expanding on the already existing marvels of nature. Allah has warned against the destruction of the Earth, and the *Qur'an* specifically says: "And of humankind there is he whose conservation on the present life will please you and he would call Allah to witness as to that which is in his heart; And when he rises to power his effort in the land would be to create disturbance therein and to destroy crops and life."

Conservation as part of preserving nature is part of the Islamic view on the use of nature and its resources. The Prophet Muhammad declared the trees around Mecca and Medina as protected by decrees such as: "I declare Medina to be sacrosanct throughout the area between its two mountain paths. . . . Leaves may not be eaten off them except for fodder. The game of Mecca is not to be molested nor its fresh herbage cut" (quoted in Masri 1992, 12, as *Mishkat al-Masabih).*

Based on such religious injunction, Islamic jurists in later years formulated various laws covering the conservation of forests, water bodies, and animals. One interesting juristic rule of conservation relates to land. According to Islamic *Sharia'h* there are seven types of land: Two of these types are the protected zones *(Haram)* and the reserves *(Hima)* established for public purpose and for preservation of natural habitat.

Regarding conservation and preservation, the Islamic paradigm includes an active element, in that there is an emphasis on the extension of God's creation. Such an extension is a good deed and is rewarded. As it directly relates to land, for example, the Prophet declared that "whoever revives dead land it shall be his" (Bukhari, sahih). The Prophet also declared that "whoever plants a tree and looks after it with care until it matures and becomes productive, will be rewarded in the hereafter" (Bukhari and Muslim). Also in relation to the extension of natural resources, the Prophet said: "If any one plants a tree and men, beasts, or birds eat from it, he should consider it as a charity on his part" (Bukhari, sahih).

Islamic religious injunctions, social history and scholarly work due to Qur'anic influence is full of examples and prescriptions of environmental awareness. The Medical Botanist, al-Razi (ninth century A.D.) used to collect flowers, leaves, and roots from nature and mix them to prepare medicines. Ibn Baytar of Malaga, the Arab/Muslim Botanist who lived in the thirteenth century A.D., mentioned more than 1,400 medicinal drugs derived from nature in his book: *al-Mughani fi al- Adwiyah.* Jabir Ibn Hyyan, the father of chemistry, was concerned with toxic effects on humans. He concluded in the ninth century A.D. that chemical laboratories should be located away from populated places. al-Jahiz, a famous Arab Muslim thinker, wrote as early as the eighth century the *Book of Animals.* He suggested in this book that environmental change eventually will alter the behavior and characteristics of animals. But the *Qur'an, Hadith, Sunnah,* and the old juristic rules do not address directly the modern issues that are arising with regard to the nature and its use. The results of modern development, including pollution, chemical wars, and technological hazards, have not yet been addressed systematically by Islamic nations and states, although the *Qur'an* views such actions as the abuse of God's creation. The following section discusses some of the efforts and guidelines that have been put forward by modern thinkers, jurists, religious men, and Muslim governments.

MODERN EFFORTS AND GUIDELINES
FOR ISLAMIC ENVIRONMENTAL ETHICS

Efforts among modern Muslim scholars to bring forward the issue of environmental depletion have gained momentum in the past decade. In 1983, a joint publication of the International Union for Conservation of Nature and Natural Resources (IUCN) and the Meteorology and Environmental Protection Administration (MEPA) of Saudi Arabia appeared in three languages, Arabic, English, and French. The work, entitled "Islamic Principles For the Conservation of the Natural Environment," recommends Islamic legal rules and procedures for the protection of the environment against modern challenges. The rules include stipulations as well as procedures for governments ruling over Muslim communities to follow.

Other efforts include the UNESCO meeting in 1991 in Cairo, Egypt, that revolved around environmental ethics. The conference produced many publications and policy papers. The paper on the Egyptian culture co-authored by Tawfik, Ebeid and Kamel recommends "Environmental Education" (EE) that is culturally relevant. They note that: "Although the ultimate goals of EE are the same everywhere, yet the objectives differ according to the particular conditions of the nations, the learners' capacities, and the characteristics of the target group" (Tawfik et al. 1991, 63).

Books written for Muslims in the various indigenous languages of the citizens are being produced. During the past year I have come across at least two major publications written in Arabic.[7]

Beyond the intellectual debates on environmental ethics, the issue remains a crisis that Muslim citizens suffer from silently. Governments of Muslim citizens have implemented very few guidelines to address the internal crisis. And Muslims know from the Qur'anic injunction that unless they actively participate in solving the internal problem it will not change. The *Qur'an* says: "Never will Allah change the condition of a people until they change themselves."[8]

CONCLUSION

To include Muslims in the global discussion about the environmental crisis, the dialogue needs to be culturally sensitive. This sensitivity requires that we look at what the Islamic texts have to offer with regard to the depletion of the environment, and not impose on the Muslims a discourse that is only suitable to American, Canadian, and European scientists and humanists. If we examine the Islamic texts, we will note that the Islamic religion declares that the environment/nature should be used in a manner that does not disturb its order, balance, and function. This declaration is a clear religious/moral value found in Qur'anic revelations and the other sources of Islam. All the sources of Islam point to the entrusting of nature to humans.

The Islamic view of utilizing nature is compatible with the idea of preservation. Islam makes the connection between the economic well being of the community (at the time of Qur'anic revelation in the seventh century, this was eating and drinking) and the conserving order of nature. The Qur'anic verse says: "Eat and drink but waste not by indulging in excess" (7:31).

Fundamentally, the Islamic view is based on the premise of discipline in the utilization of nature. Nature was created, according to Islam, and entrusted to humans as a test of their ability to use it in a moral way. Such a moral test requires humans to utilize nature in a utilitarian/functional way, but at the same time maintain their esthetic respect for it as the creation of God. Such a use model emphasizes moderation in, kindness to, and preservation of nature. The perplexing phenomenon to numerous thinkers is how a tradition that is being revived can forget such a clear prescriptive methodology of utilizing nature. The resurgence of Islamic ideals during the past two decades has emphasized issues of justice and democracy. The Islamic viewpoint is being put forward as an alternative to Western-industrial ideals. But if we as Muslims are going to advance

Islam as a serious alternative we need to advance it in its totality, and not use only austere and fragmented values from the tradition. It is thus essential to remember that a sound environmental policy in Islam is a very important component of the religion. Preserving nature is more of a central theme in the Islamic tradition than the notion of "*Jihad*" (holy war).

Hence, just as it is time for non-Muslims to become sensitive in their dialogue, it is time that we as Muslims reexamine our traditions carefully in light of their true character and peaceful direction. This chapter is one small effort in such a direction.

NOTES

1. The seven principles are:

(a) *Al-tamassuk bil asl*, the rule that originally and essentially all beneficial actions are legitimate, all harmful ones are illegitimate;

(b) *Istihab al-hal*, the rule that laws are permanently valid unless there is evidence challenging their beneficial nature;

(c) *Al-masalih al-mursulah*, the rule that a benefit is deemed legitimate if the shari-a'h is not known to have established or denied it;

(d) *Al-dhara'i*, the rule that the legitimacy of that which is instrumental is directly affected by the benefit or harm implicit in the final end to which it leads;

(e) *Al-istiqra al-naqis*, the rule that a universal law may be derived from a particular law through ascending generalization, if no exception is known to challenge the generalization;

(f) *Al-istuhsan*, the rule that a weaker qiyas may be preferred to a stronger one if it fulfills the spirit of the law better;

(g) *Al- u'ruf wal' adah*, the rule that custom and established practice may be legitimate sources of law. (al-Faruqi and al-Faruqi 1986, pp. 267–68)

2. The numbers in the quotation refer to the *Ayah* and *Surah* references in the *Qur'an*.

3. In Islam, the soul develops after the first 120 days of pregnancy; as a result, abortion is permitted only prior to soul development.

4. Sufism is Islamic Mysticism.

5. The Day does not mean human days. In another Qur'anic declaration the day was determined to be equivalent to 50,000 years: "the angels and the spirit ascend unto him in a Day the measure where is as fifty thousand years." (70:4)

6. Islam says very little in relation to population control as a means to protect nature. Actually, Islamic injunctions are very clear about multiplying as a means of fulfilling religious obligations. The words come as clear as having children, or to multiply.

7. These are:

Abu Majd, K. 1992. "The Cultural Dimensions of Human Rights in the Arab World." In *The Civil Society Journal*, a newsletter issued by the Ibn Khaldun Center for Developmental Studies, Cairo, Egypt. No. 6 (June 1992).

Hasab Alnabi, M. M. 1991 *The Holy Qur'an and Modern Science*. Cairo, Egypt: Alhaiah Almisriah lilkitab.

8. Indonesia (a Muslim country), during the first week of August 1993, announced that banks will loan money only to companies that have environmentally sound policies.

BIBLIOGRAPHY

Bakader, Abou Bakr Ahmed et al. 1983. Basic Paper on the Islamic Principles for the Conservation of the Natural Environment. Gland, Switzerland: IUCN and the Kingdom of Saudi Arabia.

Faruqi, Ismail, and Lois Lamya Al Faruqi 1988. *The Cultural Atlas of Islam*. New York: Macmillan Publishing Company.

Iqbal, S. M. 1977. *The Mission of Islam*. Bombay: Vikas.

Izzi Dien, Mawil 1992. "Islamic Ethics and the Environment." In *Islam and Ecology*. Edited by Khalid Fazlun And Joanne O'Brien. New York: Cassell Publishers Ltd.

Llewellyn, Othman 1992. "Desert Reclamation and Conservation in Islamic Law." In *Islam and Ecology*. *Op. cit.*

Masri, al-Hafiz 1992. "Islam and Ecology." In *Islam and Ecology*. *Op. cit.*

McDonough, Sheila 1984. *Muslim Ethics and Modernity, Comparative Ethics Series: Vol. 1*. Waterloo, Ontario: Wilfrid Laurier University Press.

Naseef, Abdullah Omar 1989. "The Muslim Declaration of Nature." In *World Religions and the Environment*. Edited by Dwivedi, O. P. New Delhi: Gitanjali Publishing House.

Nasr, Seyyed Hossein 1992. "Islam and the Environmental Crisis." In *Spirit and Nature: Why the Environment is a Religious Issue: An Interfaith Dialogue*. Edited by Steven Rockefeller and John Elder. Boston: Beacon Press.

Negus, Yunus 1992. "Science within Islam." In *Islam and Ecology*. *Op. cit.*

Rafiq, M., and M. Ajmal 1989. "Islam and the Present Ecological Crisis." In *World Religions and the Environment*. *Op. cit.*

8

Hinduism, Population, and the Environment

KLAUS K. KLOSTERMAIER

In January 1992, before going to Shantiniketan, where I had been invited to deliver that year's Sudhakar Chattopadhyay Memorial Lecture, I spent a week in Delhi, India's capital, and a week in Vrindaban, the holy town of Krishna, where I had lived for two years in the sixties. When I mentioned to my acquaintances in Delhi, that I was to speak on "Dharma and Ecology" at Vishvabharati Vishvavidyalaya, I was informed about the efforts of the Union Government's Ministry of Environment, about the World Wildlife Foundation, which has its center right beside the India International Centre, where I was staying, and the activities of state ministries for environment. The big Indian dailies have regular writeups on environmental issues, as well. Mentioning the topic in Vrindaban, I was treated to an instant lecture by Swami Muktananda, secretary general of the *Akhand Bharatiya Sant Samiti,* an India-wide association of *samnyāsis* (monks). He reminded me that Hindus, since Vedic times, have prayed to the forces of nature, and did not attempt to dominate and exploit them. He also pointed out that Hindus have always striven to minimize their needs, and that it was wrong to use the consumption of goods as yardstick for the state of development of a society. Dr. Srivatsa Goswami, a well-known Vaishnava scholar, expressed the opinion that Krishna's total concern was for the environment. Referring to well-known landmarks of Vrindaban like the Kaliya-ghat, he suggested that Krishna had killed the anti-environmental forces, so as to make *ras-līlā,* the highest bliss, possible. When I finally delivered my lecture at the Rabindranath Tagore University, I became aware of another

137

problem: my audience at Shantiniketan, situated in West Bengal, a state that for many years has had a Communist-led government, associated with the term *dharma* notions of right-wing, conservative Hindutva politics, none too popular in that part of India.

Considering the magnitude of the problem, the complicated situation worldwide, the sophistication of our technology and the simplistic teachings of traditional religions concerning these issues, one is tempted to suggest that we throw out all tradition and begin afresh with no other presupposition but the facts, and no other hope but science and technology. However, this does not seem to work either. We cannot escape our own history, we cannot get rid of the ideas that have guided the lives of the generations before us. If traditions can be identified as part of the problem, they must also become part of the solution. Hinduism, that large and varied family of religions that have grown on the soil of India, is too much a part of Indian reality to be overthrown by any modern argument.

HINDUISM, THE MAJORITY TRADITION OF INDIA

If someone, unacquainted with India and Hinduism, would ask me, "What is Hinduism?" I would be hard pressed for a short answer, even after a lifetime of study of Hinduism. Hinduism is not a uniform and centrally regulated religious institution. It does not hold to a single set of doctrines, does not have a unifying creed, does not subscribe to a common canon of scriptures. It consists of, quite literally, hundreds of smaller and larger *sampradāyas* (communities, sects), possesses thousands of holy books, accepts dozens of inspired teachers, and continues to develop ever new branches. While for centuries it appeared mainly as an inward looking spirituality, interested in the development of love of God, high moral character, and insight into the mysteries of existence, it has developed during the last few decades a political interest which has led to its being compared with fundamentalism in other parts of the world, for its ambition to establish a theocratic dictatorship under the Hindu banner.

It may be impossible to provide a definition of Hinduism, but one can generalize some of its features: Hinduism is a way of life, embracing all aspects of private and corporate existence (not only "religion" in the Western sense), and it is becoming increasingly exclusivistic, distancing itself from other religions, such as Islam and Christianity. It is essentially pre-modern, and pre-technological, but it has shown a great ability to incorporate aspects of modernity and technology to its advantage.

The traditional foci of Hinduism were neither on population nor on resources, which were taken for granted or seen as not under human dominion, but on *dharma* and *moksha*, i.e., the ethico-religious order of society, and spiritual emancipation. One might also add *bhakti,* love of God, as the central concern for at least a large segment of Hinduism, past and present. If we question traditional and present-day Hinduism on the issues of population pressure and resource consumption, we must keep in mind that the answers are largely extrapolations from teachings focused on quite different issues, and that there is little by way of systematic doctrine that might be relied on.

Traditional Hinduism has held a fairly pessimistic view of the present and the future. According to widely shared beliefs, humankind has been going downhill from its beginnings, some million years ago. Some thousand years ago, we reached the Kaliyuga, the age of strife, which is to last for another several millennia, before the final cataclysm occurs. The *Vishnu Purāna,* a text from the fifth century C.E., characterizes the present age in those terms:

> Wealth and piety will decrease day by day, until the world will be wholly depraved. Property alone will confer rank, wealth will be the only source of devotion, passion will be the only bond of union between the sexes, falsehood will be the only means of success in courts, and women will only be the objects of sense gratification. Earth will be treasured only for her mineral resources, dishonesty will be a universal means of subsistence, presumption will take the place of learning. Thus in the Kali age decay will constantly proceed, until the human race approaches annihilation.[1]

Hinduism on Population Pressure

The centrality of *vivaha* (marriage) as the most important *samskāra*[2] (sacrament) both for men and women, with a clear notion of procreation as the purpose of marriage, is indicative of the Hindu attitude toward population increase: children are welcome, a childless marriage is reason for divorce, a great number of children, especially sons, is both a social and an economical asset (except in post-medieval times, when the custom of dowry developed and put a great burden on parents with many daughters). Virtually all traditional Hindu *sampradāyas* condemn abortion or other attempts to limit the number of children.[3] With a high infant mortality rate and generally a low life expectancy, population increase in pre-modern India was slow. Nevertheless, both the absolute number of people and the density of population in certain areas of India has been high throughout historic times, and there are *purānic* accounts which mention that at one time the weight of the population became too heavy for the earth to carry: in modern parlance, population pressure outstripped available resources.[4]

Also, in pre-modern times, there had been frequent droughts followed by extensive famines, floods, and wars and other natural and human-made calamities that reduced the span of lives and diminished the quality of life. Buddha's profound insight *sarvam duhkham* ("all is sorrowful") reveals a deep unhappiness with life as lived even by the privileged, and his advice not to cultivate any attachments but to concentrate on solitary spiritual enlightenment as the aim of life also had a direct influence on population. We read of complaints by elderly people in the countryside, about so many young men and women joining the Buddhist *sangha* that many villages were depopulated and there was danger that there would not be enough children to fill the vacancies left by the departed. Exact figures are hard to come by, but the number of unmarried monks and nuns belonging to Buddhist and Jain communities must have been in the millions — large enough to bring about a reduction in population. The Hindus, too, recognized *samnyāsa* as ideal. However, Hindu orthodoxy declared *samnyāsa* lawful only after a person had fulfilled his or her marital duties and had procreated offspring according to *dharma*. Possibly under Buddhist influence, and certainly since the time of Shankara, it became common in Hinduism, to take *samnyāsa* as a young person and remain celibate throughout life. It may have been population pressure in certain parts of South India from the fifth century on, or merely adventurous spirit, which made Hindus establish colonies throughout South and Southeast Asia. While, later on, laws forbade Hindus to cross the seas, and punished those who did with excommunication, the founders of the Hindu Kingdoms in Java, Thailand, Cambodia, and Burma apparently did not labor under any such constraints. Hinduism in general considered population increase as desirable, and we do not know of any instance of artificial population control recommended by any Hindu rulers or sages. Marriage was seen as a religious duty, and it equally was the duty of a father to have all his children married to suitable partners. Sons, especially, played an important role not only in continuing the family lineage on earth, but also in securing a good afterlife for the ancestors. The very word *putra* (son) was interpreted as meaning the one who saves *(tra)* from hell *(pu)*.

What do the leaders of contemporary Hinduism have to say on the recent population increase, so evident in India?[5] Not much, in fact. Some condemn the introduction of modern "Western" medicine, which not only saves many lives of children who otherwise would have died, but also extends the life span generally. Most would condemn family planning measures, and all would abhor abortion. Some might recommend *samnyāsa* as an ethically acceptable way of reducing population growth. Overall, there would not even be agreement that the population is too large and that, given modern means of increasing the productivity of the soil, India could not comfortably sustain an even larger number of people.

Hinduism on Resource Consumption

All traditional ways of life were "conservative" in the literal sense of the word: they used resources carefully and circumspectly, and tried to preserve and conserve them for the future. The daily necessities of life demanded a great investment of time and energy by almost everybody, and society at large could not afford to squander these hard-earned goods. The technology available before modern industrialization was largely small-scale and fairly unobtrusive: it could not inflict any damage that nature, especially tropical nature, would not be able to repair. One exception, possibly, were wars in which — at least since Muslim times — trees were systematically cut down and the earth was scorched. Hindu ethics recommended frugality. Traditional Hindu homes, built of locally available renewable materials, had hardly any furniture, and the amount of fuel used to cook the meals, as well as foodstuffs consumed, were kept to the minimum. Fasting, i.e., total abstention from all cooked food, was a popular, frequent, and widely observed practice, and for *samnyāsis* in particular utmost restriction of all wants was mandatory.[6] The ideal *samnyāsi* would not possess any human-made objects, would not consume anything but what grew in the wild, would not build a hut or otherwise interfere with nature. Non-use of resources, taking only of the surplus freely given by nature, non-interference, accommodation to nature, were seen as belonging to the highest ideal. Some of this attitude also transpired into the lifestyle of Hindu families.

The reasons for this behavior were complex. Certainly, there was always a respect for nature, which induced Hindus to restrict interference to a minimum. Numerous groves, individual trees, rivers, animals, and mountain peaks were considered sacred and received worship. Sacredness implied that one could not with impunity damage or pollute the object of worship. In the case of sacred groves, it meant that no one could harm any animal living there, nobody could cut down a tree or take out any other materials for consumption. The number and extent of sacred groves was fairly large in pre-modern times. The British government appropriated many of these as government forests, and applied its own rules of utilization to them. Epidemics and natural calamities were often thought to be the consequence of violation of such sacred natural objects. There also was another constant: the concern for purity and purification, which could be obtained through abstention from the use of natural objects, reduction of consumption of resources, voluntary limitation of enjoyment, introspection rather than outward activity.

Exploitation of resources on a large scale was made possible and necessary by modern industry. Industrial development coincided with progress in medicine and consequent large-scale increase in population. A vicious cycle was set in motion: a growing population needed more food, more clothing, more housing. The increased demand could not be met by traditional methods but required modern science-based technology. The growth of industry increased the demand for resources: the nature of big industry required the concentration of large work-forces in big cities. The big city attracted more people from the country. The pressure of population in the big cities led to the growth of slums and a degradation of the city environment, while, at the same time, depleting the countryside of human and material resources, leading to an impoverishment of the rural areas. Not until relatively late was scientific-industrial attention directed toward agriculture and rural development. The process moved so rapidly, and was driven by its own inner logic to such a degree, that hardly anybody could or would suggest any alternative.

Hinduism as a religious tradition shut its eyes: it kept repeating ancient teachings and encouraging ancient ideals. The centers of Hinduism became centers of resistance to progress, centers of conservatism, and not centers of fresh thought. Hindu leaders bewailed the negative effects of the change, blamed it all upon "Western materialism" in general and the British in particular, and exhorted their own people to return to the old ways of life.

Some prominent Hindus, however, who would not consider themselves "Hindu leaders," though they belong to this tradition, showed greater insight. Rabindranath Tagore, early on saw, and denounced, the effects of technology not only on nature but also on the human psyche. As a poet and a person with higher sensibilities, he realized more than a generation ago that the escalation of industrial civilization was harmful, and even suicidal.

Likewise Mahatma Gandhi, early in his life, became aware of the social cost of industrial progress. He had the opportunity as a student to observe the degradation of humans and of nature in the industrial heartland of England, and he did not want to see India transformed into a gigantic replica of this. Again, his hostility toward progress and technological development was not so much dictated by concern for nature as such, but by concern for the people who were the victims of progress. Gandhi subscribed to the ancient Hindu ideals of frugality and restriction of wants, and he trusted nature to provide for the best of humans.

Few contemporary Hindu leaders have come out with any advice on this matter. The spiritual leaders continue to dispense traditional spiritual advice. The political Hindus adopted Savarkar's plea to militarize Hinduism, and to propel industrial development to such a degree that India would be the most powerful state if not on earth, then at least in the region. They advocate, among other things, the development of an Indian atomic bomb.

Hinduism and the Environment

A fairly substantial literature exists today which deals with traditional Hindu regulations of the natural environment.[7] Locally and regionally, many environmentally sound cultures existed in pre-modern India. Many of these were destroyed or damaged by the introduction of modern industrial processes, which more often than not proceeded without any environmental concerns whatsoever. The industrial transformation and degradation of vast areas in India has progressed to such an extent that it does not appear possible to reverse the process, and attempts must be made to limit the damage and to contain the development. India's population keeps growing at a tremendous pace and, with it, the need to feed, clothe, and house it. India's big cities are becoming ever bigger, traffic is becoming denser, air pollution in some areas has reached hazardous levels. Neither big cities nor large-scale industry figure in the repertoire of traditional Hinduism, and in the absence of any doctrinal positions, Hinduism is largely silent on these modern phenomena.

The Indian ecologist Madhav Gadgil, who sees in government-allotted subsidies the cause for much of the economic/ecological distortions of India, refers in this connection to an "iron triangle" which prevents ecological and economic sanity from being realized: "A collusion of: 1. Those who benefit from the subsidies: the industry, urban populations, rich farmers; 2. Those who decide on who is to be subsidized at whose cost: the politicians; and 3. Those who administer the subsidies: the bureaucracy."[8] He also speaks of "Indian islands of prosperity, surrounded by the Bharatiya ocean of poverty." By the very choice of these words, one could identify the former with the Western-trained and Western-thinking Indians, the latter with the traditional, largely Hindu people.

There are, by now, many grass-roots movements in India, which are active on behalf of protection of the environment. They are usually led by courageous individuals, some no doubt with Hindu background, like "Baba" Amte, but more often than not belonging to the *adivāsis,* the "tribals," whose existence depends much more immediately on the land. Thus, the Chipko Movement in the Himalayan foothills, and the agitation against the Narmada project, which would have flooded thousands of square miles of *adivāsi* lands, were all initiated by "tribals," often by women, who are most directly affected by the degradation of the environment.[9]

Hinduism and the World

While India's problems are large and manifest, they are not unique: in fact, they are the world's problems. Some years ago, half tongue-in-cheek, I wrote an essay, "Will India's Past be America's Future?"[10] I argued that India, due to the long duration of its civilization, had gone through many developments which America still has to go through. More and more, I come to believe that the Indian situation is, for better and for worse, exemplary for the world at large. India's problems will sooner or later be the world's problems, and India's solutions may be solutions also for the rest of the world. That is where Hinduism comes in, not only as the traditional religion of India, but as a spiritual tradition of humankind with a message for the world at large. Almost everywhere today the pressure of population leads to an overexploitation of resources and a degradation of the natural environment. What happened to Hinduism — its lack of growth and its fear to face challenges in the area of religion and spirituality — has also been the fate of most other traditional, institutionalized religions.

One of the basic, unarticulated presuppositions of Hinduism had been that everything not only follows an eternal law — *sanātana dharma* — but that it perfectly knows that law, and that nothing ever really changes so that, therefore, Hinduism need not change either. A look at history and especially at the history of the last one hundred years would suggest that almost everything once taken for granted has changed and that religions, in order to remain meaningful, have to change, too. We can anticipate even more drastic changes. The new biotechnologies that aim at changing the genetic structures of living organisms, and the communication technologies based on electronics, are likely to bring about a profound change of not only the natural environment but also the social life of most of humankind. As a consequence, humans, more and more, will live in, and depend on, a human-made world, and will be less aware of and less connected with the original creation, on which the traditional religions are based. If traditionally religious people express thanks to the Creator before they sit down for a meal, the modern person — if capable of gratitude at all — will consider the human effort that went into creating the strain of cereal or vegetable forming the raw material of the meal, the human work required to bring these largely manmade crops to maturity, the producers of fertilizers and pesticides, the manufacturers of sowing and harvesting machinery, the chemical and industrial engineers processing the foods, the chain of merchants and sales people making the food available at that particular place. It requires a major metaphysical effort to add, as the last link in the food-chain, a creator of earth and heaven. Does religion consist only of this last link? Or is it not a genuine (and also more consequential) spirituality to be aware of the manifold dependencies from human minds and hands to whom one owes what one needs? And, by conclusion, would it not reinforce the motivation to also contribute one's share to keep this web of mutuality intact and sound?

Obviously, Hinduism (as other religions, but more visibly so) operates at different levels for different people. It neither speaks with one voice nor advocates one way of salvation for all. For the sake of structuring my chapter — without claiming to exhaust the levels at which Hindu traditions operate — I shall identify five levels of Hinduism that seem relevant in connection with our theme, levels which I call the vedic-mythical, the puranic-religious, the dharmic, the yogic, and the vedantic.

The Vedic-Mythical

Myths are still a powerful reality in much of India. A great many people in India still see the world through the eyes of the Vedic *rishi*. As Kapila Vatsyayan has convincingly shown in a recent essay on "Ecology and Indian Myth,"[11] most, if not all of Indian mythology can be understood as having ecological dimensions, and all natural phenomena have been taken up by Indian mythology as religiously meaningful. The basic elements, water, earth, fire, wind, as well as space and time, have been endowed with mythological meaning in the Vedas; the names of trees and shrubs, of the months and of the days, the features of the landscape, the seas and the mountains, all connect nature with gods and supernatural powers. The majority of Indians even now spontaneously associate natural calamities like epidemics and floods with the wrath of gods, and attribute good luck and prosperity to their blessing. It is this mythic world view which tends to accept things as they are, restricting human influence on the course of events to imploring the supernatural powers by means of prayers, sacrifice, and self-mortification. All these are major facts of life also in today's India. While in Europe the Enlightenment totally dissolved the original mythic world view in the acid of rationalism, and Pragmatism dissuaded the Modern world from investing its energies in anything but economically profitable activities, in India life is still largely lived in the world of myth and symbol. We have come to appreciate not only the ecological wisdom of the myths but also the power of symbols to direct people's actions. One need not be naive, fundamentalist, or hopelessly romantic to appreciate the holistic, universalist, and reverential dimensions of mythical and symbolic thinking. The absence of reverence for things higher than pleasure and profit has much to do with the degradation of life in the so-called advanced countries. The mythic-symbolic world view is essentially reverential, world-valuing, and appreciative of natural reality for its own sake, rather than for its economic potential.

How would the mythic world view affect population? Is it not largely responsible for the resistance against any form of population control, by maintaining a purely passive attitude towards population increase? No doubt, but mythmakers can learn and symbols can change meaning. The traditional myths and symbols owe their origins to insights into nature gained at a particular time under particular circumstances, with specific modes of production and within a specific social organization. Myths in India have changed over the millennia. Gods have come and gone. Symbols have been transformed and adapted.

Preserving the reverential attitude toward the mystery of life, harmonizing the mythical with the scientific world view, adapting traditional symbolism to today's societal needs, will not only provide continuity within Indian culture but also infuse our present praxis of life with a deeper meaning.

The *Purānic*-Religious

While the vedic-mythical world view certainly could be called "religious" from the standpoint of philosophy, I am using the term "religion" here in a more specific sense, corresponding to the Indian notion of *sampradāya,* that of a community centered on worship of a specific deity, with a well-defined (particular) set of doctrines and a fully worked out theology, such as Vaishnavism, Shaivism, or Shaktism. While the mythico-symbolic universe described above supplies the foundation of the "religious" world view, it becomes overarched by a theology that claims to rest on a specific revelation, and that promises transcendental salvation to the practitioners of specific rituals. The sources of this world view are the *Purānas,* later augmented by the Vaishnava *Samhitās,* the Shaiva *Āgamas,* and the Shakta *Tantras.*

While much of the attention of the religious world view is directed toward intra-psychic and trans-mundane concerns, it too has dimensions that are relevant to questions of population, resource consumption, and environment. To begin with the latter: the religions of India have developed a strong aesthetic sense. Temples are often situated in the most beautiful spots: on the banks of rivers, on the tops of hills, on the shores of the oceans. Their architecture itself — an effort to create a microcosm — manifests the highest artistic achievement of India. Where natural surroundings were not attractive by themselves, the temple became the center of a human-made environment combining beauty and religious function: tanks were added, flower gardens and canopied courtyards, many-pillared halls and processional grounds. Aesthetic sensibilities certainly have much to do with an ecological conscience. There is a vicious circle of violence toward nature and violence toward humans, of lack of sensibility toward nature and ugliness of architectural style, of brutality and unhappiness.

The *Purānas,* the Bibles of the Indian religions, recommend the planting of trees and gardens as pleasing to God, as an activity that is meritorious as well as useful. They teach the sacredness of nature not only as creation of God, but as God's own body. The *Bhāgavata Purāna,Purana* in particular, identifies the mountain ranges, the courses of the rivers, the plains and the forests, as the bones and veins, the limbs and the hairs of the deity: humans are to meet nature with reverence as something divine, and doing harm to nature is equivalent to sacrilege. Ramanuja, the greatest of the Vaishnava theologians, has given a metaphysical backing to this world view: everything in the universe, including humans, relates to God as the body relates to the soul; human activity directed toward the world has salvific import.

How does the religious world view judge increase in population? When the major *sampradāyas* originated and flourished, population increase appeared to be desirable: God needs worshipers, the more the better. The belief in *punar-janma* (rebirth), the need to provide bodily vehicles for souls that had to work out their *karma,* would also prohibit any interference with the process of pro-creation. Abortion was considered an abominable crime, to be punished in this world and the next by specific sufferings.

Shaktism in Bengal did encourage a form of population control that strikes us today as inhuman: the offering of female infants to the Ganga. Likewise, the practice of *sati,* the (supposedly voluntary) burning of often young wid-ows together with their husbands, certainly is a form of population control that would go against our ethical sensibilities.

Indian religions in centuries past mobilized millions to pay homage to God in a specific guise and to lead a life of *bhakti,* accepting the Lordship of Vish-nu and seeing nature as His image. In our time, they mobilize millions in the pur-suit of political power, the establishment of a *Rām Rājya* along the lines of right-wing Hindu fundamentalism. It is doubtful whether these people possess the ecological sensibilities of the traditional religions or the respect for life, flowing from the recognition of God's overlordship.

The *Dharmic*

Dharma is possibly the most central concept of Hinduism in all its expressions: they may differ in almost everything else, but they affirm their adherence to *dharma,* a term which in fact is used to identify Hinduism over and against other faiths.

Leaving out discussions of etymology and history, a general definition of *dharma* is "that which sustains," comprising both society and nature, this world and the world beyond. It is a universal, cosmic as well as transcendental prin-ciple. As the well-known adage has it "*dharma* when kept, protects, when vi-olated, destroys." It is a conviction of the fairness and equitableness of the un-folding of the universe. *Dharma,* as cosmic principle as well as detailed in thousands of particular injunctions, was the backbone of Hindu society through-out the ages. Restoration of Hindu *dharma* was the concern of the great Hindu reformers of the nineteenth and twentieth centuries. One of the strengths of the Hindu notion of *dharma* was that although it was believed to be grounded in un-changing reality — *sanātana dharma,* eternal law — it was flexible and adapt-able to changing circumstances. Up until the twelfth century, there existed the institution of the *dharma-mantri,* the minister in charge of *dharma,* whose duty it was to effect changes in accordance with the principles of *dharma.* Modern Indian thinkers and sages have attributed the ills of the present age to a breakdown in *dharma,* partly caused by the mistaken belief that *dharma* was fixed once and for all, and that traditional *dharma* was out of sync with modern times and its requirements. Modern law, important as it is for the regulation of a religiously diverse secular society, cannot be a substitute for *dharma,* not only because the latter is more comprehensive, but also because it reflects natural growth, articulates the historically conditioned social reality of India, and can appeal to more profound strata of consciousness.

Can we entertain the notion of an ecological *dharma* not only for India but for humankind as well? A contemporary ecological *dharma* must incorporate all of our present knowledge of nature as well as the accumulated wisdom of the ages. It must also reflect the actual life-experience of those who are striving to lead ideal lives, and must sustain and uplift the deepest in ourselves. Ecology, in its true meaning, must be more than a branch of economics or of biology; it must be expressive of, and give support to, our concern for truth, goodness, and beauty. It must recover a holistic vision.

One of the connotations of *dharma* is that its statements are not to be understood as mere philosophical opinion or contributions to a discussion, but as norms and commands. The traditional understanding of possibly the most typical of all Hindu schools of thought, Purva Mimamsa, was that the Veda, revealed scripture, was identical with *vidhi,* injunctions to perform (rightful) actions and abstain from unlawful actions, and that these injunctions were normative: part of them normative for all *(sadhāraṇa dharma),* part of them normative for specific groups of persons *(svadharma).* Norms must be enforceable to be meaningful: a society, and humankind in general, cannot exist without such enforceable rules. No doubt, if we are sure that we have reached the level of *dharma* in matters dealing with ecology, we also have an obligation not only to follow an ecological *dharma* but also to see to it that it is followed by others.

The *Yogic*

Yoga, in one form or another, is part of virtually all branches of Hinduism and in its general sense is virtually identical with religion as structured form of life. In its basics, Yoga is restraint, self-control, the establishment of the rule of higher reason over sensual impulses, striving toward higher states of consciousness. In its specific development, Yoga, especially as systematized by Patanjali, is a way of transcendental liberation, leading to a blissful, contemplative state of mind, a condition in which a person makes no demands on the environment at all, but rests happily in self-contentment.

Reading the Indian ecologist Madhav Gadgil's perceptive essay on "Population, Resources and Environment,"[12] I was struck by his repeated emphasis on "discipline" as a requirement for ecological well-being and his castigating the "highly indisciplined fashion" in which, currently, demands are met, which causes much of the ecological damage we see around us. Whether India or America, it is obvious that lack of discipline is rampant, and cause not only for indignation but of serious harm. Against the traditional brahmin's completely disciplined life, one has to set the total lack of inhibition and self-discipline of typical modern pop idols. Again, it becomes clear, indiscipline not only affects the individual itself, but has social and ecological consequences. Ecology, understood as a mode of thought as well as a way of life, demands discipline, and engenders discipline in its turn. Nature may look random to the superficial observer; in reality it is not only a highly complex, but also a highly disciplined, whole.

This is not the place to go into details of Pātanjala Yoga, but some elements of interest in connection with our topic might be highlighted. The eightfold Yoga begins with the practice of *yama* and *niyama* — basic ethical rules to be kept by everybody, embodying respect for life, property, and truth, among other things. The notion of *ahimsā* ("not-killing") includes all life, and in and by itself has implications with regard to our theme.[13] In its higher forms, it inculcates not only a suppression of aggression but positive relations with all that lives, human as well as non-human. Yoga also insists on self-control and continence, something which extends to life-long celibacy in the professional Yogis. This may not be a very popular notion in our age of permissiveness, but continence would not be the worst way to keep populations from growing.

The *Vedāntic*

Vedānta is better known in the West than most other expressions of Indian thought, and more often than not it is understood as radical solipsistic idealism, disinterested in, or even hostile to, the world in which ecologists live. True, there are statements attributed to Shankara and his school of thought, in which the visible world is radically devalued as *māyā*, illusion and deception, a seduction and hindrance to the spirit in quest of its goal. Not all of *Vedānta* is of that nature. For some, nature is means to salvation, a marvel in and by itself, the basis for everything.[14] Awareness of a higher reality need not result in contempt for everything else. On the contrary, by insisting that everything that is real is *brahman*, ultimate reality, nature gains infinite stature and dignity. To the extent that the natural and social are taken as realities, they have to be seen as *brahman* and not as illusion. They must be taken as seriously as *brahman*, or one would fail to understand them properly. Mere numerical relations do not confer reality; mere utility cannot be equated with reality either. That adds a seriousness to the issues at hand — it confers ultimate value to that which is real in our lives.

Vedānta represents the concern of an elite, more specifically, the concerns of an elite of people advanced in age. They have reached a high plateau in life, where the mundane concerns of everyday life appear distant and unimportant. As the notion of the mathematical infinite is important even in very practical engineering calculations, so the consciousness of reality as *saccidānanda* is important for leading a humanly meaningful life. There are ramifications for population and resources implied, even if it is difficult to spell them out or make people see them, who are themselves struggling with the entanglements on the lower ranges of life-experience.

CONCLUSIONS

There is little doubt that, at various levels, Hindu traditions contain deep ecological wisdom and the seeds of ideas that might be developed into a contemporary ecology. There is also no doubt that a good deal of practical wisdom and land management skills have been accumulated by Hindu farmers and workmen over the ages, and that often they possess acute insight into quite complex situations. However, looking at the widespread incidence of overuse of land, of neglect of maintenance, of overgrazing and deforestation by Hindu farmers, of lack of resistance against the unecological methods taken over from other cultures for the sake of increased profit, one begins to doubt the effectiveness of Hindu ideas of ecology. In order to be successful, ecological regulations have to be legislated and enforced. India is simply too large and too diverse a country to expect any such legislation to be feasible, and a long tradition of circumventing and undercutting existing regulations has created a climate which does not offer much hope for success of such measures.

The best case for a made-in-India "sustainability," to use that buzz word of the nineties, has been made by *adivāsis,* the Indian indigenous people, who, quite literally, have developed a lifestyle sustained over thousands of years. As a recent study of the Warlis[15] shows, *adivāsis* tribals learned their ecological wisdom from day-to-day contact with their environment, developing a genuine symbiosis. Contrary to caste Hindus, who often see the world through the glass of a particular abstract philosophy developed not from immediate knowledge of the physical environment but from notions of ritual purity and caste ideology, the tribals have remained true to nature, and their myths reflect more closely the experience of a people that successfully lived on a particular tract of land for very long periods of time. Tribal populations also remained fairly stable over the years. They developed subsistence economies with a great deal of equality in the group, fairly good health, and high spirits. Their physical stamina as well as their *joie de vivre* compares well with the majority Hindu population. In many areas their lands have been encroached upon by Hindu farmers, and state legislation, since British times, disadvantaged many of them by restricting their traditional ways of life. They constitute ecological isles of sustainability which might have model-value for the rest of the country. Like the tropical rain forests, they need protection as important ecological resources. They may already have answers for many questions — the message which they give to the rest of the world is quite clear: live in harmony with your environment, in peace with your fellow men, return to the earth what you take from her, avoid greed, stress, and artificiality. Much of ancient tribal myth and lore has become part of traditional Hinduism — the *Purānas* have probably preserved many such tribal memories — and the fact that much of Hindu tradition is locally diverse, reflects its tribal and regional past. It may well be the starting point of an ecology suitable for India. On the other hand, much of India has already moved so much in the direction of modernity that present day India cannot risk the enormous disruption that a return to a pre-modern, pre-industrial past would entail. Neither Kampuchea under Pol Pot nor China under the Cultural Revolution are models to be followed.

As regards population control, that explosive topic of the late twentieth century, Indian tradition offers mostly resistance to modern methods of preventing further growth. The sanctity of life, especially of human life, is a fundamental tenet of all Indian religions, and nothing seems to alarm religious people more than a perceived violation of this sphere. A visit to one of the countless, extensive slums surrounding every major Indian city, an encounter with hordes of undernourished, ragged beggar children, the presence of millions of destitute, homeless people camping in the streets of India's megalopolises — not to speak of statistics listing huge armies of unemployed, underemployed, and unemployable — all these impressions and figures can be taken as proof of a massive overpopulation. Most of post-independence India's gigantic efforts to improve its economy have been nullified by an enormous growth in population. The more optimistic among India's planners believe that India's population growth will soon level off and that an increase in prosperity — and, especially, in economic security — will lead to a decrease in family size, as has happened in Europe. Others believe that only a massive family planning program that includes all the options for preventing more births would be the only way to prevent further catastrophic population growth and the risk of an economic and ecological collapse of India. Siding with the first, I would think that one of the most effective and most humane means of controlling population growth in India would be universal old age security and health care.

The crucial question for Hinduism today is how to wed local ancient tradition with modern science and technology, how to align age-old sensibilities with the realities of the late twentieth century, so as to have continuity as well as sustainability, decency as well as prosperity. Perhaps it is possible to harmonize nature and humankind, economy and ethics, on the basis of wisdom as well as science and create a more humane world for our children to live in than we have known it in our lifetime.

NOTES

1. *Vishnu Purāna* IV, 24.

2. In vedic religion, husband and wife together formed the ritual unit: only together were they "complete." Later Hindu gods were always depicted as married, with children.

3. Aborting a fetus was considered a *mahāpātaka* (deadly sin), equal to *brahmahatyā* (murdering a brahman), and unforgivable in this life.

4. Cf. J. Jong, "The Overburdened Earth in India and Greece," *JAOS* 105/3 (1985): 397–400.

5. According to the 1991 census, the population of India was 843,930,861, increasing by ca. 25,000,000 per year.

6. *Bhukti* (sense enjoyment, consumption) and *mukti* (liberation) were generally considered incompatible.

7. See the writings of Krishna Caitanya, S. C. Crawford, Tiwari, and others.

8. Madhav Gadgil, "Population, Resources and Environment," *Seminar* 365: *Towards 2000 AD* (Delhi, January 1990): 52–56.

9. See N. K. Singh's special feature on environment, "A New Militancy," in *India Today*, 31 October 1989: 174–76.

10. In *Journal of Asian and African Studies* 14 (1980): 94–103.

11. *Indigenous Vision*, 157–80.

12. *Seminar* 365: *Towards 2000 AD* (January 1990): 52–60.

13. See the special issue of the *Journal of Dharma* on "Ahimsā and Ecology," 1991.

14. See *Pancādaśī* VI, 147.

15. Winin Pereira, "The Sustainable Lifestyle of the Warlis," *Indigenous Vision*, 189–203.

BIBLIOGRAPHY

Arzhookiel, A. "Nature — Sacred and Profane." *Religion and Society* 24/1 (March 1977): 32–54.

Bapat, Jyotsna. "Towards a Critical Ecology." *Journal of the Indian Anthropological Society* 23 (1988): 1–16.

Buch, M. N. "Rise of Predator Cities." *Indian International Quarterly.*

Chaitanya, Krishna. "The Earth as Sacred Environs." *Indigenous Vision: Peoples' of India Attitudes to the Environment. India International Centre Quarterly* (Spring-Summer 1992): 35–48.

Chengapp, Raj, et al. "Urban Decay: A Mega Collapse." *India Today* 31 (January 1988): 114–21.

Crawford, Cromwell. "The Ecological Conscience of Hinduism." *Indian Philosophy and Culture* 16/2 (June 1971): 147–58.

D'Monte, Darryl. "Green at the Grassroots." *Seminar* 355 (March 1989): 16–25.

Dwivedi, O. P. "Human Responsibility and the Environment: A Hindu Perspective." *Hindu-Christian Studies Bulletin* 6 (1993): 19–26.

Engineer, Rusi. "Ecology and the Renewal of Politics." *Seminar* 353 (January 1989): 63–66.

Gadgil, Madhav. "Population, Resources and Environment." *Seminar* 365 (January 1990): 52–60.

Gadgil, Madhav, and M. D. Subah Chandran. "Sacred Groves." *Indigenous Vision,* 183–87.

Klostermaier, Klaus K. "Bhakti, Ahimsa and Ecology." *Journal of Dharma* 16/3 (1991): 32–39.

——— "Ecological Dimensions of Ancient Indian Thought." In *Religion and Society: Sudhakar Chattopadhyay Commemoration Volume,* ed. P. Jash. Calcutta 1984, 347–60.

——— "Possible Contributions of Asian Traditions to Contemporary Environmental Ethics." *Bulletin of the Humanities Association of Canada* (1992): 35–49.

——— "The New Master Paradigm: Ecology." *Hindu-Christian Studies Bulletin* 6 (1993): 5–6.

Kothari, Rajni. "Challenge of the Nineties." *Seminar* 365 (January 1990): 24–26.

Mathew, Thomas. "Energy, Environment and Development." *India International Centre Quarterly* 10/3 (1983): 359–70.

Pereira, Winin. "The Sustainable Lifestyle of the Warlis." *Indigenous Vision,* 189–203.

Prime, Ranchar. *Hinduism and Ecology: Seeds of Truth.* London: Cassell, 1992.

Singh, N. K. "A New Militancy." *India Today* (31 October 1989): 174–76.

Skolimowski, Henryk. "World Views and Values for the Future." *Indian International Centre Quarterly* (Spring 198): 155–65.

Tiwari, B. N., and O. P. Dwivedi. "Hindu Culture and Ecology." *South Asian Horizons* 4 (1986): 95–106.

Vatsyayan, Kapila. "Ecology and Indian Myth." *Indigenous Vision,* 157–80.

9

Buddhist Resources for Issues of Population, Consumption, and the Environment

RITA M. GROSS

This short chapter applying basic Buddhist teachings to questions regarding fertility control and resource utilization is written by a feminist academic scholar of religion, for whom Buddhism is the long-standing religion of choice. Therefore, I bring to this chapter the perspectives of both an insider trained in Buddhist thought and an outsider with allegiance to the cross-cultural comparative study of religion and broad knowledge of major religious traditions.

As is the case with all major traditions, conclusions relevant to the current situation cannot be quoted from the classic texts; rather, the *values* inherent in the tradition need to be applied to the current, unprecedented crises of overpopulation and excessive consumption that threaten to overwhelm the biosphere upon which we are dependent. This task of applying the traditional values of Buddhism to such issues in the contemporary context is not difficult, in my view, since classic Buddhist values suggest highly relevant ways of responding to the current situation. In this essay, I will work to some extent as a Buddhist "constructive theologian," interpreting the tradition in ways that bring the inherited tradition into conversation with contemporary issues and needs. Reflecting my own standpoint both as a Buddhist and as a scholar, I will include materials not only from early Buddhist thought, but also from the Mahayana and Vajrayana perspectives within Buddhism. At the same time, I shall try to be as nonsectarian as possible.

DEFINING THE ISSUES:
ENVIRONMENT, CONSUMPTION, AND POPULATION

When we try to bring traditional Buddhist values into conversation with the current situation, it is important to have a clear understanding of that situation. The assignment of this chapter is to address the interlocked issues of the environment, resource utilization, and population growth, from a Buddhist point of view. Since Buddhism always suggests that we need to deal with things as they are, not with fantasies, it is appropriate to begin with some brief consideration of how the ecosystem, consumption, and population actually interact. When relating these three concerns to one another, one can imagine three alternatives: a sufficiently small population living well on a stabile, self-renewing resource base, an excessive population living in degraded conditions on an insufficient resource base, or the present pyramid of a few people living well and large numbers of people barely surviving. Obviously, only the first option contains merit. How people could value reproduction so much that they could prefer the second option to the first is incomprehensible, and the current pyramid of privilege is morally obscene. It should also be clear that population is the only negotiable element in this complex. In other words, when we look at the three factors under discussion — the environment, population, and consumption — there are two non-negotiables and one negotiable. Fundamentally, it is not negotiable that the human species must live within the boundaries and limits of the biosphere. However it is done, there is no other choice, because there is no life apart from the biosphere. Morally, it is not negotiable that there be an equitable *(equitable,* not *equal)* distribution of resources among the world's people. These two non-negotiables mean that population size is the negotiable factor in the equation. It is hard to question the proposition that a human population small enough so that everyone can enjoy a decent standard of living without ruining the environment is necessary and desirable. We cannot increase the size of the earth and can increase its productivity only to a limited extent, but we, as a species, can control population. All that it requires is the realization that many other pursuits are at least equally as sacred and as satisfying as reproduction.

Religions commonly criticize excessive consumption, but commonly encourage excessive reproduction. Therefore, though I will note the Buddhist values that encourage moderate consumption, I will emphasize the Buddhist values that encourage moderation and responsibility regarding reproduction, which are considerable. I emphasize these elements in Buddhism precisely because there has been so little discussion of religious arguments that favor restraining human fertility. The example of a major, long-standing world religion whose adherents lead satisfying lives without an overwhelming emphasis on individual procreation certainly is worth investigating. Buddhism can in no way be construed or interpreted as pro-natalist in its basic values and orientations. The two religious ideas that are commonly invoked by most religions to justify pro-natalist practices are not part of basic Buddhism. Buddhism does not require its members to reproduce as a religious duty. Nor do most forms of Buddhism regard sexuality negatively, as an evil to be avoided unless linked with reproduction, though all forms of Buddhism include an implicit standard of sexual ethics. Therefore, fertility control through contraception as well as abstinence is completely acceptable. The practices regarding fertility and reproduction that would flow from fundamental Buddhist values favor reproduction as a mature and deliberate choice, rather than an accident or a duty. Because of the unique ways that Buddhism values human life, only children who can be well cared for, physically, emotionally, and spiritually, should be conceived. Few Buddhists would disagree with the guideline that one should have few children, so that all of them can be well cared for without exhausting the emotional, material, and spiritual resources of their parents, their community, and their planet.

By contrast, pronatalism as an ideology seems to be rampant on the planet; those who mildly suggest that unlimited reproduction is not an individual right and could well be destructive are derided. Suggest that there is a causal relationship between excessive reproduction and poverty and watch the fallout. Pronatalist ideology includes at least three major ideas, all of which are subject to question. Pro-natalists always regard a birth as a positive occasion, under any circumstances, even the most extreme. To suggest that reproduction under many circumstances is irresponsible, and merits censure rather than support, makes one unpopular with pro-natalists. Furthermore, pro-natalists claim that it is necessary to reproduce to be an adequate human being; those who choose to remain childless are scorned, and suffer many social and economic liabilities. Finally, pronatalists regard reproduction as a private right not subject to public policy, even though they usually insist that the results of their reproduction are a public, even a global, responsibility. The tragedy of pronatalism is that although excessive populations could be cut quite quickly by voluntary means, lacking those, they probably will be cut by involuntary means involving great suffering — disease, violence, and starvation. Therefore, it is critical to counter the mindless and rampant pro-natalist religious doctrines, socialization, peer pressures, tax policies, sentiments, and values, that senselessly assault one at every turn.

Before beginning to discuss Buddhist teachings as a resource for developing an ethic of moderation concerning both reproduction and consumption, it is important to pause to acknowledge two controversial issues. They cannot be debated in this context, even though my conclusions regarding them will be apparent in my discussion of Buddhist ethics, the environment, consumption, and reproduction.

Because the Buddhist concept of all-pervasive interdependence makes sense, I see no way that individual rights can extend to the point that an individual exercising his or her supposed rights may be allowed to threaten the supportive matrix of life — a point that has been reached in both consumption and reproduction. Whatever wealth or values a person may have that drive them to inappropriate levels of consumption or reproduction, it is hard to argue that they have individual rights to exercise those levels of consumption or reproduction without regard to their impact on the biosphere. The rhetoric of individual rights and freedoms certainly has cogency against an overly communal and authoritarian social system. But today that rhetoric and stance threaten to overwhelm the need for restraint and moderation to protect and preserve communities and species.

Furthermore, especially in the need to counter pro-natalist ideologies and policies, we have reached a point beyond relativism. In the human community, we have learned too late and too slowly the virtues of relativism whenever it is feasible. We have been too eager to condemn others for having a world view different from our own. Relativism regarding world view is virtuous because diversity of world views is a valuable resource. On the other hand, relativism regarding basic ethical standards leads to intolerable results. Are we really willing to say of a culture in which women are treated like property or children are exploited that "that's just their culture?" There would be no possibility of an international human rights movement if people really believed that ethical standards are completely relative and arbitrary. And both consumption and reproduction are ethical issues of the highest order, since their conduct gravely affects everyone's life. We can no longer afford to let individuals who believe that they should reproduce many children do so, just as we no longer condone slavery, the exploitation of children, or treating women as chattel. Certain longstanding and deeply held cultural and religious values are at stake in the claim that pronatalism is an intolerable and inappropriate ethical stance given current conditions. Some religions need to adjust their recommendations regarding fertility to the realities brought about by modern medicine, which has greatly reduced the death rate but not the birth rate, resulting in a dangerous growth in populations, all of whom want to consume at higher standards than have ever been known previously.

WALKING THE MIDDLE PATH
IN AN INTERDEPENDENT WORLD:
BASIC BUDDHIST RESOURCES FOR MODERATION

One of the most basic teachings of Buddhism concerns Interdependence (*pratityasamutpada* in Sanskrit and *paticcasamuppada* in Pali), which is said to be one of the discoveries made by the Buddha during his enlightenment experience. This teaching prepares the ground for all further comments on consumption and reproduction, since interdependence is the bottom line which cannot be defied. Rather than being isolated and independent entities, Buddhism sees all beings as interconnected with one another in a great web of interdependence. All-pervasive interdependence is part of the Buddhist understanding of the law of cause and effect, which governs all events in our world. Nothing happens apart from or contrary to cause and effect according to Buddhism, which does not allow for accidents or divine intervention into the operations of cause and effect. Furthermore, since Buddhism understands cause and effect as interdependence, actions unleashed by one being have effects and repercussions throughout the entire cosmos. Therefore, decisions regarding fertility or consumption are not merely private decisions irrelevant to the larger world. Any baby born anywhere on the planet affects the entire interdependent world, as does any consumption of resources. It cannot be argued that either private wealth or low standards of material consumption negate this baby's impact on the universal web of interdependence. Nor can it be argued that private desires for children outweigh the need to take into account the impact of such children on the interdependent cosmos, since the laws of cause and effect are not suspended in any case. Similarly, utilization of resources anywhere has repercussions throughout the entire planetary system. Often consumption of luxuries in one part of the world is directly related to poverty and suffering in other parts of the world. Thus the vision of universal and all-pervasive interdependence, which is so basic to Buddhism, requires moderation in all activities, especially reproduction and consumption, because of their impact on the rest of the universe. When the Buddhist understanding of interdependence is linked with the scientific understanding of the planet as a finite lifeboat, it becomes clear that Buddhism regards appropriate, humane, and fair fertility control as a requirement. It is equally clear that Buddhism would regard ecologically unsound practices regarding reproduction or consumption as selfish, privately motivated disregard for the finite, interdependent cosmos.

The vision of cosmic interdependence presents the big picture regarding reproduction and consumption. This vision becomes more detailed when we look more specifically at the human realm within the interdependent cosmos. On the one hand, Buddhism values tremendously the good fortune of human rebirth, and on the other hand, Buddhism sees all sentient beings as fundamentally similar in their basic urge to avoid pain and to experience well-being. Thus, birth as a human is both highly valued and seen as birth into that vast universal web of interdependence in which what relates beings to each other is much more fundamental than what divides them into species. So two phrases, "precious human body," and "mother sentient beings," need always to be kept together when discussing Buddhist views about the human place in the interdependent cosmos. The preciousness of human birth is in no way due to human rights over other forms of life, for a human being *was* and could again be other forms of life —

though Buddhist practice is also thought to promote continued rebirth in the human realm. On the other hand, all beings are linked in the vast universal web of interdependence and emptiness, from which nothing is exempt. This web is so intimately a web of relationship and shared experience that the traditional exuberant metaphor declares that all beings have at some time been our mothers and we theirs. Therefore, rather than feeling superior or feeling that we humans have rights over other forms of life, it is said over and over that, because we know how much we don't want to be harmed or to suffer, and since all beings are our relatives, we should not harm them or cause them pain, as much as possible.

As is commonly known, traditional Buddhism does believe in rebirth, and claims that rebirth is not necessarily always as a human being, but depends upon merit and knowledge from previous lives. Among possible rebirths the human rebirth is considered by far the most fortunate and favorable, favored even over rebirth in the more pleasurable divine realms. That belief alone might seem to encourage unlimited reproduction. But when one understands *why* human birth is so highly regarded, it becomes clear that excessive human reproduction destroys the very conditions that make human rebirth so valued. Rebirth as a human being is valued because human beings, more than any other sentient beings, have the capacity for the spiritual development that eventually brings the fulfillment and perfection of enlightenment. Though all beings have the inherent innate potential for such realization, its achievement is fostered by certain causes and conditions and impeded by others. Therefore, the delight in human rebirth is due to the human capacity for cultural and spiritual creativity leading to enlightenment, a capacity more readily realized if sufficient resources are available. *Mere* birth in a human body is not the cause for rejoicing over "precious human birth," since human birth is a necessary, but not a sufficient, condition for the potential inherent in humanness to come to fruition. It is very helpful, even necessary, for that body to be in the proper environment, to have the proper nurturing, physically, emotionally, and spiritually. This is the fundamental reason why a situation of a few people well taken care of is preferable to many people struggling to survive.

The conditions that make human life desirable and worthwhile are summed up in one of the core Buddhist values — that of the Middle Way or the Middle Path. This Middle Path is also discussed as right effort, not too much, not too little, not too tight, not too loose. To make the most appropriate use of the opportunity represented by the "precious human birth," a person needs to walk the "Middle Way," and to be able to walk the Middle Way. To avoid extremes in all matters is one of the core values of Buddhism, learned by the Buddha before his enlightenment experience and a necessary pre-condition to it. First he learned that a life of luxury is meaningless, but then he had to learn that a life of poverty also leads nowhere. The Buddha concluded that, in order to become fully human, one needs to live in moderation, avoiding the extremes of too much indulgence and too much poverty or self-denial.

The guideline of the Middle Way emphasizes that too much wealth or ease can be counterproductive spiritually, since it tends to promote complacency, satisfaction, and grasping for further wealth — all attitudes that are not helpful spiritually. Thus, the concept of the Middle Way provides a cogent criticism and corrective for the rampant consumerism and over-consumption that are so linked with overpopulation. However, the concept of the Middle Way also makes the fundamental point that there are minimum material and psychological standards necessary for meaningful human life. Buddhism has never idealized poverty and suffering, or regarded them as spiritual advantages. Those in dire poverty or grave danger and distress do not have the time or inclination to be able to nurture themselves into enlightenment, into actually benefiting fully from their human rebirth, which is quite unfortunate. Buddhism celebrates moderation, but it does not celebrate poverty, because it sees poverty as unlikely to motivate people to achieve enlightenment — or even to allow them enough breathing time to do so.

Therefore, Buddhists have long recognized that before Buddhist teachings can be effective, there must first be a foundation of material well-being and psychological security. Buddhism has always recognized that one cannot practice meditation or contemplation on an empty stomach, or create an uplifted and enlightening environment in the midst of degradation, deprivation, or fear. Buddhists have known for a long time that deep spiritual or contemplative practice — which is seen as leading to the greatest joy and fulfillment possible to humans — is usually taken up after rather than before achieving a certain basic level of Middle Way comfort. Before that, people really do think that once they have enough material things, they won't suffer. One has to reach a certain basic level of satisfaction of basic desires before one begins to realize that desire and its attendant sufferings are much more subtle. At a point after basic needs have been met, when people begin to experience that desire and suffering are not so easily quelled, the basic message of Buddhism begins to make sense.

This point dovetails quite nicely with the point made by many who advocate that curbing excessive population growth is much more possible if people have an adequate standard of living. It is by now a well known generalization that one of the most effective ways to cut population growth is to improve peoples' economic lives, that people who have some material wealth can see the cogency of limiting their fertility, whereas people who are already in deeply degraded circumstances do not. Buddhist thought consistently advocates investigating cause and effect, since the entire interdependent world is governed by cause and effect. Overpopulation does not just happen; it is the result of causes, one of which seems to be too much poverty, not being able to walk the Middle Way between too much luxury and too much poverty.

However, it is equally clear that too much reproduction would overwhelm all attempts to curb poverty, because a finite earth has limited resources. Thus, we return to the need to recognize the interdependence of excessive consumption, overpopulation, and poverty. If one of these key elements is left out, as is done by religious and cultural systems that have no guidelines that limit human reproduction, then an interdependent cosmos will be severely stressed. Again, it is important to point out that all religions and most cultures do have ethical guidelines limiting consumption. Often they are not kept, but the guidelines exist. But few religions advocate limiting human fertility. Most encourage or require their members to reproduce, without providing any guidance about limits, and without any recognition that there could be too many people. Therefore, the example of religious systems that can be invoked to provide religious reasons to limit fertility are critically important.

The vision of interdependence combined with the advice to walk the Middle Way in all pursuits certainly provides such guidance. Taken together, these concepts of interdependence, of the value of human birth into appropriate circumstances, and of the Middle Way provide some sensible and obvious guidelines regarding fertility control and consumption. Regarding consumption, it is critical to see that the call for the Middle Path points in two directions. Clearly, excessive consumption violates the Middle Path. But so does too much denial. The advice to walk the Middle Path is *not* advice to pull in our belts another notch and make room for more people because reproductive rights are inviolable. It is advice to limit both fertility and consumption, which are interdependent, so as to make possible a lifestyle conducive to enlightenment for all beings. Certainly, too much fertility for the earth to sustain its offspring, and for communities to provide adequate physical and emotional nurturing, would be a contradiction of the Middle Way. It is crucial that human population not grow beyond the capacity of a family, a community, or the earth to provide a life within the Middle Way to all its members.

Simply providing sheer survival is not enough, and arguments that the earth could support many more people are not cogent because *quality* of life is far more significant than mere *quantity of bodies*. In addition to minimally adequate nutrition, sufficient space to avoid the overcrowding that leads to aggression and violence is important. Availability of the technological, cultural, and spiritual treasures that make life truly human is also basic. Therefore, globally, communally, and individually, it is important to limit fertility, so that all children actually born can have adequate material and psychological care. Not to do so would be wanton disregard for the spiritual well-being of those born into a human body. Neither the poverty nor the emotional exhaustion that result from trying to raise too many children are helpful to anyone — least of all to the children resulting from unlimited or excessive fertility. In Buddhist terms, this basic fact far outweighs private wishes for "as many children as I want" or pro-natalist societal and religious norms and pressures.

These guidelines strike me as impeccable advice on how to negotiate problems of population pressure and resource utilization, though, clearly, reasonable and kind people could agree on the guideline and disagree on its implementation. Obviously, that Middle Way does not mean the mindless consumption of the first world, but neither does it mean the mindless pronatalism of much of the rest of the world, including large segments of the first world. And it does, in my view, include some technological basics that really enhance the quality of life — flower gardens, pets, computers, good stereo systems, international travel, electricity, refrigeration, cultural diversity, and humanistic education — things that cannot be provided to unlimited populations without extreme environmental degradation. Since many things in life are more sacred and more satisfying than reproduction, it would seem ludicrous to give up such cultural treasures in order to have large populations that lack those treasures.

TRANSMITTING THE "ENLIGHTENED GENE": THE MAHAYANA BODHISATTVA PATH AND MOTIVATIONS TO REPRODUCE

Many religions, including major Asian traditions with which Buddhism has coexisted, command perpetuation of one's family lineage as a religious obligation. For a Buddhist to have any children at all is not a religious requirement. In the Buddhist vision, one does not need to reproduce biologically to fulfill the acme of one's responsibilities to the interdependent web of Mother Sentient Beings, or to realize the most exalted possibilities of human life. In fact, though the arguments, in their traditional form, elevate celibacy over the householder lifestyle, rather than childlessness over biological reproduction, a great deal of Buddhist tradition suggests that biological reproduction may interfere with helping the world or realizing one's highest potential. Since Buddhists are like other human beings, it is important and interesting to explore what inspires them to embrace religious ideas that do not require reproduction, and also to investigate Buddhist discussions of appropriate reproduction.

The command to perpetuate family lineage is quite strong in some traditions, and fuels pro-natalist behaviors. Usually this command coexists with a complex of ideas and practices, including the judgment that one is unfilial and seriously remiss in one's religious obligations if one does not have a male heir, that everyone must marry and reproduce, and that women have few or no options or vocations beyond maternity. Traditions that insist that one must reproduce biologically to fulfill one's obligations rarely, if ever, also include the corollary command not to reproduce excessively, which could bring the preferred behaviors back from an extreme into some variant of the Middle Way. In fact, often such traditions discourage any attempts to limit fertility and people who want to do so are made to feel unworthy if they limit reproduction, even if they already have produced an heir to the family lineage. Buddhism, which sees such absolute concern with perpetuating the family lineage as merely an extension of ego, of the self-centeredness that causes all suffering, has never enjoined its adherents to do so. And Buddhism has come in for major criticisms from Asian neighbors for not requiring biological reproduction of its members.

The Asian criticism of Buddhists for being selfish in not requiring reproduction strikes Buddhist sensibilities as very odd. The Buddhist reply would be twofold. First, to contribute that which is most valuable to the interdependent web of mother sentient beings is in no way dependent on biological reproduction. Furthermore, biological reproduction is often driven by very self-centered and selfish motivations. Let us examine both of these ideas closely, because I think they are both important resources in countering the self-righteous moralism of much pro-natalist thinking.

These conclusions regarding reproduction are not negative limits demanded of unwilling subjects. Rather, from the Buddhist point of view, they are rooted in deep knowledge of what people ultimately want, of what satisfies our deepest longings. Buddhists would say that the simultaneous pursuit of wisdom and compassion, to the point of enlightenment and even beyond, is what satisfies our deepest longings because it speaks to our fundamental human nature. Buddhists, contrary to much popular thinking, both Asian and Western, do not live their preferred lifestyle of moderation, meditation, and contemplation out of a self-centered motivation seeking to avoid pain. Buddhists do not reject family lineage as an ultimate value to seek individual fulfillment instead. Buddhists claim that we can never find fulfillment through reproducing or, equally important, through economic production and consumption, no matter how popular these pursuits may be, or how rigorously religious or social traditions may demand them. Instead, we need to realize our spiritual potential. Finding life's purpose in either consumption or reproduction simply strengthens what Buddhists call "ego," the deeply rooted human tendency to be self-centered in ways that ultimately cause all our suffering.

Rather, Buddhists see perpetuating family lineage as trivial compared with cultivating and perpetuating our universal human heritage and birthright — the tranquility and joy of enlightenment. Rather than seek self-perpetuation through biological reproduction, Buddhists are encouraged to arouse *bodhicitta,* the basic warmth and compassion inherent to all beings. Then, to use a traditional Buddhist metaphor, having recognized that we are pregnant with Buddha-nature *(tathagatagarbha),* we vow to develop on the *bodhisattva's* path of compassion pursuing universal liberation. Rather than regarding this choice as a personal loss, it is regarded as joyfully finding one's identity and purpose in a maze of purposeless wandering and self-perpetuation. "Today my life has become worthwhile," reads the liturgy for taking the *bodhisattva* vow, the vow that is so central to Mahayana Buddhism. Upon taking this vow, one is congratulated for having entered the family and lineage of enlightenment.

Given that *bodhicitta* is regarded as the basic inheritance and potential of all sentient beings, including all humans, rousing and nurturing *bodhicitta* in oneself and encouraging its development in sentient beings is fostering family lineage in its most profound sense, beyond the narrow boundaries of genetic family, tribe, nation, or even species. The way in which such values actually foster perpetuation of our most valuable traits is pointed out by an idiosyncratic modern translation of the term *bodhicitta.* Usually translated "awakened heartmind," my teacher sometimes translated *bodhicitta* as "enlightened gene," a translation that emphasizes *bodhicitta* both as one's inherited most basic trait and as one's heritage to the "mother sentient beings." Who could worry about transmitting family genes when one can awaken, foster, and transmit the gene of enlightenment?

By contrast, the motivations to biological reproduction are often quite narrow and unenlightened. Many religious traditions have criticized material consumption as spiritually counterproductive. Few traditions have seen that biological reproduction can be equally self-centered and ultimately unsatisfactory, or that excessive reproduction stems from the same psychological and spiritual poverty as does excessive consumption. Buddhism, however, can easily demonstrate that biological reproduction is often driven by self-centered motivations, particularly by a desire for self-perpetuation or for the expansion of one's group. And self-centered desire always results in suffering, according to the most basic teachings of Buddhism. To expose the negative underbelly of emotionality and greed motivating much reproduction, to name it accurately, and to stop perpetuating false idealizations of the drive to biological reproduction is more than overdue. Such idealization is part of the pro-natalist stance that drives many people for whom parenthood is not a viable vocation into reproduction. Regarding all reproduction as beneficial was always illusory, even in times of stable and ecologically viable population density; to continue to encourage or require everyone to reproduce their family lineage under current conditions is irresponsible.

Driven by a desire for self-perpetuation, parents often try to produce carbon copies of themselves, rather than children who are allowed to find their own unique lifeways in the world. The suffering caused by such motivation to reproduction is frequently unnoticed, and perpetuates itself from generation to generation. As someone reared by parents who wanted a child who would replace them and reproduce their values and lifestyle, which I have not done, I am quite well acquainted with the emotional violence done to children who are conceived out of their parents' attachment, to fulfill their parents' agendas. Buddhist literature is filled with such stories. Frequently, personal neediness is the emotion fueling the desire to reproduce. Certainly, the mental state of some people who want to reproduce is far from the calmness and tranquility recommended by Buddhism. I am deeply suspicious of people who need and long to reproduce biologically, of their psychological balance, and of the purity of their motives. In my experience, most of my yuppie friends think population control is a vital issue — for some other segment of the population — but that their drive to reproduce as much as they want to is unassailable. The level of hostility and defensiveness that wells up upon the suggestion that maybe they are motivated by desire for self-perpetuation, rather than by *bodhisattva* practice, convinces me that, indeed, my suspicions are correct. My suspicions are deepened even further when such people endure extreme expense and go to extreme measures to conceive their biological child, instead of adopting one of the many needy children already present in the world. Finally, many people simply are overwhelmed by religious, family, or tribal pressures to reproduce, and don't even make a personal decision regarding reproduction. Instead, they are driven by collective ego, which is not essentially different from individual ego. Like all forms of ego, collective ego also results in suffering.

Implicit in this call to recognize the negative underbelly of motivations to reproduction is the call to value and validate alternative non-reproductive lifestyles, including lesbian and gay lifestyles. One of the most powerful psychological weapons of pronatalism is intolerance of diversity in lifestyles and denigration of those who are unconventional. People who are childless should be valued as people who can contribute immensely to the perpetuation of the lineage of enlightenment, rather than ostracized and criticized. As a woman who always realized that, in order to contribute my talents to the mother sentient beings, I would probably need to remain childless, I am certainly familiar with the prejudice against women who are childless by choice. It begins with badgering from parents or in-laws about how much they want their family lineages perpetuated and how cheated they feel. It continues with continual feedback that one is self-indulgent to pursue one's vocation and will come to regret that supposed self-centeredness eventually. Then there is the loneliness, the outcasting, that results from friends who are too busy with their nuclear families to be proper friends. And, finally, most especially, there are the self-centered, self-indulgent middle-aged men whose goal in relationships, approved by many, is to have second families with young women. Patriarchal pronatalism is deeply prone to such prejudices.

Needless to say, of course, reproduction can be an appropriate agenda in Buddhist practice and much contemporary Buddhist feminist thought is exploring the parameters of reproduction as a Buddhist issue and practice. In my view, for reproduction to be a valid Buddhist choice and alternative lifestyle, it must be motivated by Buddhist principles of egolessness, detachment, compassion, and *bodhisattva* practice, not by social and religious demands, conventional norms and habits, compulsive desires, biological clocks, or an ego-based desire to perpetuate oneself. I also believe that such detached and compassionate motivations for parenthood are fully possible, though not anywhere nearly as common as is parenthood. In my own work as a Buddhist feminist theologian, I have also consistently stressed the need to limit both biological reproduction and economic production, as well as to share those burdens and responsibilities equitably between men and women so that meaningful lay Buddhist practice can occur.

The lifestyle that promotes the attainment of detachment, the Middle Way, wisdom, compassion, and the development of *bodhicitta* is encouraged and valued by Buddhists. Therefore, in many Buddhist countries, celibate monasticism is preferred over reproductive lifestyles. Though the Buddhist record is far from perfect, in many, but not all Buddhist societies, this option is also available to women, who are no more regarded as fulfilled through childbearing than men are regarded as fulfilled through impregnating. In much of the contemporary Buddhist world, lifelong monasticism is less popular and less viable, but the movement toward serious lay Buddhist meditation practice is growing dramatically, not only among Western Buddhists, but also in Asia, not only among laymen, but also among laywomen. Serious Buddhist meditation practice is difficult and time-consuming. When lay people become engaged in such practices, they must limit both their economic and their reproductive activities appropriately. Thus, both excessive consumption and overpopulation, the twin destructive agents rampant in the world, can be curbed at the same time by coming to value the human potential for enlightened wisdom and compassion and striving to realize them.

Enlightened wisdom sees the interdependence of all beings, and forgoes the fiction of private choices that don't impinge on the rest of the matrix of life. Enlightened compassion cherishes all beings, not merely one's family, tribe, nation, or species, as worthy of one's care and concern. The great mass of suffering in the world would be dramatically decreased if the detached pursuit of the Middle Way more commonly guided the choices people make regarding both consumption and reproduction. According to the Buddhist vision of *bodhicitta* as inalienable enlightened gene, both inheritance from and heritage to the mother sentient beings, that which makes life fulfilling is developing compassion and being useful — not self-perpetuation, whether through individual egotism or biological perpetuation of family, tribe, or nation. In case it is not completely clear, this compassion is not regarded as something one has a duty to develop, but as one's inheritance, the discovery of which makes life worthwhile and joyful. pronatalism as religious requirement or obligation can have nothing to do with this membership in the lineage of enlightenment. Freed of pro-natalist prejudice and valued for their contributions to the lineage of enlightenment, not their biological reproduction, human beings who have sufficient talent and detachment to become parents could do so freely, out of motivation more pure than compulsion, duty, or self-perpetuation — and those who make other, equally important contributions to the mother sentient beings would also be celebrated and valued equally.

SEXUALITY AND COMMUNICATION: A FEW COMMENTS ON VAJRAYANA BUDDHISM

A commandment to perpetuate the family lineage, combined with criticism of people who limit or forego biological reproduction, is only one of the major religious sources of pronatalism. The other is at least equally insidious. Antisexual religious rhetoric is quite common in religion, including some layers of Buddhism. Frequently, sexual activity is claimed to be somehow problematic, evil, or detrimental to one's spirituality. Such guilt, fear, or mistrust surrounding sexual activity and sexual experience, grounded in religious rhetoric or rules, leads to several equations or symbolic linkages, all of which foster the agenda of pronatalism, among other negative effects. Regarding sexual experience as forbidden fruit in no way fosters mindful and responsible sexuality.

The first of the major equations that grows out of religious fear of sexuality is the identity between sexuality and reproduction that is so strong in some religious traditions. Some religions espouse the view that the major, if not the only valid, purpose of sexuality is reproduction. Sexual activity not open to reproduction is said to produce negative moral and spiritual consequences for people who engage in them. Therefore, the potential link between sexual activity and reproduction cannot and should not be questioned or blocked. Non-reproductive sexual activities, such as masturbation, homoerotic activity, or heterosexual practices that could not result in pregnancy are discouraged or condemned. The effect of such views, however, often aids the pro-natalist agenda. Encouraging people to feel negatively about their sexuality does not seem to curb sexual activity significantly. But because people have been trained to link sexual activity with reproduction, or even forbidden to take steps to disassociate them, their sexual activity results in a high rate of fertility, which, combined with the current lower death rates, contributes greatly to excessive population growth.

Breaking the moral equation between sexual activity and reproduction is a most crucial task, since as long as non-reproductive sexuality is discouraged or condemned, high birth rates are likely to continue. That equation is easily broken by re-asking the fundamental question of the function of sexuality in human society. It seems quite clear, when we compare human patterns of sexual behavior with those of most other animal species, that the primary purpose of sexuality in human society is communication and bonding. Unlike most other species, sexual activity between humans can, and frequently does, occur when pregnancy could not result because a woman, though sexually active, is not fertile. These non-reproductive sexual experiences are actually crucial to bonding and communication between human couples and thus to human society. In addition, sexuality, properly understood and experienced, is one of the most powerful methods of human communication. Reproduction is, in fact, far less crucial and far less frequently the outcome of sexual activity. Thus, it is quite inappropriate to rule that sexual contact must be potentially open to pregnancy if sexual activity is not to involve moral and spiritual defilement. Instead, mindful sexuality, involving the use of birth control unless appropriate and responsible pregnancy is intended, should be the sexual morality encouraged by all religions.

The view that sexuality should be inextricably linked with reproduction is closely tied with several other equations that are equally pro-natalist in their implications. When sex cannot be dissociated from fertility, and when females have no other valid and valued identity or cultural role than motherhood, most women will become mothers. Therefore, a symbolic and literal identity between femaleness and motherhood is taken for granted. Not many years ago, everyone assumed that a female deity would inevitably be a "Mother-goddess." I remember well that such platitudes were commonplace when I began my graduate study in the history of religions. However, the assumption that even all divine females would be mothers proves to be incredibly naive and culture-bound. When mythology and symbolism of the divine feminine is investigated free of prevailing cultural stereotypes about the purpose of females, it is discovered that divine females are many things in addition to, sometimes instead of, mothers. They are consorts, protectors, teachers, bringers of culture, patrons of the arts, sponsors of wealth . . . . Nor in mythology is their involvement in other cultural activities dependent on their being non-sexual. In mythology, one meets many divine females who are quite active sexually, but who are not mothers or whose fertility is not stressed. Clearly, such religious symbolism and mythology of sexually active, but non-reproductive, females would not promote pronatalism. Therefore, a final caution is necessary. Great care must be taken in symbolic reconstructions of motherhood in contemporary feminist theology, lest the symbols again reinforce the stereotype that to be a woman is to be a mother, literally.

The third equation links nurturing with motherhood, an exceedingly popular stereotype in both traditional religion and popular culture and psychology. The negative and limiting effects of this equation are various, not the least of which is the way in which this equation plays into the pro-natalist agenda. If nurturing is so narrowly defined, then those who want to nurture will see no other option than to become parents. The equation between nurturing and motherhood also fosters the prejudice against non-reproducers already discussed, since it is easy to claim that they are selfish and non-nurturing. However, the most serious implication of this equation is its implicit limitation on the understanding of nurturing. If nurturing is associated so closely with motherhood, then other forms of caretaking are not recognized as nurturing and are not greatly encouraged, especially in men. The assumption that nurturing is the specialization, even the monopoly, of mothers, and therefore confined to women, is one of the most dangerous legacies of patriarchal stereotyping. Because of the strength of this stereotype, it is often assumed that feminist women, who will not submit to patriarchal stereotypes, would not be nurturing. But obviously, the feminist critique is not a critique of nurturing; it is a critique of the ways in which men are excused from nurturing and women are restricted to, and then punished for, nurturing within the prison of patriarchal gender roles. Feminism is not about restricting nurturing even further or discouraging it, but about recognizing the diversity of its forms and expecting it of all members of society. Since nurturing is valuable and essential to human survival, it is critical that our ideas about what it means to nurture extend beyond the image of physical motherhood to activities such as teaching, healing, caring for the earth, engaging in social action. . . . It is equally important that all humans, including all men, be defined as nurturers and taught nurturing skills, rather than confining this activity to physical mothers.

Because some of the grounds for fear, mistrust, and guilt surrounding sexuality are in religion, a religious, rather than merely secular or psychological alternative view of sexuality, would be significant to this discussion of religious ethics, population, consumption, and the environment. A religious evaluation of sexuality as sacred symbol and experience, helpful rather than detrimental to spiritual development, would certainly inject relevant considerations into this forum. Vajrayana Buddhism, the last form of Indian Buddhism to develop, which is today significant in Tibet and becoming more significant in the West, includes just such a resource. Needless to say, it is crucial that such discussions of Vajrayana Buddhism be disassociated from the titillating accounts of "tantric sex" that actually stem from fear and guilt about sexuality.

Symbolism and practice of sacred sexuality, such as that found in Tibetan Vajrayana Buddhism, is radically unfamiliar to many religious traditions, including those most familiar to Western audiences. In Vajrayana Buddhism, the familiar paired virtues, wisdom and compassion, are personified as female and male. Not only are they personified; they are painted and sculpted in sexual embrace, usually called the "yab-yum" icon. This icon is then used as the basis for contemplative and meditative practices, including visualizing oneself as the pair joined in embrace. After many years of working with this icon personally, I am quite intensely captivated by the liberating power and joy of this symbol. Rather than being a private and somewhat embarrassing, perhaps guilt-ridden indulgence, sexuality is openly portrayed as symbol of the most profound religious truths and as contemplative exercise for developing one's innate enlightenment.

One of the most profound implications of the yab-yum icon and its centrality is the fact that the primary human relationship used to symbolize reality is that of equal consorts, of male and female as joyous, fully cooperative partners. This contrasts sharply with the tendency to limit religious symbolism to parent-child relationships, whether of Father and Son, or of Madonna and Child, that are so common in other traditions. It also contrast strongly with the abhorrence of divine sexuality that has been such a problem in those same traditions. One cannot help but speculate that this open celebration of sexuality as a sacred and profoundly communicative and transformative experience between divine partners would significantly defuse pronatalism based on a belief that sex without the possibility of procreation is wrong.

In the realm of human relations rather than religious symbols, insofar as the two can be separated, this symbolism has led, in Vajrayana Buddhism, to the possibility of spiritual or dharmic consortship between women and men. (The question of whether non-heterosexual relationships were also possible is more difficult to answer.) Such relationships are not conventional domestic arrangements or romantic projections and longings, but are about collegiality and mutual support on the path of spiritual discipline. Sexuality seems to be an element within, but not the basis of, such relationships. Though relatively esoteric, such relationships were, and still are, recognized and valued in late north Indian Vajrayana Buddhism, as well as in Tibetan Buddhism. Western Buddhists are just beginning to discover or recover this resource, this possibility of consortship as collegial relationship between fellow seekers of the way, and as mode of understanding and communicating with the profound "otherness" of the phenomenal world. To value, valorize, and celebrate such relationships would profoundly undercut pro-natalist biases regarding the place of sexuality in human life, as well as contribute greatly to the creation of sane, caring, egalitarian models of relationship between women and men.

SUGGESTIONS FOR FURTHER READING

For Buddhism in general, *The Buddhist Religion: A Historical Introduction,* 3rd edition, by Richard H. Robinson and Willard L. Johnson (Belmont, Calif.: Wadsworth, 1982) provides an academic overview. Roger J. Corless provides an innovative introduction to the same material in *The Vision of Buddhism: The Space Under the Tree* (New York: Paragon House, 1989). Interpretations and presentations of Buddhism that have been influential for the author of this paper include Chogyam Trungpa, *Cutting Through Spiritual Materialism* (Berkeley: Shambhabla, 1973) and *The Heart of the Buddha* (Boston: Shambhala, 1991). *Shambhala: The Sacred Path of the Warrior* (Boston: Shambhala, 1988), by the same author, is also highly recommended, especially for its discussions of basic goodness, meditation, and enlightened society. For the cutting edge on thinking about engaged Buddhism and Buddhist contributions to contemporary issues, see *Turning Wheel,* the journal of the Buddhist Peace Fellowship. Parallax Press specializes in publishing books on mindfulness and social awareness. This press publishes Thich Nhat Hanh's books, many of which include discussions of Buddhism and social issues. The writings of Joanna Macy and Sulak Sivaraksa are also recommended. For a fuller discussion of sexual symbolism in Vajrayana Buddhism and its implications for contemporary issues surrounding gender, see my *Buddhism After Patriarchy: A Feminist History, Analysis, and Reconstruction of Buddhism* (Albany, N.Y.: State University of New York Press, 1993).

10

Chinese Religions, Population, and the Environment

JORDAN PAPER
LI CHUANG PAPER

Typical of ethnic religions, Chinese religion has no specific term to denominate it in the Chinese language. It is so ingrained in Chinese culture that it has no separate institution apart from the family and, until modern times, the state. It has no recognizable priesthood; the eldest of families carry out its rituals, and neighborhood or village committees oversee local temples.[1] It has no doctrines; its ideology can only be understood from an analysis of the rituals. It has no texts, save for descriptions of rituals or the productions of individual temples, as well as the canons of peripheral institutional aspects. Yet Chinese religion is not amorphous; it has a specific and recognizable pattern of rituals that can be traced from the present back to at least the late neolithic period, over four thousand years. It is found wherever one finds those who identify themselves as Chinese. It is inseparable from Chinese culture, because it defines Chinese culture. Hence, Chinese religion has nothing specific to say about population and the environment, yet in its practices and the understanding that is attendant upon and basic to these practices, there is significant relevance.

This study is written from the Western perspective of comparative religion. For the above reason and for related reasons to be covered in the discussion, no similar analyses will be found in China. The oldest known analyses of ritual and of their effects on society, carried out well over two thousand years ago in China, however, are pertinent to and influential upon the following analysis.

The study is based on familiarity with Chinese religion in Taiwan over a long period of time and several trips to China, the last in 1992. This trip included

173

not only observation but discussions with Chinese ethnologists and our own extended family in regard to the topic. Interviews were also held with recent Chinese immigrants in Toronto from diverse parts of China, including a female gynecologist.

BACKGROUND:
ETHICS, RELIGION, POPULATION, AND THE ENVIRONMENT

During the formative stage of Chinese ideology, between 2,000 and 2,500 years ago, when the texts basic to ethics and other aspects of social philosophy were being formulated, underpopulation rather than overpopulation was a concern. There seems to have been undeveloped land between the competing states of the north China plain, and political theorists understood population expansion as a good for strengthening the power of a state. For example, Mengzi, in enumerating the advantages of a state that governed with the people's welfare in mind, pointed out to a king that if he so ruled, "then all the people of the Empire will be only too pleased to come and settle in your state."[2] In essence, the formulation of ethics in China is not directly relevant to the modern problem of overpopulation.

Although overpopulation was not of concern at that time, there was already an awareness of the advantages of conservation with regard to human exploitation of the environment. We also find in the *Mengzi* explicit statements that indicate awareness of ecology not unlike contemporary views:

> If you [the king] do not interfere with the busy seasons in the fields, then there will be more grain than the people can eat; if you do not allow nets with too fine a mesh to be used in large ponds, then there will be more fish and turtles than they can eat; if hatchets and axes are permitted in the forests on the hills only in the proper season, then there will be more timber than they can use. . . . This is the first step along the Kingly way.[3]

The concern with overexploitation of the environment is found within the context of class exploitation, of the elite consuming far more than necessary for a comfortable life, forcing the peasants to overproduce to their own detriment:

> There is fat meat in your [the king's] kitchen and there are well-fed horses in your stables, yet the people look hungry and in the outskirts of cities men [people] drop dead from starvation. This is to show animals the way to devour men. Even the devouring of animals by animals is repugnant to men. If, then, one who is a father and mother

to the people cannot, in ruling over them, avoid showing animals the way to devour men, wherein is he father and mother to the people?[4]

Unnecessary consumption remained a concern of officials criticizing governmental policies. In a text written more than a half millennium after the preceding, in the third century, similar criticisms abound:

> The people of the upper classes do not restrain the desires of their eyes and ears. They have been completely responsible for the development of the arts of the people, thereby exhausting the transformations [the manufacture of goods from raw and secondary sources] of the Empire. . . . Those who give reign to their passions are endless in their desires; those who employ their strength are exhausted.[5]

Contemporary with the *Mengzi,* the early strata of the *Zhuangzi* argued for a more radical solution to overconsumption and detrimental resource exploitation, a return to an egalitarian society where humans lived comfortably in harmony with nature because there was no necessity for surplus productivity to support non-producing classes. Life would be simple to the point that people of one hamlet would never bother to travel even to another village so close that the barking of their dogs could be heard. There would be no government nor any need of it. Living a life within nature, there would be no theft, murder, or raids, because nothing would be valued over anything else. Based on the mystic experience,[6] the concept was impractical, yet remains a romantic ideal to the present.

The ideal's most pervasive image is found in the introduction to a poem, popular to this day, by a fourth century poet, Tao Qian, "The Peach Blossom Spring." It describes a village in a hidden valley so cut off from the world that the villagers were unaware of the political developments of the preceding half millennium. There a steady-state population lived a simple life that not only provided all their needs from their immediate environment, but sufficient luxury to allow a banquet of chicken and wine when a stranger arrived. Although reality was far from this romantic notion, it still survives and can be found, for example, in the poetry of Mao Zedong.[7] ("The Peach Blossom Spring" is also the basis of a once popular Western novel, several Hollywood films, and the name Franklin D. Roosevelt gave the U.S. presidential retreat.)

The earliest Chinese metaphysical statements extant are also to be found in the *Zhuangzi.* As in virtually all cultures other than the monotheistic ones, humans are understood to be created from nature. In Chinese culture, like all creatures, humans are understood to receive their form from the conjunction of male Sky and female Earth and their life-force from the interaction of natural female and male energies, *yin* and *yang.* Metaphorically, humans occupy an intermediary space between sky and earth. Chinese metaphysics understands creation to be both spontaneous and continuous. Being arises from nothingness when discrimination creates first a unitary somethingness that is further discriminated into the many components of reality. In essence, Chinese philosophical understanding does not separate a creator from the created, as in the monotheistic cultures. The natural world, including humans, is the reality beyond the ultimate nothingness; there is no other world than this one. Theoretically, Chinese culture should be more sensitive to environmental concerns than those cultures whose religious understanding focuses on a world other than this one.

As with early Chinese ethics and political philosophy, there was no concern in Chinese religion with overpopulation, as the problem did not exist until relatively recently. Chinese religion, much older in origin than the texts discussed above, has a single moral imperative, to continue the patrilineal family line. The religion focuses on the patrilineal family rather than the individual to the degree that it has been called "familism." Family is a much broader concept than the English language term implies. For family includes the living, the dead, and the future unborn; it includes the members of an extended family, as well as known branches comprising a clan. Ruling clans traced their origins to spirit-beings; the clan foundation myths functioned as creation myths encapsulated in the Bible and *Qur'an* do in Western religions.

The rituals link the living members of the family to the dead through the offering and sharing of banquets.[8] The living nourish and care for the dead, and the dead protect as well as foster the prosperity of the living. In popular culture, should the living family be unable to feed the family dead, from beneficent spirits they are liable to become malevolent hungry and lonely ghosts. The individual strives for the family's prosperity, and if any glory is attained, it reflects on the family's dead. In turn, the family cares for the individual not only upon death but so long as the family continues. Without family, life for the individual has no meaning. Hence, if a male, especially an eldest son, has no son to continue the family, his own death as well as the death of his wife is truly terminal; more important, he has terminated the nexus of existence, the timeless family. In the past, if a woman had no son and daughter-in-law, she had no one to care for her in her declining years and upon and following death.

Chinese ideology maintains a focus on political philosophy, developing a synthesis approximately two thousand years ago that combined three major as well as lesser divergent viewpoints: one oriented toward gaining and keeping power; one oriented toward minimalist government exemplified in the *Zhuangzi;* and one oriented toward understanding the purpose of government to be the welfare of the governed, as in the *Mengzi.* This later orientation is that of *rujia,* mistakenly translated as Confucianism, and this term was used for the synthesis as well. Ruist philosophy expanded the notion of family to the state, both to secure the loyalty of clansmen who were government officials to the state and out of a sense of paternalism. The family rituals of the emperor and empress, the "father and mother of the people," were the primary state rituals as well. This in turn reinforced familism, and it expanded from the aristocratic clans to the population as a whole.

With the formation of the first successful Chinese empire, there developed an understanding of a common culture, one based on the religion of family. All rituals, both year-cycle and life-cycle changed to focus on food if they did not already do so, particularly a family meal that included the deceased of the family. As the Chinese empire spread and developed the longest continuing governmental system in human experience, lasting until 1911, one thread held together this huge country with diverse cultural backgrounds, terrain, and spoken languages, and created a people (in the anthropological sense): a common religion.

Familism synthesized with local practices and cosmogonic concepts. Family members also worship at temples devoted to local deities, offering uncooked food to be brought home, cooked and re-offered at the family altar, and some travel to pilgrimage centers dedicated to major spirits. The purpose of the worship is for the prosperity of the family and, particularly at pilgrimage centers, for the family to have sons. It is in this regard that religious practices concerning the environment are found.

Fengshui (lit.: wind & water) is the practice of situating buildings and graves in a harmonious relationship with its immediate natural environment. All aspects of the earth are spiritually alive; an appropriate correlation between human-made structures and these natural energies is essential for well-being. The siting of a grave, in particular, will have major consequences, good or bad, on the fortunes of the relevant family.

The understanding of Earth as a numinous being paired with Sky is ubiquitous in Chinese religious understanding and found in several modes. At the imperial level to the early part of this century, only the ultimate human powers, the Emperor and Empress, could sacrifice to the ultimate numinous powers, *Tiandi* (Sky and Earth). The Emperor also sacrificed at the altar to Soil and Grain, which was on a par with his clan temple. On the more mundane level, farming families had images of Grandmother and Grandfather Soil on their family altars and in small shrines in the fields to whom offerings were made. In other words, the earth was understood in numerous ways to be both alive and sacred. From the imperial family to farming families, rituals were performed to acknowledge human appreciation to Earth and other natural spirits for their sustenance and survival.

As religions from other cultures came into contact with Chinese culture, the interrelationship, in large part, was determined by the effects on the family.

Buddhism, because of its focus on monasticism and other individualistic practices, was viewed by traditionalists as un-Chinese. Buddhism rapidly spread
among the Chinese after the collapse of the first major empire and the domination
of the north by a foreign regime (as it also began to do in the early twentieth century, following the collapse of the traditional governmental structure). When,
after a half-millennium of cultural domination and institutional development, the
re-unified state removed Buddhism's financial underpinnings, its importance in
China rapidly waned. What predominantly remained of Chinese Buddhism *(fo-
jiao)* were ideology and rituals directed towards enhancing the "life" and lifestyle
of the families' dead. Monasteries remained a refuge for orphans and other
poverty-stricken children, females without family, and a place for retirement for
the elite, when other circumstances were not available. Monks and nuns support
themselves by saying perpetual masses for the family dead in the monasteries
and reciting sutras in the home as part of the extended mortuary rituals.

Institutional Daoism *(daojiao)*, in part influenced by Buddhism, also sur-
vived by offering mortuary services for the families and by absorbing the rituals for communicating with the family dead. This set of religious institutions
is not to be confused with ideological Daoism *(daojia)*, which offered an orientation towards individualism for the elite for re-creation, within the context
of intense involvement with the affairs of family, clan and state (always discussed
in family terms and functioning with family rituals). Recently, however, the
term "Daoism" has been used by some Western scholars oriented towards Daoism as an umbrella term for all aspects of indigenous Chinese religion, to the
delight of the Daoist clergy.

Islam, although the religion of hundreds of millions within China as a political entity, effects a relatively small number of Han Chinese (ethnically Chinese). Christianity appealed to Chinese from the mid-nineteenth to mid-twentieth centuries, when the "unequal" treaties offered many advantages to those who
converted, but those who did so were often motivated by the thought of the financial, legal, and educational (Western colleges were run by Christian missionary
organizations) benefits that would accrue to the family. Christianity in and of itself, with its emphasis on individual salvation, could only appeal to those who
had already become disaffiliated with Chinese culture for any number of reasons.

POPULATION AND CONTROL

From two thousand years ago until approximately three and a half centuries
ago, the population remained relatively stable, from somewhat under one hundred to one hundred and fifty million persons. Then, as in many other places in
the world, the population began to increase geometrically. Much of this increase was due to the crops Europeans discovered being grown by Native Amer-

icans. The new foods brought by the Spanish from the Americas had major effects within a century of their introduction. While the adoption of hot peppers in the west and tomatoes in the south of China had notable effects on cuisine, the replacement of the traditional millet with maize in the north and the ability to raise sweet potatoes and peanuts on marginal arable lands in the south, had the same effects as white potatoes in northern Europe: a population explosion.

At the same time, the conquest of China by a foreign, the Manchu, regime, incorporating China into an empire which included China's bordering countries and peoples, virtually ended the constant border wars of the past regime. A period of political stability and peace was engendered that also facilitated an increase of population. This period lasted until a century and a half ago, when the combination of internal political decay, in part probably due to a greatly increased population, and European and American expansionism led to wars to force opium and Christianity on China. The loss of these wars by the now ineffectual Chinese government, and the resultant highly disadvantageous treaties, engendered revolts and further government weakness.

After a century of increasing internal chaos and foreign domination, fragmentation with major internecine strife, conquest by Japan immediately followed by a major civil war, China reunified under the present government. The new stability, together with policies that led to the end of famines and universal, if minimal, health care, along with changes in marriage laws that removed many of the negative aspects of marriage for females, again led to a geometric growth of the population. Between the censuses of 1952 and 1982, the population had doubled. China's present population of well over a billion people, approximately one quarter of the world's population, creates enormous problems — problems of which the government and the people are well aware.

The Chinese realized that they could not improve their standard of living, their international security in the context of rapid technological development, as well as their place in the highly competitive global economy, unless they could not only bring their population under control, but actually reduce it. Those outside of China and aware of the deterioration of the environment realized that if the population of China achieved the standard of living of North America and western Europe, the resultant massive degradation of the environment, particularly given China's present inability and disinclination to control pollution, would lead to the demise of humanity.

In China, the growth of the population was not only understood as a policy problem but also in human terms. The most common popular statement when confronted with massive crowding, etc., is *"ren tai duo"* (too many people). Hence, the government's solution to the problem has met with popular support, except as it impinges on individual families; that is, the support is perhaps more theoretical than practical.

The census of 1982 indicated a bulging population of young people. The number of women of childbearing age, given that families were having multiple children, could lead to a doubling of the population every generation. By the late 1970s, the government was encouraging limitations in the size of families. In 1980, Hua Guofeng gave a speech to the National People's Congress which articulated the "one-child policy." To bring the population under control in a generation or two, and after that to begin to reduce it, the government developed a unique, far-reaching response: each family would be allowed only a single child. Late marriages were encouraged. The timing of the single child was under the control of factories and/or communes, who were required to adhere to quotas. Those couples that had more than one child would lose many of their privileges. More effective, in urban areas, neighborhood committees intervened to prevent couples from having more than a single child. The policy is not applied to "minority" peoples (that is, non-Han Chinese), and the policy was modified in 1984 for farming couples, which are allowed two children under certain circumstances. As with any public policy in a vast country with a huge population there have been abuses and non-compliance of many sorts, but overall the policy is supported as undesirable but necessary.

Population Control and Religion

A recent study (1993) of Chinese birthing practices found the following attitude still present:

> Among the Han in Beijing, people have the expression, *"You ren bi you qian geng you xiwang* [Better than money is children (lit.: people) for a hopeful outlook]." This wish refers to a family's future. To have children means one is not poor; to have money in and of itself is not considered *fu* [prosperity, happiness, good fortune]. If a person has money but lacks children, he or she has no protection in the future. Therefore, it is not difficult to understand why people living in poverty wish to have children.[9]

A similar common expression is *"Duo zi duo fu* (The more the children, the more the prosperity)." *Fu* is one of three major goals of prayers to non-family spirits for the family, along with *lu* (favorable occupational position, emoluments) and *shou* (longevity). On the temporal level, it is necessary to have children to be cared for in old age, reflected in the expression, *"Yang zi ban lao* (Rear children to care for one in old age)." On the spiritual level, without children to nourish one's souls (China being a multiple souls culture) following death, death means termination or a hungry, miserable continuation.

There can be no greater contention than between the one-child policy and traditional Chinese religion, particularly if the single child is female. For without a son, not only would a person cease upon death, but, unless there is a brother with a son, so would a male's parents, grandparents, ad infinitum. In Chinese culture, there can be no greater moral crime than familicide.

Abuses of the policy are publicized in Chinese newspapers. For example, as this essay is being written, one can read of an official who has eleven children; he used his privileged position to manipulate the system. The fact that this crime, and it is a serious legal crime, is published indicates that it is unusual and dealt with when discovered. On the whole, the policy seems to be adhered to, particularly in urban areas, although the rural partial exemption, as well as other specific exemptions, and the abuses have resulted in a population that is still increasing, albeit significantly more slowly than before (in the late 1980s, almost half the births were of second and third children).

The policy could not have continued for this length of time and be moderately successful, were the people not, to a large degree, supporting it.[10] China is not the highly centralized totalitarian state depicted in the Western press. Regional governments can and do ignore central directives, and the police, usually unarmed, can only enforce laws which are supported by the population, for to do otherwise can lead to being beaten by the populace. Change and compliance take place primarily through education and moral suasion. However, once the populace is in general agreement with regard to a policy, a combination of worker incentives and neighborhood committees ensures individual compliance. Chinese culture, different from modern Western culture, emphasizes social good over that of the individual. Indeed, the Western concept of the individual is not to be found in Chinese culture, for the underlying religions, Christianity and Chinese religion, widely differ in this regard.

A number of factors are involved in limiting or attempting to limit the conflict between traditional religious values and the one-child policy: urbanization and modernity, social welfare, the attempts by the Chinese Communist Party (CCP) to eradicate traditional religion, and the change in gender values and attitudes.

Urbanization and Modernity

As the population continues to shift toward urban residency, the limitation in housing, both in number and size, does not encourage large families. Furthermore, without grandparents in the same residence to look after small children, often the case in urban areas, it is virtually impossible to care for more than one child. It has long been common for both genders of a marital couple to work, and factory day care centers are not available for families with a second child.

As in Europe and North America, modernity also tends to limit the number of children. The costs of raising a child to a modern standard of living plus the costs of extended education are incentives to have but a single child. In this regard, the recent shift in the economy from socialism to privatized industry has led to the fear of losing one's job, already a reality for millions in the rapidly changing economic system. This fear of being unable to support children mitigates the desire to have more than one child.

Moreover, a change is taking place in parent-child relationships due to the "one-child" policy. The concentration of parental love on a single child has led to the frequently discussed "spoiled-child" syndrome. Parental authority has eroded, and parental expectations in regard to behavior may be ignored. Support by grown children is no longer certain. Rather than children caring for older parents, grown children often want to live with retired parents, to share their pensions, and have the parents take care of the grandchildren and do all of the housework. Hence, one now can hear expressed that children are "too much trouble."

In rural areas, among farming families, none of these factors apply. Moreover, having several children who can assist in the farming is another incentive toward large families. The government, by allowing two children in farming families, clearly acknowledges the difficulty of enforcing the policy in rural areas. The exemption may also exist to encourage people to remain on farms rather than move to the enormously overcrowded cities, where unemployment is becoming endemic.

Social Welfare

From the time the CCP came to power until recently, old age pensions mitigated the need for several children to support a couple in old age. Retirement tends to be early: sixty for males and fifty-five for females. Relatively generous pensions from agricultural or industrial communes allowed continuation of the same lifestyle as before retirement. This situation assisted in promoting the one-child policy.

The privatization of the economy has currently created confusion in this regard. Will private companies continue pension practices? What happens to pensions if companies go bankrupt? Who will support farmers in their old age with the dissolution of communes? As there is no government social security system per se, one assumes that these questions, as well as others, will be addressed in the near future if the population control policy is to continue.

The CCP and Religion

The major difficulty in maintaining the one-child policy is that it conflicts with the primary ethic of normative Chinese religion, the very basis of Chinese culture. For a number of reasons, the CCP has attempted to eliminate this aspect of Chinese culture and thus radically change Chinese culture per se.

Although the Chinese constitution explicitly guarantees freedom of religion, religion is understood as essentially a foreign phenomenon. The contemporary term, adopted from a Japanese term (itself taken from an obscure Chinese Buddhist text) as a translation for "religion," *zongjiao,* is applied only to Buddhism, Daoism, Confucianism, Islam, and Christianity. (Daoism here refers to institutional Daoism, and Confucianism now refers to a Western concept that has no actual Chinese referent, although there were temples to Confucius and related sages in major cities.) All of these traditions are maintained under centralized government control to appeal to and serve overseas Chinese, Japanese, and other foreigners, both to enhance foreign relations and as a source for foreign exchange. For example, there are Buddhist "nuns" in tourist-oriented temples who have families and only don the garb when they daily go off to work in the "monasteries" for their government salaries.

Chinese religion in and of itself, that is, the vast majority of religious practices, is termed *mixin* (superstition), and sporadically there have been policies to eradicate it. The attitude of the government is the result of a number of converging factors: the Marxist-Leninist-Stalinist doctrine of atheism, based on a realistic evaluation of the role of the Church of England and the Russian Orthodox Church in maintaining the status quo of worker oppression and serfdom of a century or more ago; the assumption that religion, from the model of pre-modern Christianity, is incompatible with science; and the attitude of the traditional Chinese educated elite, that the practices of the non-elite were *ipso facto* superstition, notwithstanding that their religious practices were in the main identical.

Behind all of this lay the realization that the focus of Chinese religion on family was inimical to a focus on society as a whole. A similar problem was faced by the first successful Chinese empire, the Han, when they backed away from the absolute centralism that led to the collapse of the first, short-lived Chinese empire, the Qin, twenty-two hundred years ago. The problem of the Han was how to obtain the loyalty of the clan-based aristocracy. They did so by placing the central government, symbolized in the emperor, at the apex of a hierarchy based on filial piety; that is, they extended the notion of family to the state. The ideological system, to a large extent, worked as long as there was political stability. In periods of political chaos, it was each family for itself.

The CCP gained control of China in such a period. The warlords and the opposing central government, the Guomindang under Chiang Kaishek married to the powerful Soong family, were all regimes oriented to benefiting one or a few families (the Guomindang slowly changed in this regard after its defeat and *de facto* exile to Taiwan). On the whole, people with power strove to advance their families, not society.

The CCP sought to create a new ethic, to shift loyalty from the family to the people as a whole. While the goal was laudable, the effect was to undercut the very basis of Chinese culture and society. The most radical of these attempts was the Cultural Revolution, in which the goal evolved to be the eradication of all traditions of the past. Its collapse left a generation with no sense of identity, no sense of social responsibility, and no norms for interpersonal behavior. Since that time, for the last dozen years, there has been a gradual weakening of government opposition to traditional practices, which have been slowly allowed to gain visibility, in part to deal with the social problems engendered by the Cultural Revolution.

In a period of economic expansion, technological development, and privatization of the economy with enhanced standards of living for many but increasing economic differentials between families, one might expect the decline of traditional Chinese religion. Instead, there is a resurgence of traditional religious practices. Chinese religion is not based on ideology, but on rituals to enhance reciprocity between the powers that affect life and the living. As long as the concept of family remains the basis of Chinese life and culture, the rituals of family can be expected to continue. This resurgence is far more evident in Taiwan, but there are increasing signs of this resurgence on the Chinese mainland as well.

Those Chinese males who attained maturity prior to the Cultural Revolution usually feel it necessary to continue to have children until there is a son. (This statement should not be understood to imply that Chinese males do not also esteem daughters.) Should the first child not be a male, there is a conflict between the moral imperative of Chinese religion and the one-child policy. Some will be satisfied with a female child if they are not the oldest son, considering the religious duty to fall on their oldest brother. But the very situation of having older brothers predates population control. The conflict between values may lead to attempts by their wives to skirt the law.

Those of the younger generation affected by the Cultural Revolution, particularly if they are urban, may not feel part of Chinese tradition, or any tradition for that matter. For these people, lack of a male child is not a problem. In 1989, there were indications that some of the rootless generation sought to adopt American culture, of which they actually knew virtually nothing. But the collapse of the Soviet Union, and the resultant near-anarchy, has also illustrated to many Chinese the danger of the lack of a unifying culture.

In the last few years, Chinese religion has become both visible and ubiquitous, and its viability is demonstrated by contemporary developments. For example, Mao Zedong, typical of deceased culture heroes, has become a deity, one of success. Given the changes in economic policy, he is the new God of Wealth.[11] Nevertheless, the most popularly worshiped deities continue to be female, and female deities tend to be, at least in part, fertility deities. Many Chinese women are praying for sons to carry on the patrilineal family line.

Changes in Gender Values and Attitudes

Although traditional Chinese culture was patrilineal, patrilocal, and patriarchal, these descriptive terms should be understood as relative rather than absolute. The Western understanding of Chinese culture is based, in the main, on the reports of sixteenth- and seventeenth-century Catholic monks and nineteenth-century Protestant missionaries. All were androcentric; many were misogynist. The portrayal of China as totally patriarchal, particularly with regard to religion, fit their preferences but was not accurately descriptive of Chinese culture.[12]

Chinese culture has a strong tendency towards complementary dualities, as is well known with regard to ideology; e.g., the yin-yang concept. This tendency imbues religious practices and understanding. In theory, rituals to family spirits, the dead of the family and clan, are carried out by a married couple. It was the emperor and empress together who performed the primary state rituals, sacrifices to the dead of the imperial clan. On the altars of traditional homes, the central room, or single room in a one-room dwelling, being the family temple, are found a tablet bearing the names of the most recently deceased. Often these are dual, one directed toward the deceased parents or grandparents, if the parents are still alive, of the husband and one toward those of the wife.

This duality also affects space and gender. The female space is the interior of the home, which she dominates; the exterior of the home is the male's realm. Hence, most often all of the rituals for the sacrifices in the homes are carried out by women, while males perform the sacrifices in the clan temples. Footbinding physically reinforced these expectations, literally hobbling the woman to the home.

That the clans are patrilineal, the clan temples male domains, and clan spirits predominantly male, is partially balanced by the fact that the most important deities, outside of the family dead, are female: Guanyin, Mazu, Bixia Yuanjun, Nüwa, and Xiwangmu are but some of the major female deities. There was not a male high god as depicted in Western world religion textbooks, because Tian is but part of the binomial pair: Tiandi (Sky-Earth). Moreover, these particular cosmological forces do not affect normative religion to any degree, as their worship was an imperial prerogative; for any one else to worship the pair was treason.

Clan patrilineality, however, did increasingly lessen the value of women over the last three millennia. That women were not to leave the home, except for peasants, servants, and laborers, meant that the only access women had to power was through the control of the family finances. The revolution that overthrew the last imperial government also slowly overthrew many of these practices and attitudes. Footbinding and the confinement of women to the home ended in the first third of this century. Women theoretically have equality and are taking on roles held exclusively by men in the past, although more slowly than in the West. Nonetheless, the majority of pilgrims to the major shrines of the important pan-Chinese deities (Bixia Yuanjun, Guanyin, Nüwa, etc.) are female;[13] there they pray to have sons to continue the patrilineal family succession.

In China today there are recent laws that require the direction of institutions of varying sorts to be overseen by both a female and a male. A new college is being set up specifically to train women to oversee the implementation of gender equality policies. What effect will all of this have on religion and population control?

As indicated above, Chinese family religion, albeit patrilineal, incorporates the wife into the patrilocal home and sacrifices. In traditional culture, it is she who daily offers incense to the spirits at the family altars in her husband's home (family spirits, local and major deities, stove deity, soil and grain or other occupational deities), and she will be incorporated into the family lineage of her sons. She also, depending on local variations, worships her natal lineage. For example, in the Guangzhou area, a married woman sacrifices at her husband's family tomb on the first week of the Qingming festival, and he, with her, sacrifices at her family tomb on the second week. In Fujian Province, at least in some parts, if women live in the vicinity of their natal home, they may return there to sacrifice to their natal family spirits.

In this century, there is evidence of even more far-reaching changes. In northern China, we have encountered an extended family that has maintained a matrilineal sacrificial tradition for three generations. Although one cannot generalize from a single example, discussions with the husbands of these women indicated that this development was not unique. They understood a recent development of potential as well as actual matrilineal sacrificial rituals to be due to two factors: the changing status of women and the single-child policy.[14]

SUMMARY AND CONCLUSIONS: POPULATION AND THE ENVIRONMENT

More than any other economically developing country, China has not only understood the dire consequences of an expanding population, but has developed an effective program, the one-child policy, designed to control the expansion of the population and ultimately reduce it to a level commensurate with its resources. This policy, however, conflicts with Chinese religion's ultimate moral imperative, the continuation of the patrilineal family line. A number of factors impinge on the degree of this confrontation.

Increasing modernization and urbanization, in conjunction with the attempts of the CCP to terminate Chinese religion *per se,* as well as to diminish the significance of the family, have moderated the clash of values. Nevertheless, economic and cultural liberalization is resulting in a resurgence of Chinese religion, which went underground but never disappeared. As evident in Taiwan, Hong Kong, and Singapore, modernization is not inimical to Chinese religion; indeed, an increased standard of living enhances its practice.

One factor in particular might ameliorate the situation. If gender equality continues to remain a goal and continues to become a reality, then Chinese religion may undergo an organic evolution. Should the patrilineal clan base of Chinese religion shift to a gender-neutral extended family concept, as is possibly starting to happen, then the single-child policy will not threaten the fundamental religious value and need. The concept of family will remain basic to the sense of power and reality, but it will come to be understood from the standpoint of bilateral descent. Such a concept will mean that the perception of family lineage will be considerably shortened, but that is already taking place.

The concept of patrilineal Chinese religion possibly stems, as in other parts of the world, from the development of agriculture combined with the shift from an egalitarian society. As human habitation becomes permanent, with the dead buried on the land that nourishes the family with produce, a linkage is developed between ancestors, life, and continuity. Living humans feed ancestors, who in turn see that the living are fed. The further development of a class society, based on surplus agricultural produce supporting a hereditary, professional military elite, presumably led to the patrilineal clans and an increasing patriarchal social order.

In modern times, thousands of years after the above hypothetical development, the expanding movement away from a land base, the diffusion of children to jobs distantly located, the erosion of hereditary class distinctions, the reduced size of urban dwellings, the growth of employment in industry and commerce, all work toward a lineage of several generations rather than the theoretical long lineages of the past, which the peasants and laborers never possessed in any case. It seems that Chinese religion will inevitably shift to a concept of family that will not necessitate a single-gender base. Hence, lineage could be maintained by either gender, without substantially altering the practices and ideology of Chinese religion.

Should this shift not take place, not only is there a major conflict between religious values and population control, but a serious gender imbalance will become apparent in Chinese demographics. Already in those cities with modern prenatal testing facilities, gender is being determined prior to birth, with the intention of terminating female fetuses. This is a contemporary phenomenon not unique to China, but the primary religious compulsion to have a male child undoubtedly exacerbates the problem there. If the majority of single children are to be male, China's population may well be reduced, but to the detriment of females and the gender balance, and the resultant creation of social chaos. One hopes that the manifold destructive consequences of prenatal gender testing will come to the attention of those influential on Chinese cultural practices.

Another factor with regard to religion working against the single-child policy, although far less important, is the continuing attempt by Christians to replace Chinese religion with their own. Beginning with the Opium Wars of the nineteenth century, Christian missionaries insisted on their right to convert Chinese not only to becoming Christians but to becoming non-Chinese (those who converted to Christianity no longer being subject to Chinese jurisprudence, according to the "Unequal Treaties"). This paralleled the views of Western merchants, who understood China to be their exclusive, God-given commercial domain.

In spite of revolution, unification, and growing strength in China, those Western countries that had been most involved in economic development and missionary activity in China, particularly the United States, seem never to have changed this attitude. For example, the United States, under the influence of fundamentalist Protestants and conservative Catholics, insists that limiting the size of families violates human rights. The United States government, even under a new administration, continues to threaten economic sanctions to enforce this Christian value, as well as others, on the Chinese people. So far, these threats have but served to strengthen the Chinese resolve to maintain their independence, to the benefit of the West. For should the Chinese population continue to grow geometrically, as it did for the first three decades following unification, from the degradation of the global environment, and the international turmoil[15] that massive Chinese overpopulation would cause, the West would ultimately suffer as much as China. It is important to note that forecasts by demographers for population expansion, dire as they are, assume that Chinese population policies will remain in place.[16] Should this situation change, explosive population growth in another quarter of the population would lead to immediate catastrophe. A Senior Research Fellow at the International Institute for Global Peace in Tokyo has written,

> Those who have criticized the one-child policy from the standpoint of human rights should not forget that they have been on the receiving end of its benefits. . . . China's aggressive policies to limit population growth and restrict departures from the country should be praised rather than censured.[17]

While the major factor detrimental to the Chinese environment has been the massive expansion of the population (one thousand percent over the last three and a half centuries), other factors are also of consequence. Although periodic internal disorder combined with foreign invasions have led over time to major deforestation and resultant soil erosion, the Chinese, on the whole, have maintained a successful agrarian economy on land farmed for many thousands of years, since the inception of horticulture among humans. Chinese were early aware of the importance of nitrogen-fixing plants, of the use of manure, both human and animal, and other positive agricultural practices. An understanding of the soil and the earth as spiritual entities at all levels of society undoubtedly enhanced environmentally benign farming strategies.

Technologically in advance of the West until the mid-eighteenth century, Chinese industry also tended towards practices less destructive of the environment; for example, the Chinese early used coal rather than charcoal for smelting ores. However, the influence of and economic competition with the West has reversed this situation. After conquering China twice in the mid-nineteenth century, consequent on the wars to force opium on the Chinese people, Western powers began to heavily industrialize China. Repeated treaties forcing reparations on the Chinese led to Western and later Japanese control over industry in China, with no concern for its impact on the environment or the people.

Following the consolidation and independence of China in the mid-twentieth century, war with the United States to prevent an invasion via Korea, a continuing economic blockade of China by the United States until the mid-1970s, and military tension with the former Soviet Union from the mid-1960s until its recent dissolution, led to industrialization under emergency conditions, with the resultant unconcern for the environment. The present massive industrialization is taking place under factors highly inimical to the environment.

First, a socialist economic orientation has been replaced with a free-market ideology; any remnant of centralized control is on the verge of collapse. Second, much of the industrial growth is taking place in partnership with foreign firms which have no reason to have any concern over the long-term Chinese situation. Third, traditional Chinese values and attitudes toward nature are not applied to industrial planning: in China, it is often assumed that to be scientific requires the adoption of nineteenth-century Western Christian attitudes towards nature, and the Cultural Revolution left an ideological vacuum that is now being replaced by modern capitalist notions of immediate profit, with no concern for the environment, and increasing wealth for its own sake.

Together, these factors are leading to environmental degradation on an enormous scale. We can but hope that China will take the same initiative toward environmental problems that they have taken toward controlling the population.[18]

NOTES

1. There are recent trends toward institutionalization of peripheral aspects of Chinese religion. In Taiwan, after ineffectual attempts at suppression of local religious practices for several decades, by a government under the sway of a family nominally oriented toward the U.S. Methodist church, following the end of martial law, local temple mediums, unpaid or dependant upon gratuities, organized into an association to gain respectability. In mainland China, publicly operating temples, slowly being opened over the last decade, are served by salaried professional priests, either Buddhist or Daoist, who are part of government-controlled, centralized church organizations.

2. IIA5. D. C. Lau, translator, *Mencius* (New York.: Penguin Books, 1970): 82.

3. IA3. Ibid., 51.

4. IA3. Ibid., 52.

5. Jordan D. Paper, translator, *The* Fu-tzu: *A Post-Han Confucian Text* (Leiden: E. J. Brill): 63–64.

6. Jordan Paper, "From Shamanism to Mysticism in the *Chuang-tzu,*" *Scottish Journal of Religious Studies* 3 (1982):27–45.

7. Jordan Paper, "Riding on a White Cloud:Aesthetics as Religion in China," *Religion* 15 (1985):3–27.

8. For description and analysis, see Jordan Paper, "The Ritual Core of Chinese Religion," *Religious Studies and Theology* 7/2&3 (1987): 19–35.

9. Wang Xiaoli, personal communication (November 1992), translated from the Chinese original.

10. For those unfamiliar with Western history, it is to be noted that the concept that the purpose of government is to benefit the people governed, was introduced by Jesuit missionaries in China to Europe from their understanding of Chinese political philosophy. Well over two thousand years ago, Mengzi said:

> The people of are of supreme importance; the altars to the gods of earth and grain come next; last comes the ruler. That is why he who gains the confidence of the multitudinous people will be Emperor. . . . When a feudal lord endangers the altars to the gods of earth and grain he should be replaced. When the sacrificial animals are sleek, the offerings are clean and the sacrifices are observed at due times, and yet the floods and droughts come, the altars should be replaced. (VIIB14; Lau: 198)

11. See Jordan Paper, "Further Notes on Contemporary Chinese Religion — 1992," *Journal of Chinese Religions* 20 (1992): 215–20/216–17.

12. See Jordan Paper, "The Persistence of Female Spirits in Patriarchal China," *Journal of Feminist Studies in Religion* 6 (1990): 25–40.

13. Over the last two millennia, there has been a continuing unsuccessful patriarchalization of these major deities, as can be evidenced at pilgrimage centers. For example, the nominal deity at Mount Tai is the God of Mount Tai, but most worship is directed toward Bixia Yuanjun, supposedly his daughter but functionally the actual deity of the mountain (see J. Paper, "The Persistence . . ."). At the Taihe Mausoleum in eastern

Honan of Fuxi, of the cosmic creative pair Fuxi and Nüwa, the worship is primarily directed toward Nüwa (Yang Lihui, personal communication, 1993). Of course, the feminization of Guanyin is indicative of the influence of Chinese culture on Buddhism, but she has gained a pan-Chinese recognition beyond and outside of Buddhism itself. All three share a common function as fertility goddesses to whom women pray for male progeny.

14. See Jordan Paper and Li Chuang Paper, "Matrifocal Rituals in Patrilineal Chinese Religion: The Story of an Early 20th Century Chinese Feminist," *International Journal of Comparative Religion* 2 (1994): in press.

15. Signs of this potential development, of hundreds of millions of people seeking a better situation, are already in evidence. There are now relatively large-scale attempts to smuggle illegal Chinese immigrants into the United States. Many have been prompted to claim political refugee status (perhaps their only memorized English-language statement) on the grounds that the number of children their wives are allowed to have is limited (their wives being left behind in China).

16. See Mahendra K. Premi, "Projected Population Patterns, North-South Relations and the Environment," in this volume.

17. Takashi Sugimoto, *Mass Migration Pressures in China* (Toronto: York University, Joint Centre for Asia Pacific Studies, NPCSD Working Paper No. 5, 1992): 25. He notes that:

China's enormous population tops 1.13 billion and estimates of its surplus labour force go as high as 160 million. This is greater than the entire population of Japan. Given the great numbers of unemployed, should large-scale political and economic turmoil occur, or complete freedom to go in and out of the country be granted to the masses, massive outflows of Chinese would be inevitable. (p. 25)

18. As yet, there is no reason to be sanguine; every time the Chinese government attempts to control its problems, it is immediately criticized by the West. It would not be surprising that, if the government did crack down on massive industrial pollution, it would be again be criticized as it has for controlling the population, this time for violating the rights of humans to pollute the environment. Western, particularly American, criticism of China over human rights began soon after the United States ended the state of war with China. It has recently been reported, unverified, that China dropped plans for a major campaign against the recent rise in violent crime (rape and murder) because the last time it did so several years ago, it was again criticized for violating human rights, with the usual threats of economic sanctions. Hence, China understands Western criticism over human rights to be a weapon for the destabilization of China, to allow a Western takeover, as in the nineteenth century. Moreover, it is to be noted that Chinese and Western notions of human rights arise from different religious bases, as the professor of international politics at Beijing University points out: "The Chinese government stands for the promotion of human rights based on stability and economic development." (Yang Kai, *Human Rights in China: History, Disputes and Regional Influence* [Toronto: York University, Joint Centre for Asia Pacific Studies, NPCSD Working Paper No. 9, 1992]: 11.)

III

Secular Responses

11

Prescriptions from Religious and Secular Ethics for Breaking the Impoverishment/Environmental Degradation Cycle

MICHAEL McDONALD

> What kind of planet we want is ultimately a question of values. How much species diversity should be maintained in the world? Should the size or the growth rate of the human population be curtailed to protect the global environment? How much climatic change is acceptable? How much poverty? Should the deep ocean be considered an option for hazardous waste?
>
> Science can illuminate these issues but cannot resolve them. The choice of answers is ours to make and our grandchildren's to live with. Because different people live in different circumstances and have different values, individual choices can be expected to vary enormously. (Clark 1989, 2)

William Clark wrote these words as part of the introductory essay in a 1989 *Scientific American* collection entitled, *Managing Planet Earth*. Regular readers of *Scientific American* may have been surprised by Clark's claim that the basic environmental issues are ethical rather than scientific. After all, it is scientists as a group who more than anyone else have forecast and brought to public attention such major environmental concerns as the greenhouse effect, the ozone hole, desertification, and atmospheric and aquatic pollution. However, once people and their leaders generally recognize that these predictions are valid, there remain crucial questions of choice — what should be done, who is responsible, and why act? These raise ethical questions. Foremost amongst these are those involving justice or equity issues. Thus, if "sustainable development" is defined as meeting "the needs of the present without compromising the ability of future generations to meet their own needs," then, as Clark notes, it follows that:

> Sustainable development thus reflects a choice of values for managing planet earth in which equity matters — equity among peoples around the world today, equity between parents and their grandchildren.

If equity is central to sustainable development, or at least to ethically defensible versions of sustainable development, the challenge of constructing a global consensus around sustainable development is a formidable one given the different circumstances and diverse moral perspectives of the many peoples of this earth. It is against this background of different circumstances and diverse values that I have written this chapter. In this connection, I see three matters as paramount.

First, I am convinced that on a global level human beings are imprudently testing natural limits by adding too many people and by drawing down natural capital too rapidly for natural replenishment.[1] I say this after allowing for the human capacity to stretch natural limits through technological, social, and economic adaptation. Thus, for this chapter, I take the warnings of environmentalists in a weak rather than a strong form — not as having scientifically demonstrated the existence of absolutely inelastic limits to growth, but as having given sufficient reasons for believing that we human beings cannot reasonably rely on our collective adaptive capacities to continue reproducing and using resources at current rates.

Second, as a species with choices, we have a choice between two broad alternatives — either to continue as we are or sufficiently change our behavior. If we continue our present patterns of behavior, we risk exceeding the planet's carrying capacity through resource consumption, the production of waste materials, and overpopulation. This will produce serious adverse consequences for human well-being as a result of desertification, global warming, reduced species diversity, and the like. The alternative is to make a globally prudential choice to alter our behavior so as to dramatically reduce the risks of exceeding the planet's carrying capacity.

Third, the only way the globally prudential choice is going to be an ethically acceptable alternative is to address important questions of equity — between haves and have-nots, rich and poor, present and future generations, males and females, and majorities and minorities. This also means settling disputes about ownership and entitlement to various uses of the global environment — to uses of lands, seas, and atmosphere. If such crucial equity questions are not satisfactorily addressed, then various groups will ask why they should bear a disproportionate share of the costs of protecting the global environment.[2] The largest global equity question is whether the poorest peoples of the world should curb their birth rates while the wealthiest peoples of the world consume many times the amount of natural resources per capita more than the poorest.[3]

This brings me to a fundamental question: "If equity questions are central, then whose idea of equity is to prevail or be determinative? Is it the idea of equity or fairness to be found in religious or secular ethical perspectives? If so, which belief system: Christian, Jewish, Buddhist, Hindu, or Chinese; or alternatively, liberal democratic, socialist, nationalist, individualist, or communitarian? Even within these belief systems there is considerable diversity as to what counts as equity or fairness in current global circumstances. My aim is to examine some major questions of global equity within the context of moral diversity.

I will proceed as follows. First, I will offer a short overview of the conception of ethics I am advancing. Next, I will move to a brief description of the impoverishment/environmental degradation cycle that is the topic of this chapter. Third, I will offer an ethical analysis of this cycle. Finally, I will offer some prescriptions that will, I hope, both help break the impoverishment/environmental degradation cycle and be responsive to the moral diversity of the peoples of this earth.

ETHICAL METHODOLOGY

Even though my personal perspective is secular rather than religious in its orientation (although not entirely in its inspiration), my ambition is to address people from a wide range of secular and religious ethical traditions. In this spirit, I advance the following conception of ethics:

> Ethics is the science or study of morals, where morals is concerned with conduct, character, intentions, and social relations insofar as they are appraised as excellent, right, deserving, virtuous, just, or proper. In particular, ethics is concerned: with right and wrong actions, policies, and practices; with duties, obligations, and rights; with fairness in the correction of wrongs [corrective justice]; with the fair distribution of benefits and burdens within society [distributive justice]; with virtue, vice, and just desserts; with good and evil, benefits and disbenefits, welfare and illfare, the valuable and the disvaluable, for individuals and communities. It is concerned with the resolution of disputes, controversies, and uncertainties about the foregoing types of issues. Ethics is divided into normative ethics [opinions in morals] and meta-ethics [which is about morals], including both descriptive and theoretical ethics. (McDonald, Stevenson, and Cragg 1992, 5)

In my view, *ethics is knowable.* I reject a subjectivist account of ethics that cashes out moral claims as personal preferences; thus, a subjectivist would read the claim that "murder is wrong" as a simple statement of personal dislike for homicide. I also reject an imperatival and emotivist interpretation of moral claims, which reads them as directives or imperatives designed to manipulate others' preferences and express personal emotions; on this view, "murder is wrong" is read as the negative imperative, "Dislike murder!" I believe that ethics is about acting on good reasons, in particular reasons that override reasons of interest and inclination (Kurt Baier). Like scientific or other factual claims, moral claims can be true or false; they are not meaningless, not mere expressions of emotion, and they are not simple statements of individual or collective preference.

Nonetheless, I hold that our claims to moral knowledge are fallible and corrigible. Now, it might be thought this conception of ethics would be unacceptable to those who claim a religious basis for morality. Nonetheless, there are religious believers who accept that human understanding of timeless, divinely ordained moral truths can be faulty and subject to correction, whether by benefit of natural reason or through divine inspiration.

How can we test and correct claims to moral knowledge? I would suggest what can be labeled *"the four C's tests."* The first two C's are *consistency* and *coherence.* These are internal standards to be applied to secular or religious moralities. The test is whether a morality's prescriptions hang together and make sense as part of a single whole. By appealing to consistency and coherence, I do not intend to dismiss out of hand religious world views that assert that in the moral life there are elements of mystery and areas in which faith, not reason, guides. Rather, my suggestion is that such religious views should seek an integrative understanding of reason and faith.

The next two C's are *conformity* to and *confirmation* by life experiences. Especially after working as an ethics consultant to the Native peoples of Ontario on environmental issues, I have been convinced of the importance of taking a broad view of life experiences and knowledge.[4] I believe that it is essential to take into account traditional forms of knowledge and the lived experience of those actually faced with serious problems. This means a heightened moral responsiveness or sensitivity along two dimensions. First, I suggest responsiveness to the moral sensibilities of minorities, as well as those of majority or dominant communities. Second, it involves taking seriously the life experiences of lay people as well as experts. This is not to denigrate expert knowledge, but to suggest that those of us who are experts in various sciences (natural, social, or human) or the professions have our limitations and blinkers (McDonald 1989). Ultimately, I hope for convergence between traditional and expert forms of knowledge, but in real life there will be disagreements that need to be honestly addressed. Such honesty requires that the judgments of experts be regarded as both fallible and corrigible.

THE IMPOVERISHMENT/ENVIRONMENTAL
DEGRADATION CYCLE

My focus in this chapter is on the impoverishment/environmental degradation cycle. This is one of the many environmental challenges that now confront the global community. While I think the analytical tools I advance in the next section apply to some other environmental choice situations, it is important to understand that my focus is on this crisis, and not on other crises in which environmental limits are being imprudently tested. In particular, some ethical prescriptions that can be offered for dealing with this cycle may not be appropriate for dealing with other global human-environmental problems. In particular, I will suggest that it is likely that this cycle could be broken without a major redistribution of resources from haves to have-nots. Now if this suggestion is right, the prescriptions I present in this chapter for breaking this cycle will not deal directly with the major question of the overconsumption of resources by the richest people on earth. This, it seems to me, is a different and distinct problem from the one at hand.

H. Jeffrey Leonard describes the impoverishment/environmental degradation cycle as follows:

> The growing numbers of poor people living in more geographically focused poverty zones in the developing countries are not simply standing still, waiting to be touched by the magic hand of development. They are literally "loosing ground" as their lands suffer more and more from the strains of too many people, inappropriate technology, or lack of "protective" infrastructure investment. Environmental destruction has become synonymous with poverty wherever poor people cluster together. Environmental degradation — soil erosion, desertification, declining soil fertility, salinization, flooding, mud slides, fuelwood shortages, unhealthy water supplies — is now one of the most formidable constraints on productivity for rural and urban poor in developing countries. These problems sap the productive potential of the marginal and meager land resources available to poor people; they heap additional labor requirements on poor people [especially women] who already work very long hours just to meet basic subsistence needs; they threaten the physical security of people and their possessions; and they increase opportunistic diseases that debilitate adults and kill children.
>
> The longer these circumstances persist, the higher will be the remedial costs and the external social and economic costs for nations that can ill afford to foot the bill. The incalculable human suffering associated with

this process and the destruction of invaluable wildlife and natural resources in the interim can never be recouped. (Leonard 1989, 42)

Leonard thus describes the desperate situation of a considerable number of
the poorest of the poor — 780 million of the approximately 900 million people
in the world who fall into this category (1988 figures, Leonard 1989, 18). The
adverse environmental effects are not only local and regional affecting the
poorest themselves and their near neighbors, but also having global effects
through contributions to global warming and the reduction of biological diversity (Leonard 1989, 6). The net effect is that:

> *The interaction of poverty and environmental destruction sets off
> a downward spiral of ecological deterioration that threatens the phys-
> ical security, economic well-being, and health of the world's poorest
> people.* (Leonard 1989, 6; *my emphasis*)

Leonard sees three major factors contributing to the situation of too-large
rural populations with limited access to productive lands: (1) rapid population
growth, (2) agricultural modernization in high potential areas; and (3) inequitable land distribution. At the Summer Institute, participants identified
other contributory factors. These include natural (not humanly caused) changes
in the atmosphere, specifically dramatically reduced rainfalls over the Sahel. They
also include environmental degradation brought about by human activities,
such as the commercial exploitation of forests on the Indian subcontinent and
the erection of massive dams and irrigation projects in various parts of the
world.

Contributing factors vary from place to place, but the consequences are
fairly similar: pushed to the margins of survival, the poorest of the poor are
pushed into practices that dangerously degrade and destroy the few resources
they have available to them. Thus, desperate for wood for cooking, people strip
the trees bare. Once the trees are gone, there are dramatic declines in water tables; the land becomes even more marginal for farming and grazing. This creates the conditions for migration — migration often to urban slums or to even
more marginal and usually ecologically precarious lands, such as the Ama-
zonian rain forests or the highlands in the Himalayas or in Central America.

Among the poorest of the poor caught in this downward spiral, women
are often in the worst circumstances. Jacobsen describes their situation in terms
of a "gender gap" in development; she says:

> Rapid population growth within subsistence economies in turn
> compounds the environmental degradation — the unsustainable degra-

dation of soil erosion, depletion, and deforestation — first put in motion by the increasing separation of poor farmers from the assets that once sustained them. The health of women and girls, most affected by environmental degradation because of the roles they play, declines further. The cycle accelerates. This is the population trap: many of the policies and programs carried out in the name of development actually increase women's dependence on children as a source of status and security. Moreover, environmental degradation triggered by misguided government policies is itself causing rapid population growth, in part as a result of women's economically rational response to increasing demands on their time caused by resource scarcity. (Jacobsen 1993, 76)

AN ETHICAL ANALYSIS

To provide an ethical analysis of this cycle, I propose the three following categories:

- Moral patients, who suffer evils that could be removed or alleviated by human action;
- Moral agents, whether individual or institutional, who could help break the cycle; and
- Moral agendas that link moral agents to moral patients.

Although I realize that these terms are open to misinterpretation, I have chosen this language with some care. The word "patient" comes from the Latin word for "suffering," "enduring," or, in other words, "being acted on." The term "agent" describes a being who acts or has the capacity to act. Being an agent or patient requires the possession of capacities for acting or suffering, whether these be cognitive, volitional, emotional, or material. Most human beings in the course their lifetimes are both agents and patients. As individual agents, individuals perform actions that affect both themselves and others. People also act collectively through "agencies" — coordinated bodies of individual human agents like governments, corporations, churches, or communities.[5]

Moreover, I want, in the terms "agent" and "patient," to call to attention "activity" and "passivity" as human responses to adverse situations. Many enduring religious and secular moral traditions will counsel acceptance and passivity in the face of adversity and even when blessed with good fortune. Thus, there are both religious and secular traditions (e.g., Buddhist and platonic) that recommend the development of an inner self, detached from the happenings of day to day existence. Other moral traditions — in particular secular moralities prevalent in Western industrialized countries — lay emphasis on agency and the possession of power. Hobbes, for example, saw life as consisting in a ceaseless search for power after power (Hobbes 1968, 161). Indeed, critics of the secular morality prevailing in Western societies see this emphasis on agency as a dangerous and ultimately self-destructive Promethean urge (Taylor). There is also a rich feminist literature that confronts the stereotyping of males as agents and females as patients.[6]

There is a third motivation for my choice of the terms "agent" and "patient," and that lies in the problem at hand. The people who suffer most from the impoverishment/environmental degradation cycle have under current circumstances very limited opportunities for the significant exercise of either collective or individual agency. Those facing famine and the deeply malnourished have few if any meaningful choices (see Leonard, Drèze and Sen, and Nell). What I see as morally essential is removing from their situation obstacles that bar them from having a meaningful set of choices; in other words, it is their empowerment that is morally mandatory.

Finally, I have chosen the term "agenda" for a variety of reasons. Agendas are action-oriented. In keeping with what I said in the previous section about the fallibility and corrigibility of moral judgments, I believe that agendas can and should be revised in the light of new information or the realization that particular beliefs and values are mistaken. I like the term "agenda" for another reason. Setting an agenda, say for a committee meeting, involves setting priorities. Time is short. Attention spans are limited. The committee only has finite resources. Hence, the committee has to set an agenda that determines which items are for action, which to be postponed, and which to be dropped. This raises the question, "where on the moral agenda of the rich and powerful of the world is the task of helping to break the impoverishment/degradation cycle?" If we judge by actions, I am afraid that we would have to say that it is not a priority item for most agents and agencies who could break the impoverishment/environmental degradation cycle.

I have chosen the term "moral agenda" for another reason. This term highlights the need to connect agents and patients in ethical theory and moral practice. Some ethical theories insist on large and inclusive moral agendas. Take, for example, the moral agenda act utilitarians set; it requires that in any choice situation an agent must act so as to produce the greatest happiness for the greatest number. It is hard to imagine a wider, more inclusive, and more demanding moral agenda. These can be contrasted with more restrictive moral agendas that focus the attention of specific agents on specific patients. For instance, the contemporary neo-Hobbesian David Gauthier restricts moral relationships to those in which reciprocal advantage is possible (Gauthier 1986). For Gauthier, the utterly weak and helpless would have no meaningful moral claims against moral agents. Lest this be thought unduly harsh, it should be noted that in most moral systems distinctions are made between intimates and strangers; hence, it is widely believed that parents have special obligations to their children that they do not have to their neighbors' children, let alone the children of far-distant peoples. The latter, if they enter the parent's moral agenda, typically do so in a weaker form as the object of non-enforceable charitable obligations or even more weakly as acts of supererogation — good deeds above and beyond the call of obligation. I have created the term "moral agenda" to cover the wide range of moral connectedness between agents and patients from duties to acts of supererogation. I also wish to highlight the diversity of moral agendas, and to underline what to some may be an unpalatable fact, that not everyone has a widely inclusive moral agenda.

There is a further advantage in the choice of the term "agenda"; it is that agendas are primarily social rather than individual constructs. Morality, as I conceive it, is essentially social in its orientation — directed toward interaction rather than solitary reflection; hence, the appropriate mode of speech for ethics is dialogue rather than monologue. Agendas imply a context of collective action. Only derivatively do we talk about individual persons having agendas, and then only when they bring their personal agendas to collective choice situations.

Moral Patients

I divide moral patients into those directly affected and those indirectly affected. The directly affected include those caught in the impoverishment/environmental degradation cycle. Ethically, our primary concern should be for those directly affected. If I correctly understand this cycle, it is not plausible to argue that those indirectly affected — the better-off people of the world who are not trapped in this cycle — have nearly as much at stake, at least in the short to medium run, as those directly caught in this downward spiral. In this respect, the situation is unlike that posed by CFCs or greenhouse gases, where ill effects are more evenly spread between the haves and have-nots. As I will argue shortly, this makes salient the problem of moral connectivity connecting moral agents to moral patients in meaningful ways.

The most directly affected are the poorest of the poor. This includes two groups — the present generation, or those now alive, who are trapped in this cycle, and future generations, including their future children, grandchildren, etc., who will likely face the same or even worse circumstances. The present generation suffers from the evil effects of impoverishment and environmental degradation. These evil effects include poverty, reduced life-prospects, increased morbidity and mortality, misery, insecurity, fear, and hopelessness.

Bluntly, the evils surround the inability or failure to meet the most basic human needs. Beyond such needs are the gross inequities that are reinforced and even exacerbated by the depressing cycle of impoverishment leading to environmental degradation, which leads in turn to more impoverishment. It is worth noting that those caught in this cycle include three groups. There are those who are on marginal lands. Then there are those on good but underdeveloped agricultural lands. Finally, there are the growing numbers of impoverished living in urban squalor (Leonard 1989, 20).

There is the grim prospect that unless appropriate actions are taken soon these problems will affect more people in the future. With respect to moral standing or significance, I would argue that the present generation has a different moral standing in terms of rights than do future generations. An agent can only wrong existing patients — not those who do not yet exist and especially not those whose existence is dependent on the agent's putatively wrongful action (Broome 1992, ch. 2); hence, only existing patients have rights against agents. So if future generations are to occupy a place on moral agendas, they will have to do so in some other way than as holders of rights.

The impoverishment/environmental degradation cycle also has indirect effects on other persons. Included here are the better-off neighbors of those directly facing this cycle. These better-off neighbors face increased risks of disease, crime, and social instability, as well as the longer-term consequences of the "drag effect" of having substantial "poverty reserves" or "ghettos" in their vicinity. There are also trans-border and even global effects of the impoverishment/environmental degradation cycle. These include the global environmental effects of this cycle in such forms as global warming, desertification, salinization, and lessened species diversity. But there are also political or social consequences involving migration and regional conflict (Kennedy 1993, 41–46). As I said earlier, my understanding of these trans-border effects is that in purely self-centered terms the better-off peoples of the world have much less at stake here than do the worst-off.

Moral Agents and Agencies

Just as moral patients can be divided into present and future generations, so can moral agents and agencies, including governments, religious movements, and NGOs (non-governmental organizations). Included in the present generation of agents are the poorest of the poor. While it would be wrong to ignore their agency, it would be a mistake to overestimate their ability to help themselves without the help and cooperation of others. Assuming that breaking the impoverishment/environmental degradation cycle requires action over an extended period of time, those of us in the current generation should give some thought to shaping the moral agenda for the next generation. One possibility is to create new agencies to help break this cycle, especially where old agencies have failed.

Moral Agendas

It is useful to think of responsible moral agents as trying to order their practical lives according to moral standards that they accept and endorse. I will describe this ordering as a moral agenda. Individuals have moral agendas, but so also do organized groups, including international agencies like the United Nations and the Red Crescent, national governments, and corporations. I should caution that I am here using the term "moral agenda," as well as the terms "moral agent" and "moral patient," in a descriptive and neutral way rather than in a prescriptive or commendatory way. Some moral agents and agencies have dreadful moral agendas — say, those advanced by Hitler, Stalin, the Mafia, and the Khmer Rouge.

Examination of an agent's moral agenda reveals the moral sensitivities and priorities of that agent. Obviously, not all agents share the same moral sensitivities and priorities. For any agent A with respect to any patient P, we can ask the following:

1. Is patient P on A's moral agenda?

2. What priority does P have on A's agenda?

3. What does A's moral agenda prescribe for P?

The first question raises acutely the question of whether a particular religious or secular moral perspective instructs its adherents to do anything about those suffering the impoverishment/environmental degradation cycle, and what, specifically, it tells them to do by way of positive or negative injunctions. A particular moral tradition also provides reasons to agents for caring about particular patients. Consider, for example, the reasons that lie behind the injunction, "Honor your parents."

The reasons given will determine in at least rough form an answer to the second question, which concerns priorities. Agents and agencies — even the most powerful have limited time, energy, and resources to allocate. Moreover, agents and agencies are faced with incompatible demands with respect to diverse patients. For example, there is good reason to believe that there are genuine moral problems of demographic transition in developed as well as in developing countries, so that baby boomers are in the process of unfairly exploiting generation X and subsequent generations (Thomson 1992). Should dealing with this sort

of intergenerational injustice be given a lower priority than dealing with breaking the impoverishment/environmental degradation cycle simply because the
need is greater in the latter than the former case? Not obviously — at least on
moral agendas that set a priority on obligations to patients "nearer" to particular agents, say to one's own children rather the children of neighbors and
strangers.[7]

This prompts a cautionary note. It is worth emphasizing that moral agents
may well face difficult and sometimes non-obvious choices. Often, in leading
discussions about ethical issues, I meet "moral optimists" who think all moral
problems have easy and obvious solutions. I would mention three types of optimists. First, many of those who participate in discussion of business ethics think
that duty and self-interest generally coincide. On this view, good ethics means
a better bottom line; hence, morality rarely, if ever, requires self-sacrifice. The
second type of optimist I have encountered in discussions of environmental issues. These optimists underestimate the possibility of serious but sincere moral
disagreement among those from different traditions. They assume that because
environmental issues are globally pressing, they will necessarily receive a high
priority on everyone's moral agenda. The third kind of moral optimist believes
that every problem has a technological or market fix.[8] In other words, human
beings will invent their way around difficult and painful choices, or else the market will readjust demand to supply to avoid a crisis. All three strike me as dangerously naive. But I also must admit my impatience with the moral pessimism
displayed by colleagues in moral philosophy who in their efforts to differenti-
ate moral agendas see no possibility of common moral ground or constructing
shared moral agendas.

The third question — what, specifically, to do about those moral patients
who have a relatively high priority on an agent's moral agenda — raises a number of salient moral questions. Virtually every strategy for breaking the im-
poverishment/environmental degradation cycle has important moral aspects
and raises serious ethical questions within at least some agents' moral agendas.
I would suggest the following areas are relevant to the impoverishment/envi-
ronmental degradation problem.

There are strategies that may inflame cultural sensitivities. Consider, for instance, efforts to achieve population control through education for despised
minority group members or through the use of financial or legal incentives or
disincentives for sterilization. Even the most non-intrusive strategies to control
population size or to reduce gender or other inequities, may well involve challenging existing social norms. Such strategies also raise issues of paternalism
and exploitation in the form of political, economic, or cultural colonialism or
imperialism when they are imposed by those from developed countries on those
in developing countries.

Another controversial area concerns strategies that have the net effect of re-assigning entitlement patterns. For instance, it has been proposed that the impoverishment/environmental degradation cycle can be broken by altering legal or social structures with respect to land tenure, access to technology and economic assistance (Leonard 1989). It has also been suggested that partial remedies can be found in market alterations with respect to food prices, international debt repayments, and opening markets in the developed world to agricultural products from poorer countries (Drèze and Sen 1989, ch. 7). It has also been suggested that developing countries should produce less in the way of cash crops and seek agricultural self-sufficiency. Each of these proposed strategies involves the re-arrangement of patterns of existing entitlements, that is, the dramatic readjustment of at least some agents' moral agendas. In particular, each raises questions about the obligations of haves to have-nots, including not only the haves in developed countries, but also the haves within developing countries.

A further area for concern involves deciding between conflicting priorities. Should an agent or agency dealing with the impoverishment/environmental degradation cycle set a priority on (a) environmental protection strategies, such as setting up forest or wildlife reserves by removing land from agricultural protection, or (b) agriculture enhancement strategies (Leonard 1989, 4)?

In brief, effective strategies for breaking the impoverishment/environmental degradation cycle can be controversial. Given the variety of interests involved, it is unlikely that there are many optimal strategies in which everyone will be a winner. Furthermore, it is hard to find strategies that are going to be morally acceptable to all relevant agents and patients. That is, there may be disagreement about what is or is not a morally legitimate strategy. Beyond the issues of conflicting interests and conflicting moral agendas, there is the problem of uncoordinated agencies, which all too frequently plague international aid. All this said, I believe that *the basic moral issue involves linking moral agents to moral patients via moral agendas that are morally compelling to both agents and patients*. Only with compelling moral agendas will there be the meaningful action necessary to bring to a close the impoverishment/environmental degradation cycle.

BREAKING THE CYCLE: ETHICAL PRESCRIPTIONS

Much of the discussion of sustainable development has focused on the carrying capacity of the earth. The images are familiar — "spaceship earth" and "lifeboat earth" (Nell 1986, 17). Indeed, a major presupposition of this Summer Institute is that we are pressing the limited carrying capacity of the earth in two main ways: (1) the pressure of population numbers and growth in developing countries; and (2) the pressure of resource consumption in developed countries.

Human numbers and the net demands made by humans on the environment are unprecedented in human history. Annually from 1985 to 1990, world population increased by 88 million, roughly the population of Mexico; from 1995 to 2000, it is predicted that world population will be growing at the rate of 112 million per year — about the current population of Nigeria (Kennedy 1993, 23–24). To put these figures in a concrete context, it is as if every week, there was added to the world a city with the population of Vancouver — about two million people. Almost all this growth is concentrated in developing countries. But population increases alone do not explain the increase in human demands on the environment. Account must be taken of the high and increasing demands placed on the environment by the relatively stable populations of developed countries. These demands are also at record levels, despite many gains being made in the efficiency with which those in the developed world use resources. Both population growth in the developing world and resource consumption in the developed world must be curbed.

Responding to the pressures of population and resource consumption challenges the adaptive capacities of human communities and the global community of communities. I would suggest that, like the earth, human communities taken singly or collectively have limited capacities for change and adaptation to increasing pressures in sufficient time to preserve their functioning well. The adaptive capacities of communities facing the impoverishment/environmental degradation cycle are under incredible strain. While these communities take the brunt of population pressures, at least some of the pressures are transferred to other communities, particularly in developing countries, but also to the world at large. For communities pressured directly or indirectly by the impoverishment/environmental degradation spiral, it is worth asking if they have the adaptive capacities to mitigate or even escape, these pressures. Not all communities will survive — famines, diseases, wars and other catastrophes can and do destroy communities.[9] Whether a community survives and survives intact in the face of crisis situations is in part a function both of its own actions and the actions of other peoples.

If a community is thought of as a group of people who share a common moral agenda, it is plausible to suggest that the long-term survival of the community depends to a considerable degree on the contents of that agenda and community members' adherence to it. The community's survival and flourishing is also dependent on external factors both from nature and from other human communities. The community's moral agenda shapes its response, at least in part, to both internal and external factors affecting its survival. That is, a people's moral views and practices will make a considerable difference to both the viability and the livability of the community. Over a period of time, a community's moral agenda will determine whether it will meet or fail to meet the natural and human challenges it faces.

I would suggest that for a moral agenda to be adequate it must be both environmentally and ethically sustainable. But what conditions should be set for ethically sustainable moral agendas, especially those that could break the impoverishment/environmental degradation cycle? I will argue that our diverse moral agendas, whether secular or religious, should build on four important elements. These are trust, nonmaleficence, beneficence, and the encouragement of diversity.

Trust

In environmental sustainability, a crucial role is played by the notion of stewardship. Stewardship implies a trust relationship not only among human beings, including future generations, but also with respect to the environment itself. *Our Common Future* emphasizes the trust relationship that the present generation has to future generations, and that those who consume, per capita, large amounts of resources have to those who consume very little. In a situation in which resources are limited, overuse by some could well result in shortages for others. Those with the power to overuse should stand in a trust relationship to those who lack this power.

As Annette Baier has argued in her influential paper, "Trust and Anti-Trust," the moral test of trust relationships is whether they could survive full disclosure to the person doing the trusting (Annette Baier 1986, 253–60). We can ask if a religious or secular ethics that commands women to remain in a subservient position could survive the challenge of this test. Such views standardly rely on insupportable myths about the natural or divinely ordained division of familial labor and the special role of women to sustain exploitative social arrangements. In such cases, trust turns to anti-trust with the full disclosure of the motivations, beliefs, and behavior of those who claim to deserve the trust. In short, it is essential to discard those aspects of religious or secular ethical views that would block what appears to be one of the best ways of escaping the impoverishment/environmental degradation cycle, namely, through the empowerment of women through education, investment, legal reform, and health care.

A paradigm trust relation is the parent/child relationship (Annette Baier 1986, 240–44). Insofar as parenting is an option and not a necessity (as it still is for many of the poorest of the poor), one ought to avoid bringing people into existence whose lives are likely to be filled with misery and unhappiness. History shows that, given an option of producing fewer children with better life-prospects or more children with greatly diminished life-prospects, people will choose the former (Kennedy 1993, 3–11). Again, it is fair to ask if there are religious or secular moral perspectives that proscribe access to the means of controlling population, not only by denying men and women access to the means of birth control, but also by denying impoverished peoples the opportunity to make the "demographic transition" from poor, overpopulated societies to reasonably prosperous, less populated societies (Brown 1987, 20–24).

The same test for trust should be applied to those who occupy positions of power in countries where the impoverishment/environmental degradation cycle is endemic. Do government officials and local power-brokers deserve the trust of those caught in such cycles? Do the prevailing ethical views in these societies counsel acquiescence on the part of the poorest of the poor? Because the abuse of such trust does play a significant role in continuing and even worsening the lot of the poorest of the poor, it is crucial to call into question moral views that condone and even promote the abuse of positions of political and economic trust. I have in mind here first and third world regimes that promote tribal hatreds and engage in militaristic adventures. It is also essential for first world representatives in third world countries — be they from the private, public, or not-for-profit sectors — to ask themselves if they honor or abuse the trust placed in them by their hosts? It is not enough to say that host populations agreed, albeit reluctantly, to the terms and conditions proposed by their first world guests. It seems to me that any worthwhile moral view will also define and denounce unconscionable bargains particularly with the poorest of the poor and not simply rely on their silent and often coerced acquiescence.[10]

Non-Maleficence

"Reduce waste" and "eliminate pollution are environmental injunctions that would be endorsed by adherents of most contemporary religious and secular ethical perspectives. Sometimes this endorsement is grounded on an intrinsic concern for nature itself; in other cases, it is grounded on a more instrumental, anthropocentric rationale. In either, it is based on doing no harm to moral patients — be they persons, animals, ecosystems, or the global environment (on the Gaia hypothesis). This non-maleficence condition is connected to the environmental limits' hypothesis presented above. If we were not imprudently testing the biosphere's limits, then we could plausibly believe that some forms of pollution were morally acceptable so long as no harm was inflicted on any being that had the status of a moral patient; but this, as I have noted, is not the case for human beings today.

With respect to those caught in the impoverishment/environmental degradation cycle, it is important to see what non-maleficence demands. For instance, it would require governments, corporations, and individuals not to engage in or permit actions that would destroy the rain forest habitats of indigenous groups in Asia and the Americas. It certainly requires refraining from actions that worsen the lot of those caught in the impoverishment/environmental degradation cycle. The avoidance of policies that abet and encourage strife and warfare in developing countries is extremely urgent (Drèze and Sen 1989, 273–75). It requires not using their lands as a repository for harmful wastes. It also requires compensation for past harms that have exacerbated or even brought about such cycles, e.g., the construction of dams that have wrought havoc on downstream dwellers.

Beneficence

So far the prescriptions I have suggested for breaking the impoverishment/environmental degradation cycle have been fairly conservative. I have argued that an acceptable ethical view would require those who hold positions of trust to deserve that position, and generally would require agents and agencies not to worsen the situation of the worst-off. I want to move beyond these negative imperatives to positive ones that encourage doing good for others. Agents can do good for others — act beneficently — in two ways: either with the expectation of reciprocity on their part in the form of an exchange relationship, or without such expectation in the form of a gift relationship.

It is important to avoid either under- or over-estimating the value of exchange or market forms of beneficence. Some criticize all free market exchanges as inherently exploitative and demeaning. Such criticisms strike me as over-general and question-begging. When parties to an exchange freely and knowingly agree to the exchange, and the bargain is struck in a condition in which the parties have reasonable alternatives to making the exchange (so the bargain is not an unconscionable one), it seems to me that there is no cause for complaint on grounds of justice. Indeed, to deny people the right to make such exchanges would be an unconscionable interference with the freedom of both parties.[11] Much could be done to help the situation of those caught in the impoverishment/environmental degradation cycle by way of fair, mutually beneficial exchanges through trade, investment, as well as reciprocal research and educational ventures. One of the problems most affecting the lot of a significant number of the poorest of the poor is the lack of public and private investment in the development of an adequate infrastructure to enable them to exploit such resources as are available (Leonard 1989, 32). Not all the poorest of the poor live in marginal rural regions or in overcrowded cities. Some are in areas of high agricultural potential (Leonard 1989, 18). The creation by public authorities of conditions in which that potential can be realized through local and international investment is important, but so also is the opening of markets in developed countries.[12]

Unfortunately not all the poorest of poor are very bankable even over the long term (Leonard 1989, 6). We need to think about gift-relationships because market solutions are inadequate for ameliorating the lot of those without real bargaining power. Nonetheless, we must remember that, like exchange relationships, gift-relationships can be used to exploit the weak or to treat them paternalistically. Aid directed to those caught in the impoverishment/environmental degradation cycle has to aim at self-reliance and empowerment, both as a means of breaking the cycle and as a morally significant goal in its own right. To plausibly frame moral imperatives urging or requiring sharing, I would urge six considerations:

1. It is essential to distinguish and prioritize meeting needs over satisfying optional wants or preferences. A number of ethical theories and a variety of functioning moral systems unfortunately treat desires for luxuries on a par with desires for necessities (Braybrooke 1987).

2. Agents from diverse moral communities need enough moral space to (a) pursue other projects important to them,[13] and (b) identify those moral patients whose needs they can meet best.[14] (a) is important because people have different but legitimate moral agendas. People need the freedom or space in which to pursue their moral agendas.[15] (b) matters because our situations vary as agents and as members of agencies; different social skills and roles have to be taken seriously. This is why the specific resolutions from this Summer Institute are directed to specific parties, such as government officials, business leaders, religious figures, educators, those working in NGOs, and citizens.

3. We must allow and encourage a wide variety of direct and indirect efforts to break the cycle. It is important not to put all our eggs in one basket. It is also the case that the impoverishment/environmental degradation cycle occurs in diverse circumstances. what works in one set of circumstances may not work in a different context. The problems in mobilizing agents and agencies are extremely complex. Sometimes, the best things that can be done to help internationally involve the clearing of domestic moral agendas. Thus, it is unfair and unrealistic to think that we will open markets to third world products unless we address in developed and more economically advanced developing countries the situation of our own worst-off producers of similar goods.

4. We should take a broad view of the resources needed to break the impoverishment/environmental degradation cycle. Much of what is desperately needed to break the impoverishment/environmental degradation cycle involves the transfer of soft goods like information and low-cost technologies. Think, for example, of medical knowledge important to reproductive control. In other cases, the need is for public health measures or for relatively simple agricultural or urban technologies, e.g., to provide minimally adequate shelter in slums.

5. We need to have appropriate moral reward structures in our moral traditions. One of the salient failures of highly ascetic moral traditions is the failure to develop such reward structures. In large part, this is due to leaving no room for moral options. It is also due, I believe, to a mean view of human nature.

6. It is crucial that there be genuine responsiveness to the needs of the moral patients in question. All too often, foreign aid has been a means of satisfying domestic needs; sometimes even at the expense of recipients. Thus, the provision of surplus foods may swamp local markets, depressing prices and undermining agricultural self-sufficiency. Aid is sometimes provided to prop up corrupt regimes or to forward the donor's essentially self-centered agenda. To repeat a point made earlier about trust, it is essential that individual and collective paternalism (read "colonialism") be avoided.

It is important to understand that the situations of moral agents and patients involved in the impoverishment/environmental degradation cycle are many and diverse, both materially (thus the needs of urban and rural poor are different) and spiritually, in that our diverse and sometimes divergent moral agendas direct us in different ways. If the impoverishment/environmental degradation cycle is to be brought to a close, it is essential to identify ways in which the moral agendas of agents and patients can be hooked together without sacrifice of the moral integrity of any of the parties involved.

It should be remembered that religious and secular moral traditions offer diverse ways of adapting to life circumstances. From the point of view of encouraging human well-being, there is much to recommend "different experiments of living" (Mill 1962, 115). We should remember that moral traditions are themselves adaptable. Traditions, prescriptions, and standards are all subject to reinterpretation. Thus, contemporary Christian theologians have responded to the charge that Christianity displays an anti-environmental bias (Coward, 46–47). In this volume can be found a number of feminist reinterpretations of traditional religious perspectives with respect to the issues of population growth and resource consumption. Yet a caution. There are psychological and moral limits to adaptability. Psychologically, if pushed too hard too fast, people can become resistant to change. Cynicism and skepticism can result. Morally, if an ethical perspective has any integrity or wholeness, it will have a core character or spirit that must remain intact.

Finally, I must be true to my own ethical inclinations and insights by mentioning virtue and limits. Much of what matters in the case of the impoverishment/environmental degradation cycle as in other moral challenges will require steadfast, coordinated, and adaptable action over a protracted period of time. For that, people need more than simply good intentions and good information.

We require good judgment and good character. We need to cultivate those characteristics in ourselves and in the next generation. The virtues cultivated and the communities constructed will be based on specific moral agendas. I have suggested that such agendas should be framed by the reasonable acceptance and recognition of limits — environmental, epistemic, personal, and cultural; acceptance of individual and collective fallibility in the formation of moral agendas and an openness to correction are essential.

Breaking the impoverishment/environmental degradation cycle is an important moral goal. It is important for environmental protection. It is important for future generations. Most of all, it is important because we can individually and collectively, both directly and indirectly, ameliorate the situation of those facing these terrible conditions and bring to an end this horrendous but preventable cycle.[16]

NOTES

1. I prefer putting the question of global limits in prudential rather than absolute terms. In this way, I can avoid arguments about whether there are absolute limits to growth in particular areas — in particular, population numbers and resource consumption. I can also allow for the ability of humans to find new ways to support greater numbers of people or higher resource consumption through, for example, improved methods of agriculture (as in the Green Revolution) or new technologies that substitute efficient for inefficient processes (alternative fuels and computers). In short, this way of phrasing the global limits question puts front and center normative, as opposed to predictive, questions.

2. For purposes of this chapter, the crucial equity questions are those connected with global limits, in particular the impoverishment/environmental degradation cycle.

3. Two issues are raised. First, there is a practical question of whether population control without resource consumption control is an adequate response to our global situation. In effect, is overpopulation a greater or lesser threat than resource consumption? The consensus at the 1993 Summer Institute was that resource consumption was a far greater threat to human well-being than overpopulation. Second, the example raises a moral question about the fair distribution of burdens between rich and poor.

4. During 1991 and 1992, three of us in moral philosophy — Jack Stevenson at the University of Toronto, Wesley Cragg at York University, and I — acted as ethics consultants for the Aboriginal Research Coalition of Ontario, which had intervener status before the Ontario Environmental Assessment Board in regard to Ontario Hydro's Demand/Supply Plan. The Plan mapped a major expansion of Ontario Hydro's generating capacity from nuclear, hydroelectric, and fossil fuel sources. In our view, many of the proposed expansion alternatives would have had a major impact on the well-being of various native groups. Due to dramatically worsened economic prospects for both Ontario Hydro and the Province of Ontario, the Plan has been withdrawn from consideration before the Environmental Assessment Board. As ethics consultants, we prepared a report

entitled, "Finding a Balance of Values," which tried to provide a common ethical perspective on the divergent perspectives of native peoples and Hydro planners.

5. As a "deep communitarian" (by which I mean to suggest a parallel to "deep ecology"), I don't think there are individual moral agents apart from communities. I do not then take an atomistic view of human agency. See my paper, "Should Communities Have Rights?" which develops a communitarian approach.

6. See Will Kymlicka, Chapter 7, for a helpful survey of feminist perspectives.

7. "Nearness" can be cashed out in terms of kinship, historical, or other ties between particular agents and patients. There is a significant divide between deontological ethical theories that see "nearness" as morally legitimate and relevant, and those that assert a universalistic ethic, such as utilitarianism (cf. Smart and Williams). The same divide occurs between social contractarians like Rawls, who regard natural endowments as subject to the conditions of justice, and those like Gauthier, who do not.

8. Brunk has an elegant and penetrating discussion of "technological" and other kinds of "fixes."

9. "Communities" has normative or moral force here, implying the continued existence of people peacefully cooperating in order to survive and achieve at least a minimum modicum of well-being.

10. There is an excellent discussion of the responsibilities of trans-national corporations in Donaldson.

11. I am also assuming that the exchange does not harm non-consenting third parties.

12. The issues here are complex. See, for example, Drèze & Sen 89–93 on private trade and famine relief.

13. Vide Bernard Williams' criticisms of utilitarianism.

14. This is a point well made by Nell among others.

15. Nell develops a Kantian theory of imperfect duties to account for this.

16. I wish to thank participants at the Summer Institute for all their helpful comments on this paper.

BIBLIOGRAPHY

Baier, Annette (1986). "Trust and Antitrust." *Ethics* 96, 2 (January): 231–60.

Baier, Kurt. *The Moral Point of View.* Cornell University Press, Ithaca, N.Y., 1957.

Braybrooke, David. *Meeting Needs.* Princeton University Press, Princeton, N.J., 1987.

Broome, John. *Counting the Cost of Global Warming: A Report to the Economic and Social Council.* The White Horse Press, Cambridge, U.K., 1992.

Brown, Lester. "Analyzing the Demographic Trap." *State of the World 1987: A Worldwatch Institute Report on Progress Toward a Sustainable Society.* Lester Brown et al, eds. W. W. Norton & Co. New York, 1987, 20–37.

Brunk, Conrad G. "Professionalism and Responsibility in the Technological Society." Benjamin Eby Lecture. *Conrad Grebel Review.* Conrad Grebel College, Waterloo, Ontario, 1985.

Clark, William C. "Managing Planet Earth." *Managing Planet Earth: Readings from Scientific American Magazine.* W. H. Freeman and Co., New York, 1989.

Coward, Harold. "Religious Responsibility." *Ethics and Climate Change: The Greenhouse Effect.* Wilfrid Laurier University Press, Waterloo, Ontario, 1993, 39–60.

Donaldson, Thomas. *The Ethics of International Business.* Oxford University Press, New York, 1989.

Drèze, Jean, and Sen, Amartya. *Hunger and Public Action.* Clarendon Press, Oxford, 1989.

Gauthier, David. *Morals By Agreement.* Oxford, Clarendon Press, 1986.

Hobbes, Thomas. *Leviathan.* C. B. Macpherson, ed. Pelican Books, Harmondsworth, U.K., 1968.

Jacobsen Jodi. "Closing the Gender Gap." *State of the World 1993: A Worldwatch Institute Report on Progress Toward a Sustainable Society.* W. W. Norton & Co., New York, 1993.

Kennedy, Paul. *Preparing for the Twenty-First Century.* Random House, New York, 1993.

Kymlicka, Will. *Contemporary Political Philosophy: An Introduction.* Clarendon Press, Oxford, 1990.

Leonard, H. Jeffrey. "Environment and the Poor: Development Strategies for a Common Agenda." *Environment and the Poor,* H. Jeffrey Leonard et al. Transaction Books, New Brunswick, N.J., 1989,

McDonald, Michael (1989). "Ethics versus Expertise." *Ethics and Technology: Ethical Choices in the Age of Pervasive Technology,* J. Nef, J. Vanderkop, and H. Wiseman, eds. Wall and Thomas, Toronto, 1989, 119–24.

McDonald, Michael (1992). "Should Communities Have Rights? Reflections on Liberal Individualism." *Human Rights in Cross-Cultural Perspectives,* A. A. An-Na'im, ed. University of Pennsylvania Press, Pennsylvania Studies in Human Rights, Philadelphia, 1992, 133–61.

McDonald, Michael, Stevenson, J. T., and Cragg, Wesley. "Finding a Balance of Values: An Ethical Assessment of Ontario Hydro's Demand/Supply Plan." Report to the Aboriginal Research Coalition of Ontario. November 1992.

Mill, John Stuart. *Utilitarianism; On Liberty;* and *Representative Government.* Everyman's Library, Dent & Co., London, 1962.

Nell, Onara. *Faces of Hunger: An Essay on Poverty, Justice and Development.* Allen & Unwin, London, 1986.

Rawls, John. *A Theory of Justice.* Harvard University of Justice. Cambridge, Mass., 1971.

Smart, J. J. C., and Williams, Bernard. *Utilitarianism: For and Against.* Cambridge University Press, New York, 1973.

Taylor, Charles. "The Politics of the Steady State." Beyond Industrial Growth, A. Rotstein, ed. University of Toronto Press, 1976. Reprinted in *Ethical Issues: Perspectives for Canadians,* Eldon Soifer, ed. Broadview Press, Peterborough, Ont., 1992, 251–71.

Thomson, David. "Generations, Justice, and the Future of Collective Action." *Justice Between Age Groups and Generations,* Peter Laslett and James Fishkin, eds. Yale University Press, New Haven, 1992, 206–35.

12

Projected Population Patterns, North-South Relations, and the Environment

MAHENDRA K. PREMI

POPULATION PROJECTIONS OF THE UN

The worldwide rate of population growth has been essentially the same since 1975, at about 1.7 percent a year. Fertility has actually declined slightly from a total fertility rate (TFR) of 3.8 in 1975–80 to 3.3 in 1990–95. Because of past growth, however, the number of people added each year is still rising. In 1975, the annual addition was about 72 million. In 1992, it was 93 million. It will peak between 1995 and 2000, at about 98 million.

Rapid population growth is therefore still the dominant feature of global demographics, and will continue to be so for at least the next thirty years. The 1993 global population of 5.57 billion is projected to increase to 6.25 billion in 2000, 8.5 billion in 2025 and 10 billion in 2050; significant growth will continue until about 2150 and a level of about 11.6 billion would be reached if the assumptions under the medium variant hold good (UNFPA 1993, 1).

If the population continues to increase according to the high variant, with continuously high growth rates in most developing countries, the world population is likely to be about 12 billion in 2050. This will be more than the projected population in 2150 under the medium variant. If, however, the countries make an effort to slow their growth rates in right earnest from now on, the world population will be just about 8 billion, which would be a little less than the projection for 2025 under the medium variant. These vast differences in the population size and its pressure on natural and other resources would easily be noticed by the younger generation who have already started entering into

217

Table 12-1. World population and growth rates by regions and selected countries.

REGION/COUNTRY	POPULATION (MILLIONS) 1992	2025	AVERAGE GROWTH RATE (%) 1990–95	TFR (1990–95)
World total	5479.0	8472.4	1.7	3.3
More developed countries	1224.7	1403.3	0.5	1.9
Less developed countries	4254.3	7069.2	2.0	3.6
Africa	681.7	1582.5	2.9	6.0
North America	282.7	360.5	1.1	2.0
Latin America	457.7	701.6	1.8	3.1
Asia	3233.0	4900.3	1.8	3.2
Europe	512.0	541.8	0.3	1.7
Oceania	27.5	41.3	1.5	2.5
U.S.S.R. (former)	284.5	344.5	0.5	2.3
Bangladesh	119.3	223.3	2.4	4.7
Bhutan	1.6	3.4	2.3	5.9
India	879.5	1393.9	1.9	3.9
Nepal	20.6	40.1	2.5	5.5
Pakistan	124.8	259.6	2.7	6.2
Sri Lanka	17.7	24.7	1.3	2.5

Source: UNFPA 1993, 48f.

the labor force and the reproductive ages. Hence, the actual size of the world population after the next half century or so will depend on decisions of the people currently in the reproductive ages, and those who will be entering into this age group in the near future.

The developing countries' proportion of this increase grew from 77 percent in 1950 to 93 percent in 1990, but, between now and the end of the century, it will be 95 percent. Africa and South Asia alone account for 53 percent (UNFPA 1993, 1).

In terms of growth rates, the biggest variation has emerged between the industrialized countries of Europe and North America, and the rest of the world. In the industrialized countries, population growth has slowed down or stopped altogether, and fertility is at or below the replacement level. Their populations increased by 43 percent between 1950 and 1990, compared to 162 percent among the least-developed 47 countries (officially designated as such by the United Nations), and 140 percent in the other developing countries (UNFPA 1993, 2).

Table 12-1 presents a summary of the world population in mid-1992 and in 2025, according to the medium projections of the United Nations for the world, the continents, and the countries of the Indian subcontinent. The table also gives the population growth rates as estimated by the U.N. for the 1990–95 quinquennium and their TFRs. The population of the African continent will be 2.3 times larger in the next 33 years as the growth rate has remained almost at three percent per annum.

Sri Lanka having achieved an estimated growth rate of 1.3 percent per annum and a TFR of 2.5 children (Table 12-1), its population will grow by only 39.5 percent by 2025, whereas India's population, currently growing at 1.9 percent per annum, will increase by 58.5 percent by that year. The other four countries of the region — Bangladesh, Bhutan, Nepal, and Pakistan — will all have almost double their 1992 estimates.

Among developing countries, the lowest growth rates are in East Asia and the Caribbean (1.3 percent). East Asia's growth rates largely reflect the situation in China, which is 85 percent of the region. Central and South America, South-East and South Asia, and Southern Africa lie between 2 and 2.5 percent; North Africa, and West Asia between 2.5 and 3 percent; and the rest of Africa over 3 percent (UNFPA 1993, 2). Most African countries have, however, not yet felt the fast population growth as any serious threat to their economic development or to their ecosystems.

As birth rates and growth rates decline in most parts of the world during the next quarter- to half-century, the issues relating to population distribution (urbanization and migration) should gain much greater importance. While a number of environmentalists have opined that population concentrations in the cities and metropolises have led to greater environmental degradation, we must also realize that most innovations and discoveries in the world have originated in the urban centers. Moreover, the pace of urbanization cannot be stopped or even slowed down, at least during the next half century or so. For example, in 1950, 83 percent of the developing world's population lived in rural areas. By 1975, rural areas still accounted for nearly 75 percent of the population; by the end of the present decade, it is expected that this will be down to 60 percent. By the early decades of the next century, more than half of the world's people will live in cities (UNFPA 1993, 5).

By the year 2000, the 125 cities in developing countries with more than one million people will have increased to some 300. In Africa alone, the least urbanized continent, there are now 37 such cities, as compared with only two in 1950. The increase in urban populations will continue going up even after annual additions to overall world population have started to decline, reaching 95.5 million per year between 2020 and 2025 (UNFPA 1993, 5).

Although it is difficult to say whether the major share of future urbanization will be accounted for by natural increase or by migration and the emergence of new towns, still, migration will play an important role in future population distribution patterns, both internal and international. Of the estimated one billion poor people in developing regions, some 450 million live in low potential agricultural areas. A similar number live in ecologically vulnerable areas susceptible to soil erosion, floods, and other environmental hazards. These "critical zones" cannot sustain current inhabitants, let alone future additions (UNFPA 1993, 7). In the cities and metropolises, on the other hand, a large proportion of migrants live in slums and squatter settlements where they do not get proper housing, sanitation worth its name, or even the minimum necessary quantities of water, which results in poor quality of life. When people talk of environmental degradation due to urbanization, probably their major focus is on these people.

Global warming is expected to make certain islands, coastal areas, and river deltas uninhabitable due to rising sea levels. This alone could turn some 16 percent of Egypt's population and ten percent of Bangladesh's into environmental refugees. The United Nations Conference on Environment and Development (the "Earth Summit") in Rio de Janerio in June 1992 called attention to the scale of these possibilities. Hence, early and determined action along the lines of the strategies for sustainable development (Agenda 21) adopted at Rio will be needed if human and ecological catastrophe are to be prevented (UNFPA 1993, 7).

INDIA'S POPULATION AND ITS GROWTH PATTERN

India's population around 300 B.C. was estimated somewhere between 80 to 100 million. In 1650, it was still estimated between 100 and 125 million. These estimates included those parts of the Indian subcontinent that now constitute Bangladesh, Pakistan, and Sri Lanka. About a fourth of the above population lived in those areas in 1650.

Table 12-2 gives India's population for the past 90 years, since the beginning of this century. India's population increased from 238 million in 1901 to double that size in a little over 60 years but, if one considers the growth in population after Independence in 1947, it became 2.3 times between 1951 and 1991. In fact, India's population growth pattern can be easily divided into three broad periods. The first was up to 1921, when the country had a high birth rate and a high death rate, and population was growing very slowly. The second period relates to the 30 years from 1921 to 1951, when the population started growing at a moderate level, with the death rate declining thanks to the control of various scourges and famines. The period after 1951 saw a big jump in the population growth rate, with further control and elimination of certain diseases and the birth rate not declining. A susceptible decline in the birth rate in India is observed from 1971 onward and one can probably say that the decline in birth rate during the 1980s was slightly higher than the decline in the death rate, leading to a slight, but only slight, decline in the growth rate.

Table 12-2. Population of Indian Republic and its average annual growth rate, 1901–91.

YEAR	POPULATION (MILLIONS)	GROWTH RATE (%)
1901	238.4	—
1911	252.1	0.56
1921	251.3	-0.03
1931	279.0	1.04
1941	318.7	1.33
1951	361.1	1.25
1961	439.2	1.96
1971	548.2	2.22
1981	683.3	2.20
1991*	846.3	2.14

Source: Census of India 1991 (1993).

Note: The population figures for the period prior to Independence also refer to the present boundaries.

* Although no census could be conducted in Jammu and Kashmir in 1991, the total for the country includes the projected population for that state.

India's estimated population of 879.5 million for mid-1992 (by the U.N.) is somewhat higher than the officially projected population of 852 million. If one takes account of the expected roughly two percent undercount in the censused population, the actual population of India and the U.N. estimate would be very similar.

India's growth rate of 1.9 percent per annum for 1990–95, projected by the U.N., seems to be in order as the natural growth rate (difference between the birth rate and the death rate) estimated in the Sample Registration System for 1990 and 1991 is just a little below two percent. With a birth rate falling at a faster pace than the death rate in recent years, one can say that the country has positively entered the third stage of demographic transition.

POPULATION ENVIRONMENT INTERRELATIONSHIP

"How many is too many?" The answer to this question is not easy at all, as one might say that the population we have on our planet today is already "too many," and should be reduced one way or the other so that those who survive might live an enriched life. In contrast, people living in the villages and slums very often say, "leave us to our fate and we shall mold our future the way we like." These are, however, two extreme positions, as outlined by Harold Coward in his Introduction to this volume.

The difference in the forecasts is extreme: a boundless population increase that rapidly exhausts the Earth's carrying capacity unless a "zero-sum game" is adopted, or a world of vastly increased population yet supporting a sustainable economy and ecology by virtue of scientific, technological, and social changes. According to the medium projections of the United Nations, as indicated in the beginning, the world population is likely to be 6.25 billion in 2000, 8.5 billion in 2025, and 10 billion in 2050, and will still not become stationary. The future population size may vary greatly depending on the decisions of those who are in the reproductive age group now and will be entering it in the years to come. The policies of various governments may also play a dominant role in this regard.

I am not in a position to comment on the future population-environment balance as I am not an ecology student and have no knowledge about the earth's known and unknown resources. I may, however, say that even if we were able to tap solar energy commercially, and succeeded in nitrogen fixation from the atmosphere and, thus, revolutionized agriculture, there would still be questions related to water availability, particularly in poor countries, as well as the manner in which human activities in future would affect the global water systems. The other issues relate to housing and clothing the vast populations.

Coming to water availability, a recent publication of the Population Reference Bureau indicates how environmental preconditions, like climate and geography, limit human access to water; and how human activities affect the global water systems. According to Falkenmark and Widstrand, water is a finite resource, and the tiny fraction suitable for drinking or irrigating crops is distributed unevenly throughout the world's regions. For example, with a harsh hydroclimate and increasing population pressure, arid and semi-arid regions of Africa are already living on the hydrological margin. The continuous famine conditions in Somalia over several years have forced people to leave their hearths and homes in search of water, and created a riot situation. Further, there have been reports of people begging for water from passing vehicles in western Kenya, which is suffering the brunt of the drought. In parts of Zimbabwe, drought has caused industries to shut down. Collapse of the water system in the Zimbabwean city of Bulawayo may cause residents to be evacuated (Falkenmark and Widstrand 1992, 9). By 2025, over one billion people worldwide may be living in areas subject to extreme water scarcity. The authors, however, conclude that there are many ways to soften the effects of both the current water crisis in selected world regions and the more widespread problems that loom ahead. These require active management of existing water resources and a slowing of population growth in water-scarce areas. As water systems transcend national boundaries, their management will require the cooperation and commitment of local, national, and international governments, industries, and other organizations (Falkenmark and Widstrand 1992, 32).

THE ENVIRONMENTAL ISSUES

There are several types of environmental issues before us, which can be put into three broad categories: (a) macro level, (b) meso level, and (c) micro level. At the macro level the discussions have largely concentrated on global warming; the rise of sea water level, with small islands and coastal lands getting submerged in oceans by the melting of glaciers; greenhouse effect; and the depletion of the ozone layer. The global warming effect of the "greenhouse gases" and, consequently, the depletion of the ozone layer, basically comes from the production of carbon dioxide created by the burning of fossil fuels in automobiles and factories. The future effects of global warming, indeed the estimated extent of it, are vigorously debated, but some change is certain to occur. The recent efforts of the developing countries toward industrialization and overall economic development have also been named as major factors in global warming by a number of scholars from the developed countries.

The meso level ecological/environmental issues can be classified as below:

1. Flow of city waste and industrial effluents into rivers and other water bodies.

2. Denudation of forests due to large-scale felling of trees. This has led to landslides in the mountains, and flooding during heavy rainfalls of regions which had never experienced this earlier. In contrast, there has been a substantial increase in drought-prone areas. There are reasons to believe that deforestation has led to reduction in rainfall in certain areas, leading to frequent drought situations.

3. Commissioning of multipurpose river valley projects, including construction of dams for better resource utilization and, sometimes, to check flooding in certain areas. In contrast, building a major dam often involves changing the water table near the dam site, leading to waterlogging in certain areas, especially near canal systems, and altering the balance of plant and animal species in the natural habitat up and down the stream. Alteration of groundwater systems and river deltas is an unavoidable outcome of the building of dams.

The micro level issues are altogether different in nature than the macro or meso level issues. Here the common man's perspective might be more useful. In India, as in several other developing countries of the world, there are a large number of villages which do not have a safe drinking water supply of their own, and it is a part of the daily chores of women and children to fetch water from a distance, sometimes a few kilometers, to meet the daily household needs. The problem is partly the topography, partly it is scarcity of rainfall and non-availability of subsoil aquifers at a reasonable depth. Further, in most villages in India, there is hardly any drainage system worth its name. The waste water from the households flows into the village lanes, and forms cesspools of stagnant water. The water of the village pond is used by the human beings and the cattle alike. There is no knowledge of the various types of diseases which may be prevalent in the area because of this common use of water. It is, however, a commonly known fact that roughly half the deaths caused by cholera in the world occur in India and Bangladesh. Malaria, gastroenteritis, fijaria, etc. are quite common in many parts of India.

NORTH-SOUTH RELATIONS AND THE ENVIRONMENT

The question of North-South relations in the context of the environment has been discussed on several occasions. The debate has basically been confined to the macro level issues; that is, how much the developing countries have been responsible for the unabated damage to the ecosystem and the environment. In contrast, scholars in the developing countries raise the issue of great consumerism in the industrialized and developed countries, and opine that if the people in the developed countries modified a little bit their way of life, things might improve a lot. The share of the developing countries in the utilization of fossil energy compared to that of the developed countries, if computed per capita, is just a small fraction. The allegation from the other side is that the absolute size of the developing countries' population is three and a half times that of the developed countries and, therefore, even if the per capita consumption is higher in the developed countries, the difference in the absolute amount of consumption is not that large.

Further, the developed countries, through improved technology, have limited environmental damage, whereas the developing countries have not yet been able to adopt the prescribed standards in this regard. While there may be a certain amount of truth in this contention, there are various constraints on the developing countries as regards adopting those standards. The major problem of this debate is in computing the amount of damage to the environment by the use of different sources of energy as opposed to, for instance, deforestation, etc. What the specific processes of the lifestyle in the developing countries are that probably cause global warming and "greenhouse effects" is something that has not been properly studied and understood yet; consequently, we have no knowledge as to how the same might be minimized without completely over-hauling that living style. The solutions to these questions have to be within the means of the people. Nobody has easy answers to these questions yet, but this might require a close examination of Aboriginal traditions on the one hand and secular ethics on the other. One might also like to consider the role of religion in this regard. Religion is one of the most important aspects of India's social struc-ture. As we know, most of the religions of the world that play significant roles in human development have encouraged birth. Under the current population growth regimes, and the need to modify them very substantially in the other di-rection in India and in other developing countries, religion has to play a role op-posite what it has in the past.

Besides emphasis on human reproduction, almost all religions in the world emphasize protecting the natural environment by limiting our needs and con-suming only that which is necessary for sustenance. In the developing countries, as we know, people below the "poverty line" cannot afford even subsistence level consumption; consequently, the question of consumerism for a large section of the population does not apply at all. It is the developed countries' people, and those belonging to the upper and upper-middle classes in the developing coun-tries that have forgotten the above religious tenet.

As I indicated earlier, besides the macro level issues in which the world's coun-tries have shown deep concern, the meso level and the micro level environmen-tal issues are also very important from the nations' and peoples' perspectives.

If one considers the problem from the perspective of the common person, one sees that that person is not concerned with what will happen to the world a few centuries hence, but is concerned about his or her daily woes. In a majority of developing countries, the common person's concern is how to achieve even a subsistence living, how the government or society can help by providing potable water in the village or hamlet, how the death toll due to various com-municable diseases can be minimized, if not eliminated completely. If the household does not have electricity, the concern is how to get it. There are mil-lions of households in rural and urban India that do not have electricity. Even if there is electricity in the village, a majority of households are unable to af-ford the initial investment needed to acquire the utility. These are some of the realities of the life of the masses in the developing countries, but little attention has been paid to such issues in international forums.

At the meso level, issues are much bigger in magnitude, and it is largely the national governments or the state (regional) governments that have to tackle them. At the first level, various governments are involved in different types of de-velopment projects, related to, for instance, multipurpose river valley projects, the opening up of hitherto isolated areas by developing road systems or laying new railway lines, or exploiting mineral resources in the resource-rich regions. In every case, there is a modification of the existing environment and a disturbance of the existing ecological balance. A basic question here is: Should the government proceed with the necessary developmental strategies or not? The answer is not very easy and, therefore, there have been tensions of various types. In India, current examples include the Tehri Dam project in Uttar Pradesh, and the Narmada Dam project, covering the states of Gujarat, Madhya Pradesh, Maharashtra, and a little of Rajasthan.

The second important question relates to stripping of forests and afforestation. In India, contrary to the religious teaching outlined in chapter 8, governments in the past have not been very careful in this regard, which led to large-scale felling of trees to meet various needs without requiring replanting in those areas. Increasing population pressure in the hills and mountains also led to a certain amount of deforestation, to get more and more land for cultivation. There have been some peoples' movements against large scale deforestation, like the *"Chipko Andolan"* in the Garhwal area of Uttar Pradesh, but such movements, being localized, have not been able to make much of a dent against deforestation. There is a need to have a stronger commitment to afforestation than in the past.

Regarding the discharge of industrial and urban wastes into the rivers, recently there has emerged a major concern at the government level. The governments have developed programs for cleaning the rivers on the one hand, and have instituted acts calling for more rigorous punishments for those who discharge industrial wastes into water bodies before properly treating the same. The implementation of these acts, however, requires even greater effort, because many times the governments themselves have been the major culprits.

CONCLUDING REMARKS

The above discussion of the environmental issues indicates clearly that there has been little concern by either the governments or the people with long-range environmental questions. For the people, their immediate present is more important. If their life can become a little more comfortable, they might start thinking of other environmental issues. Hence, from the viewpoint of the people, efforts should be made to provide them safe, potable water where the same is not available yet, a cleaner environment so that a number of communicable and water-borne diseases, etc., might be controlled, a livable house, and the ways and means to have a sustainable living. All this requires both government and community involvement.

Industry in India, whether public or private, has not shown any concern about environmental issues. The thermal powerhouses, for example, discharge a lot of soot, and there has been little effort to control the same. Similarly, if the Union Carbide factory at Bhopal had followed the prescribed rules and regulations, there would not have been the major gas disaster in 1984. There is, therefore, a need to direct the concern of the industry toward such problems, and also to implement regulative measures with full vigor.

Finally, at the individual level, the fatalistic attitude of "what can I alone do" needs to be molded to a positive, active attitude of working out one's own action plan. Here, religion and religious ethics can play an important role.

BIBLIOGRAPHY

Census of India 1991 (1993). Series I, *India, Final Population Totals:* Brief Analysis of Primary Census Abstract. Delhi: Controller of Publications.

Falkenmark, Malin, and Carl Widstrand (1992). Population and Water Resources: A Delicate Balance. *Population Bulletin* 47, No. 3. Washington: Population Reference Bureau.

United Nations Population Fund (UNEPA) (1993). *The State of World Population 1993.* New York: United Nations Population Fund.

13

Environmental Degradation
and the Religion of the Market

A. RODNEY DOBELL

FRAMING THE PROBLEM

In reporting periodically on the state of human affairs, the Human Development Reports produced by the United Nations Development Program serve in some respects as companions and complements to the economically-oriented World Development Reports of the World Bank. Figure 13-1 shows the figure used on the cover of the 1993 Human Development Report. In explanation, the inside front cover of that Report notes that the diagram refers to weighted averages of regional GDP (gross domestic product) and employment growth, and notes:

> The cover design reflects the disturbing phenomenon of jobless growth in the world. The upper curve represents GDP growth (1975–1990) and its projected trend (1990–2000) weighted for major regions [OECD countries, Latin America, Sub-Saharan Africa, South Asia and East Asia]. The lower curve represents employment growth, weighted by region. Since 1975, employment growth has consistently lagged behind output growth, and this gap is likely to widen during the 1990s.

Interestingly, however, one could speculate that the same design, with exactly the same variables and shapes, might appear on the cover of the World Development Report, but with a different explanatory note. Inside its front cover, the WDR might say something like:

229

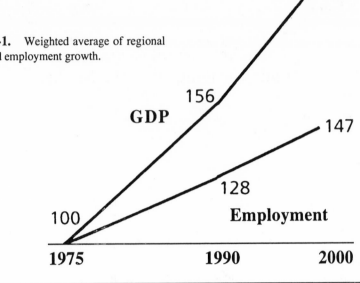

Fig. 13-1. Weighted average of regional
GDP and employment growth.

The cover design depicts the success with which industry and national governments have pursued aggressive adjustment measures to downsize operations, trim excess staff, de-layer hierarchies and achieve more efficient operations. . . . Since 1975, output growth has consistently outpaced employment increases, and this gap is likely to widen in the 1990s and beyond. This record of rising productivity makes possible continuing increases in wages for those employed, and creates an environment favorable to continued new investment and economic progress.

Thus, depending on whether one interprets employment as someone's opportunity to participate in production, and thereby claim a social role and a share of the world's material resources, or as simply a cost of doing business, the record of the last fifteen years will be read either as a disturbing trend toward jobless growth or as an encouraging indicator of steady increases in productivity and rising incomes per person employed.

The problem with the latter view, of course, arises in its emphasis on income per person employed. It is this which raises all the concerns about the emerging dual economy and enclave society where rising incomes for a falling

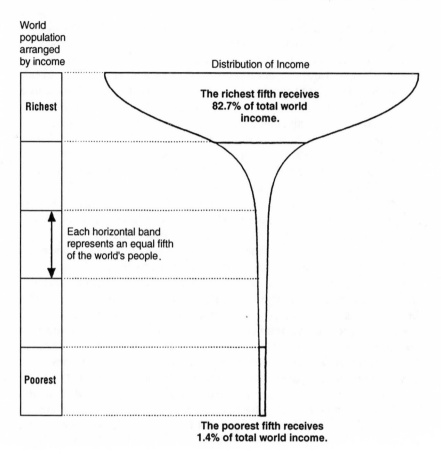

Fig. 13-2. The diagram shows the global distribution of income. The richest 20% of the world's population receives 82.7% of the total world income, while the poorest 20% receives only 1.4%. Global economic growth rarely filters down. The global income distribution by quintile is as follows:

WORLD POPULATION	WORLD INCOME
Richest 20%	82.7%
Second 20%	11.7%
Third 20%	2.3%
Fourth 20%	1.9%
Poorest 20%	1.4%

proportion of the population lead to an increasingly polarized and strained community. (See Homer-Dixon [1991] for a research agenda linking these concerns with issues of environmental degradation and global security.)

The Human Development Report for the previous year (1992) reveals starkly the massive gap between two economic worlds, the industrial countries (mostly) of the economically developed North and the less economically developed countries (mostly) of the South. This is the reality behind the issues of environmental stress and resource management to be discussed here. Figure 13-2, reproducing the inside cover of the 1992 Report, portrays a startlingly inequitable world, a world of maldistribution and disparity which underlies a so-called "ticking time bomb" of potential ecological degradation and collapse. The situation portrayed by the diagram seems on its face to be an unjustifiable result of indefensible policies. Yet day by day we accept these outcomes and live placidly (more or less) with their consequences. Why is that so?

It will be argued here that the explanation lies largely in our embrace of a peculiarly European or Western religion, an individualistic religion of economics and of markets, which explains all of these outcomes as the inevitable results of an intricate but objective system in which discretionary collective intervention is counterproductive. In particular, the explanation resides in the adoption of a perspective or frame that rests on an economic calculus in which employment is simply a cost of doing business, and Nature is merely a pool of resources for use in production. In this calculus, the world of business is so fundamental and so separate from the environment or the biosphere that intervention in the ongoing economic system is a threat to the natural order of things, and hence to future human welfare. In this way of thinking, that outcome is just (or at least inevitable) which emerges from the natural workings of this economic system, and the "wisdom of the market" on which it is based. The hegemony achieved by this particular intellectual construct — a "European religion" or economic religion — is remarkable; it has become a dogma of almost universal application, the dominant religion of our time, shoring up and justifying what would appear to be a patently inequitable status quo. It has achieved an immense influence which dominates contemporary human activity.

Core elements in the dogma of this religion of the market include two counter-intuitive but basic propositions:

1. That it is right and just, through the medium of the limited liability corporation, to separate one's personal morality from responsibility for acts undertaken in the name of corporate objectives. Contemporary rhetoric may be weakening the phrasing of this proposition, but the expression "the market made me do it" remains a fundamental element of explanations for actions that would otherwise seem morally unjustifiable. This proposition leads on to the pri-

macy of corporate-form bookkeeping, which, as will be noted below, is a long way from any concept of full environmental accounting.

2. That value can be adequately signaled by prices, and exchange of value can be adequately accomplished by free transactions on impersonal market mechanisms.

What is necessary as an antidote to this strange world view is to shift to a dramatically different frame, in which the economic sphere is inexorably embedded in the biosphere, and the functioning of the larger ecological system provides the natural benchmark; intervention in that functioning for economic purposes will be acceptable only when demonstrably not threatening to the natural order. Before dealing in detail with this process of inversion or reframing, however, it is useful to look more closely at the relationships between human activity and environmental stress.

ENVIRONMENTAL DEGRADATION: DECOMPOSITION INTO COMPONENT FACTORS

It is clear that increasing population and the increasing scale of human activity are straining dramatically the carrying capacity of the Earth. The increasing pressure of the anthroposphere on the biosphere is undeniable, and persistent environmental degradation is an observable consequence. But that stress reflects not one simple problem of population growth, but four problems, of which population is only one. These four are:

1. The scale of population and its still-too-high rates of growth;

2. Dramatic inequity in employment opportunities, income and wealth, leading to the coexistence of absurd "absolute affluence" and grinding "absolute poverty";

3. Excessive material content and resource use in consumption;

4. Wanton, wasteful stress imposed on the environment and ecological systems as a result of inappropriate technologies in the harvesting of renewable resources and the utilization and disposal of material resources or energy.

In attempting to examine the relative roles of population and technology in the explanation of environmental stress and degradation, there is a little trick which, though simple, is illuminating. Used already by Ehrlich and Ehrlich in their path-breaking 1972 book, *Population, Resources and Environment,* and subsequently employed in various descriptive comparative studies at OECD and elsewhere, it consists of breaking down or decomposing a complex notion like environmental stress into component elements for separate analysis. Although it is tautological, it is useful for expository purposes to examine the formula on the following page.

This formula simply reminds us that several factors go into determining the level of environmental stress in any one region: the scale of population itself, the level of income per person to be maintained, the material content of the goods and services on which that income is spent, and the stress generated directly by the choice of technique by which the resources will be harvested or extracted to provide that material throughput. Or, in other words, the point is that the link between the scale of population and the extent of environmental stress is mediated through several key intervening determinants: income, or the scale of the consumption/production system; the quality of development, or the material content of consumption; the technological choices determining the environmental impact associated with the flow of material and energy through the production system, including harvesting or extraction and discharge or disposal.

Of course, in this formula none of these elements is independent of the others; they are all determined in a simultaneous system. Indeed, the formula is not offered as an operational concept; it is illustrative, not necessarily computable (although it does seem to offer some possibly fruitful approaches to organizing the results of empirical research). Our contemporary economic religion has created a system of social organization and individual incentives which has enjoyed unparalleled success in a drive toward rapid growth of per capita incomes (Y/P), and it is clear that aspirations for higher incomes and material well-being are widely shared around the world.

But the major impact of the religion of the market on environmental degradation is probably in the latter two terms of the formula, which reflect income aspirations and technological choices more than they do population. The first of these (M/Y) can be thought of as representing the material content of consumption and production, thus reflecting choices on production techniques; the second (S/M) represents the environmental stresses associated with the utilization of resources and ecological services, reflecting decisions on the technologies adopted for harvesting or conservation.

Relevant to the first of these two are discussions of dematerialization and reduction of resource demands in production — increasing energy and resource efficiency. (See Schmidt-Bleek [1993] for examples and references.) Relevant to the second is the concern with wasteful and destructive, non-selective resource extraction or harvesting techniques. Because ecological resources and natural capital are unpriced, harvesting techniques like driftnets and draggers, clearcuts and strip-mines, are not only tolerated, but forced in the name of com-

Table 13-1.   S = (Y/P) x (M/Y) x (S/M) x P

DECOMPOSITION OF PRESSURES LEADING TO
ENVIRONMENTAL DEGRADATION OR STRESS

Where

S – denotes some measure of environmental stress

Y/P – stands for income per capita

M/Y – stands for the material content or resource
use per unit of income or output

S/M – denotes the environmental stress per unit of material
output or resource input

and

P – represents total population

NOTES

(S) – It must be remembered, of course, that environmental stress is experienced differently in different places: in the North concerns may be abstract and global — e.g., CFCs and ozone depletion problems; in the South they are more immediate and local — e.g., the loss of communal grazing land or fuelwood.

(Y/P) – Obvious distributional issues are central in examining the impact of changing levels of income per capita.

(M/Y) – Represents a choice of lifestyle (materialistic consumer society versus a conserver society (Science Council 1977) and orientation to production (Wuppertal Institute 1993).

(S/M) – Relates to the question of appropriate technologies (Schumacher), "wanton by-catch" and social or environmental stress.

---

petitiveness. The extent to which market forces can lead in this area to what would seem obviously irrational, if not obscene, practices, such as the harvesting of species to the point of extinction, has been clearly demonstrated by Colin Clark, for example, in his book *Mathematical Bioeconomics* (Clark 1976).

The economic religion thus seems to push inexorably toward high incomes, highly material-intensive and environmentally stressful modes of production — toward the adoption of technologies that are unselective and wasteful of ecological resources and ecological integrity. At the same time, it leaves behind absolute poverty on a large scale, from which environmental degradation also flows inevitably. Within the framework of this religion, it seems, the conserver society is not commercially viable, and the consumer society is largely inevitable.

Interestingly, and paradoxically, it is in the harvesting of renewable, rather than exhaustible, resources, that we appear to go most wrong and put ourselves most at risk. Examples are all around, in the adoption of destructive technologies such as strip-mining on land, strip-mining of oceans (draggers, driftnets), massive clearcutting of forests, and so on. Thus, environmental choices are embedded in and driven by the economic religion, though not explicitly articulated in the process. At the same time, it can be argued that economic adjustment processes, technological progress, and substitution of more plentiful materials have consistently generated, and will continue to generate, increasing supply and decreasing real supply prices for almost all minerals and exhaustible resources (Moore 1992). Some observers would extend this argument not only to wood products but to water and other renewable resources. Doubts are greater with respect to concerns about biodiversity and the functioning of ecosystems more generally.

It is obvious that religious teachings and traditions influence the last term (P) of the formula, through impacts on rates of population growth, but it is also widely recognized now that the level and distribution of income, and social factors such as the treatment and education level of girls and women, probably influence it more. (References dealing with this question of demographic transition can be found in several other chapters in this volume. (See also Margaret Catley Carlson.)

Examining this formula, then, we note that traditional religions appear pro-natalist, and press towards high total population (P). Western individualist consumer-based religions, on the other hand, press towards the joy of high Y/P, high income and high consumption per capita, though there may be some possibilities of promoting the conserver society as an alternative. Technological developments offer considerable promise of reducing the material content of output and consumption, for example, through "dematerialization." (Schmidt-Bleek 1993.) But the pressures toward efficiency and competitiveness in a world economy with a religion based on a bizarrely incomplete price system seem to condemn us to continuing problems in the methods of resource utilization.

Thus it seems that the biggest difficulties arise precisely where one or another religious tendency is strongest. In the name of authority, traditional religions appear, at least to some, to press a pro-natalist view and encourage excessive population growth. In the name of efficiency, on the other hand, economic religions encourage environmentally wasteful, destructive technologies for the harvesting of renewable resources, utilization of ecological services, and extraction of exhaustible resources. So we turn to a closer look at that peculiar intellectual perspective.

ECONOMIC (European) RELIGION

The basic posture or orientation of the economic religion is well captured in a recent comment of Jagdish Bhagwati, who notes "There are at times philosophical differences between the two [proponents of free trade on the one hand and of the environment on the other] that cannot be reconciled, as when environmentalists assert nature's autonomy, whereas most economists see nature as a handmaiden to humankind." (Bhagwati 1993). The economist's outlook, as so described, can be illustrated as in figure 13-3.

It is by now widely recognized in the economics literature — though much less so in practice — that this model itself demands attention to the costs and prices of many resources and ecological services previously treated as free. Given its claim to scientific rationality, this economic religion rests on a surprisingly small base of information (even though it may be vast relative to what can be handled within a central planning agency). Interestingly, more or less everybody now knows that market systems are profoundly flawed, in the sense that, left on their own with present pricing and practices, they will lead inevitably to environmental damage and destruction of irreplaceable ecological systems. (See Solow 1992, and Daly 1993.) In particular, market mechanisms are widely recognized to be incomplete with respect to prices, property rights, and accounting information when it comes to environmental concerns. Indeed, on examination, prices, markets, and market principles appear to cover such a small portion of overall human activity, even economic activity, that the hegemony achieved by the religion over all social action is startling, as noted earlier. It is a puzzle that Western society has bought so fully into the particular intellectual construct, but the undercurrent of dissent that has always been present does now seem to be moving toward a stage of much more fundamental questioning. (The political philosopher Charles Taylor [1991] offers one critique, as does the more popular volume of John Ralston Saul [1992].) (See also Sagoff 1988.)

In the school of "Free Market Environmentalism" (figure 13-3), these problems are to be remedied by completing the market through the introduction of prices and property rights that attach appropriate market signals to resources presently not properly valued in economic calculation. In particular, property rights governing the use of common pool resources, and property rights governing the exploitation of ecological services for waste disposal are all to be created in order to ration access in socially optimal fashion. One can consult Ostrom (1990) and Block (1990) for two views, and the seminal work of Dales (1968) for the origins of much of this thinking.

From Ostrom's work, it is clear that we need to take much more fully into account the richness of the social institutions, beyond the market, involved in

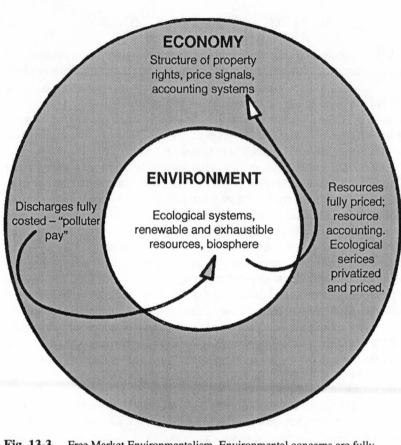

Fig. 13-3. Free Market Environmentalism. Environmental concerns are fully integrated into economic decisions. Environmental objectives are pursued without distorting trade or creating protectionist barriers.

such regulation. But in any case, it is also clear that we need to know much more about the dynamics and interactions of ecological resources with the natural processes of the biosphere. For this purpose, then, it is essential to consider an alternative frame or world view.

Indeed, Stevenson (1991) emphasizes the necessity to recognize a whole range of common property arrangements, which represent alternative institutional solutions to the difficulties of open access resources, short of the full private property (FME) solution. Such intermediate arrangements include as alternatives not just general access through a structure of government regulation, but also more restricted access governed formally by well-defined organizations or community groups, or informal access controlled by less well-defined traditional or cultural groupings. It is these last which have been of particular interest to Ostrom and her colleagues in many settings.

THE ECOLOGICAL FRAME

The alternative, then, is to construct a broader frame of reference. In figure 13-4, the economy is portrayed as one set of structures and activities, developed within a broader set of social institutions, all of which in turn operate within the context of a biosphere with its own internal logic and natural dynamics.

Within this framework, one can view the economic system, as just noted, as meeting the needs of current generations by utilizing produced means of production (physical, human, and intellectual capital), drawing on natural ecological systems as a source of raw materials, and on the absorptive capacity of the natural environment as a source of waste disposal services, with the whole set of activities governed by a well-established set of property rights, price signals, and market exchange mechanisms, but mediated also by a set of social institutions and traditions. The point of the "free market environmentalism" idea is that this process can, with appropriate prices and accounting, achieve appropriate utilization of environmental resources, taking into account intangible benefits, option values, and the like. Indeed, in a theoretical ideal world, it can be argued that the very short term pursuit of maximum net national product, appropriately priced, can lead to the long term objective of sustainability. (In a model focused particularly on pollution costs, Hartwick [1990] demonstrates this mathematical result; in a more general argument, Solow [1992] suggests an "almost practical" definition of sustainability drawing on the same analysis.) Even in this ideal setting for free market environmentalism, however, the argument does depend both on assumption of the "right" prices for all ecological and social, as well as physical, goods, and on the existence of a social rule that provides for appropriate social reinvestment to maintain the value of society's capital stock, including natural capital. (And all of this therefore requires the assumption of appropriate repricing of resource flows from South to North, for example, to reflect the scarcity value of natural resources as well as compensation for pollution costs customarily unpriced.)

With some such understanding about a better contemporary balance in resource flows, one can turn to the question of sustainability and intergenerational equity more directly. The starting point is simply that, to meet the needs of current generations without compromising the capacity of future generations to meet their own needs, it is necessary to undertake sufficient investment to maintain the capital stock of society undiminished. A generation ago, Solow (1973) noted that the normal pattern of economic growth entailed a

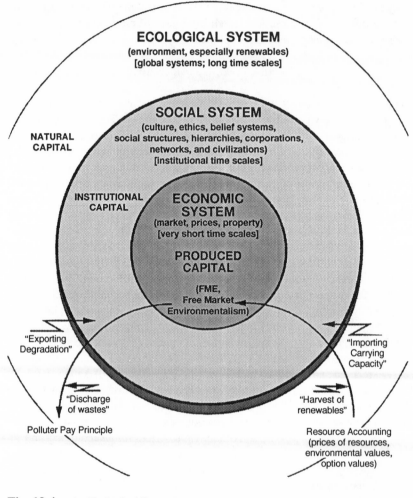

Fig. 13-4. An Ecological Frame

process of transformation whereby existing natural resources are drawn down and converted to manufactured goods (produced means of production), thereby creating a constructed capital stock capable of generating the flow of goods and services necessary to meet the needs and desires of growing numbers of people with rising incomes. The key to sustainability is simply that in this process of transformation, the consumption of natural resources is matched by a sufficient buildup of physical capital and industrial capacity. In his "An Almost

Practical Step toward Sustainability," Solow (1992) spells out how this calculation can be accomplished, noting the correspondence with what has become known as "Hartwick's Rule." (See Hartwick [1990] for references.) The logic is evident, and the process natural. That logic corresponds directly to an obvious industrial strategy for oil-based economies like the Middle East or Alberta, the transition strategies of which obviously must build up heritage funds sufficient to assure adequate income when the oil runs out.

A minimal concept of sustainability, therefore, would be one which insists on at least a "constant capital" rule, or on the responsibility of current generations for passing along an aggregate capital stock no smaller than the present. But as figure 13-4 emphasizes, it is important to keep in mind not only a general social asset which might be called institutional capital, reflecting a history of social organization and social relationships, but also a potentially still more fundamental asset called natural capital which reflects the continuing productive capacity flowing from the maintenance of biodiversity and the integrity of the natural ecological processes of the planet. It is not clear that we can treat all these forms of capital as fully interchangeable and easily substitutable.

In particular, it is not clear that produced means of production (physical capital) can fully replace critical natural capital, or ecological systems indispensable for human well-being and, ultimately, for human survival. Examples of such critical natural assets often cited include the ozone layer, the carbon cycle, and biodiversity, but also might relate simply to fisheries, or wilderness. Following up earlier work of David Pearce (see for example, Pearce et al. [1989, 1991]), Pearce and Atkinson (1993) suggest specific constraints on the preservation of critical natural habitat.

Thus, a notion of "weak sustainability," or a rule of non-decreasing capital per capita, assures an undiminished productive potential for future generations by requiring a sufficiently high rate of reinvestment, essentially that total resource rents be reinvested, in addition to appropriate physical depreciation allowances (Pearce and Atkinson 1993). Such a rule is adequate if in fact physical capital can always be substituted for natural capital, and there exist no critical natural capital stocks the sacrifice of which would represent an irreversible loss of capacity to meet the needs of future generations.

If this assumption is not warranted — as it seems it clearly might not be — then something more is needed. If forms of capital stock are not easily substitutable, then Pearce and Atkinson argue for a requirement of "strong sustainability" which insists on preservation of a minimum stock of critical natural capital as such. Since it is probably too much to hope for a pricing system which can adequately value critical natural capital stocks, the requirement of strong sustainability translates into an imposed ceiling on the rate of exploitation or transformation of natural resources, and a floor on the preservation of critical natural capital. The Brundtland target for wilderness preservation — now adopted formally by the Government of British Columbia — is one obvious example of such a constraint on the utilization of natural capital.

Adopting this approach to natural capital also leads inevitably, it might be noted, to the inversion of the frame or image of the free market environmentalism approach. Rather than viewing the environment as a pool of resources embedded in the economy, the utilization of which as raw material or as disposal capacity should be properly priced and rationed, it becomes more natural to see our pool of natural capital as a continuing heritage or bequest to future generations, a fund from which withdrawals can be made on a continuing basis for investment, for example in a "working forest" base or a commercial fishery. In this image, the maintenance and continuity of the fund constitute the fundamental social obligation and the natural starting point; withdrawals for current production can be warranted only so long as the continuity of the fund is not compromised. In this image, one does not "withdraw" land from the "working forest" for parks or wilderness preservation purposes; those purposes form the starting point, and "withdrawals" from the fund for commercial forestry (or settlement) can be contemplated only when they do not jeopardize the integrity of the overall commitment to sustainability.

The conclusion from all this is that even with the fullest pricing of ecological goods and services, some form of social valuation or target is required to guide the market system in its interactions with the biosphere. It is interesting that this result, developed here from consideration of environmental and social values, seems to be, in fact, a general property of economic models with many durable goods. In an old paper which anticipated somewhat the application of butterfly theorems and chaos theory in economic analysis, the present author and colleagues working in economic growth theory noted that even in the purest of models of economic dynamics, the inescapable requirement for a competitive economic model to pursue an optimal (or even a stable) path of growth is that the terminal valuations of capital goods be fixed from outside the economic model. That is, in effect, a society must be prepared to specify the values of its resources in the longest run (for future generations) before it can be argued that decisions about resource allocation can responsibly be delegated to the wisdom of the market (Burmeister, Dobell, et al 1973).

In the absence of such a valuation, we are forced to respond to the impossibility of a so-called rational or scientific analytical solution by falling back on a more pragmatic mechanism: adaptive (participatory) management — perhaps at community level and employing economic instruments — but within an overall resource use framework and conservation constraints that "preserve the heirlooms" — the basic natural capital.

SOCIAL RESPONSE

A first social response, then, is to set up ground rules to guide the market. The discussion in the previous section suggests two such rules to begin with, one requiring adequate reinvestment to assure maintenance of the productive capital stock, and the other to require preservation of a minimum stock of critical natural capital (parks, wilderness, biosphere reserves, etc.) in its original form, even if current market signals suggest that its highest and best use lies in some other application. This use of a preemptive rule on minimum "set-asides" of biosphere reserve or wilderness as an overriding constraint on land and resource use decisions in place of market calculations raises some serious questions about the perceived rationality of the proposed constraints, and has given rise to a vast literature in a wide range of applications. In the Uruguay Round of trade negotiations, for example, the idea of "tariffication" to replace rules (import quotas) by prices (tariffs) is central, as a way to achieve a better allocation of agricultural resources more appropriately geared to the circumstances of different countries.

Similar controversies arise in arguments about regulations governing waste disposal, for example. Rules like the Basle Convention, which restricts or prohibits international traffic in toxic wastes, even though some countries may be enthusiastic about the revenues which might accrue from trade in waste disposal services; or like the Ontario government's regulations precluding transport of waste from Toronto to Elliot Lake, even though both communities seem keen on the respective benefits which might be realized from the transaction; or like proposed regulations requiring massive investment in sewage treatment facilities for the city of Victoria, even though scientific evidence is cited to show that there is no discernible harm from current discharges into the ocean — all these have the effect of preempting economic decisions and preventing economic activity which might leave all parties to the transactions feeling better off. Such rules are seen as lacking variety, flexibility, differentiation; failing to reflect the differing ecological circumstances and assimilative capacities in different environments; ignoring scientific evidence and economic reason — in short, they are argued to be unscientific, offering an irrational response insufficiently sensitive to calculable consequences of alternative actions. Equal treatment, in circumstances that differ radically, it is argued, is neither sensible nor equitable; equal outcomes might call for different actions or different sacrifices in different circumstances.

The counterargument to the suggestion that such rules are irrational and overlook current opportunities to achieve a better allocation of resources is often to the effect that pricing is simply an inefficient way to achieve prohibition of actions we truly want to prohibit (witness the problems of smuggling generated by high cigarette taxes). Rules may be necessary to change behavior directly, to force acceptance of individual responsibility for waste, for example, in ways that price systems (given existing inequities in wealth or resources) may not. In such a situation, the perception of equal sacrifice may be essential to social acceptance of action, even if this demonstrably leads to wasteful social expenditures by failing to take advantage of differences in circumstances, assimilative capacity of the environment, or preferences.

In the case of waste treatment, for example, an absolute prohibition on transport of hazardous waste might be seen in some longer-run sense as a risk-minimizing strategy. The loss of precise optimality is of less concern than the mobilizing of popular support that might come with a perception of equal treatment and equal application of the rules to all, or with acknowledgment of a concern to avoid the exploitation of the poor that would occur through the application of economic mechanisms in the absence of an absolute social prohibition. This concern for an offloading of fundamental human responsibilities is widespread. It underlies controversies like the volunteer army or procedures for a fair draft. Should wealthy individuals be able to compensate poorer ones to assume their responsibilities in something so fundamental? Is this different from simply a division of labor and the operation of comparative advantage? Should we be able to buy our way out of an obligation to change our own lifestyles by funding the poor to pick up the slack? "Debt for nature" swaps or "guardian of the rain forest" schemes seem to be of this character, for example, or schemes for acquisition of land in Paraguay to offset industrial development in Indiana, while staying within overall emissions limits. More generally, the idea of "joint implementation," whereby rich countries might fund more cost-effective measures for reduction of greenhouse gas emissions in poorer countries, figures very strongly in the recent Framework Convention on Climate Change. Other such schemes are discussed in a recent volume on *Ethics and Climate Change* (Coward and Hurka 1993). In short, these questions pit the argument that the poor should not be denied opportunities for increased income through pollution-intensive or risky activity against the argument that there should be no opportunity to escape our individual responsibilities for environmental sustainability — the obligation to clean up one's own emissions and wastes — by transferring these responsibilities through an exchange of funds.

It is these perplexing issues which lead on to the second social response to the need for social ground rules. The problem raised by the above examples is that equal treatment, at this moment, of people who have been unequally treated before now, need not be fair or equitable. In the debate around the goal of equal outcomes versus the rule of equal opportunity or equal treatment, it has been argued that one's position in the social spectrum now — and hence one's ability to participate effectively in an individualistic market-driven world — depends critically not just on history up to now, but also on a social lottery at birth: life chances differ widely, and consequently, the mere assumption of equal treatment cannot assure either equal outcomes or even fundamental fairness. As the initial endowments with which individuals participate in the market system may be thought unfair, both absolute rules of access (e.g., to health care) and absolute prohibitions (e.g., against transfer of social responsibilities for waste disposal) may reasonably be adopted by a society, despite all the valid arguments about opportunities forgone thereby.

Indeed, in the end, it seems that societies are willing to give up much of the fine-tuning and precise optimization promised by market calculation in favor of broader but possibly more robust guidelines such as social rules or religious precepts. In some cases this amounts to giving up on opportunities to adapt to differing ecological circumstances and alter treatment according to different assimilative capacities, or to realize gains from trade. In effect, it is giving up on a scientific or consequentialist approach in favor of broader social goals seen as more fundamental. (See Taylor [1991], Saul [1992], or even Lindblom [1976].) In work identified after this chapter was completed, Sagoff (1988) sets out, from a philosophical perspective, a much fuller analysis of this issue. Two subsequent publications by Sagoff (1991 and 1993) are also directly relevant to the topic of this present chapter.

A second dimension of the social response, however, requires us to address the other challenge, which is the inequity in initial endowments, the problem of North-South disparity that must be addressed if the distribution of initial property rights is to be contemplated. To create property rights in the larger natural assets of concern to the North creates a truly formidable challenge.

We have argued above that our future interests and the interests of future generations both demand preservation of requisite biodiversity and natural capital, and pursuit of an environmentally responsible path of economic development throughout the world. To achieve this purpose, free market environmentalism envisages a new (and final) enclosures movement, one which will establish ownership, and hence rational allocation, not only of global open-access resources, but also of the elements of basic ecological systems such as the oceans, the atmosphere and biodiversity itself.

In the context of this question, an observation attributed to Ruskin, quoted by Ivan Head in his recent book *On a Hinge of History* (1991), is interesting:

> "Whereas it has long been known and declared that the poor have no right to the property of the rich, I wish it also to be known and declared that the rich have no right to the property of the poor."

The property of the poor, for the most part, is the commons. Recognizing the claim of the poor to their share of such property is simply recognizing some part of intrinsic human claims to a share of the earth's life-support systems. And the idea of creating property rights for the poor by restricting access to the global commons is not new. It goes back in international discussions at least to the International Sea-Bed Authority created as part of the UN Convention on the Law of the Sea, which recognized the "common heritage of humankind." But these concepts came fully to the fore in the negotiations leading up to the 1992 United Nations Conference on Environment and Development meetings in Rio.

In those discussions, the South Commission (1991) set out a negotiating position featuring a number of basic propositions grounded on the central principle that developing countries have an inherent right to adequate environmental space to accommodate their basic development needs. These included:

- Recognized right of access to world's atmospheric resources for the South;
- Recognition by the North of the enormous environmental debt already incurred as a result of the allegedly irresponsible development path followed thus far;
- Recognition of special property rights systems and appropriate compensation mechanisms, in particular in respect of biodiversity and genetic materials.

There exist, by now, many analyses of the redistributional consequences of the various schemes proposed. On climate change, for example, one may see Dobell and Parson (1988) for a preliminary discussion of a world atmosphere fund, and Grubb (1990) for a more detailed analysis. On biodiversity and related questions of intellectual property, negotiations and controversy continue. Overall, however, it seems fair to conclude that the degree of redistribution entailed in recognition of anything like equal per capita claims on the global commons, or even the principle of adequate environmental space put forward by the South Commission would be far too great to be acceptable to the developed economies of the North.

For the time being, therefore, the debate remains centered on possibilities for a sharing of the responsibilities for sustainability through joint implementation, technical assistance, and transfers of resources, technology, and intellectual property through individual efforts or official development assistance, where guidelines like those of Singer (1979), mentioned above, may be brought to bear.

SUMMARY AND CONCLUSIONS

The conclusions from this discussion can be summarized as follows:

1. We do face a crucial situation, and it is centered on the problem of scale — the scale of human numbers, activity, and appetite — all pressing the limits of a finite biosphere.

2. Numbers and the growth of numbers — the expansion of population — are key factors contributing directly to this crisis. But if other factors can be addressed, a demographic transition to population stabilization may be accomplished quickly enough to avoid catastrophic collapse of human society. Key determinants of such demographic transition are more equitable income distribution, and more equitable treatment of women (including higher levels of education for girls and women).

3. A key factor in other components of the problem is the pervasive influence of a flawed — probably fatally flawed — religion or belief system: the European religion of the market. Interestingly, the proponents of this religion individually recognize its flaws and incomplete nature, but "in the absence of other measures," insist on its continued application in social decisions.

4. "Free market environmentalism" — the introduction of prices and property rights for ecological services and natural capital as steps toward filling some of the recognized gaps and completing the information base for social decision — is a necessary step in a social response to the current crisis, but is not, and cannot be, enough.

5. Beyond such steps to complete the market, we require measures to embed the market in a larger vision. We need acceptance of more fundamental principles, amounting to ethical guidelines, to shape our relationship with our land and control the pace of our harvesting from it. Two such basic ground rules may be sufficient to assure sustainability:

   a. "Do not eat into capital." — (Consumption must not exceed Net National Product — Solow 1992.)

   b. "Do not sell the heirlooms." — (Preserve wilderness, the gene pool, the natural systems of the biosphere, biodiversity, cultural diversity, natural capital in general — Osberg 1988; Pearce and Atkinson 1993.)

Thus, there is a two-part requirement: the substitution, transformation, or creation of a resource base must be adequate to preserve undiminished opportunities for the future, and some essential parts of the resource base must be preserved intact and unaltered.

6. Most fundamentally, in order to achieve this goal, it is essential to address current inequities in wealth and income, and hence to address a fundamental reallocation in property rights. One feasible target might be tithing for development assistance (Singer 1979). The theoretical target of equal per capita claims on the Earth's common pool of ecological resources — equal shares in the biosphere for all individuals (South Commission 1991) — seems compelling morally, but obviously is far beyond anything socially acceptable at this time.

Finally, then, the point of this chapter is that the link from population scale and growth to environmental stress and degradation is not simple — it must be recognized as affected by many social and technological considerations, of which this chapter focuses on three: the level and distribution of income, and hence consumption (the twin problems of absolute affluence and absolute poverty must be faced); the material content of consumption and hence production (the problems of inefficient resource use and the quality of development must be faced); and the choice of technologies for harvesting and disposal of the energy and material throughput and resource use in production (the problem of "wanton waste and bycatch" must be addressed, and obligations to Nature in its own right must be considered).

The key conclusion advanced here is that for a workable and responsible stewardship, some version of "free market environmentalism" is necessary, but not sufficient. Delegation of almost all environmental management responsibility to markets, or market-like community decisions, is inescapable. But the direction of those decisions ultimately demands social ground rules reflecting ethical judgments. In addressing these issues, no matter how faithfully we pursue the religion of economics, and particularly that of free market environmentalism, there are two points at which we must inevitably appeal to social ground rules of a more traditional religious character: on the question of sustainability, or the preservation of critical natural capital, where we must recognize our obligation to respect some intrinsic (or at least terminal) value to Nature in its own right — that is, we need some form of preservation ground rules such as the two noted above; and on the question of ownership of the commons, or the distribution of initial endowments, where we must recognize our obligation to others in some form — that is, we need some redistribution ground rule .

Neither of these can be found in the dogma of the market; both rest on more fundamental features of our relationships with others and with the earth around us.

BIBLIOGRAPHY

Bhagwati, Jagdish. "The Case for Free Trade." *Scientific American* (November 1993): 42–49.

Block, Walter D., ed. *Economics and the Environment: A Reconciliation.* Vancouver: The Fraser Institute, 1990.

Burmeister, E., C. Caton, A. R. Dobell, and S. Ross. "The 'Saddlepoint Property' and the Structure of Dynamic Heterogeneous Capital Good Models." *Econometrica* 41, 1 (1973): 79–95.

Catley Carlson, Margaret. *Explosions, Eclipses and Escapes: Charting a Course on Global Population Issues.* The 1993 Paul Hoffman Lecture, 7 June 1993. New York: United Nations Development Program, 1993.

Clark, Colin W. *Mathematical Bioeconomics: The Optimal Management of Renewable Resources.* New York: Wiley, 1976.

Coward, H. and T. Hurka. *Ethics and Climate Change.* Waterloo: Wilfrid Laurier University Press, 1993.

Dales, J. H. *Pollution, Property and Prices.* Toronto: University of Toronto Press, 1968.

Daly, Herman E. "The Perils of Free Trade." *Scientific American* (November 1993): 50–57.

Daly, Herman E. and John B. Cobb, Jr. *For the Common Good: Redirecting the Economy Toward Community, the Environment and a Sustainable Future.* Boston: Beacon Press, 1989.

Dobell, A. R., and Edward Parson. "A World Atmosphere Fund," *Policy Options* (December 1988): 6–8.

Ehrlich, Paul R., and Anne H. Ehrlich. *Population, Resources, Environment: Issues in Human Ecology.* 2nd ed. San Francisco: W. H. Freeman, 1972.

Grubb, Michael. *Energy Policies and the Greenhouse Effect.* London: Royal Institute of International Affairs, 1990.

Hartwick, John. *Degradation of Environmental Capital and National Accounting Procedures.* Ottawa: Economic Council of Canada, 1990.

Head, Ivan. *On a Hinge of History.* Toronto: University of Toronto Press, 1992.

Homer-Dixon, Thomas F. "Environmental Scarcities and Violent Conflict." *International Security* 19, 1 (Summer 1991): 5–40.

Huntington, Samuel P. "The Clash of Civilizations." *Foreign Affairs* (Summer 1993): 22–49.

Keyfitz, Nathan. "A Short Course in Population Policies: How the Systems Approach Differs." Photocopy. 16 August 1989.

Lindblom, Charles E. *The Policy-Making Process.* Englewood Cliffs, N.J.: Prentice-Hall, 1976.

Moore, Stephen. "So Much for 'Scarce Resources'." *The Public Interest* 106 (Winter 1992): 97–107.

Osberg, Lars. "Remarks on the Cost of Inaction." In *The Brundtland Challenge and the Cost of Inaction,* ed. Alex Davidson and Michael Dence. Halifax: Institute for Research on Public Policy, 1988.

Ostrom, Elinor. *Governing the Commons.* Cambridge: Cambridge University Press, 1990.

Pearce, David, Anil Markandya, and Edward B. Barbier. *Blueprint for a Green Economy.* London: Earthscan Publications, 1989. (See also Blueprint II, 1991.)

Pearce, David, and Giles Atkinson. "Measuring Sustainable Development." *Ecodecision* (June 1993): 64–66.

Piel, Gerard. *Only One World.* New York: W. H. Freeman and Company, 1992.

Ramakrishna, Kilaparti, and George M. Woodwell, eds. *World Forests for the Future: Their Use and Conservation.* New Haven: Yale University Press, 1993.

Rees, William E. "Ecological Footprints and Appropriated Carrying Capacity: What Urban Economics Leaves Out." *Environment and Urbanization* 4, 2 (October 1992): 121–30.

Sagoff, Mark. *The Economy of the Earth.* Cambridge: Cambridge University Press, 1988.

Sagoff, Mark. "Nature versus the Environment." Report from the Institute for Philosophy and Public Policy, University of Maryland, 1991.

Sagoff, Mark. "Population, Nature and the Environment," *Report from the Institute for Philosophy and Public Policy,* University of Maryland, special issue, Fall 1993.

Saul, John Ralston. *Voltaire's Bastards: The Dictatorship of Reason in the West.* New York: Free Press, 1992.

Schmidt-Bleek, F. "Revolution in Resource Productivity for a Sustainable Economy." *Fresenius Environmental Bulletin,* August 1993 (and other related papers in this special issue of the journal).

Singer, Peter. *Practical Ethics.* Cambridge: Cambridge University Press, 1979.

Solow, Robert. "Intergenerational Equity and Exhaustible Resources," *Review of Economic Studies,* Symposium on the Economics of Natural Resources, Special Issue, 1974, 29–45.

Solow, Robert. "An Almost Practical Step Toward Sustainability." An invited lecture on the occasion of the fortieth anniversary of Resources for the Future, 8 October 1992. Washington, D.C.: 1992.

Stevenson, Glenn G. *Common Property Economics.* Cambridge: Cambridge University Press, 1991.

South Commission. *Environment and Development: Towards a Common Strategy for the South in the UNCED Negotiations and Beyond.* Geneva: South Centre, November 1991.

Taylor, Charles. *The Ethics of Authenticity.* Cambridge, Mass.: Harvard University Press, 1991.

United Nations Development Programme (UNDP). *Human Development Report 1992.* New York: Oxford University Press, 1992.

United Nations Development Programme (UNDP). *Human Development Report 1993.* New York: Oxford University Press, 1993.

14

Ethics, Family Planning, Status of Women, and the Environment

JAEL M. SILLIMAN

Most of the chapters in this volume have taken us back to the wellsprings of religious doctrine and practice to explore what they may contribute to contemporary problems. The values and wisdom they contain might help us heal the wounds inflicted on each other and on our fragile planet. To restore broken relationships between North and South, between people and their communities and the natural world, and to counter violence are major global challenges before us that will require multifaceted solutions.

Women have much to contribute in restoring broken relationships, opposing violence in all its forms, and in redirecting development. In the area of population thinking and policy, women's voices are, and must be, heard, because they will be most affected. Women's views and vision of population policies are not drawn from ancient doctrines and traditions, but have been forged on the anvil of experience, and reflect harsh political realities. Women are demanding a different kind of development — one that places values and ethics at the core of development, population, and environmental policies.

This chapter[1] challenges simplistic thinking on population and environmental interactions, because simplistic thinking gives rise to simplistic and misguided solutions. Without denying the need and the right for women and men to control their fertility, slowing population growth rates cannot be a solution to the world's environmental ills. The limitations of previous population policies are sketched impressionistically. A "woman-centered" approach to population concerns is then presented as a constructive way to address population and

251

environmental goals simultaneously. The efforts of women's health and human rights advocates to restructure and redirect population policies in the drive towards attaining sustainable development is highlighted.

POPULATION/ENVIRONMENT DEBATE: A STALEMATE

The last few years have witnessed a plethora of articles, conferences, and research on the negative effects of population growth on the environment. A great deal of attention has been devoted to the high rates of population growth in the South and their negative environmental impacts. The controversial nature in which the debate has been cast has pitted North against South. The North has sought to protect its standard of living and lifestyles, while the South demands the rights of its people to a decent standard of living. To meet their immediate development needs, poor countries need to expand their economies, thereby increasing their resource consumption, energy use, and waste. It is in this political context that the debate on the extent and nature of population environmental/interaction rages on, locking people and countries in ideologically inflexible positions. This highly charged and politicized debate is counterproductive — it cannot move thinking or policy forward. It is at the program level, in the actual delivery of services, that consensus can be forged and appropriate actions taken.

Aside from the political volatility of the subject, consensus cannot emerge on the nature of the relationship between population growth rates and environmental deterioration. The nature of this relationship is highly location and culture specific, and varies according to resource use patterns, hinging on the type of social structures in place and the technologies employed by a particular population. As the examples below indicate, there is no evidence for asserting that high rates of population growth or high population densities necessarily hasten environmental decay, nor do low growth rates or population density guarantee sustainable resource management.

> In parts of Nepal, for example, it is the depopulation of mountainsides through migration — not population increase — that is leading to less sustainable resource management and greater environmental destruction; there simply are no longer enough people to maintain agricultural terraces, replant trees, and carry on the practices that have sustained mountain agriculture for thousands of years. Conversely, in the dry Kaakaamega District of Kenya, the greatest density of trees is associated with greatest density of settlement." (Janice Jiggins, " Don't Waste Energy On Fear of the Future," in *Conscience* XIV, 3 (1993): p. 27)

Moreover, the North's consumption and capital are often more responsible for resource depletion in the poorer countries than are the growing populations of those countries. The example of global deforestation is especially pertinent. While local populations can nibble around the edges of rain forests, it takes enormous capital investments to deforest on a major scale . . . rapidly growing numbers of peasants contribute to tropical deforestation but on a global scale their activities are probably akin to picking up branches and twigs after commercial chain saws have done the work. (Mark Sagoff, "Population and Nature," in Conscience XIV, 3 (1993): p. 24)

Population and environment interactions can only be understood in specific contexts. Experience has shown that particular patterns of consumption and production can lead to environmental destruction at any level of population growth or at any level of poverty or wealth. Therefore, to halt environmental decay, it will be necessary to forge policies at the local level to respond to the specific situation to be effective. Reducing population cannot be the stock answer for halting environmental decay, and in and of itself cannot be an effective strategy.

Some believe that time is running out to save the environment, and call for population control to solve the crisis. Their zeal should he tempered by the following facts:

1. Slowing population growth will have no immediate short-term impact; and

2. There are limits to what family planning programs can achieve in curbing population growth.

Because so much momentum is built into demographic processes, efforts to limit population growth, however determined, take a generation or two before they begin to show results at the aggregate level. Even if by some miracle worldwide TFR fell to 2.1 tomorrow, world population would approach eight billion in 2050 — bigger by almost half than today's population." (Mark Sagoff, "Playing the Numbers," in Conscience XIV, 3 (1993): p. 16)

In addition, to place the role that population reduction can play in environmental decline in perspective, it is important to understand the role that population growth rates play in fertility decline. Declining death rates, not rising birth rates, are causing rapid population growth. Furthermore, studies indicate that family planning programs account for somewhere between ten percent and forty percent of decline in birth rates. Economic and cultural changes are also important determinants of fertility decline.

Though by no means a quick and easy solution to our environmental ills, fertility regulation programs are important for many other reasons. First and foremost, these programs are essential so that women and men may control their fertility and determine what is best for their family and community. Fertility regulation programs are a prerequisite for expanding women's rights. Furthermore, at some point in the future, if fertility regulation services are not provided, population growth will take a toll on the environment. No problems are made easier given high rates of population growth. Therefore, a broad cross-section of people, whether or not they agree on the nature of the relationship between population and environment, would concur that it is important to ensure access to fertility regulation services to improve the quality of life of the individual, the society, or the global commons — or all simultaneously.

In the final analysis, whether motivated by a concern to avert environmental disaster or to meet development goals, such motivating factors must not impinge on the quality of services provided to the client, or on the client's right to determine family size. Where demographic considerations have driven and determined the policies and programs put in place, abuse has been rampant as individual needs are compromised to meet other goals. The Population Council underlines the moral imperative for providers to respond to the client's needs, rather than letting demographic objectives be the primary motivator.

> Conflicts may arise when family planning program managers are convinced that they can achieve higher rates of contraceptive use by ignoring the needs of individuals. The international community should not be carried away by success in fertility reduction through programs that do not pay attention to individual welfare. . . . If . . . a program justifies a course of action solely in terms of fertility reduction, we should refrain from labeling it a success." (Population Council, 1991 Annual Report, p. 22)

To ensure broad access to family planning, it is necessary to step back and review the foundations upon which current population programs were built. Population programs are part of a flawed development model.

POPULATION POLICIES AND PROGRAMS IN POLITICAL AND HISTORICAL CONTEXT

Population policies and programs cannot be understood in isolation. They were a component of development policies and thinking that took root in the fifties. "Development" policies in the "third world" were an outcome of Europe and America's relative success in rebuilding Germany after World War II. Development plans, built on the European model, were designed and imposed on third world countries to usher in social and economic well-being in the South. The North would have much to gain from development in the South, because it would open up huge markets for Northern manufactured goods. This development model has been a relentless force over the last forty years, shaping, and often distorting the political, economic, social, and cultural structures of much of the South. Though critiques of this model have prevailed since the outset, it is only now that the very foundations of the development model are being seriously challenged.

Central features of the development model were: a focus on economic indicators such as the gross national product (GNP) as the most important measure of progress; an emphasis on growth and high consumption at all costs; and the exploitation of the environment, which was considered as a resource for exploitation. By and large, development policies failed to acknowledge and build upon local knowledge, resources, and traditions. The pivotal role that women play in different social and economic sectors was not factored-in in development plans and programs. Population policies and programs were an essential part of this development framework, and therefore reflected many of the errors and biases of the development model.

In the quest for "development" that started in the fifties, population policies and programs were established and designed to counter "rapid population growth rates" in the "developing world." These policies were considered essential for countries to "take-off" into "self-sustained growth." In keeping with the thinking of that time, technological advances were seen as the key to alleviating social and economic problems. In the field of population, one such technological breakthrough with great promise was the birth control pill. Population policies and programs together with improved contraceptive methods were considered the "magic bullets" that would enable countries to climb out of poverty and usher in prosperity for their populations.

The primary objective of population programs in the South and among poor people in the North was to reduce fertility. The emphasis, therefore, was to deliver family planning services to the greatest number of women possible in the most "rapid" and "efficient" manner. To deliver family planning services to the widest number of "contraceptive acceptors," investments were made in centralized family planning structures. The number of contraceptive acceptors was the yardstick for measuring the success of a program, and less attention was given to the quality of services delivered.

In retrospect, it is easy to see how the very language of population policies and programs robbed women of their right to make reproductive choices. Programs were not conceptualized and framed in terms of enabling women to exercise their "reproductive rights" (still an alien concept in many parts of the world and among many cultures). "Reproductive rights" include: the right to control one's own sexuality; the right to choose whether or not to bear children; and the right to decide the number of children, given the constraints and pressures a woman confronts. As the primary objective of population programs were to reduce fertility, the primary targets of programs were women's bodies. "Control" over fertility was not invested with women, but with family planning authorities and with clinic personnel. Women's behavior, not men's, was, and still is, the focus of attention.

POPULATION POLICIES AND WOMEN'S LIVES

The results of traditional population programs and policies have been less than ideal and, in many cases, have abused women's dignity, health, and human rights. A few hypothetical, but fairly typical examples, attest to this reality. While there is some understanding and acknowledgment that there have been specific cases of widespread violation of human rights in population programs, the public is less aware of the many subtle and not so subtle ways in which traditional family planning programs consistently undermine the rights and dignity of women.

Ameena, a poor woman in Bangladesh, is offered a radio if she agrees to be sterilized. Knowing that she can sell the radio to meet her daily needs, Ameena agrees to the procedure. What does this example tell us? While the incentive system may indeed help the family planning workers to meet the targets on which their own salaries depend, it does little to address Ameena's health needs, nor does it respect her right to make an independent an appropriate contraceptive decision. If anything, it takes advantage of her poverty, pushing her to make an irrevocable decision she might not otherwise choose.

Mary, a woman from Kenya with three children whose contraceptive fails, decides she cannot afford to have another child. Unable to attain a legal abortion, she seeks assistance from a neighbor and ends up in a hospital with a septic abortion and permanent damage to her health. What does this example tell us? No contraceptive is one hundred percent reliable. Contraceptives do fail, and abortion is a necessary back-up. Despite social and religious strictures, women have always had, and will continue to have, abortions. Where public health systems do not make safe abortions available, women must and do resort to having unsafe abortions. The lack of safe, legal abortion services take an enormous toll on individual women, their families, and societies. Over 200,000 women a year die from unsafe abortions, and countless more suffer lifelong disabilities. Nevertheless, family planning clinics in many parts of the world do not offer women this essential reproductive health service.

North America is not immune from many of the abuses rampant in family planning programs. My third example is based on a recent U.S. case. Anita, a thirteen year old African-American girl, had Norplant inserted. Shortly thereafter she went to a clinic complaining about discomfort and irregular bleeding. The doctor did not take her complaints too seriously. She was told she would get used to the pain. Birth control pills were prescribed to control the bleeding! What does this tell us? First, that young Anita probably did not receive adequate counseling, which would have warned her of the potential side effects like breakthrough bleeding, and would have enabled her to choose whether she wished to use Norplant as a birth control method. Second, that even if she did receive counseling, just as she was entitled to make an informed decision to use Norplant, it had to be her decision to decide whether and when to have it removed. The doctor should have considered her complaints seriously and provided her with the option to have the Norplant removed. Third, that there are still many unresolved medical questions about the safety of long-term use of hormonal contraception for teenagers. Given this fact, the doctor's decision to combine the pill and Norplant leads one to wonder about the doctor's competence and judgment. One can only hope that the doctor counseled Anita to use condoms to protect herself against STDs and AIDS.

Each of the cases demonstrates how programs that focus on limiting women's fertility, rather than attending to their broader health needs, undermine women's rights and foster a climate where coercion is permissible and racism acceptable. This has made many women distrustful of family planning programs, causing them to avoid rather than seek out services. The examples also illustrate how the responsibility and risks of contraception are borne mostly by women. Women have been given all of the responsibility for controlling fertility, without the power or authority to implement decisions around sexuality and child-bearing. For, ". . . people without resources do not have choices, and people without choices cannot be asked to take responsibility" (Marge Berer, "Population and family planning policies: women-centered perspectives," in *Reproductive Health Matters* 1 (May 1993): p. 10). Much must be done by reproductive health and social programs/services to sensitize men to their sexual, parental, and household responsibilities. And governments must seek to provide the social, political, and economic conditions in which individuals may be able to act in a manner that is consistent with public interest.

WOMEN-CENTERED PERSPECTIVES AND PROGRAMS — AN ALTERNATIVE APPROACH

Women around the world are interested in controlling their fertility and exercising their reproductive rights. According to the United Nations Fund for Population Activities, a World Fertility Survey, twenty-five percent of the women in twenty-three countries said they would prefer small families, and up to half of the women aged forty to forty-nine did not want their last pregnancy. Yet, despite broadbased support for fertility regulation programs, many women's health advocates have and continue to reject family planning programs that are motivated by demographic considerations. Such programs have emphasized targets and incentives, and promote long-acting methods to reduce fertility, with less concern for women's health.

Women's health and rights advocates are developing programs that are sensitive and aware of the reality of women's lives. They start from the premise that:

> myriad circumstances beyond [women's] individual control influence [women's] decisions about childbearing and contraception: economics, family dynamics, relationships with men, access to health services and transportation, media images, etc. . . . (Jacqueline Pitanguy and Rosalind Petchesky, "Women and Population: A Feminist Perspective," in *Conscience* XIV, 3 (1993): p. 5)

Therefore, more broadly based programs have been designed. Women's health advocates underline the fact that reproductive issues encompass fertility control, sexuality, and reproduction. Such programs seek to enable women to control their fertility, which often entails challenging unequal gender relations. Alternative services help women cope with male resistance to family planning and encourage male responsibility for fertility control and child rearing. Efforts are directed toward empowering women and reducing gender inequities. Enabling women to exercise control over their fertility may mean helping women seek economic independence or freeing women from violence, or offering legal assistance when necessary. Such programs take into account the ways in which society and men directly influence and control the reproductive responsibilities of women. Women's health centers also seek to offer women a range of contraceptive methods in an atmosphere of trust and respect. Counseling and follow-up are essential components of "quality of care" that women's health advocates have promoted both in their own health centers and among other family planning institutions.

Not only have women designed alternative approaches and clinics to meet women's reproductive health care needs, they are beginning to be heard in policy circles. In preparations for the 1994 UN population meeting in Cairo, feminist voices are being heard through non-governmental organizations and through some national delegations. In preparation for Cairo, an international network of women's health activists representing women's networks in Asia, Africa, Latin America, the Caribbean and U.S., and Western Europe have put forth a "Declaration on Population Policies" that has been widely circulated and received overwhelming support.

The Declaration calls for a "fundamental revision in the design, structure and implementation of population policies, to foster the empowerment and well-being of all women." They declare that "women's empowerment is legitimate and critically important in its own right, not merely as a means to address population issues." They put forward a set of ethical principles to serve as a basis for establishing population policies that are responsive to women's needs. They include the following:

1. Women can and do make responsible decisions for themselves, their families, their communities and . . . women must be subjects, not objects of any development policy, and especially of population policies.

2. Women have the right to determine when, whether, why, with whom, and how to express their sexuality. Population policies must be based on respect for the bodily integrity of girls and women.

3. All women, regardless of age, marital status, or other social conditions, have a right to information and services necessary to exercise their reproductive rights and responsibilities.

4. Men also have a personal and social responsibility for their own sexual behavior and fertility, and for the effects of that behavior on their partners and children's health and well-being.

5. Sexual and social relationships between men and women must be governed by principles of equity, non-coercion, mutual respect, and responsibility.

6. The fundamental sexual and reproductive rights of women cannot be subordinated, against a woman's will, to the interests of partners, family members, ethnic groups, religious institutions, health providers, researchers, policy makers, the state, or any other actors.

7. Women committed to promoting women's reproductive health and rights, and linked to the women to be served, must be included as policy makers and implementers in all aspects of decision making, including definition of ethical standards, technology development and distribution, services, and information dissemination.

Positioning women's organizations to affect the development of international population; population policies will be critical in tipping the balance away from population control toward more democratic principles, reproductive health, sexual self-determination, and bodily integrity. (Pitanguy and Petchesky, "Women and Population: A Feminist Perspective," in Conscience XIV, 3 (1993): p. 7)

Women's health advocates have achieved much over the last three decades in redirecting population thinking and practice. However, major challenges remain. The rhetoric of the population proponents and governments is changing. There is greater awareness and sensitivity to women's health and rights needs and concerns. However, these rhetorical changes must be operationalized. The "notion of reproductive autonomy for every woman must seep into the structures of the government, the fabric of health care systems and the thinking of women themselves" (Shanti Dhairam, "Managing Gender Sensitive Family Planning Services," in *Feedback — ICOMP Newsletter on Management of Population Programmes* XIX, 2 (June 1993): p. 6). This will require restructuring of services, retraining of staff from the top level to the clinic in the field. It will also require the reallocation of services for the empowerment of women. Another enormous challenge that the international women's health movement must confront is the issue of how to reconcile women's rights to determine their fertility in the context of social and global welfare and limits. This debate is now in full swing among women's health advocates. Moreover, women's health and rights advocates are now in dialogue with other groups about population and environmental concerns, which bodes well for the future.

By paying attention to what women want, and showing greater sensitivity to the contexts in which people live, demographers, environmentalists, and policy makers can forge vital alliances with women's health advocates in both the North and the South. Together [they] can meet the population environmental challenge in an effective yet democratic way." (Janice Jiggins, "Don't Waste Energy on Fear of the Future," in Conscience XVI, 3 (1993): p. 27)

NOTE

1. While I have learned from many people about this complex set of issues, those who have provided me with constant encouragement, guidance, and clarity of thought are Shira Saperstein, Stephen Viederman, Jamie Fellner, and Pat Corozzo. To them I am most grateful.

BIBLIOGRAPHY

Conscience — A Newsletter of Prochoice Catholic Opinion, Women, Population and the Environment, Vol. XIV, No. 3. Washington D.C., 1993.

Feedback — ICOMP Newsletter on Population Programmes, Vol. XIX, No. 2. Kuala Lampur, Malaysia, 1993.

Hartmann, Betsy. *Reproductive Rights and Wrongs: The Global Politics of Population Control and Contraceptive Choice.* New York: Harper and Row, 1987.

Jacobson, Jodi L. *Gender Bias: Roadblock to Sustainable Development,* World Watch Paper 110. Washington D.C.: World Watch Institute, 1992.

Jiggins, Janice. *Women and Sustainable Development.* Washington, D.C.: Island Press, expected in 1994.

Sen, Gita. "Women, Poverty and Population: Issues for the Concerned Environmentalist." Written for a collaborative project of the International Social Sciences Association, the Social Science Research Council, and Development Alternatives With Women for a New Era, December 1992.

Reproductive Health Matters. *Population and Family Planning Policies,* Number 1. May, London 1993.

Women's Global Network for Reproductive Rights. Newsletter 42. Amsterdam, 1993.

Women's Voices '94. Declaration on Population Policies in preparation for the 1994 International Conference on Population and Development.

15

International Law, Population Pressure, and the Environment

ELIZABETH A. ADJIN-TETTEY

Since the 1960s, humanity has grimly discovered the damage done to the environment. The causes of today's environmental problems include the rapid increase of the world's population, especially since the 1950s, and excessive consumption of natural resources. The international community has become aware that these environmental problems have global implications and must be resolved collectively.[1] This has been a driving force for the convening of international conferences regarding the environment, and the adoption of declarations and conventions on the subject.

Ostensibly, pressure on natural resources resulting from population growth is a problem mostly confronting the developing world.[2] These countries lack resources to improve their standards of living which, as evidenced in the industrialized countries, is an important factor in reducing population growth. The developing world needs financial and technological assistance to improve their standard of living, reverse exponential rates of population growth and pressures on the Earth's resources resulting from sheer numbers. The urgency of the population-environment problem dictates that such assistance must not depend on the benevolence of the industrialized countries but on a legal regime obliging the rich to do so.

Since the developing countries began to demand a New International Economic Order, there has been a debate as to whether they have a legal right to the transfer of financial, technical, and technological resources from the rich countries to aid their general economic development. Ostensibly, there is no established principle of international law which can be pointed to as requiring the rich to do this. However, I argue that the need for environmental protection, together with the emerging state practice whereby the rich "undertake" to help poorer nations clean up the environment, may constitute the bases for requiring the industrial countries to transfer resources to poorer countries for their general development. As well, the moral obligation to eliminate poverty from the world and preserve the environment for humankind demands that the rich help poorer countries to get to that point.

This chapter focuses on the predicament of the developing world. It proceeds by looking at the relationship between population pressures and environmental degradation in these countries, and then looks at some approaches to the problem. The balance of the paper discusses some international responses to the population-environment issue and the environmental problem as a whole, especially as it pertains in developing countries.

POPULATION PRESSURES AND THE ENVIRONMENT

The fact that the world is experiencing rapid increases in population can hardly be overstated. It is a truism that the relationship between population growth and environmental degradation is not well understood. However, at the very least, higher population growth generally implies greater demands on the Earth's resources. Meanwhile, "the amount of natural resources with which to sustain life on Earth, improve the quality of human lives and eliminate mass poverty remains finite."[3] Admittedly, technological advancement and human ingenuity are increasing the productivity of resources. Nevertheless, the increasing number of people in the world has resulted in tremendous pressures on natural resources and their ability to satisfy human needs.[4] The population forecast for the next few decades presents an even more grim effect on the Earth's resources.[5]

The picture is more gloomy in developing countries where, as mentioned, most of the population growth is occurring. Population pressure in these countries is creating an ever-increasing but impoverished peasantry who are compelled to depend on a dwindling natural resource base. This has tremendous effects on ecosystems. As humans and plant and animal species compete for the same habitation and resources, the latter is marginalized by virtue of the survival of the fittest. In the process, some plant and animal species have suffered severe reduction in their population, while others are driven to extinction.[6] If this trend persists, ecosystems are likely to become less complex and less diverse.

Exponential rates of population growth, mostly in the rural communities, which apparently constitute the majority of the developing world's population, result in a scarcity of natural resources and increased poverty. As such, most of the populations, especially the young, migrate to urban areas in search of better living conditions. The urban population in these countries is growing at about 3.6 percent a year.[7] For the most part, urban dwellers aspire to affluent lifestyles which are resource intensive, and thereby exacerbate pressure on already dwindling resources. Consequences of this phenomenon include the loss of valuable agricultural land, mostly by putting up structures for settlement, over and above land lost through overuse and mismanagement.[8]

Population growth in the developing world has occasioned mounting pressures on fuelwood, the major source of energy in these countries.[9] The growth in human population is outpacing the growth of new trees, and this is raising serious ecological problems. As the poor deplete the supplies near their homes, the scavenging process is intensified, accelerating the depletion of the world's forest cover and contributing to deforestation.

Pressures on natural resources do not only stem from the sheer numbers of people on Earth. Poverty and underdevelopment prevent the developing world from using the natural resources they command sustainably,[10] notwithstanding the fact that the developed world is increasingly moving toward greater efficiency in their use of natural resources.[11] Thus, pressures on the Earth's resources are as much a result of population increase as is the lack of development for the majority of humanity.

Although the poor have the highest fertility rates and, in their struggle to survive, subject the natural environment to considerable stress and destruction, it must also be acknowledged that the North exerts enormous pressures on the environment through their opulent lifestyles. In fact, the rich consume far more than their fair share of natural resources. It has rightly been pointed out that a child born in a rich, industrialized country, or in a rich family in a developing country, where per capita consumption of energy and materials is high, consumes far more and places far greater pressure on natural resources than an additional person in a poor country.[12]

APPROACHES TO THE POPULATION/ENVIRONMENT PROBLEM: INTERGENERATIONAL AND INTRAGENERATIONAL EQUITIES

The international community has adopted a precautionary approach that emphasizes that exponential growth in the world's population and unsustainable use of natural resources must be reversed because it increases pressure on the environment and places future generations at risk.[13] Protecting the interest of future generations regarding the use of the Earth's resources emerged in the preparations for the 1972 Stockholm Conference on the Human Environment.

The Stockholm Declaration states that we not only have a right to a life of dignity and equality in an environment of quality but also a "solemn responsibility to protect and improve the environment for present and future generations," and that this responsibility has become an imperative goal for humanity.[14] Ten years after Stockholm, the world community reaffirmed the validity of the Declaration and called upon

> all Governments and peoples of the world to discharge their historical responsibility, collectively and individually, to ensure that our small planet is passed over to future generations in a condition which guarantees a life of human dignity for all.[15]

Protecting the environment for the benefit of present and future generations was a recurrent theme in the work of the World Commission on Environment and Development (WCED). The crux of the Commission's Report was to point the way to sustainable development, which was defined as "development that meets the needs of the present without compromising the ability of future generations to meet their own needs."[16] Article 1 of the Legal Principles and Recommendations adopted by the Experts Group of the WCED declares the fundamental human right to an environment adequate for their well-being.[17] As such, all states have to "ensure that the Earth's resources are used and conserved for the benefit of present and future generations."[18] Intergenerational equity was also prominent at the United Nations Conference on Environment and Development, 1992.[19]

Intergenerational equity upholds that there be fairness in the use of our "common patrimony" — the earth's resources — among and within generations.[20] This obliges every generation to ensure that succeeding generations have available to them at least the options and uses the former derives from the natural environment. These options should at least be comparable in quality and diversity to those received by preceding generations.[21] Thus, we (the present generation) must prevent and/or abate anything that will degrade the natural environment, and thus reduce the options of future generations or require them to clean the environment after us.[22]

Intragenerational or current equity emphasizes that there be fairness in the use of the Earth's resources within each generation. Though current equity may appear to be in conflict with intragenerational equity, the two can coexist and must go together. Indeed, fairness within each generation is implied in intergenerational equity.[23] To a significant extent, the realization of the latter depends on the degree to which the former is recognized and promoted.

The duty to future generations implies that impoverished members of the present generation must be assisted to gain effective access to the Earth's resources so that we can collectively fulfill said obligation. However, there has been an unfortunate tendency to pay little or no attention to current equity issues. Finding solutions to the problems of unborn generations while rejecting the realities of the present, in which the majority of humanity have no future prospects, is a "myopic world view [and] presumptuous."[24] Gundling reminds us that "without equity within the present generation, we will not be able to achieve equity among generations."[25] One sure way to remove pressure from the Earth's resources, and to pass on an environment capable of meeting the needs of future generations, is to eliminate inequities within the present generation.[26]

The experience of the industrialized nations has shown that improved standards of living and socioeconomic conditions can bring about a decline in birth rates.[27] Thus, socioeconomic growth is required in developing countries, in order to break the cycle of poverty and high rates of population growth in these countries, which itself intensifies pressure on natural resources.[28]

Admittedly, the developing countries have to put their own house in order to enable them to achieve meaningful long-term socioeconomic development, reduce birth rates, and prevent environmental degradation. For example, they must increase environmental awareness, cut military expenditure, and eliminate corruption in their own countries. However, this chapter does not address these domestic issues; it focuses on how to deal with the environment-population problem in developing countries at the international level in the context of North-South relations.

It is axiomatic that the developing countries lack the technological and financial resources required to improve their living standards without intensifying pressures on natural resources.[29] If these countries are left to base themselves on resources they presently command, their development will, no doubt, intensify pressures on natural resources and, consequently, result in further environmental deterioration. Clearly, the situation demands that the developing countries must pursue sustainable socioeconomic growth. Indeed, the world community expects them to do this. Inasmuch as the developing countries must be encouraged, and in fact desire, to be self-sufficient, their inability to meet their present needs dictates that they must be assisted to get to that point.

The necessity to assist poor nations calls for significant transfers of financial, technical, and technological resources from industrial to developing countries. Admittedly, development assistance programs have, for the most part, failed to achieve their intended objectives; mostly, they address the symptoms rather than the roots of the problems of the developing world. These programs have also created deleterious impacts on the environment, due to the neglect of environmental and social concerns in the planning and implementation of these activities.

In spite of these shortcomings, development assistance is indispensable in eradicating poverty and improving living standards in developing countries.[30] This means that the international community must change the focus of its political and economic policies to accommodate the development needs of the

South and promote global environmental well-being. Development assistance must be seen to be temporary and aimed at promoting long term self-sufficiency in recipient countries. Funding institutions and donor governments must encourage sound environmental practices in recipient countries, by ensuring that environmental assessment processes and criteria are integrated into the planning and implementation of projects funded by them.

Intended beneficiaries of development assistance must be allowed to determine for themselves the kinds of projects that will best meet their needs, and they should be actively involved in the planning and implementation of same. Attention must also be given to small-scale projects which respect not only the environment but also traditional lifestyles of the recipients. As well, considerable percentages of development assistance must be committed to improving birth control technology, women's health, and medical care generally. Efforts should be made to improve the status of women by promoting their socioeconomic independence.

To promote these objectives, aid must be "untied" in most cases so it will satisfy the actual needs of recipient countries and not merely promote the economic and political interests of the donors.[31] Development assistance must no longer be seen as a manifestation of sporadic voluntary generosity by rich nations. Rather, such transfers should be obligatory, consistent, and automatic, and perceived as something expected of industrialized nations in their relations with poorer countries.

INTERNATIONAL JUSTICE

The obligatory transfer of resources from North to South is mandated by international justice in view of our obligation to present and future generations. The leading sociopolitical philosopher in the contemporary Anglo-American tradition, John Rawls, rightly points out that "Justice is the first virtue of social institutions."[32] The primary concern of Rawls' theory of justice is to evaluate "the way in which the major social institutions distribute fundamental rights and duties and determine the division of advantages from social cooperation."[33] Rawls admits that people do not only have a right to life, but also to the resources required to provide their basic needs.

There has been comparatively little attention given to the international application of Rawls' theory of justice, though there is much room for applying the theory in international relations. The application of Rawls' notion of justice in the international context would require applying the "difference principle" at a global level. According to the difference principle, inequalities in social and economic benefits are justified insofar as they work to the maximum benefit of the least advantaged members of the society, because, other things being equal, it is morally wrong for some people to be worse off than others in the society.[34] As such, the disadvantaged must be placed in a position in which they may not be any better off. Insofar as inequalities in the community of nations are not to the benefit of poorer countries, a situation of injustice can be said to be perpetuated, and the "difference principle" requires that there be a fundamental restructuring of international economic relations. Admur points out that:

> . . . [the] global application of the difference principle...is almost certain to require a far more egalitarian distribution of wealth than that which presently prevails. . . . Justice is likely to require monetary and trade reforms . . . and more important, massive development aid; in short, a substantial redistribution of wealth from the rich nations to the poor.[35]

The claim of the developing countries for assistance can also be premised on past and present economic relations between developed and developing nations. Most developed countries were colonial powers, and the colonies became the developing nations of today. The colonial powers exploited the resources of their colonies for their own economic development without considering the long-term interest of the colonies. Zheng-Kang notes that:

> This method of exploitation permitted developed countries to take almost all of the benefits and left developing countries to bear almost all the burdens, especially the environmental destruction that such rapid resource development caused. When the colonies became independent in the twentieth century, the environment that they inherited was already severely damaged. The economic success of the developed countries has in large part been built on the poverty of their colonies, which are the developing nations of today.[36]

A historical application of the "Polluter Pays Principle" requires that the developed countries must assist the developing ones, through the transfer of resources, to clean up their environment and achieve economic growth. It could therefore be argued that the developed countries are morally obliged to help the poorer countries address the population-environment problem plaguing the latter. In the absence of such assistance, the developing nations would be disadvantaged by pursuing population control and environmental protection measures expected of them by the international community.

The South has insisted on fair access to financial and technological resources, in order to improve living conditions in their countries and enhance their environmental protection abilities,[37] through their demand for a new international economic order (NIEO). Unfortunately, the adoption of the NIEO instruments have not helped the cause of the South.[38] While the developing nations regard these instruments as establishing legal principles in favor of their development, the developed nations see them as mere recommendations having no binding force. It is admitted that the debate on the legal effect of the NIEO instruments has not decided the issue of transfer of resources in favor of either side. Thus, at a doctrinal level, no firm conclusions emerge.

ASSISTING DEVELOPING COUNTRIES IN CONTEMPORARY INTERNATIONAL RELATIONS

Notwithstanding this impasse, the industrialized countries have themselves recognized the necessity to help poorer countries deal with environmental degradation and to encourage them to pursue sustainable development.[39] To do this, the North acknowledges that they have to give poorer countries economic incentives which may include the use of aid mechanisms and the transfer of specific technology.[40]

The international community has moved beyond rhetoric to establish funding mechanisms to help poorer nations preserve the environment while meeting their development needs. One most significant achievement in this regard has been the World Bank's establishment of the Global Environment Facility (GEF) to promote environmental causes in developing countries. Specifically, the GEF is intended to help developing countries adopt environmental protection and enhancement measures which could not be subsumed under existing development assistance or environmental programs.[41] The GEF will be implemented by the World Bank, UNEP, and UNDP.[42] Projects to be funded by the GEF will be appraised to determine their environmental appropriateness.[43]

The GEF provides funds to developing countries in the form of grants or concessional loans for ozone layer protection, control of greenhouse gas emissions, protection of biological diversity, and international waters. For example, the GEF will assist developing countries in obtaining cleaner fuels and modern and efficient energy technologies, which developing countries would otherwise not be able to afford as a means of limiting the greenhouse gas effect.[44]

Other achievements include the establishment of the financial mechanism under the 1990 London Amendment to the Montreal Ozone Protocol, to help developing nation parties (Article 5 parties) to implement their obligations under the Montreal Protocol by facilitating the transfer of technology needed to achieve this very purpose.[45] The mechanism establishes a trust fund financed by contributions from the parties. Prior to the coming into force of the London amendment establishing the fund and a formal secretariat to administer the same, the parties adopted an "interim financial mechanism" that will last for three years, starting from 1 January 1991.[46]

The drafters of the *Framework Convention on Climate Change*, considered it important to include provisions that will ensure that developed country parties extend financial and technological assistance to developing country parties to aid the latters' compliance with the treaty obligations, and to meet the costs involved in so doing.[47] Developed country parties to the *Biological Diversity Convention* also undertook to make available new and additional financial resources to help developing country parties bear the extra costs to them in the fulfillment of their treaty obligations.[48]

There appears to be a consensus that funds to be transferred to poorer countries for this purpose must be "new and additional" to existing development assistance programs.[49] This is because the elimination of poverty and the achievement of economic growth in developing countries are imperative and must be fundamental if population and environmental problems are to be successfully addressed in these countries.

These developments set valuable precedents for an evolving norm in international relations, in which both rich and poor nations accept the common responsibility for stewardship of the environment. They also establish a general need, and corresponding understanding, to transfer financial and technological resources to poorer countries to enable them meet their needs without intensifying pressures on natural resources.

POLICY CONSIDERATIONS IN TECHNOLOGY TRANSFER

Most of the resources to be transferred must take the form of technology, or be directed toward the purchase of technological knowhow aimed at promoting self-reliance in developing countries. The availability of funds to purchase technology does not by itself decide the debate over intellectual property rights. For the most part, intellectual property rights are owned not by the developed countries *per se,* but by multinational corporations (MNCs) that are unwilling to transfer them to the developing countries on favorable terms. This reflects the sanctity of private property rights, and also suggests a particular view of intellectual property rights.

International law accords a more extensive protection to intellectual property rights than is consistent with the needs of the South for technology, and is prejudicial to socioeconomic development in developing countries. Since the notion of property is merely a legal construct of society, the international community must define intellectual property rights in a way that accommodates the urgent needs of developing countries.

In the meantime, the industrial countries in whose jurisdictions these MNCs are registered should encourage them to make their intellectual property available to nations of the South by giving them incentives such as tax breaks. Since the primary concern of industrialized countries relates to the protection of intellectual property rights, developing countries must establish legal regimes which will adequately protect the rights so transferred. This does not mean industrialized countries should unduly restrict developing countries in the use of technology transferred. Both sides should reach compromises that respect the property rights of the owners and at the same time leave room for developing countries to sufficiently benefit from the technology. When such an atmosphere of trust has been established, developed countries will presumably be more willing to transfer modern and efficient technology to developing nations.[50]

Most importantly, the North must help train developing country nationals to develop technology suitable for their domestic needs without disrupting established markets of the former. Developing countries must also share their intellectual property rights with other nations similarly situated.

CONCLUSION

Notwithstanding opposing juridical positions between North and South on transfer of resources, the recognition that this has become a part of relations that have evolved in the context of cooperation between both sides to preserve the environment seems to be fairly well settled in contemporary international relations.

Generally speaking, international law is an imperfect but indispensable system. For the most part, the enforcement of international law depends on the political will of individual states. If the obligation to transfer resources to the South is seen as emanating from treaties,[51] only state parties may be bound by it.

My thesis is that the obligation to assist developing nations to deal with factors that compel them to degrade the natural environment is an emergent customary norm in North-South relations.[52] There are no strict requirements regarding the duration of the practice which may be accepted as law. A custom may develop within a relatively short period of time in response to changing international circumstances, such as the need for environmental protection, provided the uniformity and generality of the practice are proved.[53] Once such practice passes into the general *corpus* of international law and is accepted as such by *opinio juris*, it becomes binding even for states that did not participate in the formation of the same, and they cannot unilaterally terminate their obligation by withdrawal.

Given this position, the obligation to assist developing countries in the interest of global environmental quality can be enforced just like any rule of custom. Consequences of breach, such as advisory opinion by the International Court of Justice denouncing the same, public embarrassment, and the imposition of sanctions on the violating country, may serve to enforce the said obligation.

To avoid misuse of resources transferred, recipient countries must be made to account for assistance received, showing how such transfers have promoted domestic self-sufficiency which respects the environment, and the nature of subsequent assistance, if desired. Assisting developing countries in this way will help break the cycle of poverty, population increases, and environmental degradation, and will be in the long-term interest of humankind.

NOTES

1. Historically, international environmental protection was premised on the principle of national sovereignty over natural resources, and the obligation of states regarding the environment was considered largely in terms of the doctrine of state responsibility. In general, the law is that the state is responsible, and therefore liable, to another for damage to its environment resulting from activities within the former's jurisdiction; see *Trail Smelter Arbitration, Canada v U.S.,* 3 UNRIAA 1905 (1943); *Corfu Channel Case* (U.K. v Alb.) [1949] ICJ Rep. 4; and *Lake Lanoux Arbitration* (Fr. v Spain) 12 UNRIAA 281 (1956).

2. The term "developing world" as used interchangeably with "developing countries" refers to the over 120 politically diverse States of Africa, Asia (except Japan and China), and Latin America, most of whom achieved independence since World War II. These countries share similar characteristics to the extent that they are subject to widespread poverty; high rates of population increase; low levels of capital and technology; unequal income distribution, and slow industrial growth. They are also referred to as the "South" in contrast to the "North," used to indicate the industrialized nations.

3. The World Commission on Environment and Development, *Our Common Future* (Chair: G. H. Brundtland) (Oxford: Oxford University Press, 1987), p. 95.

4. See C. S. Silver and R. S. DeFries, *One Earth, One Future: Our Changing Global Environment* (Washington, D.C.: National Academy Press, 1990), p. 50. The authors point out that the ability of humans to change the environment increases along with our numbers, and our desire to achieve affluence.

5. See UN, Agenda 21, Chapter 5.3, A CONF.151/1 (1992). The Brundtland Commission noted that if per capita use of energy remains unchanged, by 2025 a global population of about 8.2 billion would need about 14TW of energy; *Our Common Future,* pp. 169–70; Second World Climate Conference, Geneva, 29 October–7 November 1990, 2(6) ENVT'L POL'Y & LAW, 220, para. 21 (1990).

6. There are no precise figures on current rates of extinctions. In the past, extinctions have occurred as part of natural processes. Today, however, anthropogenic activities seem overwhelmingly the main cause of extinctions. *Our Common Future,* pp. 150–52.

7. The United Nations has predicted that at this rate of growth, by the year 2000, urban areas in the developing world are likely to reach 17 million hectares, more than twice the size in 1980. M. K. Tolba, *Saving Our Planet: Challenges and Hopes* (London: Chapman & Hall, 1992), p. 188; UNFPA, *Population and the Environment: the Challenge Ahead* (New York: United Nations Population Fund, 1991).

8. Tolba, *Ibid.*

9. About seventy percent of the developing world's population depend on fuelwood for domestic uses. *Our Common Future,* p. 189. Indeed, wood has been referred to as the "people's fuel"; B. Munslow et al, *The Fuelwood Trap: A study of the Southern African Development Coordination Council (SADCC)* (London: Earthscan, 1988), pp. 5–6.

10. *Our Common Future,* p. 49. Underdevelopment is as much a cause as it is a sign of environmental deterioration; See G. Handl, "Environmental Protection and Development in Third World Countries: Common Destiny — Common Responsibility," 20 NYU J. INT'L L. & POL'Y, 603, 607 (1988). This makes the poor both agents and victims of resource scarcity and environmental degradation generally: a "desperate ecocide" of the poor. P. Blaikie, *The Political Economy of Soil Erosion* (London: Longman Publishers, 1985), p. 138. For a catalog of how this operates in various developing countries, see A. B. Burning, *Poverty and the Environment: Reversing the Downward Spiral,* Worldwatch Paper 92 (Washington, D.C.: Worldwatch Institute, 1989), 40–54.

11. Though industrialized societies require more energy than developing nations, the availability of sophisticated technology to use these resources efficiently and to control emissions from their use, at least more than the developing countries, has led to significant declines in the amount of resources required and the environmental degradation arising from their use. See L. Schipper, "Improved Energy Efficiency in the Industrialized Countries: Past Achievements, Carbon Dioxide Emission Prospects," 19 ENER. POL'Y 127, 128–29, 130–31; R. E. Benedick, *Ozone Diplomacy* (Cambridge, Mass.: Harvard University Press, 1991), p. 209; C. Flavin and N. Lenssen, *Beyond the Petroleum Age: Designing a Solar Economy* (Worldwatch Paper 100, December 1990), p. 17; U. Hansen, "Delinking of Energy Consumption and Economic Growth: the German Experience" ENER. POL'Y, 631 (1990), p. 18.

12. See Tolba, *supra* note 7, p. 183; Silver and DeFries, supra note 4, p. 53; J. MacNeil, "Strategies for Sustainable Economic Development," *Scientific American,* 105 (1989), p. 261; For example, average persons in the industrialized market economies consume about eight to ten times the energy used by their counterparts in developing countries. To take the point even further, the developed world as a whole, with about one-quarter of the world's population, consumes about three-quarters of the world's primary energy, while developing countries, containing three quarters of the world's population use one-quarter of global primary energy: *Our Common Future,* p. 169.

13. See G. Handl, "Environmental Security and Global Change: the Challenge to International Law," in W. Lang et al, eds. *Environmental Protection and International Law* (Gt. Britain: Graham & Trotman, 1990), pp. 59, 60; E. Brown-Weiss, "Global Environmental Change and International Law: The Introductory Framework," in E. Brown-Weiss ed. *Environmental Change and International Law,* 392 (UN University Press, 1992); "Our Rights and Obligations to Future Generations for the Environment," 84 A.J.I.L. 198 (1990); *In Fairness to Future Generations: International Law, Common Patrimony, and Intergenerational Equity,* 25–26 (1989).

14. *Declaration of the UN Conference on the Human Environment,* Stockholm, 1972, para. 6 of Preamble and Principle 2. See also, *1972 Convention for the Preven-*

tion of Marine Pollution by Dumping from Ships and Aircraft; and, *Convention on International Trade in Endangered Species of Wild Fauna and Flora,* 1973.

15. *The Nairobi Declaration on the State of Worldwide Environment,* 1982, para. 10, 21 I.L.M. 676 (1982).

16. *Our Common Future,* p. 43. Concern for future generations is also typified by statements such as ". . . the time has come to take the decisions needed to secure resources to sustain this and coming generations" (2); and the call to use natural resources in ways that "foreclose as few future options as possible" (46). The Commission also urges the present generation to refrain from borrowing environmental capital from future generations with no intention or prospect of repaying (8).

17. *Environmental Protection and Sustainable Development,* Legal Principles and Recommendations adopted by the Experts Group on Environmental Law of the WCED, 40 (Chairman: R.D. Munro) (Graham & Trotman, 1986).

18. *Ibid.,* Article 2.

19. See Principles 3 and 5 of the *Rio Declaration on Environment and Development, 1992.*

20. See C. Tinker, *Making UNCED Work: Building the Legal and Institutional Framework for Sustainable Development at the Earth Summit and Beyond,* no. 4, chapter III (United Nations Association of the USA, March 1992).

21. D'Amato, "Do We Owe a Duty to Future Generations to Preserve the Global Environment?" 84 A.J.I.L. 190, 195 (1990).

22. Some writers have argued that the extension of rights to unborn generations appears absurd because we cannot protect the interest of an unknown group of people. See Sagoff, "Conflict and Contradiction in Environmental Law," 12 ENVTL L. pp. 283, 297–98 (1982); L. Gundling, "Our Responsibility to Future Generations," p. 84 A.J.I.L. 207 (1990). However, it suffices to know that other things being equal, some people will inherit the Earth after us and we are morally obliged to ensure that they also benefit from the fruits of the planet.

23. Conservation of access (one of the tenets of intergenerational equity) ensures that each generation obtains a reasonable non-discriminatory right of access to the Earth's resources, while protecting the interests of future generations; Brown-Weiss, (1992) *supra* note 13, p. 405. The Brundtland Commission pointed out that "even the narrow notion of physical sustainability implies a concern for social equity, a concern that must logically be extended to equity within each generation"; *Our Common Future,* p. 43.

24. J. Ntambirweki, "The Developing Countries in the Evolution of an International Environmental Law," 14 HASTINGS INT'L & COMP. L. REV. 905, 924.

25. Gundling, *supra* note 22, at 211.

26. Gundling observes that "the inequities of the present imply that we cannot solve the problems of the future simply by postulating a global collective sacrifice. For many countries, restrictions would not be possible and would even deteriorate the economy and, thus, the environment. Many countries need development for the very reason that it is an essential prelude to finding long-term solutions to environmental problems." *Ibid.,* pp. 211–12; see also World Bank, *World Development Report 1992: Development and Environment* (Oxford University Press, 1992), p. 8.

27. For instance, parents would no longer require big families to ensure their financial security, a condition very common in developing countries.

28. The Brundtland Commission pointed out that growth is needed in the South because that is where the links between economic growth, the alleviation of poverty and environmental conditions operate the most; *Our Common Future*, pp. 50–51.

29. See "Consultation Group on Special Needs of the Developing Countries," ENVT'L POL'Y & L. 20, 6 (1990): pp. 230, 231.

30. See *WEST AFRICA*, "Main Reasons for Third World Aid," 1675 (20–26 September 1993). Indeed, the developing countries maintain that their lack of resources prevent them from meeting their own needs in an environmentally sustainable way, let alone to protect the interest of future generations.

31. Donor governments usually have mixed motives — political, economic, etc. — in extending aid and, therefore concentrate on the realization of these motives. In most cases, aid programs are used to expand export markets of donor countries and job opportunities for their citizens, to the detriment of the domestic economy of the recipient country. This is achieved by "tying" aid to the purchase of goods and services from the donor. For example, until 1988, Canada required that eighty percent of its aid be used to purchase Canadian goods and services, regardless of the needs of recipient countries. Under the new ODA Charter, 1988, the percentage of tied aid, with the exception of food aid, has been reduced to fifty percent for Sub-Saharan Africa and other developing countries. Food aid continues to be tied at 95%. *Sharing Our Future: CIDA*, 52–3 (Ottawa: Minister of Supply and Services, 1987). This makes aid funding politically saleable in donor countries while determining the kinds of projects chosen and how they are delivered.

32. J. Rawls, *A Theory of Justice* (Cambridge, Mass.: Harvard University Press, 1981), p. 3.

33. *Ibid.*, p. 7.

34. See R. Arneson, "Symposium on Rawlsian Theory of Justice: Recent Developments," 99 ETHICS (1989): pp. 695, 709.

35. R. Admur, "Rawls' Theory of Justice," 29 WORLD POL. (1977): pp. 439, 455; see also J. Cohen, "Democratic Equality," 99 ETHICS (1989): pp. 727, 728.

36. C. Zheng-Kang, "Equity, Special Considerations, and the Third World," 1 COLO. J. INT'L ENVTL L. & POL'Y (1990): pp. 57, 58–59.

37. See D. B. Magraw, "Legal Treatment of Developing Countries: Differential, Contextual, and Absolute Norms," 1 COLO. J. INT'L ENVTL L. & POL'Y (1990): pp. 69, 77.

38. The NIEO instruments include the *Programme of Action on the Establishment of a NIEO*, G.A. Res. 3202 (S-VI), 1974, 13 I.L.M. 720 (1974); *Declaration on the Establishment of a NIEO*, G.A. Res. 3201 (5-VI), 1974, Ibid, 715; and the *Charter for Economic Rights and Duties of States*, 1974, 14 I.L.M. 251 (1974).

39. Third World Needs financial Help for Sustained, Ecological Development," in INT'L ENV'T REP. 13, 4 (1990): p. 160; *EC: Council Resolutions on the Greenhouse Effect and the Community*, 21 June 1989, para. 6, in 28 I.L.M. 1306 (1989); Section XV(2) of the *World Conservation Strategy*, 1980; *Nairobi Declaration*, *supra* note 15, at para. 7.

40. See *Paris Economic Declaration: Economic Declaration,* 1989, para. 38, 28 I.L.M. 1292 (1989); "Strong Statement from the EC Environment Council," in NET-WORK '92, 13 (January 1992): p. 11.

41. The World Bank, Establishment of the Global Environment Facility, 1991, Section 1(1)&(5), in 30 I.L.M. 1735 (1991). For an analysis of what the GEF is, how it works and what it does, see M. T. El-Ashry, "The GEF and Its Future," NETWORK '92, 14 (February 1992): p. 5.

42. The World Bank is the Trust Fund Administrator, while UNEP and UNDP will see to the strategic planning of projects to be implemented under the GEF, to ensure that they are consistent with overall environmental protection and enhancement goals; *Ibid.,* Section II, p. 1748.

43. *Ibid.,* pp. 1742, 1744.

44. *Ibid.,* Section 1(1)(ii).

45. *Montreal Protocol on Substances that Deplete the Ozone Layer,* 1987, in 26 I.L.M. 1541 (1987); *Helsinki Declaration on the Protection of the Ozone Layer,* 1989, in 28 I.L.M. 1335 (1989); See D. S. Bryk, "The Montreal Protocol and Recent Developments to Protect the Ozone Layer," 15 HARV. ENVTL L. REV. 275, 287 (1991). See also the financial arrangement under the *Convention Concerning the Protection of the World Cultural and Natural Heritage,* 1972, 11 I.L.M. 1358 (1972), which provides assistance for the conservation of cultural and natural heritage of outstanding value, situated in the territory of a party unable to protect the same. Though the UNESCO Convention makes no mention of assistance to developing countries *per se,* it recognizes their inability to protect natural and cultural heritage and the need for the international community to assist them in that regard; Articles 13(4) & 21.

46. Second Meeting of the Parties to the Montreal Protocol, London, 26–29 June 1990, UNEP/OzL.Pro. 2/3, para. 40.

47. *UN Framework Convention on Climate Change,* 1992, in 31 I.L.M. 849 (1992), Article 4(3). Funds for this purpose are to be channeled through the World Bank's Global Environment Facility, until definite arrangements will be made.

48. *Convention on Biological Diversity,* 1992, 31 I.L.M. 818 (1992), Article 20; see also the *Basel Convention on the Control of Transboundary Movements of Hazardous Wastes and their Disposal,* 1989, in 28 I.L.M. 657 (1989); *Bergen Ministerial Declaration on Sustainable Development in the ECE Region* 1990, in 1 Y.B. INT'L ENVTL L. 430 (1990).

49. The Report of the ad hoc Working Group of Experts on Biological Diversity, UN Doc. UNEP/Bio.Div.2/3 (1990) stated that funds to be allocated for conservation should not be taken from existing funds for other development assistance programs. See also the 1992 World Development Report, *supra* note 26, pp. 172–76.

50. At the Uruguay GATT Round the industrialized countries urged the South to provide enhanced protection for their intellectual property rights in exchange for concessions in technology transfers and even to grant them more favorable terms in other GATT negotiating area(s); See F. A. Abbot, "Protecting First World Assets in the Third World: Intellectual Property Negotiations in the GATT Multilateral Framework,"

22 VAND. J. TRANSNAT'L L. 689, 733–34, 739–42 (1989); M. Kakabadse, "Current Status of the Uruguay Round," 19 GA. J. INT'L & COMP. L. 292, 293 (1989).

51. A treaty is an international agreement concluded between two or more subjects of international law in writing, governed by international law and intended to create legal rights and obligations for the parties; *Vienna Convention on the Law of Treaties 1969,* Article 1(a).

52. Article 38(1) (b) of the *Statute of the International Court of Justice* refers to "custom" as "evidence of State practice accepted as law." This requires consistent and constant State practice, pursued by two or more States, acting on the conviction that it is obligatory under international law.

53. See the dissenting opinion of Judge Sorenson in the *North Sea Continental Shelf Cases* (Ger. v Den & Neth.) [1969] ICJ Rep. 242, 244–45.

16

The Northern Consumption Issue after Rio and the Role of Religion and Environmentalism

YUICHI INOUE

THE "MYTHS"[1] OF POPULATION AND TECHNOLOGY IN JAPAN

There are two environmental "myths" in Japan. One concerns population, and the other technology. The first states that the population problem belongs to the South.[2] The second says that constant economic growth and environmental protection can be made compatible by means of technological innovation and scientific resource management. These two myths exempt a strong belief in constant economic growth and material affluence from close examination, and thereby keep the Japanese from serious considerations of their social and moral obligations in the global community, which should lead to drastic reductions in resource consumption within the country.

Japan is one of the most densely populated countries in the world. However, the problem of overpopulation is largely thought of as somebody else's problem, not Japan's. The excess of people is not felt as a serious problem there, because it results in only minor inconveniences. On the contrary, people enjoy one of the world's highest material standards of living.

Japan has experienced rapid and geographically uneven urbanization in the second half of this century, which has resulted in depopulation of the countryside. It has also experienced a sharp decline in the birth rate, which is expected to result in rapid aging of the society in the short run. It is going to be increasingly difficult to maintain the level of social service, for example, because of a rapid shrinkage of the labor force relative to the senior population.

279

These are what might be meant by "population problems," if any, within the country.

When the Japanese are shown what is known as the exponential growth curve of the world's population and are informed that more than seven births are occurring in the South while one baby is born in the North,[3] they tend to feel that the future of the planet is being threatened by the population growth in the South and something must be done there. Here, they conveniently forget that the ecological carrying capacity of their own country is being significantly overburdened. This fact is largely eclipsed by the inter-regional transfer of commodities (e.g., import of natural resources) and wastes (e.g., discharge of pollutants into the atmosphere and the sea). The Japanese thereby tend to fail to understand the double-sided nature of the current global environmental "crisis," or the essential link connecting the two major issues of population and consumption.

The technology myth works as a complement to the view that something must be done in the South rather than in the North. Japan is widely regarded as a technologically successful country. Technology is believed to have played a crucial role in combating the toxic nightmare in the 1970s without sacrificing economic growth. If technological fixes (such as catalytic converters), "scientific" resource management (such as "sustained" yield forestry), and mild changes in lifestyle (such as recycling) are sufficient to achieve both ecological soundness and constant economic growth, there is nothing the Japanese have to worry about seriously, as long as Southern demographic patterns are stabilized.

These two "myths" are shared by Northern residents in general. However, the myths can be dangerously misleading, especially when they work together. They can result in a naive, exceedingly optimistic view, which totally neglects the global economic and ecological context in which Japan and other Northern countries are located. The ecological balance of a Northern country is often reached by consuming resources from beyond its boundaries, a substantial portion of which come from the South. These myths do not necessitate any major change in the belief in constant economic growth and the current exceedingly affluent lifestyle. They tend to work adversely, by eclipsing social responsibilities and moral obligations that must be assumed by the Japanese and other Northern residents in the global community.

If these "myths" are tenable without qualifications, there is not much room left in the North for religions to make contributions to environmentalism. It is not the case, however.

THE POPULATION/CONSUMPTION ISSUE
AS PERCEIVED BY THE SOUTH

The Earth Summit was held in June 1992 in Rio de Janeiro, Brazil. Governments, international organizations, industry, and citizens' groups, with a wide range of values and interests, gathered from the South and the North under the same banner of sustainable development. The UNCED (United Nations Conference on Environment and Development) process, consisting of inter-governmental negotiations, preparations of national reports, and various meetings of citizens, scientists, and industry representatives, lasted two years, and attracted different views and interpretations of environmental problems and sustainable development.

Southern governments, as represented by the G-77 countries (then composed of 128 "developing" nations), basically demanded economic equity in international society. This agenda emerged in the form of claims for the right to development, the national sovereign right to exploit natural resources within a nation's territory, and the fulfillment of the North's moral obligations and environmental responsibilities.[4] "Differentiated responsibilities" corresponding to "the different contributions to global environmental degradation"[5] was the baseline of their position. Southern environmental NGOs (non-governmental organizations) put social justice, both international and domestic, at the top of their agenda. Priority was placed on basic human needs rather than economic growth as measured by conventional indicators such as GNP and GRP. They often rejected Northern development models,[6] and explicitly demanded that the North give up wasteful lifestyles and other economic privileges.[7]

From the Southern point of view, it is not development or population growth in the South, but excessive resource consumption in the North, that has to be halted first, because the latter is the prime cause of environmental degradation on the global scale. This position is reinforced by the current North-South imbalance in resource and wealth distribution, which is too obvious to be politically ignored and too large to be morally neglected. This inequality has been illustrated in many ways.[8]

Although the problem of population growth has other important aspects than its impact on environmental sustainability, when we look at this problem in terms of pressures on the planetary environment, it is inappropriate and unacceptable to base our argument on simple size or growth rate of population. We instead need to talk about the size of the negative impact of each population on the environment, which may be defined, for example, as a product of population size and consumption rate. Under circumstances where one person in the North may consume many times more resources than one person in the South, we naturally need to talk about population size adjusted by consumption rate (and the composition of consumption, where appropriate), if we hope to make our argument environmentally meaningful, socially justifiable, and morally acceptable.

Here we can try a thinking experiment. Suppose one Japanese consumes ten times as much of a certain resource as one third world resident does; one Japanese baby should be counted as equivalent to ten third world babies in terms of impact on that resource. This way of thinking might help keep the Japanese from conveniently attributing current and future environmental degradation to the South for no other reason than that fertility is high in the third world and low in Japan. When we multiply 125 million, which is the population of Japan, by 10, which is obviously a modest multiplier,[9] we get 1.25 billion. When we imagine 1.25 billion people living in an area approximately the size of Montana, it is not difficult to see that Japan is truly "overpopulated."[10]

In the North, fortunately, demographic patterns have largely stabilized. However, the rate of resource consumption remains both environmentally unsustainable (global environmental degradation) and socially inequitable (North-South imbalance). The problem of Northern consumption patterns is at least as serious as and likely more serious and urgent than the problem of Southern demographic patterns in terms of planetary ecological sustainability.

The above argument is by no means intended to deemphasize the problem of overpopulation, but to emphasize that the Southern population problem must not be used for distracting attention from what has to be done in the North, which claims a disproportionate share of the world's wealth and environmental space (i.e., room for resource consumption and waste generation).

INDUSTRIALISM AND THE DEEP ECOLOGY MOVEMENT

In the UNCED process, however, Northern countries largely failed to listen to the South's argument that the North should substantially reduce resource consumption so that some environmental space or natural capital could be transferred to improve living standards in the South.[11] The reluctance of Northern governments to adopt a policy to substantially reduce the size of their economy is understandable. It would be political suicide for a government or political party to try to sell a policy that initiated drastic reductions in resource consumption and reverse economic growth, though these may be logical answers if we really want to achieve an environmentally sustainable and socially equitable future.

Industrialism, with a strong belief in economic growth, is firmly rooted in Northern society. Thus, the environmental problem transcends the domain of technological fix, and ultimately becomes a question of values and beliefs within our society and ourselves: as Neil Evernden summarizes, "instead of saying that we face an environmental crisis, it might be a more appropriate verbal convention to say that we are the environmental crisis."[12]

This understanding is articulated by Arne Naess, using the term "deep ecology movement."[13] He argues that there are two main forms of environmentalism. One is the "shallow," or mild reform movement,[14] which advocates continuous economic growth and environmental protection mainly by means of technological innovation. It avoids serious fundamental questions about our values and world views; it does not profoundly examine our sociocultural institutions. The other is the deep, radical, and long-range movement, which is based on the ecocentric, holistic awareness that the ecological crisis is truly a crisis of our culture and consciousness, and we need to make fundamental changes in our values and world views.[15]

This distinction, made over twenty years ago, has become even more important today because the above-mentioned technology myth may adversely affect any motivation to initiate actions to reverse the overconsuming mode of current Northern societies, despite the deepening global environmental crisis. Humankind has benefited tremendously from technology, and there is no doubt that an ecological future will not be achieved without technological innovation. The importance of ecologically sound technology must not be deemphasized. The point, however, is that an environmentally sustainable society can not be achieved by employing technological innovation alone, without questioning and redirecting dominant values, assumptions, and institutions within our society.

Despite our strong belief in technological solutions to pollution and resource depletion, it is becoming evident that technological innovation can not provide ultimate solutions to environmental problems as long as economic growth — increase in consumption — is presupposed.[16] Our belief in economic growth and material affluence is almost "religious," and obviously hard to depart from. If a religion means "a specific fundamental set of beliefs and practices generally agreed upon,"[17] industrialism has become a religion in many parts of the world. If the global environmental problem is a problem at that fundamental level, rather than merely a matter of technological application, it needs to be treated accordingly. It is necessary to examine the level of world views and religions.

AMBIVALENCE TOWARD RELIGION IN ENVIRONMENTALISM

For environmentalists with an ecocentric world view, religions have primary importance as they explore for alternative environmental values related to spiritual richness and the sacredness of being. Some religions can work as valuable guides for this exploration. Environmentalism has been inspired and enhanced by the holistic values and world views of spiritual traditions such as North American native cultures and ancient Eastern religions/philosophies. Considerable interest in religions and spiritual traditions exists in environmentalism.

For example, some supporters of the deep ecology movement articulate the relevance of rituals and ceremonies to the effort to construct an ecological culture based on criticism of Western industrial civilization. Dolores LaChapelle advocates retrieving the "old way," in which rituals and ceremonies play a crucial role in sustaining the sacred and spiritually rich relationship of a human community to its land. She argues that rituals, which are the pattern that connects, are indeed a sophisticated social technology for maintaining communication between all beings, including human and non-human, and between human communities and natural environment.[18] Workshops have been organized in which rituals and other religious practices are employed and the potential of religion to transform awareness and behavior is explored.[19] To this exploration into the transformative potential of rituals and spiritual values, existing religions are likely able to make uniquely valuable contributions.

On the other hand, however, environmentalists often try to avoid commitment to organized religions. This is because religions, in their dark side, can accompany authoritarian, dogmatic, hierarchic, and chauvinistic values, which are essentially incompatible with ecological values — egalitarian and libertarian — which emphasize symbiosis and diversity.

Shinto, Japan's original religion, is a good example. Today, Shinto has two main phases, quite distinct from each other. One is an animistic, popular, and more traditional version, which we may call Folk Shinto. The other is an institutionalized, authoritarian, and more recent one, or State Shinto.

Folk Shinto sees "gods" *(kami)* in every entity in nature, and is characterized by a strong reverence for nature. It has developed a rich spiritual tradition and promoted the concept of the oneness of humanity with nature. Local communities usually have their own Shinto shrines, often surrounded by age-old sacred woods that no one has dared to develop despite full utilization of the surrounding areas. Many of the local shrines are voluntarily maintained by community members and used as the venues of community events and festivals. Folk Shinto thus has a rich potential to help environmentalists develop ecological values that depart from anthropocentric and materialist values and retrieve community ties of mutual enhancement, which have been demolished by the process of industrialization.

State Shinto, on the other hand, was established by intention as a vehicle to subordinate people to the authority of the emperor who is designated as a living god, in order to enhance and secure the state's power to control people. Especially in the World War II period, State Shinto was fully mobilized to unite the whole population into one solid body. Grandiose shrines were constructed and Folk Shinto was, though not completely, co-opted by the centralized Shinto system. The authenticity of the emperor was never to be questioned because he was a god, sacred and inviolable. The government of the "divine" empire was by no means to be challenged or questioned in any manner, either. Thus, Shinto played a crucial role in totalitarian Japan.

Ambivalence toward Shinto is widely shared by Japanese environmentalists. Although they are aware of the critical relevance of Shinto to ecological values and world views, the dark memory of totalitarianism haunts them and prevents their commitment to the religion. This is a paradox of religion in environmentalism.

RELIGION AND ENVIRONMENTALISM

On the one hand, it might be ideal for ecocentric environmentalists if ecological values were established in us to the extent that our behavior becomes completely ecological almost unconsciously. With ecological values buried deeply inside ourselves, we might "automatically" behave in an ecological manner every time we take action, rather than consciously making the hard choice to subordinate our "selfish" interest to environmental values.[20] This might happen if the ecology movement ever became a "religion." If industrialism has become today's dominant religion, there seems to be no reason for environmentalists to object to an effort to replace industrialism (as a religion) with environmentalism (as a religion).

On the other hand, many environmentalists would not be happy to see the ecology movement become a "religion." Organized religions often refuse to be challenged, especially to be questioned regarding their ultimate premises. Ultimate premises are to be either adopted or rejected, but by definition not to be logically derived from other norms or values. Adherence to a specific set of ultimate premises can result in narrowminded, dogmatic, and chauvinistic response to those who hold a different set of ultimate premises. Environmentalists are aware of the danger of rigid inflexibility that potentially accompanies a religion. Democratic values, with respect for diversity, are widely shared by radical environmentalists. Both open-minded understanding and level-headed questioning are thought of as necessary for coping with differences.[21]

Arne Naess observes that there are four levels in the ecology movement: (1) ultimate premises (philosophies/religions), (2) core principles, (3) general views, and (4) practical/concrete decisions, presented in order of logical derivation.[22] This formulation, which was initially developed to represent a total view of the deep ecology movement, and is known as the "Apron Diagram," is useful for understanding the relationship of religions to environmentalism. It helps to clarify the whole spectrum of the ecology movement ranging from philosophical/religious inquiries to concrete judgments and daily actions.

Naess advocates unity at the level of principles (Level 2), while allowing plurality/diversity at the other levels. At Level 1, the premises of Christianity,

Buddhism, Spinoza's philosophy, and Ecosophy T (i.e., Naess' own version of ecological philosophy and wisdom), for example, can be placed. General views (Level 3) and daily actions (Level 4) may vary, reflecting situational, personal, and cultural differences. On the other hand, core principles (Level 2) can be represented by something like a platform of the movement, which is supposed to promote consensus among supporters despite their different backgrounds, whether these differences are philosophical, religious, cultural, or occupational.

The sets of ultimate values, beliefs, and world views of existing religions and spiritual traditions may widely differ and can even contradict each other. Nevertheless, each religion can make a uniquely significant contribution to environmentalism by informing and enriching the ecological platform comprising core principles, which in turn inform people, living with different backgrounds, of an ecological way of seeing and doing things. In this process, religions will need to constructively reexamine their relationships with industrialism: for example, how their major premises have been interpreted under industrialism, and how relevant or irrelevant their teachings are to industrialist doctrines. This reexamination will provide a solid ground on which religions can make contributions to the ecological platform.

Here, the meaning of the term "ecological" needs to be understood on at least three levels: that is to say, "being ecological" is composed of *physical sustainability* (i.e., meeting environmental imperatives in terms of resource consumption and waste generation); *social equity* (i.e., promoting fundamental human rights starting from satisfying basic human needs [e.g., air, water, food, clothes, shelter, health and education] and increasing citizens' political access to decision making that affects their future); and *ontological richness* (i.e., providing ample opportunity to realize oneself as one wishes, to achieve personal growth in many directions, and to deeply appreciate and enjoy a spiritual web of intrinsic connections with other beings). The ecological platform basically contains holistic, egalitarian, non-hierarchical, and non-authoritarian values with explicit emphasis on the essential connection, both physical and spiritual, of humanity to nature.[23]

At the '92 Global Forum, the NGO version of the Earth Summit in Rio de Janeiro, representatives of religious organizations constituted a substantial portion of the participants, and many gatherings were held on religion and spirituality. The interchange and cooperation between environmentalism and religions will be crucially important to the effort to create an ecological future beyond the current crisis. This exchange will become truly fruitful when the paradox of religion in environmentalism has been successfully addressed.

In response to the Earth Summit, the United Church of Canada, for example, developed a set of ethical principles for environment and development.[24] This is one of the prominent efforts to enhance the above-mentioned ecological platform principles. The Japanese Committee of the World Conference on Religion and Peace, present at the '92 Global Forum, articulated the need to achieve "inter-religious cooperation and a kind of international solidarity in which each other's religious teachings and traditions are respected" in an effort "to contribute to the salvation of human beings, establish world peace, and enhance culture."[25] This type of open-minded approach is required of religions to break down the wall now separating environmentalists from religion.

Religious organizations have shown serious concern about the current environmental crisis, in the UNCED process and on other occasions.[26] On the other hand, as seen above, there is substantial concern among environmentalists for potential contribution of religions and spiritual traditions to the ecology movement. Creative and constructive interaction is needed today between religions and environmentalism to get over the high hurdles set by the current ecological crisis, which are in the North epitomized in the task of departing from the strong belief in constant economic growth and unlimited material affluence.

NOTES

1. "Myth" is used here in its second *Oxford English Dictionary* sense of "illusion" or "fallacy."

2. In this paper, the South means the so-called "developing" or "less developed" countries, and the North means "more developed" countries. The South includes roughly three-quarters of the world's population, while the North comprises the richer quarter. Although these terms are primarily employed for differentiating one group of countries from another, they are used with full knowledge of uneven distribution of wealth and resources within a country as well as between countries, as summarized in one of the Alternative Treaties established at the '92 Global Forum in Rio de Janeiro in June 1992: "The terms South and North presuppose that there is a North in the South and a South in the North" (International Non-Governmental Organization Forum, "NGO Debt Treaty," *Alternative Treaty-Making: A Process in Support of Sustainable Societies and Global Responsibility* (Mill Brook, Nr. Ampthill, Bedfordshire, U.K.: International Synergy Institute, 1992), p. C-11).

3. The ratio of the births in the North to those in the South was 1:7.3 in 1990, and is estimated at 1:7.9 in 2000 (United Nations Development Programme, *Human Development Report 1992* [Oxford: Oxford University Press, 1992], as quoted in Michael Keating, *The Earth Summit's Agenda for Change* [Geneva: Centre for Our Common Future, 1993], p. 9).

4. These claims were largely incorporated in the UNCED agreements such as the Rio Declaration on Environment and Development. This position is also often articulated in documents prepared by international organizations from the Southern point of view. See, for example, Latin American and Caribbean Commission on Development and Environment, *Our Own Agenda* (Washington, D.C.: Inter-American Development Bank; and New York: United Nations Development Programme, 27 August 1990).

5. See Principle 7 of Rio Declaration on Environment and Development.

6. Excellent criticism of Northern mainstream development models made by Southern thinkers from the grass-roots perspective includes Vandana Shiva, *Staying Alive: Women, Ecology and Development* (London: Zed Books, 1989); and Rajni Kothari, *Rethinking Development: In Search of Humane Alternatives* (New York: New Horizon Press, 1989).

7. See, for example, Martin Khor Kok Peng, *The Future of North-South Relations: Conflict or Cooperation?* (Penang, Malaysia: Third World Network, 1992).

8. As for inequity in resource distribution, for example, the United States, with only 5% of the world's population, "uses 25% of the world's energy, emits 22% of all CO_2 produced and accounts for 25% of the world's GNP," while for India the equivalent figures are 16%, 3%, 3% and 1% in order *(Time,* vol. 139, no. 22 [1 June 1992], pp. 22–23). The Brundtland Report states that: "The growth of energy demand in response to industrialization, urbanization, and social affluence has led to an extremely uneven global distribution of primary energy consumption. The consumption of energy per person in industrialized market economies, for example, is more than 80 times greater than in Sub-Saharan Africa. And about a quarter of the world's population consumes three-quarters of the world's primary energy" (World Commission on Environment and Development, *Our Common Future* [Oxford: Oxford University Press, 1987], p. 169). According to UNDP statistics, 82.7% of the world's income belongs to the richest 20% of the world's population and 11.7% to the second 20%, while the rest of the world (the poorest 60%) is left with only 5.6% of the income, in 1989; and the income disparity between the richest and the poorest 20% almost doubled from 30:1 in 1960 to 59:1 in 1989 (UNDP [1992], as quoted in Keating [1993], p. 1).

9. According to an estimate made by the Brundtland Commission, per capita consumption averages of "developed countries" (then, 26% of the world's population) were approximately 15 times (paper), 11 times (steel), 13 times (other metals), and 12 times (commercial energy) as much as those of "developing countries" in 1980–82 (WCED [1987], p. 33).

10. This thinking experiment is heuristic by nature and is intended to work as an educational tool for dramatization. The multiplication is oversimplified and is by no means intended as an algorithm or a formula to serve as a policy formulation tool.

11. The reluctance of the North to give a pledge in the UNCED process for commitment to the consumption/lifestyle issue was heavily criticized by Southern NGOs. See, for example, Martin Khor, "The North-South Battles that Dominate Earth Summit," *Earth Summit Briefings* (Penang, Malaysia: Third World Network, 1992), no. 1; and "North Unwilling to Meet Some Southern Environment Demands," *Earth Summit Briefings,* no. 3. The North, especially the United States and Canada, resisted the South's demand to make the question of consumption and lifestyles a major issue in the UNCED agreements, such as Agenda 21. At the fourth Preparatory Committee (PrepCom IV), "the U.S. and Canada succeeded in deleting from Agenda 21 nineteen paragraphs on consumption and lifestyles, especially the one that proposed a U.N. monitoring system for these trends" (Angela Harkavy, *A Progress Report on Preparatory Negotiations for the United Nations Conference on Environment and Development: The Final Effort* [Wash-

ington, D.C.: National Wildlife Federation and CAPE '92, 1992], p. 7). At the Rio Conference, the "compromise brokered by Canada on paragraph 2.33 eliminate(d) the phrase 'to restrain consumption' in developed countries, yet retained the need to 'generate resources to support the transition to sustainable development'" (*Earth Summit Bulletin* [N.p.: Island Press; and Winnipeg: International Institute for Sustainable Development], vol. 2, no. 6 [8 June 1992], p. 1).

12. Neil Evernden, "The Environmentalist's Dilemma," in Evernden (ed.), *The Paradox of Environmentalism* (Downsview, Ontario: York University, 1984), proceedings of a symposium (2 May 1983) at York University, pp. 13–15 (emphasis in original).

13. Arne Naess, "The Shallow and the Deep, Long-Range Ecology Movement. A Summary," *Inquiry,* vol.16 (1973): pp. 95–100. The deep ecology movement can be represented by the "platform" or the eight basic principles for the movement: see Bill Devall and George Sessions, *Deep Ecology: Living as if Nature Mattered* (Salt Lake City: Peregrine Smith Books, 1985), pp. 69–73.

14. The supporters of the deep ecology movement and those of the shallow technological approach share many concerns, and they should cooperate where necessary and appropriate. Although the distinction articulated by Naess is important, it is not always wise nor even necessary to drive a wedge between these two groups. This is well understood by supporters of the deep ecology movement, and so the term "reform" is often used as an alternative to "shallow," which has a negative, insulting tone.

15. Two excellent elaborations on Naess' thesis in this context are: Alan R. Drengson, "Shifting Paradigms: From the Technocratic to the Person-Planetary," *Environmental Ethics,* vol. 3 (1980), pp. 221–40; and Andrew McLaughlin, *Regarding Nature: Industrialism and Deep Ecology* (Albany, N.Y.: State University of New York Press, 1993).

16. For example, while the Automobile Industry Association (Japan) has announced that they expect to reduce the amount of carbon dioxide (CO_2) from an automobile by 10% (to the mile) with new technology by the year 2000, it is also expected that the number of automobiles in the country will increase by 30% in the same period of time (*Asahi Shinbun,* 29 October 1990). In this case, despite technological innovation, the overall pollution is expected to increase. In order to cope with global warming, the industry has proposed major technological countermeasures such as replacing fossil-fuel power stations with nuclear power plants and dumping liquefied or frozen CO_2 deep into the ocean. These measures, just like what is called circuitous production in economics, may seem to work for the time being, but only deceivingly. This kind of resource-intensive approach with potential environmental destructiveness will likely result in inducing unexpected and more unmanageable difficulties in the long run. We can understand that unconditional belief in technology is dangerous only by remembering that chlorofluorocarbons (CFCs), once believed to be one of the most benign substances that humankind had ever created, has now been identified with a major threat to organisms on the planet by destroying the life-protecting ozone layer. It is in this last decade that the limitations of technological solutions have become evident in many ways. It is estimated that "organic material equivalent to about 40% of the present net primary production in terrestrial ecosystem is

being co-opted by human beings" and "humans also affect much of the other 60% . . . often heavily" (Peter M. Vitousek, et al, "Human Appropriation of the Products of Photosynthesis," *BioScience*, vol. 36 [1986], p. 372). Whether thermodynamically or biologically, we may be approaching the absolute limit of the planet today, which we cannot go beyond by any means without causing lethal disasters.

17. *Random House Webster's College Dictionary* (New York: Random House, 1991), p. 1138.

18. Dolores LaChapelle, "Ritual is Essential," an appendix to Devall and Sessions (1985), pp. 247–50.

19. For example, Pat Fleming and Joanna Macy, "The Council of All Beings," in John Seed et al. (eds.), *Thinking like a Mountain: Towards a Council of All Beings* (Philadelphia: New Society Publishers, 1988), pp. 79–90, describes details of a Council of All Being ritual, which is a form of such "psychotherapeutic" workshop. Dolores LaChapelle, *Sacred Land, Sacred Sex: Rapture of the Deep* (Silverton, Colo.: Finn Hill Arts, 1988) also gives examples of these ritual practices, and introduces various traditional rituals and ceremonies that could be employed in an effort to retrieve ecological consciousness.

20. Arne Naess advocates a psychological rather than moralistic approach to environmentalism. His approach is to work on our inclinations, rather than preaching the subordination of our behavior to an environmental ethic. He thinks that this will be made possible by expanding self beyond the boundaries of the narrow ego through the process of identification with larger entities such as forests, bioregions and the planetary biosphere. See Arne Naess, "Self-Realization: An Ecological Approach to Being in the World," *The Trumpeter*, vol. 4 (1987), no. 3: pp. 35–42. Also see his argument on Ecosophy T, an ecophilosophical norm-hypothesis system with "Self-realization!" as the ultimate norm, in Arne Naess, *Ecology, Community and Lifestyle: Outline of an Ecosophy*, translated and revised by David Rothenberg (Cambridge: Cambridge University Press, 1989), pp. 196–210. Naess' "Self-realization" thesis has been elaborated by supporters of the deep ecology movement: see, for example, Bill Devall, *Simple in Means, Rich in Ends: Practicing Deep Ecology* (Salt Lake City: Peregrine Smith Books, 1988), pp. 38–72; Freya Mathews, "Conservation and Self-Realization: A Deep Ecology Perspective," *Environmental Ethics*, vol. 10 (1988): pp. 347–55; and Warwick Fox, *Toward a Transpersonal Ecology: Developing New Foundations for Environmentalism* (Boston: Shambhala, 1990), pp. 249–68.

21. These values and methods for consensus formation have been developed particularly in the process of political and social commitment by radical environmentalists. See, for example, Brian Tokar, *The Green Alternative: Creating an Ecological Future*, 2nd ed. (San Pedro, Calif.: R. & E. Miles, 1992).

22. Arne Naess, "Intuition, Intrinsic Value and Deep Ecology," *The Ecologist*, vol. 14 (1984), nos. 5/6: pp. 201–3; and "Deep Ecology and Ultimate Premises," *The Ecologist*, vol. 18 (1988), nos. 4/5: pp. 128–31.

23. See, for example, the Platform of the Deep Ecology Movement (Devall and Sessions [1985], pp. 69–73). Also see core principles developed by the Greens: the "Four Pillars" of German Greens are: ecology, social responsibility, democracy, and non-vi-

olence; and the "Ten Key Values" adopted by U.S. Greens (St. Paul, Minnesota, 1984) are: ecological wisdom, grass-roots democracy, personal and social responsibility, non-violence, decentralization, community-based economics, post-patriarchal values, respect for diversity, global responsibility, and future focus (Tokar [1992], pp. 2, 53).

24. United Church of Canada, *One Earth Community: Ethical Principles for Environment and Development* (Toronto: United Church of Canada, 1992).

25. Japanese Committee, World Conference on Religion and Peace, "National Report of WCRP/Japan, 1991 Fiscal Year" (Tokyo: WCRP/Japan, 1992), p. 1.

26. A good deal of literature has been published, which examines industrialism and tries to establish an ecological perspective within the framework of a certain religion. For example, A Working Party for the Society, Religion and Technology Project, Church of Scotland, *While the Earth Endures: A Report on the Theological and Ethical Considerations of Responsible Land-Use in Scotland* (Edinburgh: University of Edinburgh, 1986), is a well-organized comprehensive response from Christianity to environmental issues, with a focus on land-use in Scotland.

IV

Conclusions

17

Conclusions and Recommendations

HAROLD COWARD

The chapters in Part II reveal many points of convergence, along with some differences in the approaches of the religions to the two-sided problem of population pressure and excessive consumption in relation to environmental degradation. In spite of their differences, however, all the religions view nature as having varying degrees of intrinsic value and therefore commanding human respect. Also, almost all religions have come to see the need for humans to limit their increase so as to leave room for other species to exist, and, indeed, for humans to live in the ways intended for them.

In spite of these rather significant points of agreement, recent commentators have observed that the views of the various religions do not seem to make much difference when we examine how humans have in fact interacted with nature. Callicot and Ames point out that in both the East and the West, the environment has been ruthlessly exploited. In their view, it is our innate aggressiveness as *Homo Sapiens,* inherited from prehuman savanna primates, that is at the root of the problem. This might lead one to the pessimistic conclusion that what religions teach about the environment does not after all matter, for we as humans are simply driven by our biological inheritance. The religions reviewed would not accept such a deterministic position. There is simply too much evidence that humans can and do change their behavior, sometimes in radical fashion. It is in this context that the question to be asked of the religions is not what their followers have done in the past in relation to population, consumption, and the environment, but what they teach today. Two questions must be considered: (1) do the religious ideas of a tradition encourage environmental exploitation and destruction? (2) do the religious ideas of a tradition offer correctives to exploitation?

When these questions are asked, we can then begin to make distinctions between religions. While all the religions reviewed here teach that nature is to be respected and not abused for human self-satisfaction, it is true that the Eastern and Aboriginal traditions are more congenial to ecology and a conservationist ethic. They teach the unity of humans and nature in ways that are quite different from the separation between humans and nature fostered in much Western religious thought. While the active domination of nature may not have been the intent of Jewish and Christian teachings, one can see how Genesis is open to such interpretations in ways that the Eastern views are not. Lynn White's contribution is useful in helping us see how Biblical views about the human domination of nature, when decontextualized, encourage us to exploit. Eastern and Aboriginal ideas are a clear corrective in this regard.

Although the traditional ideas of all religions, with the exceptions of Buddhism, Chinese Religion, and the Aboriginal traditions, have encouraged population growth in irresponsible ways, feminist scholars in all religions are introducing new readings which limit population growth out of respect for our necessary interdependence with each other and the environment.

In Part III, the chapters on the contributions that can be offered from philosophy, economics, demography, law, women and fertility planning, and a post-Rio Japanese reflection all conclude that while religions have a role to play, there are other forces, such as the economic market and the forces of international law, that must also be engaged. Inoue's study of the popular myths of Japan — that the population problem belongs to the poorer developing nations, and that technology can solve the pollution problem so that consumption patterns do not need to change — could well be generalized to other industrialized countries of the North. Here, the ability of religion to prophetically challenge and critique these myths in the service of both the environment and humanity will be strongly tested.

T. S. Eliot, in his poem "The Hollow Men," says

Between the idea
And the reality
Between the motion
And the act
Falls the shadow[1]

If, as Callicot and Ames suggest, "the shadow" obstructing the actualization of our responsibilities to the environment is our innate human aggressiveness, then the world views of the religions can only help. Each offers an assessment of our human condition in relation to the cosmos that to varying degrees would temper our aggressiveness toward nature. While there are failures within all cultures and religions, there is also evidence that what we think can affect the way we act. The shadow can be flooded with light. All of the religions reviewed show, to varying degrees, an enlightened understanding of our human duties to the environment. To meet our current crisis, the ecological resources of these religions can usefully be engaged at the levels of individual believers, religious leaders, government leaders, business C.E.O.s, and workers in NGOs. The changing of people's thinking and behavior is after all the one thing that the religions have consistently demonstrated the power to accomplish. It was with this hope that the forty representatives of the above religions concluded their ten-day seminar at Whistler. Far from being depressed by the observations of Callicot and Ames, they concluded their work inspired that the religions have important wisdom to offer the global problems of population pressure, excessive consumption, and the degradation of the environment. While necessarily lacking the quality of a transforming spiritual inspiration that infused the participants at the end of the seminar, the Whistler Conclusions and Recommendations with their Preamble read as follows:

PREAMBLE

Humanity is inseparable from the ecosphere, which it shares with all life. Conserving that ecosphere is vital.

Exponential resource consumption and population growth are rapidly destroying the interconnected web of life. The scope and scale of this current crisis are without precedent.

It is urgent that we identify, understand and rectify material, intellectual, psychological, emotional, and spiritual causes and conditions which give rise to excessive consumption and reproduction.

We human beings have a moral obligation to recognize that we are responsible for the degradation of the ecosphere and that we are called to redress the damage.

An unprecedented crisis demands an unparalleled creative response. We must search out relevant resources from ancient wisdom traditions, and current arts, sciences and technologies, in our quest for radical personal and communal transformation.

Actions must be informed by and inclusive of diverse ways of knowing.

Responsibility for action rests with all of us, individually and collectively.

CONCLUSIONS AND RECOMMENDATIONS

1. Individuals

Conclusions

A resolution of the problems of excessive population growth and consumption calls for a transformation of our social attitudes and behaviors toward the ecosphere from one of domination and exploitation to one of preservation and conservation. Such a transformation begins with the individual.

Recommendations

We urge individuals in all parts of the world to consider the following and recommend that they:

• Consider the needs of other creatures that share the ecosphere and the needs of future generations when they act.

• Reflect on the inability of humankind to satisfy its spiritual desires through material means, whether that be through consuming more goods or through bearing more and more children.

• Examine the uneven distribution and misuse of our resources and the implications that follow from these situations, and take action to reduce consumption and waste and redirect resources to those in need.

• Explore their inner resources and direct them towards making social policy more ecologically responsible.

2. Educators

Conclusions

Through example and through teaching, educators and academics hold the key to the future, because they influence both current and future generations. There is a significant gap between religious understanding and scientific discovery. There is much to be learned from both disciplines and educators on each side should work toward an integrative wisdom.

Recommendations

We invite educators at all levels to consider the following and recommend that they:

• Reflect on existing symbols in the curricula regarding the human relationship with nature and how they influence human reproductive and consumer behavior; as well, where needed, explore and integrate new symbols into the curricula that demonstrate ecologically responsible relationships with nature. Some useful symbols and knowledge can be found in the disciplines of ecology, natural history, and the world's ethical systems.

3. Religious Leaders

Conclusions

Religious leaders should address the urgent problems of population growth and overconsumption, which are almost entirely spiritual or ethical at root.

Recommendations

We encourage religious leaders to consider the following and recommend that they:

• Seriously reflect upon their traditions and the ethical implications that follow, and consider what obstacles might be removed or principles emphasized or reinterpreted so as to address the pressing problems of excessive consumption and overpopulation. This will entail putting environmental ethics at the forefront of their thinking and messages.

• Set an example of how ethical beliefs about the ecosphere can be integrated with ethical action.

• Identify and mobilize social and economic resources to address the interconnected problems of environmental degradation, consumption, and population growth.

4. Business Leaders

Conclusion

Large public and private corporations in all countries have a profound impact on ecological sustainability and social equity. As people and their governments become more environmentally aware, it is prudent as well as ethical for corporations to demonstrate their commitments to social equity and environmental sustainability.

Recommendations

We invite business leaders to consider the following and recommend that they:

• Recognize their responsibility not to promote forms of consumerism that negatively affect the ecosphere, but rather to work with each other and consumers to eliminate harmful forms of consumption and marketing, and advertising that promotes it.

• Explore new models of behaviors that are more socially and environmentally responsible. Initiatives taken by enlightened corporations already provide good models of behavior. Structured dialogue with business leaders, community representatives, ethicists, and environmental experts can help the business community produce workable ethical guidelines for their operations that have widespread public support.

• Make every effort to make their operations, marketing, and lobbying consistent with their publicly stated commitments to social and environmental goals and standards.

• Support research and development on sound/appropriate technology. Such technology would embody respect for principles of efficiency, ecological sensitivity, and meaningful work.

5. Government

Conclusions

Governments are responsible and accountable for ensuring the welfare their people and the ecosystems on which they and other living beings depend. Ecological sustainability must be an immediate and overriding goal of government policy. Government actions or inactions in such areas as trade, aid, international cooperation, and military programs have caused significant damage to the natural environment and social systems.

Recommendations

We urge governments all over the world to consider the following and recommend — for the following fields — that they:

Management/Decentralization
• Promote and adopt environmental stewardship obligations at the macro, meso, and micro levels of government, assigning greater responsibility and accountability for stewardship at the local level.

• Develop better ways of accounting for and incorporating the costs of resource consumption into price systems and national accounts.

Population/Fertility
• Recognize the importance of women's right to control their own fertility.

• Take immediate action to meet all requests for family planning, including methods for men.

Poverty/Inequity
• Take serious steps to alleviate gross national and international inequities. Highest priority should be given to the needs of the poorest of the poor, especially women and children. Particular attention should also be paid to enhancing the self-sufficiency of the poor. Helping them regain and repair their land base or improve their access to resources is an essential step in accomplishing this.

Military
• Curtail combative military expenditures and redirect these resources towards peacekeeping programs and programs that promote social equity and ecological sustainability. An environmental corps, trained to mitigate or restore environmental degradation, is one example of the latter.

Aboriginal Rights
• Respect and support the rights of the world's Aboriginal peoples and facilitate the preservation of their unique traditional wisdom.

Trade
• Develop and adopt a globally equitable trading system that provides fair prices for Southern as well as Northern producers. This will entail eliminating

certain subsidies instituted by the North and opening markets to Southern products. The trading system would also aim toward the development of common environmental and social standards for traded products.

International Cooperation/Aid
• Participate actively in the promotion of global strategies for ecological well-being and social justice (e.g., UNCED). Governments should ensure that their people participate in these discussions through public education and consultation.

• Develop aid programs that balance the immediate and long-term needs of recipients with environmental sustainability. This will entail that recipients, especially women, are involved in the design and implementation of aid programs, and that environmental standards be integrated into aid programs, where relevant.

• Support existing international organizations involved in non-violent conflict resolution. These organizations are to provide opportunities for resolving disputes peacefully and for avoiding the human and environmental disasters of war.

6. Non-Governmental Organizations

Conclusions

Non-governmental organizations are close to various segments of the population, and so can play an important role in helping to resolve the problems of consumption and population growth.

Recommendations

We urge non-governmental organizations to consider the following and recommend that they:

• Address the problems of overpopulation and excessive consumption in ways already discussed above where governments can not or will not act.

• Cooperate with governmental and other non-governmental partners whenever possible.

• Ensure accountability among governmental and non-governmental decision makers for their actions or inactions affecting growth in consumption and population.

NOTE

1. T. S. Eliot, "The Hollow Men." In O. Williams (ed.), A Little Treasury of Modern Poetry. New York: Charles Scribner's Sons, 1952, p. 286.

About the Contributors

Elizabeth A. Adjin-Tettey is a doctoral candidate at the Osgoode Hall Law School, York University, Toronto. Her research interests are international environmental law, particularly North-South relations and refugee issues, with a focus on refugee women.

Nawal H. Ammar teaches at Youngstown State University, Ohio. She is an anthropologist by training and is a specialist in Islam; women in criminal justice; corrections; and conflict resolution. Her publications include: "Women in Islam: The paradox of unity and diversity" *(Chicago Seminary Journal,* Summer 1992) and "Islam's Attitude Towards War" *(Leadership Conference of Women Religious Occasional Papers,* 1991).

Harold Coward is Professor of History and Director of the Centre for Studies in Religion and Society at the University of Victoria. His main fields are comparative religion; psychology of religion; and environmental ethics. He serves as an Executive Member of the Board, Canadian Global Change Program. His wide variety of publications include: *Ethics and Climate Change* (with Thomas Hurka) (Waterloo, Ont.: Wilfrid Laurier University Press, 1993) and *Pluralism: Challenge to World Religions* (Maryknoll, N.Y.: Orbis Books, 1985).

A. Rodney Dobell is Winspear Professor for Research in Public Policy at the University of Victoria School of Public Administration. His research interests are environmental policy and administrative ethics, in particular the reconciliation of economic analysis, environmental values and international action.

305

See e.g., his "Global Change and Local Development: Environmental grid-lock?" (paper presented to IDAC 1990 Roundtable, Victoria B.C., October 1990); and "Economic Policy Making in Canada: The case of the Canada-U.S. Free Trade Agreement" *(Processes and Problems of Economic Policy Making in the Asia-Pacific Region,* K. Lorne Brownsey ed., Institute for Research and Public Policy, 1990).

Rita M. Gross is Professor of Comparative Studies in Religion at the University of Wisconsin, Eau Claire. Her special fields of interest are Indian religious thought, women and religion, and feminist theology. She is also a long-term Buddhist practitioner. Her books include: *Buddhism after Patriarchy: A Feminist History, Analysis, Reconstruction of Buddhism* (SUNY Press, 1993); *Feminism and Religious Studies: Transformations of a Discipline* (forthcoming).

F. Kenneth Hare is Chancellor of Trent University; Chair of the Advisory Board at the Institute for International Programs, University of Toronto; Chair of the Technical Advisory Panel on Nuclear Safety, Ontario Hydro. He has served with many other official bodies, foundations and institutions. His research interests are climatic change and nuclear safety; e.g., "Contemporary Climatic Change; The problem of uncertainty" *(Resource Management and Development,* Bruce Mitchell ed., Oxford University Press, 1991, pp. 8–27); and *The Canadian Climate Program* (pamphlet to be published by the Canadian Climate Program Board).

Yuichi Inoue is a Ph.D. Student in Interdisciplinary Studies at the University of Victoria and Junior Professor at Nara Sagyo University, Japan. His field of interest is environmental philosophy and environmental education.

Catherine Keller is Associate Professor of Theology at Drew University Theological and Graduate Schools. She studies feminist, process, ecological and political theologies. She is the author of: *From a Broken Web: Separation, Sexism and Self* (Boston: Beacon Press, 1987) and is presently finishing *Apocalypse Now & Then: A Feminist Approach to the End of the World.*

Klaus K. Klostermaier is Head and Professor at the Department of Religion, Director of the Asian Studies Centre, and University Distinguished Professor at the University of Manitoba. His research interests are: India: history, culture, philosophy, contemporary issues; interreligious dialogue; science and religion. He has published many articles, including "Bhakti, Ahimsa and Ecology" (Journal of Dharma, 16:3: pp. 245–6); "Possible Contributions of Asian Traditions to Contemporary Ethics" *(Bulletin of the Humanities Association of Canada,* 18:1: pp. 35–49); and he is working on a book manuscript, *The Nature of Nature.*

Sharon Joseph Levy, B.Ed. (McGill), wife of Rabbi David J. Levi and mother, teaches senior elementary school Judaic studies, as well as adult Torah classes. She is on the Canadian board of Gifts of Life – Friends of Jay, a bone marrow recruitment charitable foundation. Sharon has previously taught general studies in elementary school, as well as having been the teacher liaison to the Kitchener-Waterloo Hebrew Day School Board. Sharon was founding coordinator of the environment network for CAJE (Coalition for Advancement in Jewish Education), as well as writer of its first publication *Leovda Uleshomra.* She has lectured to both Jewish and general audiences about Judaism and the environment. Sharon is the creator of *Misparim M'Saprim,* a numberline frieze for preschool classrooms. She is past Educational Director of Hebrew Congregation and founding President of Aleph-Bet Preschool, both of Wichita, Kansas. Sharon was the editor of *Holocaust: An Annotated Bibliography* (Montreal: Canadian Jewish Congress, 1978). She is a graduate of Gold College for Women, Jerusalem. Sharon is a student of Prof. Nechama Leibowitz. She is a product of the day school system in Montreal, graduating from Hebrew Academy School.

Michael McDonald is currently Director of the Centre for Applied Ethics and Maurice Young Professor of Applied Ethics at the University of British Columbia. He studies ethics, particularly as applied to contemporary decision making in the public and private sectors. He has published widely, especially in philosophical and legal journals; e.g., "Should Communities Have Rights? Reflections on Liberal Individualism" *(Canadian Journal of Law and Jurisprudence* IV, 2: 1991). He co-authored the report: *Towards a Canadian Research Strategy for Applied Ethics: Report for the Social Science and Humanities Research Council of Canada* (Canadian Federation for the Humanities, 1988).

Jordan Paper is Associate Professor, Division of Humanities, York University. His research interests are comparative religion: methodology, Chinese religion, Native American religions, female spirituality, ecstatic religious experience. His books include: *Guide to Chinese Prose* (Boston: G. K. Hall, 1973 & 1984) and *Chinese Religion: New Approaches* (forthcoming).

Li Chuang Paper is an Educational Consultant. She researches language and culture and comparative culture. She is also active in the fields of curriculum design and teacher training.

Mahendra K. Premi is Professor of Demography at the Centre for the Study of Regional Development, Jawaharlal Nehru University, New Delhi. His research interests are general demography; the status of women, especially from the point of view of their education and employment; urbanization and migration; population and environment. He is President of the Indian Association for the Study of Population. He is the author of ten books, the latest being *India's Population: Heading Towards a Billion.*

Daisy Sewid-Smith is Department Head, First Nations Education, School District 72 in Campbell River, B.C. She writes and lectures on the history and culture of the KʷaKʷaKᵊakʷ (Kʷaguɫ) Nation of the North West coast and the preservation of the Ligʷala / KʷaKʷala language.

Jael M. Silliman is Program Officer at the Noyes Foundation and Visiting Professor at the University of Iowa. She specializes in women's movements, with a special interest in environmental health and reproductive health concerns; she is interested in race and social justice issues in the U.S., and in movement building.

Anne Whyte is Director General, Division of Environment and Natural Resources, International Development Research Centre. Her research interests are environmental policy; natural resources management; food security; environmentally friendly technology. She has undertaken extensive fieldwork in developing countries, North America, and Europe, has published widely, especially in the fields of environmental risk assessment, human behavior in response to hazards, and public environmental attitudes. She serves on numerous national and international committees.

Index